elevate science

SAVVAS
LEARNING COMPANY

You're an author!

As you write in this science book, your answers and personal discoveries will be recorded for you to keep, making this book unique to you. That is why you are one of the primary authors of this book.

In the space below, print your name, school, town, and state. Then write a short autobiography that includes your interests and accomplishments.

YOUR NAME ....

SCHOOL ....

TOWN, STATE ....

AUTOBIOGRAPHY ....

....

....

Your Photo

Savvas Learning Company LLC, 15 East Midland Avenue, Paramus, NJ 07652

Cover: The cover photo shows a drone flying over a cultivated area. Miguel Sotomayor/Moment/Getty Images

Attributions of third party content appear on pages 532–534, which constitute an extension of this copyright page.

ISBN-13: 978-0-328-94858-1
ISBN-10: 0-328-94858-6
13 22

Program Authors

ZIPPORAH MILLER, Ed.D.
Coordinator for K-12 Science Programs, Anne Arundel County Public Schools
Dr. Zipporah Miller currently serves as the Senior Manager for Organizational Learning with the Anne Arundel County Public School System. Prior to that she served as the K-12 Coordinator for science in Anne Arundel County. She conducts national training to science stakeholders on the Next Generation Science Standards. Dr. Miller also served as the Associate Executive Director for Professional Development Programs and conferences at the National Science Teachers Association (NSTA) and served as a reviewer during the development of Next Generation Science Standards. Dr. Miller holds a doctoral degree from the University of Maryland College Park, a master's degree in school administration and supervision from Bowie State University and a bachelor's degree from Chadron State College.

MICHAEL J. PADILLA, Ph.D.
Professor Emeritus, Eugene P. Moore School of Education, Clemson University, Clemson, South Carolina
Michael J. Padilla taught science in middle and secondary schools, has more than 30 years of experience educating middle-school science teachers, and served as one of the writers of the 1996 U.S. National Science Education Standards. In recent years Mike has focused on teaching science to English Language Learners. His extensive experience as Principal Investigator on numerous National Science Foundation and U.S. Department of Education grants resulted in more than $35 million in funding to improve science education. He served as president of the National Science Teachers Association, the world's largest science teaching organization, in 2005–6.

MICHAEL E. WYSESSION, Ph.D
Professor of Earth and Planetary Sciences, Washington University, St. Louis, Missouri
Author of more than 100 science and science education publications, Dr. Wysession was awarded the prestigious National Science Foundation Presidential Faculty Fellowship and Packard Foundation Fellowship for his research in geophysics, primarily focused on using seismic tomography to determine the forces driving plate tectonics. Dr. Wysession is also a leader in geoscience literacy and education; he is the chair of the Earth Science Literacy Initiative, the author of several popular video lectures on geology in the *Great Courses* series, and a lead writer of the *Next Generation Science Standards**.

REVIEWERS

Program Consultants

Carol Baker

Science Curriculum

Dr. Carol K. Baker is superintendent for Lyons Elementary K-8 School District in Lyons, Illinois. Prior to this, she was Director of Curriculum for Science and Music in Oak Lawn, Illinois. Before this she taught Physics and Earth Science for 18 years. In the recent past, Dr. Baker also wrote assessment questions for ACT (EXPLORE and PLAN), was elected president of the Illinois Science Teachers Association from 2011–2013, and served as a member of the Museum of Science and Industry (Chicago) advisory board. She is a writer of the Next Generation Science Standards. Dr. Baker received her B.S. in Physics and a science teaching certification. She completed her master's of Educational Administration (K-12) and earned her doctorate in Educational Leadership.

Jim Cummins

ELL

Dr. Cummins's research focuses on literacy development in multilingual schools and the role technology plays in learning across the curriculum. *Elevate Science* incorporates research-based principles for integrating language with the teaching of academic content based on Dr. Cummins's work.

Elfrieda Hiebert

Literacy

Dr. Hiebert, a former primary-school teacher, is President and CEO of TextProject, a non-profit aimed at providing open-access resources for instruction of beginning and struggling readers, She is also a research associate at the University of California Santa Cruz. Her research addresses how fluency, vocabulary, and knowledge can be fostered through appropriate texts, and her contributions have been recognized through awards such as the Oscar Causey Award for Outstanding Contributions to Reading Research (Literacy Research Association, 2015), Research to Practice award (American Educational Research Association, 2013), and the William S. Gray Citation of Merit Award for Outstanding Contributions to Reading Research (International Reading Association, 2008).

Content Reviewers

Alex Blom, Ph.D.
Associate Professor
Department Of Physical Sciences
Alverno College
Milwaukee, Wisconsin

Joy Branlund, Ph.D.
Department of Physical Science
Southwestern Illinois College
Granite City, Illinois

Judy Calhoun
Associate Professor
Physical Sciences
Alverno College
Milwaukee, Wisconsin

Stefan Debbert
Associate Professor of Chemistry
Lawrence University
Appleton, Wisconsin

Diane Doser
Professor
Department of Geological Sciences
University of Texas at El Paso
El Paso, Texas

Rick Duhrkopf, Ph.D.
Department of Biology
Baylor University
Waco, Texas

Jennifer Liang
University of Minnesota Duluth
Duluth, Minnesota

Heather Mernitz, Ph.D.
Associate Professor of Physical Sciences
Alverno College
Milwaukee, Wisconsin

Joseph McCullough, Ph.D.
Cabrillo College
Aptos, California

Katie M. Nemeth, Ph.D.
Assistant Professor
College of Science and Engineering
University of Minnesota Duluth
Duluth, Minnesota

Maik Pertermann
Department of Geology
Western Wyoming Community College
Rock Springs, Wyoming

Scott Rochette
Department of the Earth Sciences
The College at Brockport State University of New York
Brockport, New York

David Schuster
Washington University in St Louis
St. Louis, Missouri

Shannon Stevenson
Department of Biology
University of Minnesota Duluth
Duluth, Minnesota

Paul Stoddard, Ph.D.
Department of Geology and Environmental Geosciences
Northern Illinois University
DeKalb, Illinois

Nancy Taylor
American Public University
Charles Town, West Virginia

Teacher Reviewers

Jennifer Bennett, M.A.
Memorial Middle School
Tampa, Florida

Sonia Blackstone
Lake County Schools
Howey In the Hills, Florida

Teresa Bode
Roosevelt Elementary
Tampa, Florida

Tyler C. Britt, Ed.S.
Curriculum & Instructional Practice Coordinator
Raytown Quality Schools
Raytown, Missouri

A. Colleen Campos
Grandview High School
Aurora, Colorado

Ronald Davis
Riverview Elementary
Riverview, Florida

Coleen Doulk
Challenger School
Spring Hill, Florida

Mary D. Dube
Burnett Middle School
Seffner, Florida

Sandra Galpin
Adams Middle School
Tampa, Florida

Margaret Henry
Lebanon Junior High School
Lebanon, Ohio

Christina Hill
Beth Shields Middle School
Ruskin, Florida

Judy Johnis
Gorden Burnett Middle School
Seffner, Florida

Karen Y. Johnson
Beth Shields Middle School
Ruskin, Florida

Jane Kemp
Lockhart Elementary School
Tampa, Florida

Denise Kuhling
Adams Middle School
Tampa, Florida

Esther Leonard, M.Ed. and L.M.T.
Gifted and talented Implementation Specialist
San Antonio Independent School District
San Antonio, Texas

Kelly Maharaj
Challenger K–8 School of Science and Mathematics
Spring Hill, Florida

Kevin J. Maser, Ed.D.
H. Frank Carey Jr/Sr High School
Franklin Square, New York

Angie L. Matamoros, Ph.D.
ALM Science Consultant
Weston, Florida

Corey Mayle
Brogden Middle School
Durham, North Carolina

Keith McCarthy
George Washington Middle School
Wayne, New Jersey

Yolanda O. Peña
John F. Kennedy Junior High School
West Valley City, Utah

Kathleen M. Poe
Jacksonville Beach Elementary School
Jacksonville Beach, Florida

Wendy Rauld
Monroe Middle School
Tampa, Florida

Anne Rice
Woodland Middle School
Gurnee, Illinois

Bryna Selig
Gaithersburg Middle School
Gaithersburg, Maryland

Pat (Patricia) Shane, Ph.D.
STEM & ELA Education Consultant
Chapel Hill, North Carolina

Diana Shelton
Burnett Middle School
Seffner, Florida

Nakia Sturrup
Jennings Middle School
Seffner, Florida

Melissa Triebwasser
Walden Lake Elementary
Plant City, Florida

Michele Bubley Wiehagen
Science Coach
Miles Elementary School
Tampa, Florida

Pauline Wilcox
Instructional Science Coach
Fox Chapel Middle School
Spring Hill, Florida

Safety Reviewers

Douglas Mandt, M.S.
Science Education Consultant
Edgewood, Washington

Juliana Textley, Ph.D.
Author, NSTA books on school science safety
Adjunct Professor
Lesley University
Cambridge, Massachusetts

TOPIC 1

Introduction to Matter xviii

MS-PS1-1, MS-PS1-2

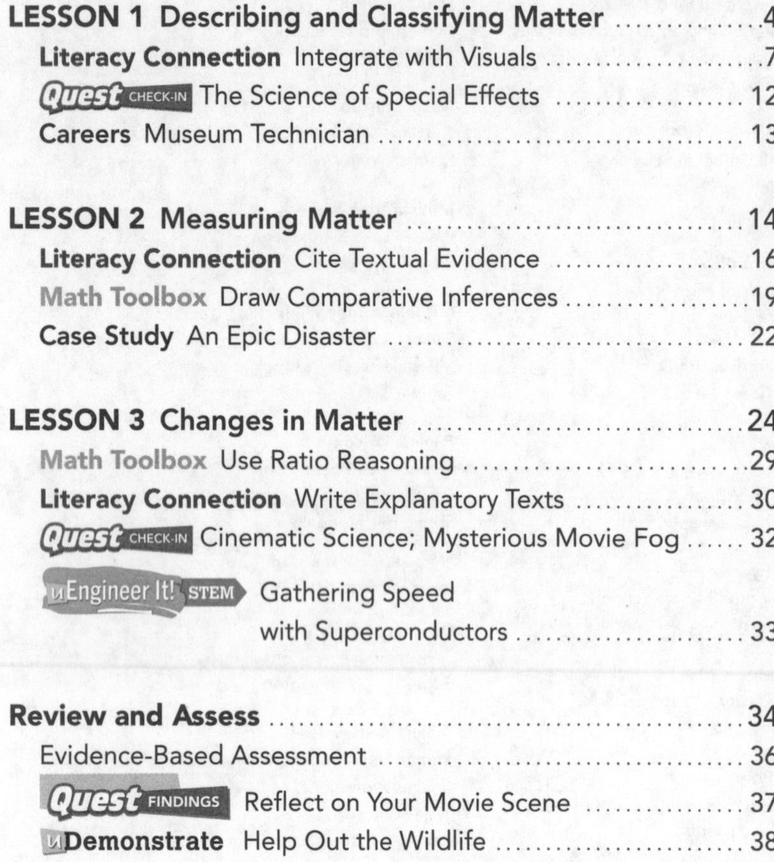

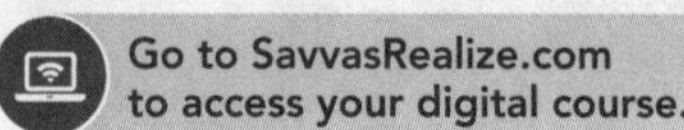

Go to SavvasRealize.com to access your digital course.

VIDEO
- Museum Technician

INTERACTIVITY
- What Makes Up Matter?
- Molecules and Extended Structures
- Calculating Density
- Weight on the Moon
- Properties of Matter

VIRTUAL LAB
- What's the Matter with My Chocolate?

ASSESSMENT

eTEXT

HANDS-ON LABS

uConnect The Nuts and Bolts of Formulas

uInvestigate
- Models of Atoms and Molecules
- Observing Physical Properties
- Physical and Chemical Changes

uDemonstrate
Help Out the Wildlife

Solids, Liquids, and Gases

MS-PS1-4

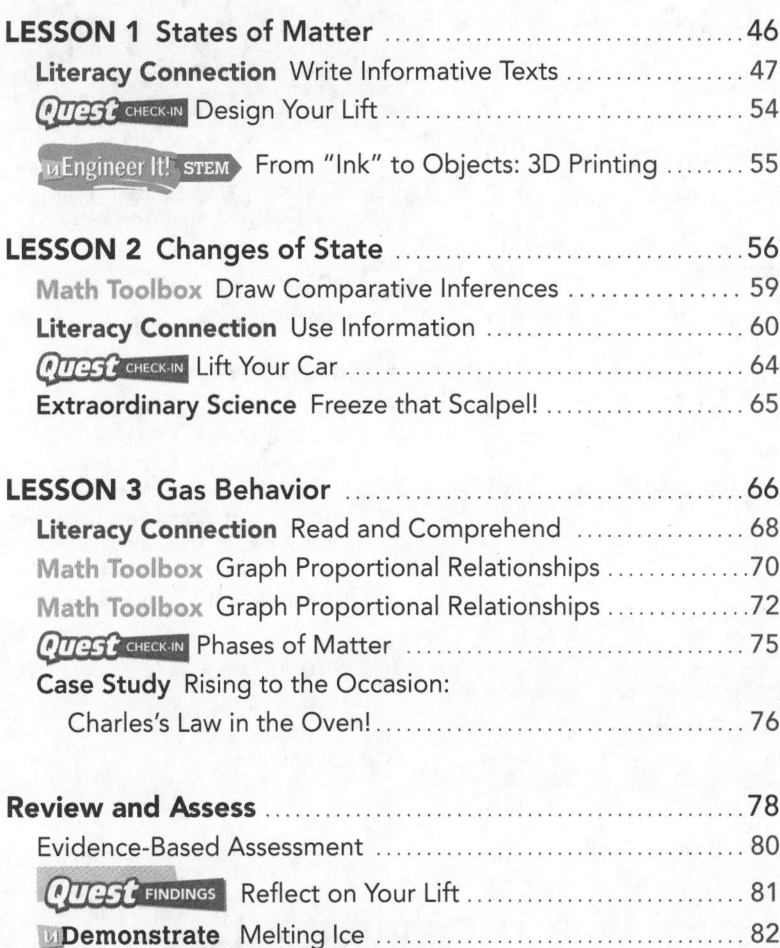

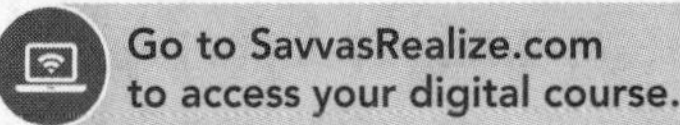

Go to SavvasRealize.com to access your digital course.

VIDEO
- Materials Scientist

INTERACTIVITY
- Particles and States of Matter
- Properties of Solids, Liquids, and Gases
- A Matter of Printing
- Particle Motion and States of Matter
- States of Matter
- Thermal Energy and Changes of State
- Gas Laws
- Hot Air Balloon Ride

VIRTUAL LAB
- Cooking and the States of Matter

ASSESSMENT

eTEXT

Connect Solid, Liquid, or Gas?

Investigate
- Properties of Matter
- Mirror, Mirror
- Testing Charles's and Boyle's Laws

Demonstrate
Melting Ice

TOPIC 3

Energy

MS-PS3-1, MS-PS3-2, MS-PS3-5

Go to SavvasRealize.com to access your digital course.

VIDEO
- Energy Engineer

INTERACTIVITY
- Get the Ball Rolling • Understanding Machines • Levers • Force and Energy • Interpret Kinetic Energy Graphs • Racing for Kinetic Energy • Roller Coasters and Potential Energy • Prosthetics in Motion • Types of Energy • Forms of Energy • Energy Transformations • Take It to the Extreme

VIRTUAL LAB
- Skate or Fly!

ASSESSMENT

eTEXT

Connect What Would Make a Card Jump?

Investigate
- What Work Is
- Mass, Velocity, and Kinetic Energy
- Energy, Magnetism, and Electricity
- Making a Flashlight Shine
- Law of Conservation of Energy

Demonstrate
3, 2, 1... Liftoff!

Thermal Energy 136

MS-PS3-3, MS-PS3-4, MS-PS3-5

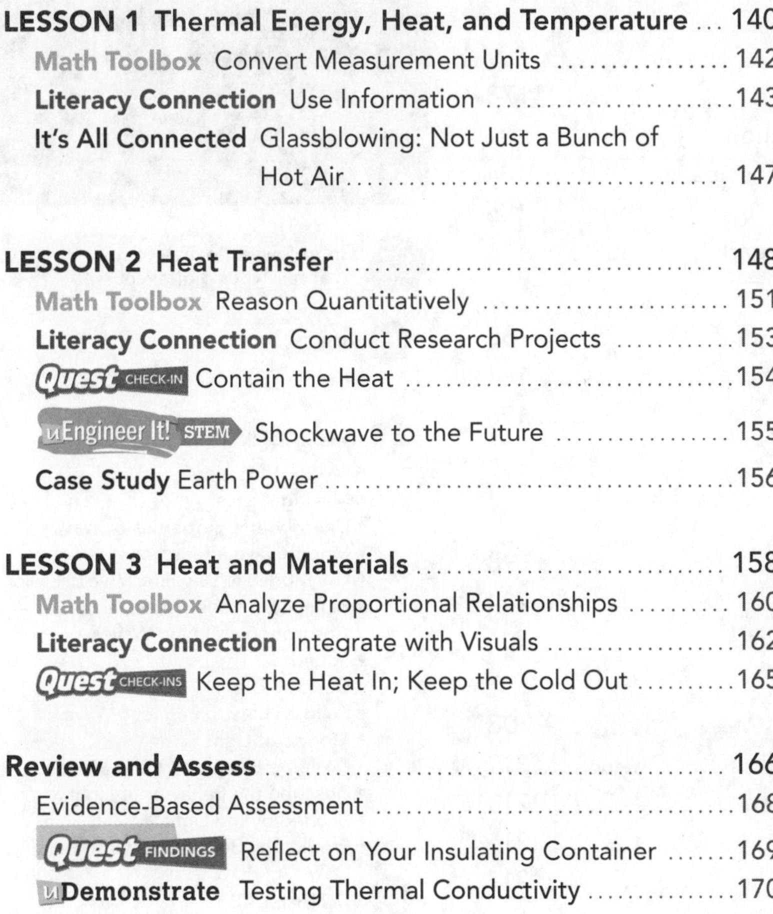

VIDEO
- Firefighter

INTERACTIVITY
- Flow of Thermal Energy
- A Rising Thermometer
- Methods of Thermal Energy Transfer
- Heat and Reheat
- A Day at the Beach
- Solar Oven Design
- Matter and Thermal Energy Transfer

VIRTUAL LAB
- Choosing a Snack Food

ASSESSMENT

eTEXT

uConnect How Cold Is the Water?

uInvestigate
- Temperature and Thermal Energy
- Visualizing Convection Currents
- Comparing How Liquids Cool

uDemonstrate
Testing Thermal Conductivity

TOPIC 5

Waves and Electromagnetic Radiation

The Essential Question What are the properties of mechanical and electromagnetic waves?

MS-PS4-1, MS-PS4-2

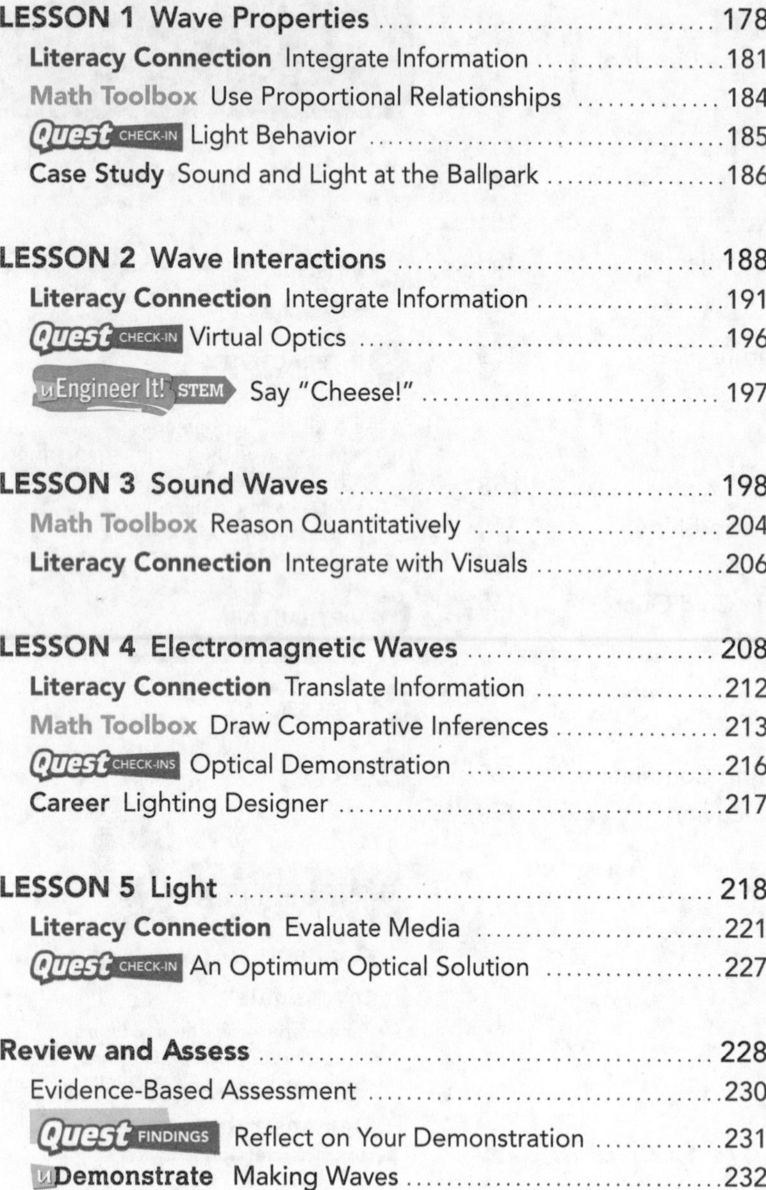

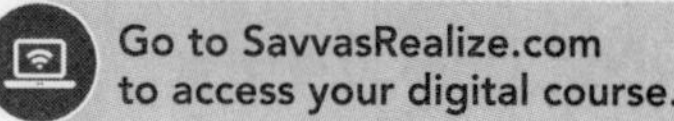

Go to SavvasRealize.com to access your digital course.

VIDEO
- Lighting Designer

INTERACTIVITY
- Modeling Waves
- Making Waves
- Describe the Properties of Waves
- Model Wave Interactions
- Use Models to Describe Wave Behavior
- Reflection, Transmission, and Absorption of Sound Waves
- Sound
- Doppler Effect
- Build an Electromagnetic Wave
- Models of Light
- Describe Electromagnetic Waves
- Describe the Behavior of Light
- Blinded by the Light
- Predict the Behavior of Light Rays

VIRTUAL LAB
- Colors of the Sky

ASSESSMENT

eTEXT

Connect What Are Waves?

Investigate
- Waves and Their Characteristics
- Standing Waves and Wave Interference
- Understanding Sound
- Build a Wave
- Light Interacting with Matter

Demonstrate
Making Waves

Electricity and Magnetism 236

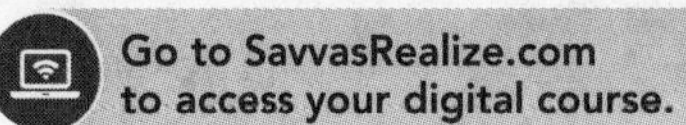
Go to SavvasRealize.com to access your digital course.

VIDEO
- Electrical Engineer

INTERACTIVITY
- Theremin
- Electric Currents
- Charged Interactions
- Interactions of Magnetic Fields
- Model Magnetic Forces
- Electricity and Magnetism
- Electromagnetism
- Electromagnetic Evidence
- Electric Motors
- Generators
- Electricity, Magnets, and Motion

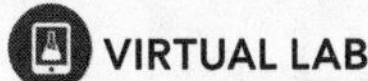
VIRTUAL LAB
- Get Your Bearings

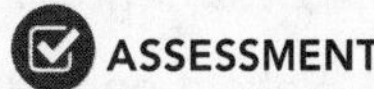
ASSESSMENT

eTEXT

Connect Magnetic Poles

Investigate
- Detecting Charges
- Detecting Fake Coins
- Electric Currents and Magnetism
- Electric, Magnetic Motion

Demonstrate
Planetary Detective

TOPIC 7

Information Technologies

The Essential Question Why are digital signals a reliable way to produce, store, and transmit information?

MS-PS4-3

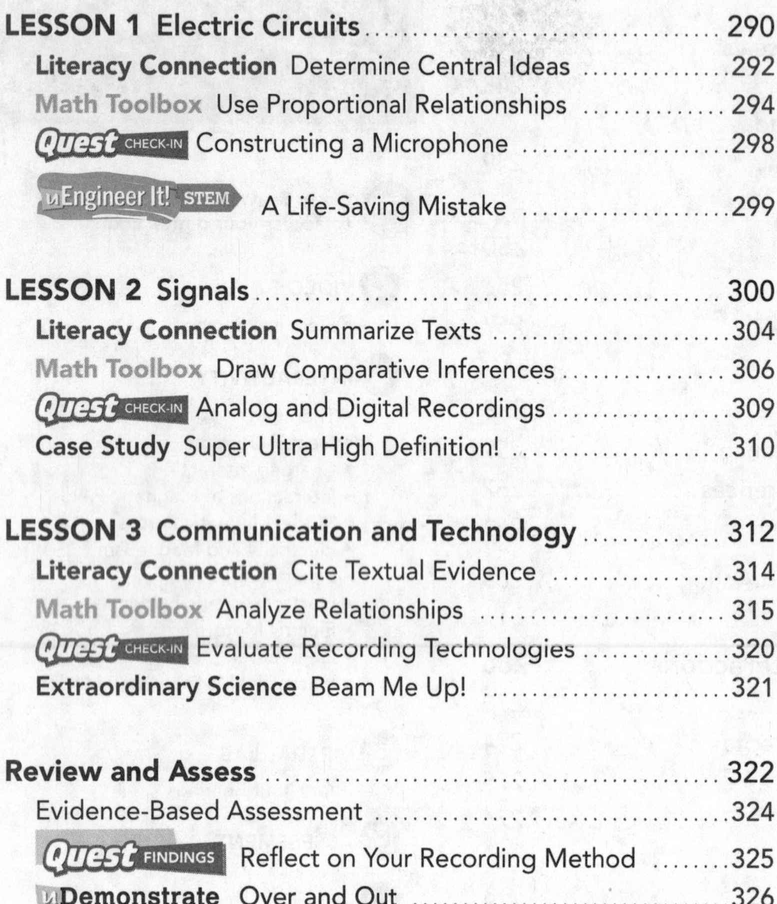

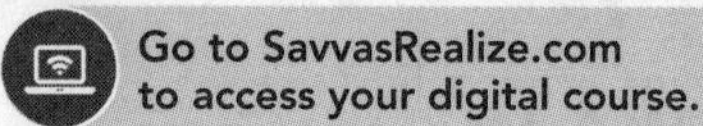

Go to SavvasRealize.com to access your digital course.

VIDEO
- Network Administrator

INTERACTIVITY
- Electric Circuits
- How Can You Light the Lights?
- Analog and Digital Signals
- I've Got to Take This Call
- Digitized Images
- Film Cameras and Digital Cameras
- Technology and Communication
- Signal Reliability

VIRTUAL LAB
- Super Spy!

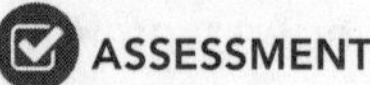

ASSESSMENT

eTEXT

HANDS-ON LABS

uConnect Continuous or Discrete?

uInvestigate
- Electric Current and Voltage
- Constructing a Simple Computer Circuit
- Let the Music Play

uDemonstrate
Over and Out

TOPIC 8

Atoms and the Periodic Table

MS-PS1-1

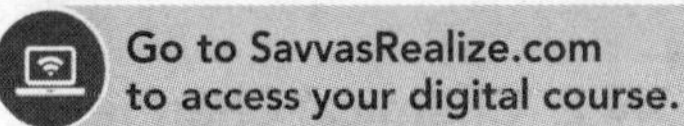

Go to SavvasRealize.com to access your digital course.

VIDEO
- Artist

INTERACTIVITY
- Build an Atom • Models of Atoms
- Organization of the Periodic Table
- Interactive Periodic Table • Groups of Elements • Valence Electrons
- Transferring Energy Through Bonding • Build an Ionic Compound
- Ionic or Covalent Bonding
- Chemical Bonding • Properties and Uses of Acids and Bases • Acids and Bases in Careers • Acid Rain

VIRTUAL LAB
- Protect the Helpers!

ASSESSMENT

eTEXT

uConnect Modeling Matter

uInvestigate
- How Far Away Is the Electron?
- Classifying Elements
- Element Chemistry
- Properties of Molecular Compounds
- Properties of Acids and Bases

uDemonstrate
Shedding Light on Ions

Chemical Reactions 394

MS-PS1-2, MS-PS1-3, MS-PS1-5, MS-PS1-6

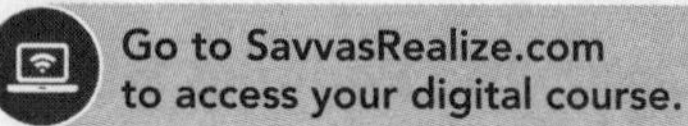

Go to SavvasRealize.com to access your digital course.

VIDEO
- Forensic Scientist

INTERACTIVITY
- Separating a Mixture
- Inside a Water Treatment Plant
- Water Contaminants and Removal Methods
- Evidence of Chemical Reactions
- Analyze Exothermic and Endothermic Graphs
- Conservation of Matter
- Model a Chemical Reaction
- Reactants and Products
- Model the Conservation of Mass
- Describe the Impact of Synthetics
- The Impact of Synthetics

VIRTUAL LAB
- Chemistry of Glowsticks

ASSESSMENT

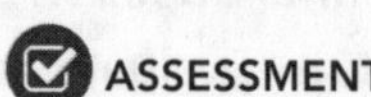

eTEXT

HANDS-ON LABS

Connect What Happens When Chemicals React?

Investigate
- Particles in Liquids
- Changes in a Burning Candle
- Is Matter Conserved?
- Making Plastic from Starch

Demonstrate
Evidence of Chemical Change

TOPIC 10 Forces and Motion 446

The Essential Question How is the motion of an object affected by forces that act on it?

MS-PS2-1, MS-PS2-2, MS-PS2-4, MS-PS3-2

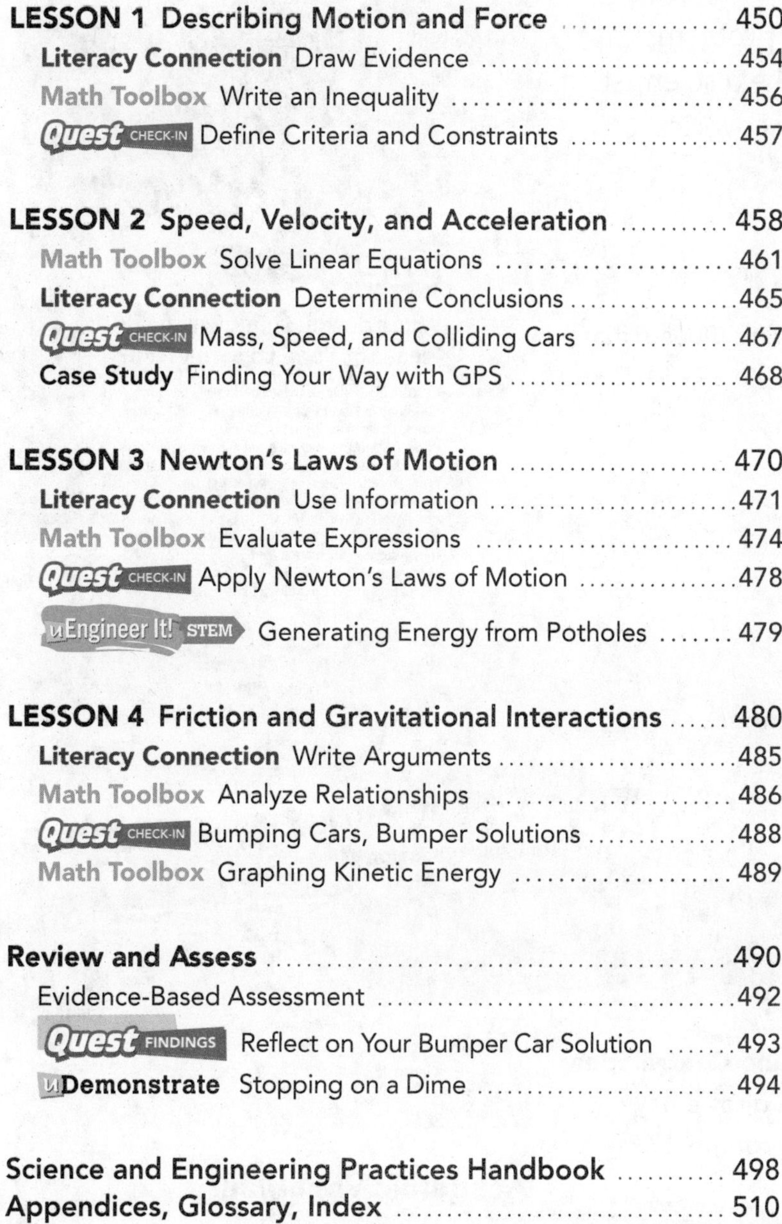

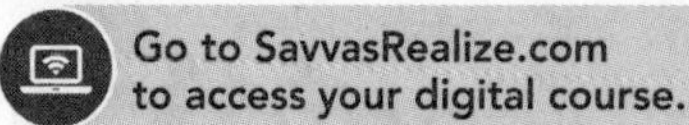

Go to SavvasRealize.com to access your digital course.

VIDEO
- Mechanical Engineer

INTERACTIVITY
- Relative Motion • Balanced and Unbalanced Forces • Explore Forces • Falling for Velocity • Motion Graphs • How Forces Affect Motion • How are Mass, Motion, and Force Related? • Going, Going, Gone! • Fuel Efficient Vehicles • Exploring Gravity • The Pull of the Tides

VIRTUAL LAB
- Launching a Spacecraft into Motion

ASSESSMENT

eTEXT

Connect Identifying Motion

Investigate
- Motion Commotion
- Walking the Walk
- Newton Scooters
- Observing Friction
- Sticky Sneakers

Demonstrate
Stopping on a Dime

Elevate your thinking!

Elevate Science takes science to a whole new level and lets you take ownership of your learning. Explore science in the world around you. Investigate how things work. Think critically and solve problems! *Elevate Science* helps you think like a scientist, so you're ready for a world of discoveries.

Explore Your World

Explore real-life scenarios with engaging Quests that dig into science topics around the world. You can:

- Solve real-world problems
- Apply skills and knowledge
- Communicate solutions

Quest KICKOFF

What do you think is causing Pleasant Pond to turn green?

In 2016, algal blooms turned bodies of water green and slimy in Florida, Utah, California, and 17 other states. These blooms put people and ecosystems in danger. Scientists, such as limnologists, are working to predict and prevent future algal blooms. In this problem-based Quest activity, you will investigate an algal bloom at a lake and determine its cause. In labs and digital activities, you will apply what you learn in each lesson to help you gather evidence to solve the mystery. With enough evidence, you will be able to identify what you believe is the cause of the algal bloom and present a solution in the Findings activity.

Make Connections

Elevate Science connects science to other subjects and shows you how to better understand the world through:

- Mathematics
- Reading and Writing
- Literacy

Math Toolbox

Graphing Population Changes

Ohio's Deer Population

Changes in a population over time, such as white-tailed deer in Ohio, can be displayed in a graph.

Deer Population Trends, 2000–2010

Year	Population (estimated)	Year	Population (estimated)
2000	525,000	2006	770,000
2001	560,000	2007	725,000
2002	620,000	2008	745,000
2003	670,000	2009	750,000
2004	715,000	2010	710,000
2005	720,000		

Relationships Use the data

READING CHECK **Determine Central ideas**
What adaptations might the giraffe have that help it survive in its environment?

Academic Vocabulary
Relate the term *decomposer* to the verb *compose*. What does it mean to compose something?

Build Skills for the Future

- Master the Engineering Design Process
- Apply critical thinking and analytical skills
- Learn about STEM careers

Focus on Inquiry

Case studies put you in the shoes of a scientist to solve real-world mysteries using real data. You will be able to:

- Analyze Data
- Test a hypothesis
- Solve the Case

Case Study

MS-LS2-1

THE CASE OF THE DISAPPEARING

Cerulean Warbler

The cerulean warbler is a small, migratory songbird named for its blue color. Cerulean warblers breed in eastern North America during the spring and summer. The warblers spend the winter months in the Andes Mountains of Colombia, Venezuela, Ecuador, and Peru in northern part of South America.

Enter the Lab

Hands-on experiments and virtual labs help you test ideas and show what you know in performance-based assessments. Scaffolded labs include:

- STEM Labs
- Design Your Own
- Open-ended Labs

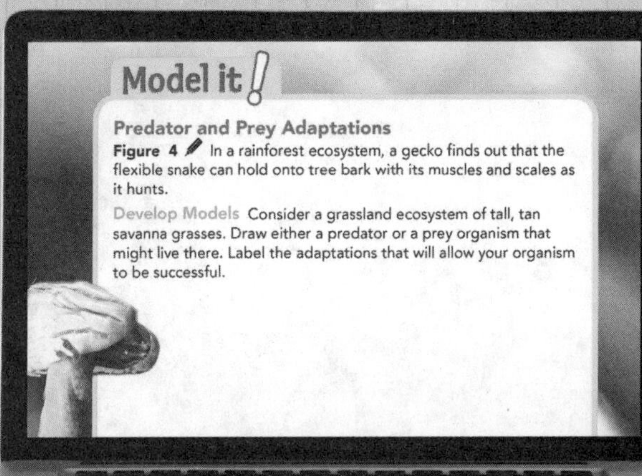

uInvestigate Observe how once-living matter is broken down into smaller components in the process of decomposition.

TOPIC 1

Introduction to Matter

NGSS PERFORMANCE EXPECTATIONS

MS-PS1-1 Develop models to describe the atomic composition of simple molecules and extended structures.

MS-PS1-2 Analyze and interpret data on the properties of substances before and after the substances interact to determine if a chemical reaction has occurred.

GO ONLINE
to access your digital course

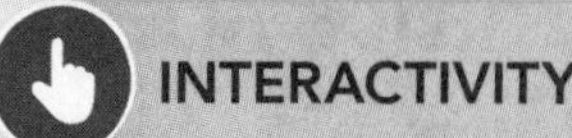

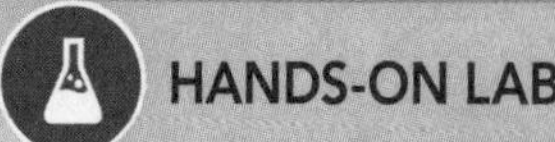

How did this ice form?

uConnect See how you can model particles that are so small you can't see them.

The Essential Question

How can we observe, measure, and use matter?

CCC Energy and Matter If you step outside when the temperature is well below freezing, you can bet it will not be raining. You are more likely to see snow if there is any precipitation at all. Water in the clouds is so cold that it turns into ice crystals. What are some of the physical differences between rain water and ice crystals such as snow?

Quest KICKOFF

How can you use science to make special effects?

Phenomenon A special effects company would like to be chosen to develop the special effects for a new movie. But first, the movie director wants to check out the company's capabilities. In this problem-based Quest activity, you will develop a movie scene that uses some amazing special effects. You will write the script and the storyboards. As you develop the special effects, you will explore different types of substances that are used to make special effects. You will understand the role that physical and chemical properties of matter play in the special effects. Finally, you will present your scene, along with an explanation of the special effects and the properties of matter behind them.

INTERACTIVITY

Lights! Camera! Action!

MS-PS1-2 Analyze and interpret data on the properties of substances before and after the substances interact to determine if a chemical reaction has occurred.

NBC LEARN VIDEO

After watching the Quest Kickoff video about special effects, complete the sentences about special effects you have seen in movies. Then discuss your answers with a partner.

1 **One special effect I have seen is**

....

....

....

2 **It added to the scene because**

....

....

....

Quest CHECK-IN

IN LESSON 1

How can substance changes play a role in special effects? Think about how you can take advantage of physical and chemical changes to create special effects.

INTERACTIVITY

The Science of Special Effects

IN LESSON 2

How will the amounts of substances affect physical and chemical changes? Consider the amounts of substances you will need to create the special effects you want.

Quest CHECK-INS

IN LESSON 3

How do substances interact? Explore substances and how they interact. Collect and analyze data to help develop your special effects.

INTERACTIVITY

Mysterious Movie Fog

HANDS-ON LAB

Cinematic Science

Smoke in movie scenes can be eye-catching and dramatic, but it is never accidental. Directors carefully manage the production and movement of the smoke to create the desired effect.

Quest FINDINGS

Complete the Quest!

Present your scene and storyboard, and include an explanation of the physical and chemical changes involved in your special effects.

INTERACTIVITY

Reflect on Your Scene

uConnect Lab

MS-PS1-1

The Nuts and Bolts of Formulas

How can you **develop a model** of particles that are so small you can't even see them?

Background

Phenomenon Have you ever noticed dust particles floating through the air? You may think nothing is smaller than a dust particle, but in fact, everything you see is made up of atoms that form molecules of substances. The atoms and molecules are many times smaller than dust particles. How can you describe something you cannot see? In this lab, you will develop a model that describes a molecule.

Materials

(per group)

- short bolt
- long bolt
- hex nuts
- square nuts

Develop and Use a Model

☐ 1. **SEP Develop a Model** Examine the objects supplied by your teacher. Assign a symbol to each type of object. Record your assigned symbols.

☐ 2. Assemble different structures using the objects you have. In the space provided, sketch your structures.

☐ 3. **SEP Use a Model** Under each sketch, write a formula for each structure using the symbols you assigned in Step 1.

☐ 4. Share the symbols you assigned to each object with another group. Write a formula using those symbols and ask the other group to build the structure.

GO ONLINE
to access your
digital course

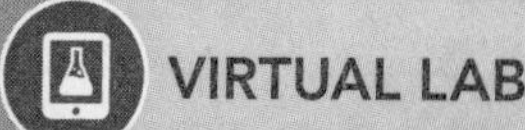

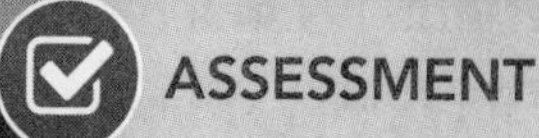

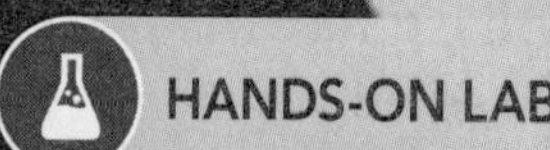

The Essential Question

What causes matter to change from one state to another?

SEP Construct Explanations You can see a cloud of your breath outside on a cold day but not on a warm day. What do you think is happening to your breath in the cold air?

Quest KICKOFF

How can you use solids, liquids, and gases to lift a car?

STEM Phenomenon Auto mechanics often need to go under cars to repair the parts in the under-carriage, such as the shocks and exhaust system. It's much easier for them to do their job if they have more room to work, so they use lift systems to raise the cars overhead. In this problem-based Quest activity, you will design an elevator or lift system that uses a solid, liquid, or gas to raise a model car. You will explore the properties of solids, liquids, and gases to see how they can be used in a lift mechanism. You will investigate how potential changes of state affect or impose constraints on your design. By applying what you have learned through lessons, digital activities, and hands-on labs, you will design, build, test, and evaluate a model elevator or lift.

NBC LEARN VIDEO

After watching the Quest Kickoff video, which examines different ways that elevators and lifts work, write down what you already know about solids, liquids, and gases.

Solids:

....

....

Liquids:

....

....

Gases:

....

....

INTERACTIVITY

Getting a Lift

MS-PS1-4 Develop a model that predicts and describes changes in particle motion, temperature, and state of a pure substance when thermal energy is added or removed.

Quest CHECK-IN

IN LESSON 1

STEM What are the properties of solids, liquids, and gases? Think about how you can use those properties in your lift device.

INTERACTIVITY

Design Your Lift

Quest CHECK-IN

IN LESSON 2

STEM How might a change in state affect a process? Consider how changes in the state of matter might affect your lift. Then develop a final design.

INTERACTIVITY

Lift Your Car

Auto mechanics raise cars above their heads to repair parts such as engines and transmission systems.

Quest CHECK-IN

IN LESSON 3

STEM What criteria and constraints affect your model? Build and test your lift device. Improve and retest as needed.

HANDS-ON LAB

Phases of Matter

Quest FINDINGS

Complete the Quest!

Demonstrate your lift and evaluate its performance. Reflect on your work and consider other applications for your device.

INTERACTIVITY

Reflect on Your Lift

uConnect Lab

Solid, Liquid, or Gas?

How can you **develop and use models** to illustrate examples of the different states of matter?

Background

Phenomenon Imagine that your little sister's class is studying matter. She asks you if all the kinds of matter in bottles are liquids. To help her understand the answer, you decide to show her examples of different states of matter that can be put in a bottle.

Materials

(per group)

- 3 clear plastic bottles with lids
- water
- ice
- seltzer
- marbles
- paper towels
- funnel (optional)

Safety

Be sure to follow all safety procedures provided by your teacher. The Safety Appendix of your textbook provides more details about the safety icons.

Develop Models

☐ 1. **SEP Develop Models** Describe how you will use the materials to make three models. Remember, you need to show materials in each state of matter. You can show more than one state in a bottle or a single state of matter in a bottle but you need to show each state of matter. See if you can get one bottle to show all three states.

....

....

....

....

☐ 2. Show your plan to your teacher for approval, and then assemble your bottles. Observe the matter inside each bottle.

☐ 3. In the observation section, draw a table and record your observations.

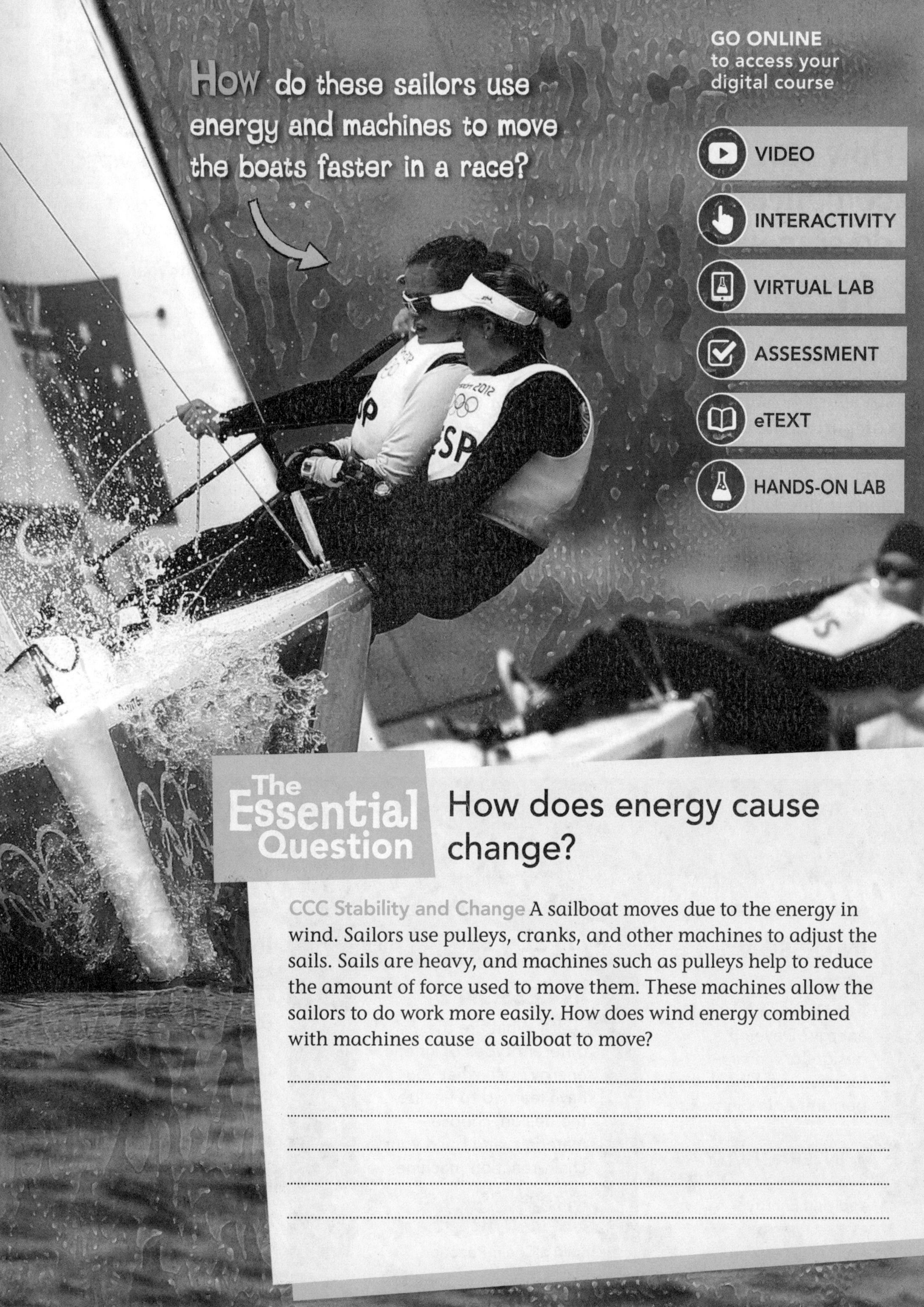
How do these sailors use energy and machines to move the boats faster in a race?
GO ONLINE
to access your digital course
VIDEO
INTERACTIVITY
VIRTUAL LAB
ASSESSMENT
eTEXT
HANDS-ON LAB
ESP

The Essential Question

How does energy cause change?

CCC Stability and Change A sailboat moves due to the energy in wind. Sailors use pulleys, cranks, and other machines to adjust the sails. Sails are heavy, and machines such as pulleys help to reduce the amount of force used to move them. These machines allow the sailors to do work more easily. How does wind energy combined with machines cause a sailboat to move?

Quest KICKOFF

How can you build a complicated machine to do something simple?

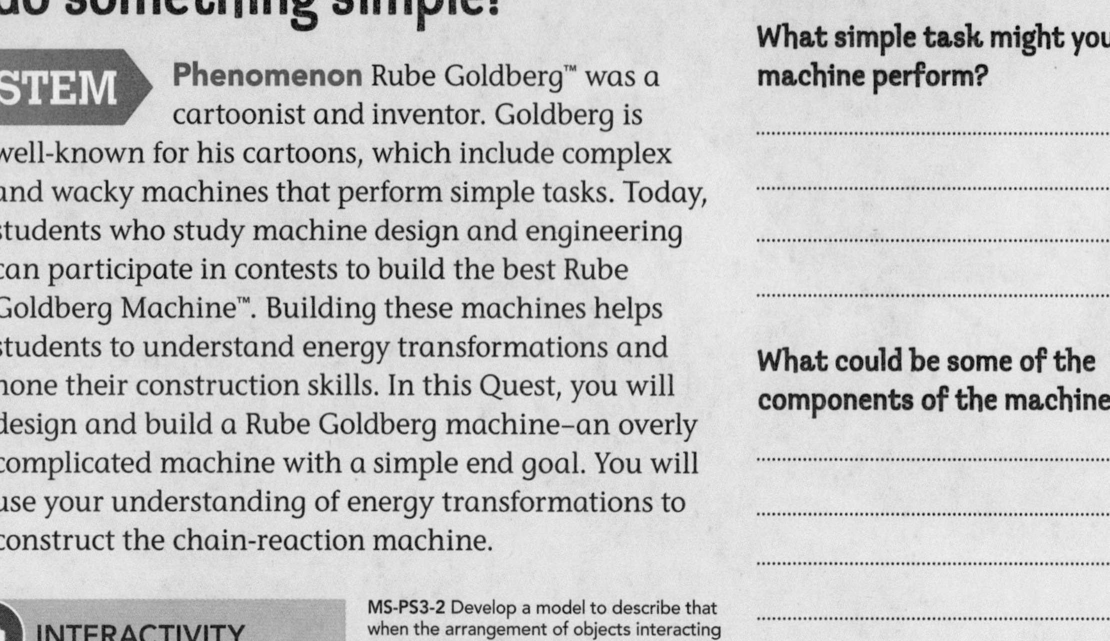

STEM **Phenomenon** Rube Goldberg™ was a cartoonist and inventor. Goldberg is well-known for his cartoons, which include complex and wacky machines that perform simple tasks. Today, students who study machine design and engineering can participate in contests to build the best Rube Goldberg Machine™. Building these machines helps students to understand energy transformations and hone their construction skills. In this Quest, you will design and build a Rube Goldberg machine–an overly complicated machine with a simple end goal. You will use your understanding of energy transformations to construct the chain-reaction machine.

INTERACTIVITY

Outrageous Energy Contraptions

MS-PS3-2 Develop a model to describe that when the arrangement of objects interacting at a distance changes, different amounts of potential energy are stored in the system.
MS-PS3-5 Construct, use, and present arguments to support the claim that when the kinetic energy of an object changes, energy is transferred to or from the object.

NBC LEARN VIDEO

After watching the Quest Kickoff video, answer the following questions.

What simple task might your machine perform?

....

....

....

....

What could be some of the components of the machine?

....

....

....

....

Quest CHECK-IN

IN LESSON 1

STEM How do machines exert force and transfer energy? Develop a design for a chain-reaction machine that can perform a simple task.

INTERACTIVITY

Applying Energy

Quest CHECK-IN

IN LESSON 2

STEM What are the different types of kinetic energy? Use what you have learned to finalize the design, choose materials, and build your chain-reaction machine.

HANDS-ON LAB

Build a Chain-Reaction Machine

Quest CHECK-IN

IN LESSON 3

STEM What energy transformations take place in a chain-reaction machine? Test your chain-reaction machine prototype and evaluate its performance. Revise and retest it.

HANDS-ON LAB

Test and Evaluate a Chain-Reaction Machine

Many energy transformations occur in this complicated device. In the end, it simply turns on a light bulb!

Quest CHECK-IN

IN LESSON 4

STEM How can an additional energy transformation improve your design? Modify your chain-reaction machine to include at least one additional energy transformation. Then test, evaluate, and finalize it.

HANDS-ON LAB

Redesign and Retest a Chain-Reaction Machine

…est FINDINGS

…lete the Q…

Determine th… your machine, and s… is used in the working of you… from start to finish.

INTERACTIVITY

Reflect on Your Chain-Reaction Machine

MS-PS3-2, MS-PS3-5

What Would Make a Card Jump?

How can you **use evidence** to make an argument that energy is transformed?

Background

Phenomenon When riding a bike, have you ever thought about what you need to get the bike moving? Or what it takes to stop the bike? Energy is needed to cause an object, such as a bike, to start moving, stop moving, speed up, slow down, or change direction. This energy can be transformed from other kinds of energy. In this activity, you will devise a model to observe energy transformations.

Materials

(per group)

- 3 × 5 index card
- scissors
- rubber band

Safety

Be sure to follow all safety procedures provided by your teacher. The Safety Appendix of your textbook provides more details about the safety icons.

Design a Procedure

☐ **1.** Using the materials given, you and your partner will devise a model that can demonstrate how energy is transformed. Discuss your ideas with your partner.

☐ **2.** **SEP Plan a Procedure** Write a procedure that describes how you will use the given materials to construct a model that will allow you to observe energy transformations. Show your procedure to your teacher before you begin.

____

____

____

____

____

____

☐ **3.** Record your observations.

Observations

Connect Go online for a downloadable worksheet of this lab.

Analyze and Conclude

1. **SEP Construct Explanations** Describe what happened to the card in your model.

2. **SEP Engage in Argument** Based on your observations, use evidence to support or refute the argument that energy was transferred from one object to another in your model.

3. **CCC Energy and Matter** What can you do to increase the potential energy of a rubber band?

LESSON 1

Energy, Motion, Force, and Work

Guiding Questions

- How is energy related to motion and force?
- What are the relationships among energy, motion, force, and work?

Connections

Literacy Determine Central Ideas

Math Solve Linear Equations

HANDS-ON LAB

uInvestigate Experiment with a soda can to see how an object's energy relates to work.

Vocabulary

energy
motion
force
work
power

Academic Vocabulary

maximum

Connect It!

Draw curved arrows on the photograph to represent the motion of the motorcycles.

SEP Construct Explanations These motorcycles need energy to move. Where does the energy come from?

....

Write Explanatory Texts Describe how the rider exerts a force on the motorcycle.

....

....

SEP Construct Explanations In what way do you think the motorcycles perform work?

....

Energy in Motion and Force

Watch this video to better understand energy.

Energy is the ability to do work or cause change. You do work when you pick up your backpack. Motorcycles do work during a race, as in **Figure 1**. The energy to do this work comes from fuel. As the fuel burns, it changes into other substances and releases energy.

Energy comes in many forms. Light, sound, and electricity are all forms of energy. Energy can also be transferred from place to place. For example, chemical energy is transferred from the food you eat to your body. Energy from the sun is transferred to Earth in the form of electromagnetic radiation. Energy is not something you can see directly. You can, however, observe its effects. When you touch something hot, you don't see the energy, but you feel the heat. You can hear the sound of a bass drum, but you can't see the sound energy itself.

Reflect Think about the different methods you used to travel from one place to another today. In your science notebook, describe two of these ways. For each, identify the energy source that caused the movement.

Energy and Motion It takes energy for motion to occur. An object is in **motion** if its position changes relative to another object. A pitched ball would not speed toward home plate without energy supplied by the pitcher. Energy supplied by food enables a racehorse to run around a track. Energy stored in gasoline allows the motorcycles in **Figure 1** to move at high speeds. In each of these examples, the more energy that is used, the faster the object can move.

Racing Around the Track

Figure 1 Energy, motion, force, and work are all involved in a motorcycle race.

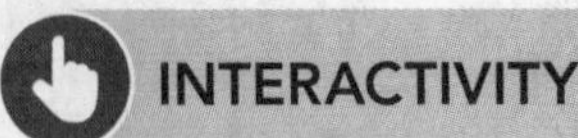

INTERACTIVITY

Play the role of a video game designer and test virtual machines.

Energy and Force The relationship between energy and motion also involves forces. A **force** is a push or pull. You can see many examples of this relationship on a construction site. Look at **Figure 2** and study the examples of how energy is used to apply a force that causes motion.

READING CHECK **Explain** How would you describe a force?

....

....

Force

Figure 2 When energy is used to apply force, objects can move.

CCC Energy and Matter Draw an arrow on each numbered picture to show the direction of the force being applied. Then label each arrow with "push" or "pull" to identify the type of force being applied.

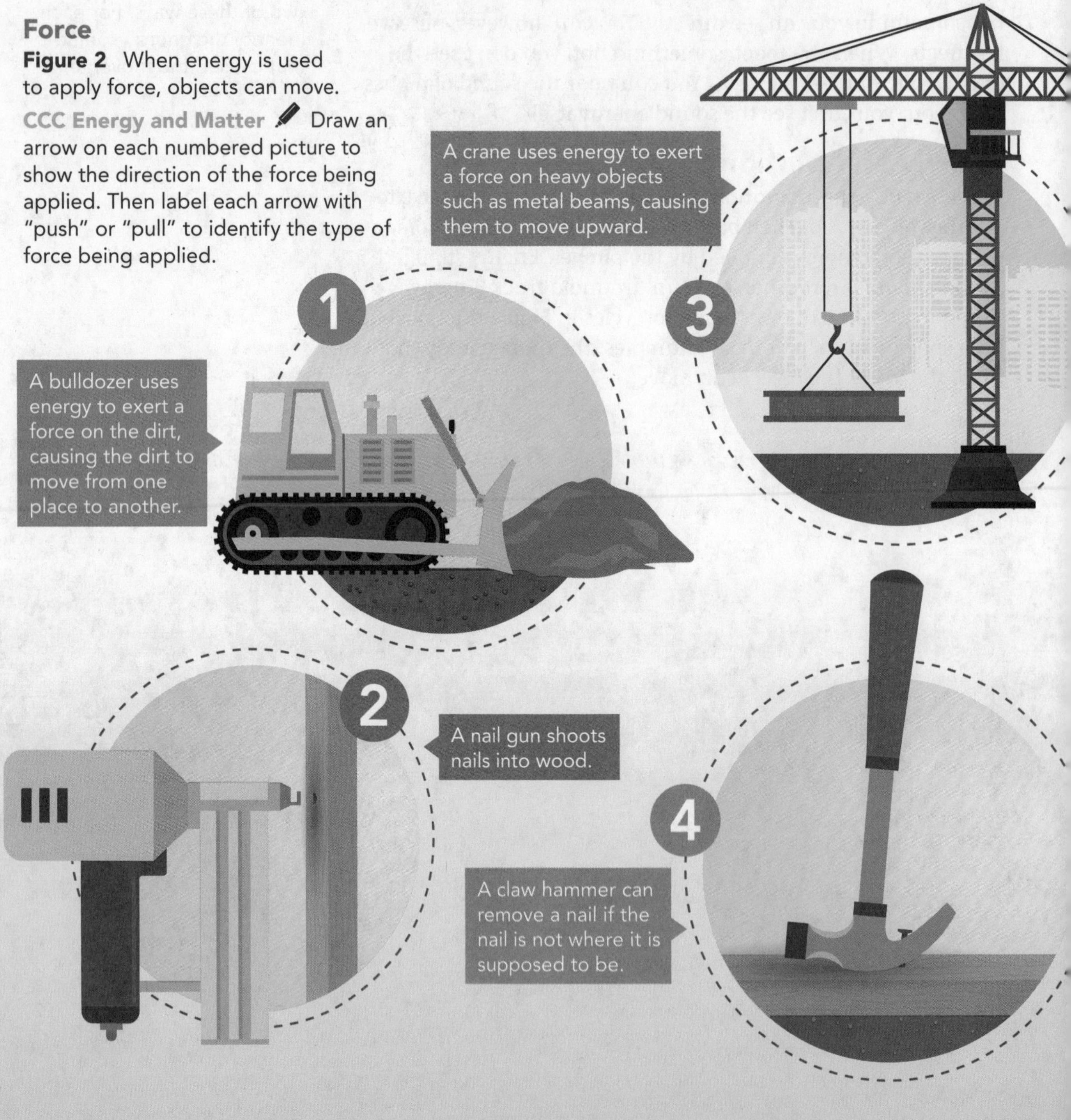

1 A bulldozer uses energy to exert a force on the dirt, causing the dirt to move from one place to another.

2 A nail gun shoots nails into wood.

3 A crane uses energy to exert a force on heavy objects such as metal beams, causing them to move upward.

4 A claw hammer can remove a nail if the nail is not where it is supposed to be.

Force and Work

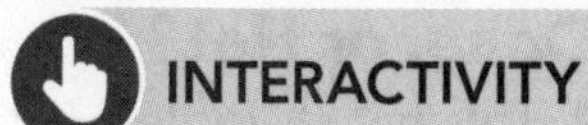

INTERACTIVITY

Explore how levers work in this virtual activity.

You might think of "work" as a job, such as teaching, being a doctor, or bagging groceries at the local supermarket. But the scientific meaning of work is much broader than that. In scientific terms, you do **work** any time you exert a force on an object that causes the object to change its motion in the same direction in which you exert the force. All of the machines on the previous page show work being done because the forces are being applied in the same direction as the motion shown.

You probably carry your books from one class to another every school day. You know that you exert a force on the books as you carry them. However, you do very little work on them because of the direction of the force exerted. When you carry an object while walking at constant speed in a straight line, you exert an upward force on the object. Because the force is vertical and the motion is horizontal, you don't do any work on the object itself.

Figure 3 shows three different ways to move a tool bin. The weight of the bin is the same in each situation, but the amount of work varies. For a given force, the **maximum** amount of work is done when both the movement and the force are in the same direction.

Academic Vocabulary

Write a synonym for maximum.

....

Force, Motion, and Work

Figure 3 The amount of work that you do on something depends on the direction of the applied force and the object's motion. In the second and third pictures, label each arrow with "motion" or "force."

Direction of motion
Force
Does no work
Does work
Only the horizontal part of the force does work to move the tool bin.
The force acts in the same direction as the motion, so the maximum work is done.
As the worker walks, the lifting force is not in the direction of the motion, so no work is done on the tool bin while it is being carried.

Work Done, or Not?

Figure 4 This girl struggles to open a jar, but the lid does not budge.

SEP Construct Explanations Is the girl doing work? Explain your reasoning.

....

....

....

....

....

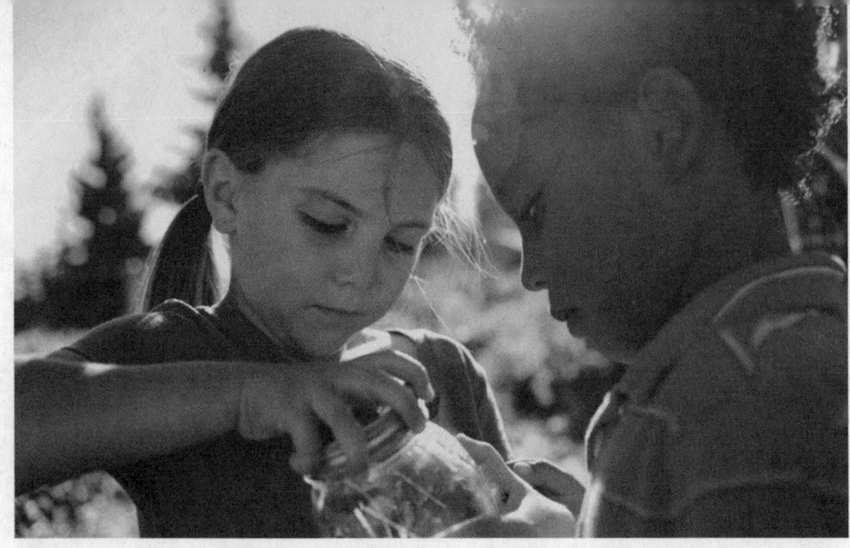

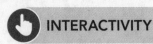

INTERACTIVITY

Explore how energy is needed to get an object to move, and discover how work on an object affects its motion.

Work Requires Motion Imagine that you are trying to open a jar, and the lid is stuck. You exert a lot of force on the lid, but it doesn't move. Are you doing work? No. No matter how much force you exert, you don't do any work if the lid does not move.

Calculating Work Suppose you bought a new painting for your room. You have to carry the painting up three porch steps to the first floor and then up another flight of 12 steps to the second floor. (See **Figure 5.**) Is it more work to lift the painting up 12 steps than three steps? As you might guess, moving an object a greater distance requires more work than moving the same object a shorter distance. The amount of work you do depends on both the amount of force you exert and the distance the object moves.

More or Less Work Done?

Figure 5 This person carries a painting up two sets of steps.

Predict Circle the image in which you think the person does more work.

The amount of work done on an object is calculated by multiplying force times distance. When force is measured in newtons and distance in meters, the SI unit of work is the newton-meter (N-m). This unit is also called a joule (J). One joule is the amount of work you do when you exert a force of 1 newton to move an object a distance of 1 meter.

READING CHECK **Determine Central Ideas** What two factors affect how much work is done in any given action?

....

Calculating Work

A grandfather lifts a baby 1.5 m with an upward force of 80 N, as shown in the third photograph below. You can use the relationship among work, force, and distance to find out how much work is done:

Work = Force × Distance
Work = 80 N × 1.5 m
Work = 120 N-m

The amount of work done is 120 N-m, or 120 J.

Use the formula for finding work to answer questions 1–2. Show your calculations. Use joules as the unit for work.

1. Solve Linear Equations This woman lifts a plant 2 m with a force of 65 N. How much work does she do?

   ....

2. Calculate How much work is done when 300 N of force is used to lift the dog 1.5 m?

   ....

3. Classify Label the photos below with the words *least, medium,* and *most* to rank them from least work done to most work done.

Investigate Experiment with a soda can to see how an object's energy relates to work.

Work Related to Energy and Power

Did you pull your shoes from the closet this morning? If so, then you did work on the shoes. As you have read, work is done when a force moves an object in the direction of the force. When an object moves, its position changes. What causes change? Recall that the ability to do work or cause change is called energy. Energy is measured in joules—the same units as work.

Literacy Connection

Determine Central Ideas As you read, underline the main idea of each paragraph on this page.

When you do work on an object, some of your energy is transferred to that object. Think about the plant shown in the Math Toolbox. When the gardener lifted the plant to the high shelf, she transferred energy to the plant.

If you carry a bag of groceries up a flight of stairs, the work you do is the same whether you walk or run. The time it takes to do the work does not affect the amount of work you do on an object. But something else—power—is affected. **Power** is the rate at which work is done, and it equals the amount of work done on an object in a unit of time. You can think of power in two main ways. An object that has more power than another object does more work in the same amount of time. It can also mean doing the same amount of work in less time. Look at **Figure 6** for other examples that compare power.

Work and Power

Figure 6 In each of these images, work is being done. For each image, give two examples of ways the people shown can increase the power being used.

These people load 10 items on the truck in 10 minutes.
Ways power can be increased:

....

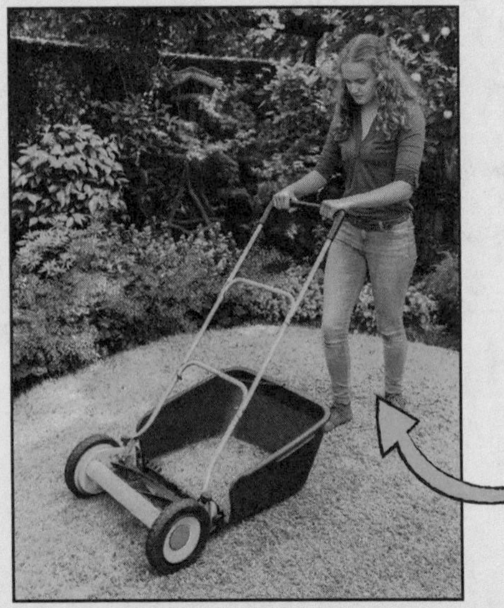

This person mows half of her backyard in one hour.
Ways power can be increased:

....

Calculating Power

All you need to know to calculate power is how much and how quickly work is being done. Power is calculated by dividing the amount of work done by the amount of time it takes to do the work. This can be written as the following formula:

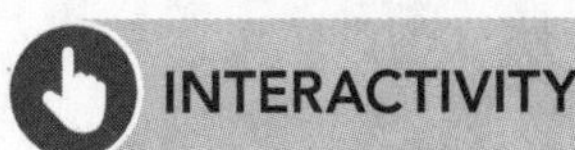
INTERACTIVITY

Examine real-world examples of energy transformations and forces.

$$\text{Power} = \frac{\text{Work}}{\text{Time}}$$

Because work is equal to force times distance, you can rewrite the equation for power as follows:

$$\text{Power} = \frac{\text{Force} \times \text{Distance}}{\text{Time}}$$

When work is measured in joules and time in seconds, the SI unit of power is the watt (W). One watt equals one joule per second (1 W = 1 J/s). Examine **Figure 7** to learn more about calculating power.

Power

Figure 7 Most climbers of the Himalayan Mountains would not make it to the peaks without the help of Sherpas.

SEP Use Mathematics Sherpas are natives of Nepal, and they carry heavy loads of equipment up the mountains for the climbers. Suppose one Sherpa uses a force of 980 N to move a load of equipment to a height of 20 meters in 25 seconds. How much power is used?

Different Types of Power

Figure 8 Leaf blowers require gasoline for power, while rakes require power from your body.

Power and Energy Recall that power is the rate at which work is done. Power is also the rate at which energy is transferred, or the amount of energy transferred in a unit of time.

$$\text{Power} = \frac{\text{Energy transferred}}{\text{Time}}$$

For example, a 60-watt lightbulb transfers 60 joules of energy per second. Different machines have different amounts of power. For instance, you can use either a rake or a leaf blower to remove leaves from your lawn (see **Figure 8**). Each tool transfers the same amount of energy to the leaves when it moves leaves the same distance. However, the leaf blower moves leaves faster than the rake. The leaf blower has more power because it transfers the same amount of energy to the leaves in less time.

READING CHECK **Apply Concepts** What is the difference in power between a 60-watt lightbulb and a 100-watt lightbulb?

Model It

SEP Develop Models In the concept map below, label each line to show how energy, motion, force, work, and power relate to each other. One line is labeled for you as an example.

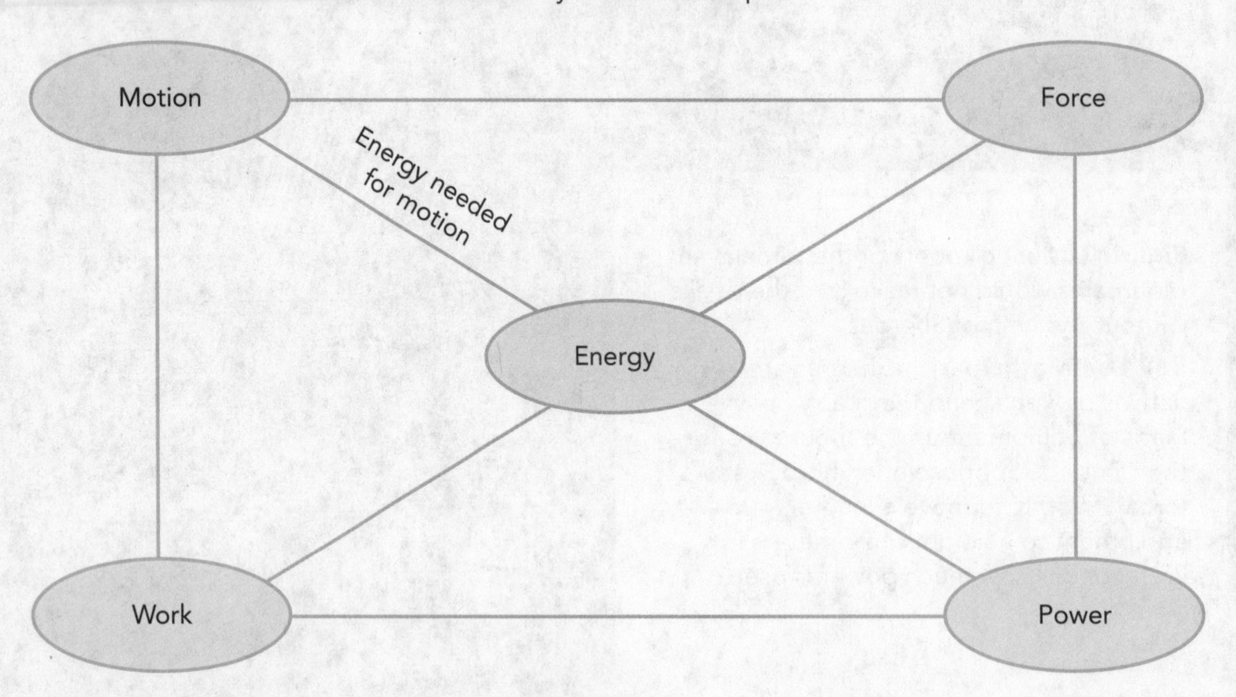

LESSON 1 Check

1. **Explain** How are energy and motion related?

2. **Apply Concepts** Give an example in which energy produces a force that causes motion.

3. **SEP Engage in Argument** Is work done when you hold a heavy object for a long time? Why or why not?

4. **SEP Use Mathematics** What force was applied to an object if 35 J of work was done and the object moved 7 m? Show your work.

5. **SEP Ask Questions** A student did 24 J of work on a chair. She applied a force of 12 N and moved the chair 2 m. What question do you need to ask to determine the amount of power used?

6. **CCC Cause and Effect** Use the terms *motion*, *power*, and *work* to complete the table.

Cause	Effect
Energy transferred over time	
Force applied to an object to change its position	
Force moving an object over a distance	

Quest CHECK-IN

In this lesson, you learned about the basics of energy and how force and motion relate to it. You also learned about how these concepts relate to how work is done.

SEP Define Problems How do the concepts of energy, force, and motion relate to the machine you will be designing? What factors will you need to consider in your design?

INTERACTIVITY

Applying Energy

Go online to learn about how energy, force, and motion relate to machines. Then, develop the design for your machine.

LESSON 2

Kinetic Energy and Potential Energy

Guiding Questions

- What determines an object's kinetic energy?
- What factors affect potential energy?
- What is the relationship between potential and kinetic energy?

Connections

Literacy Integrate With Visuals

Math Evaluate Expressions

MS-PS3-1, MS-PS3-2

HANDS-ON LAB

uInvestigate Use a skateboard to model changes in kinetic energy.

Vocabulary

kinetic energy
potential energy
gravitational potential energy
elastic potential energy

Academic Vocabulary

virtue

Connect It!

Draw an arrow on the image to show the direction that you think the rocks and dirt are moving.

SEP Construct Explanations It takes a lot of energy to move this amount of dirt and rocks. What do you think is the source of this energy?

....

....

Apply Scientific Reasoning What is another example of something that starts moving suddenly?

....

....

Kinetic Energy

Study the landslide shown in **Figure 1**. In this image, dirt and rocks are moving rapidly down the side of the hill. As you read in Lesson 1, it takes energy to cause the motion you see in this photo. When objects are in motion, they are demonstrating a certain kind of energy—kinetic energy. **Kinetic energy** is the energy that an object possesses by **virtue** of being in motion.

Examples of kinetic energy are all around us. A car moving down a road exhibits kinetic energy. So does a runner participating in a race. As you sit at your desk in school, you exhibit kinetic energy every time you turn a page in a book or type on a keyboard.

Factors Affecting Kinetic Energy The kinetic energy of an object depends on both its speed and its mass. The faster an object moves, the more kinetic energy it has. For example, if a tennis ball moves at great speed, it has more kinetic energy than if the ball had been softly lobbed over the net. Kinetic energy also increases as mass increases. A wheelbarrow full of dirt has more kinetic energy than an empty wheelbarrow has, due to its greater mass.

INTERACTIVITY

Interpret graphs to understand the relationships among a snowboarder's kinetic energy, mass, and speed.

Academic Vocabulary

The phrase *by virtue of* means "because of." In what other way have you heard the term virtue used?

....

....

....

Landslide!

Figure 1 A landslide is a sudden movement of rock and soil. Before the landslide, all the rocks and soil were in place and not moving.

Investigate Use a skateboard to model changes in kinetic energy.

Calculating Kinetic Energy Keeping in mind that the kinetic energy of an object depends on its mass and its speed, you can use the following equation to solve for the kinetic energy of an object:

$$\text{Kinetic energy} = \tfrac{1}{2} \times \text{Mass} \times \text{Speed}^2$$

The exponent "2" that follows "Speed" tells you that the speed is multiplied by itself first.

For example, suppose a girl with a mass of 50 kg is jogging at a speed of 2 meters per second (m/s). Note that $1 \text{kg}\cdot\text{m}^2/\text{s}^2 = 1$ joule (J).

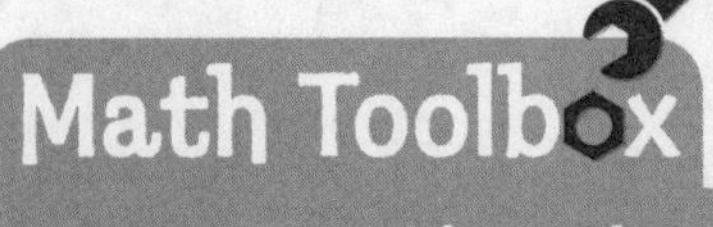

Apply Concepts
Underline the unit of energy you get when you calculate kinetic energy.

$$\begin{aligned}\text{Kinetic energy of girl} &= \tfrac{1}{2} \times 50 \text{ kg} \times (2 \text{ m/s})^2 \\ &= \tfrac{1}{2} \times 50 \text{ kg} \times (2 \text{ m/s} \times 2 \text{ m/s}) \\ &= \tfrac{1}{2} \times 50 \text{ kg} \times 4 \text{ m}^2/\text{s}^2 \\ &= 100 \ \text{kg}\cdot\text{m}^2/\text{s}^2 = 100 \text{ J}\end{aligned}$$

Do changes in speed and mass both have the same effect on kinetic energy? Use the Math Toolbox to answer this question.

Math Toolbox

Mass, Speed, and Kinetic Energy

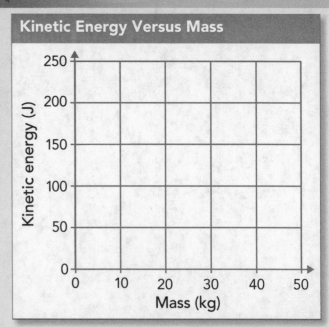

A boy and his dogs are running.
The white dog has a mass of 10 kg.
The black dog has a mass of 20 kg.
The boy has a mass of 40 kg.
They are all running at 3 m/s.

1. Evaluate Expressions Determine the kinetic energy of the dogs and the boy. Record the kinetic energy for each.

   ....

   ....

2. Construct Graphs Graph the data to show how mass and kinetic energy are related.

3. SEP Use Mathematics Suppose the smaller dog speeds up to 6 m/s. What is the kinetic energy of the dog now? How is kinetic energy related to speed?

   ....

   ....

Kinetic Energy Versus Mass

Kinetic energy (J): 0, 50, 100, 150, 200, 250
Mass (kg): 0, 10, 20, 30, 40, 50

Potential Energy

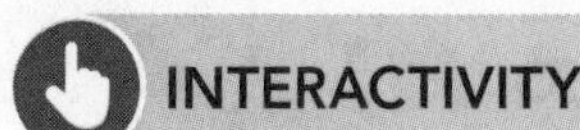

INTERACTIVITY

Investigate model racecars to see how mass affects kinetic energy.

Kinetic energy is easy to observe because there is motion involved. But an object that is not moving may still have energy. Some objects have energy simply as a result of their shapes or positions. Energy that results from the position or shape of an object is called **potential energy**. This type of energy has the potential to transform into kinetic energy, or, in other words, to do work. Recall that work involves using force to move an object over a distance.

When you raise a bottle up to your mouth to take a drink of water, or when you stretch out a rubber band, you transfer energy to the object. The energy you transfer is stored, or held in readiness by the object. It may be used later if the bottle is dropped or the rubber band is released (see **Figure 2**).

Look back again at the photo of the landslide at the beginning of the lesson. You see the dirt and rocks moving, showing kinetic energy. At some point before the photo was taken, however, the dirt and rocks were not yet moving. At that stage, they held potential energy.

Literacy Connection

Integrate With Visuals
In your notebook, draw an object with elastic potential energy.

Stored-Up Energy

Figure 2 This stretched rubber band is not moving, but it still contains energy—potential energy. Once the fingers that are stretching the rubber band release the band, what kind of energy will the rubber band have?

....

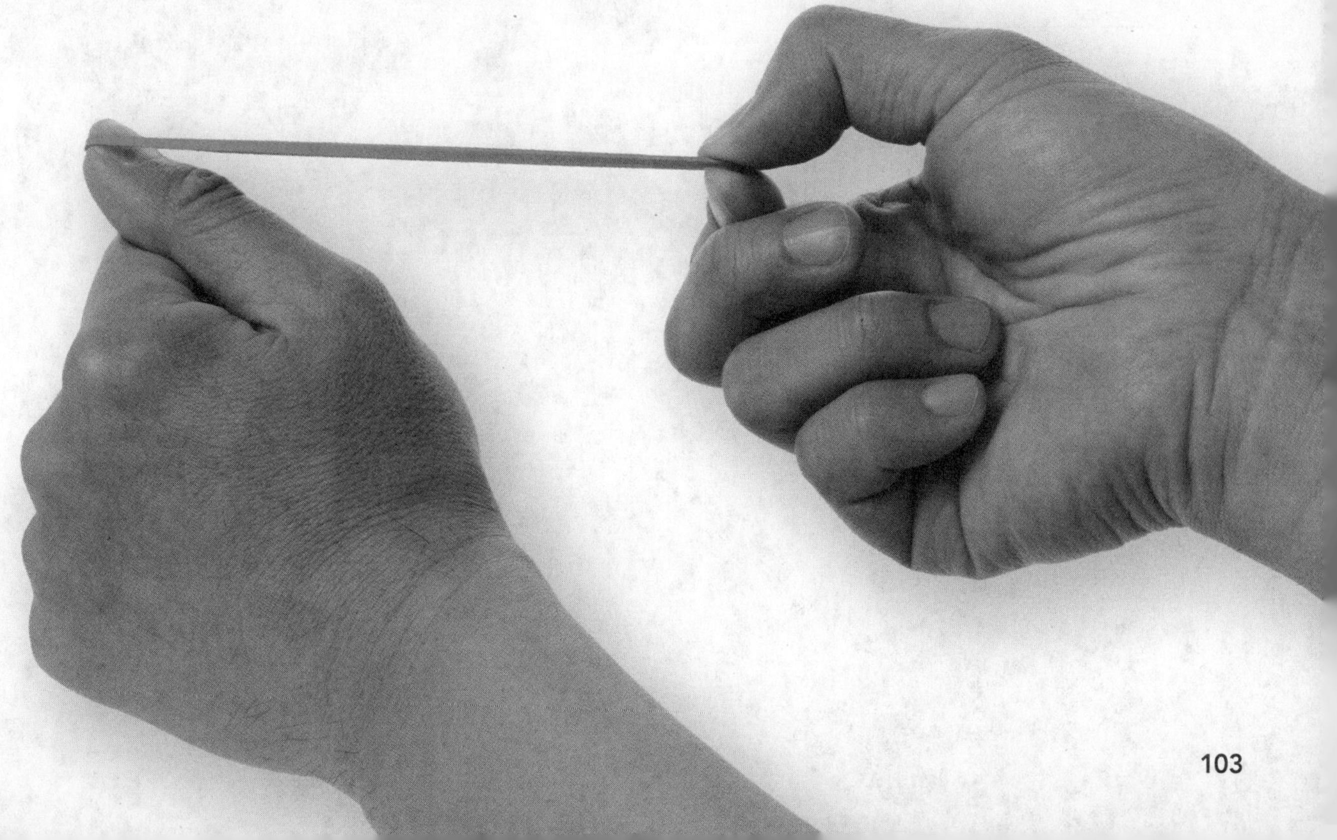

Explore gravitational potential energy on Earth and on the moon.

Investigate Develop a model with magnets to show how the arrangement of objects affects potential energy.

Gravitational Potential Energy There are two types of potential energy directly related to kinetic energy. One of these types is **gravitational potential energy**. This type of potential energy is related to an object's vertical position—how high it is above the ground. The potential energy is stored as a result of the gravitational pull of Earth on the object.

Gravitational potential energy can be measured by the amount of work needed to lift an object to a certain height. Remember that work is equal to force multiplied by distance. The force you use to lift the object is equal to its weight. Weight is the force that gravity exerts on an object. The distance you move the object is its height above ground level. You can calculate an object's gravitational potential energy using this equation:

$$\text{Gravitational potential energy} = \text{Weight} \times \text{Height above ground}$$

For example, suppose a cat has a weight of 40 newtons, which is about 9 pounds. The cat is lifted 2 meters off the ground. You can calculate its potential energy:

$$\text{Gravitational potential energy} = 40\ \text{N} \times 2\ \text{m}$$

$$= 80\ \text{N-m, or } 80\ \text{J}$$

The energy of the cyclist at the top of hill shown in **Figure 3** is another example of gravitational potential energy.

Gravitational Potential Energy

Figure 3 A cyclist sitting still at the top of a hill displays gravitational potential energy. What makes it possible for the cyclist to have this type of energy?

....

....

....

....

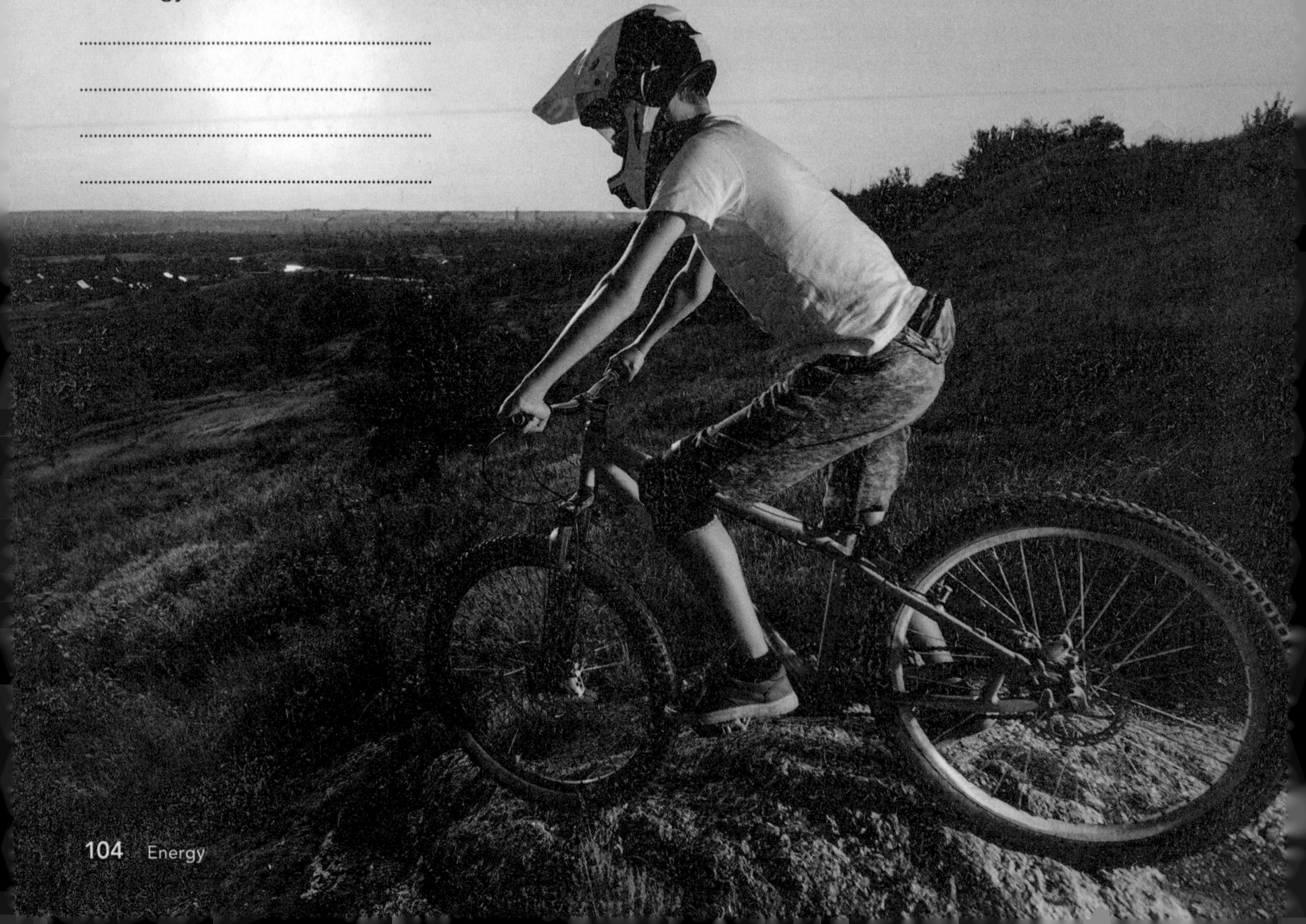

Elastic Potential Energy Sometimes, an object has a different type of potential energy due to its shape. **Elastic potential energy** is the energy associated with objects that can be compressed or stretched. This type of potential energy can be stored in such items as rubber bands, bungee cords, springs, and an arrow drawn into a bow.

Explore the potential energy of roller coasters.

Trampolines also store elastic potential energy. Take a look at **Figure 4**. When the girl presses down on the trampoline, the trampoline changes shape. The trampoline now has elastic potential energy. When the girl jumps up off the trampoline, this stored energy is transferred from the trampoline to the girl, sending the girl upward. During this energy transfer, the elastic potential energy of the trampoline is transformed into different types of energy.

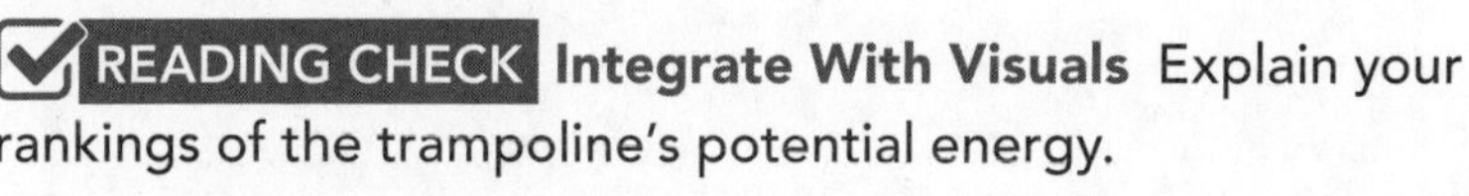

READING CHECK **Integrate With Visuals** Explain your rankings of the trampoline's potential energy.

Elastic Potential Energy

Figure 4 The energy stored in a stretched object, such as a trampoline, is elastic potential energy. Rank the amount of elastic potential energy of the trampoline from greatest to least using the words *most, medium* and *least*. Write your answers in the boxes next to the images.

LESSON 2 Check

MS-PS3-1, MS-PS3-2

1. **Explain Phenomena** Explain why a running deer has kinetic energy.

2. **SEP Use Mathematics** Imagine the running deer has a mass of 100 kg and is running at a speed of 8 m/s. What is the deer's kinetic energy, in joules?

3. **SEP Construct Explanations** Several people are using bows to shoot arrows at targets. At what point do the bows have elastic potential energy? At what point do the arrows have kinetic energy?

4. **SEP Use Mathematics** Imagine that a bowling ball needs to be lifted 1.5 meters, and its gravitational potential energy is 90 joules. How much does the bowling ball weigh?

5. **Determine Differences** What is the main difference between gravitational potential energy and elastic potential energy?

Quest CHECK-IN

In this lesson, you learned about potential and kinetic energy and the different roles they play with regard to forces and motion in everyday life.

SEP Define Problems How might the concepts of potential and kinetic energy impact the design of your machine? What factors do you need to consider?

HANDS-ON LAB

Build a Chain-Reaction Machine

Go online to download the lab worksheet. Finalize the design for your machine, choose construction materials, and build it! Then, analyze the moving parts of your machine and identify the different types of energy that come into play.

littleBits CHALLENGE

MS-PS3-2

Prosthetics on the Move

INTERACTIVITY

Discover the properties of materials and changes in energy to guide your construction of a prosthetic limb.

How might you design a prosthetic arm that meets the needs of a modern, on-the-go person? You engineer it!

The Challenge: To design a prosthetic arm based on research into current prosthetic technology.

This prosthetic leg has the shape, weight, and flexibility to allow this runner to sprint again!

Phenomenon Until very recently, prosthetics, or artificial limbs, were made of wood, rubber, or plastic. These older prosthetics were solid and heavy, and they often made movement difficult.

When you walk, your foot muscles and leg muscles provide the force to push off the ground. The potential energy stored in your body becomes the kinetic energy of motion. Using an artificial leg, however, takes practice and can be uncomfortable because other muscles strain to carry the artificial limb.

Prosthetic design has advanced thanks to new technologies. In the early 2000s, engineers developed a carbon prosthetic for track athletes. This flexible leg bends and provides elastic potential energy to help the athlete run. The lighter weight of the materials allows the runner to move more efficiently with less muscle strain. Today, advanced engineers are working on limbs that are controlled by the electrical impulses in the human brain, mimicking the way our brains signal our muscles to move!

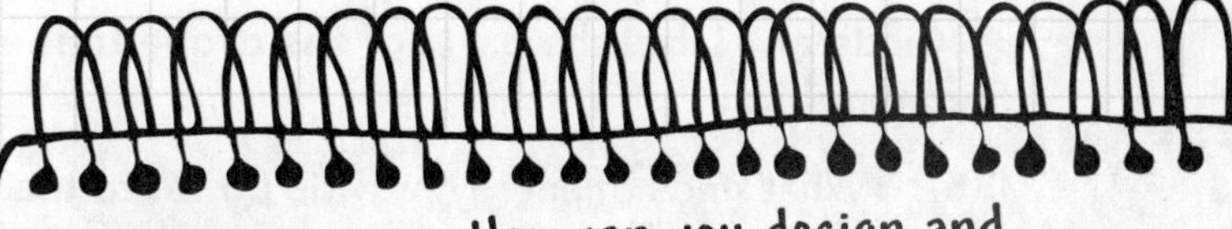

DESIGN CHALLENGE

How can you design and build a new kind of prosthetic limb? Go to the Engineering Design Notebook to find out!

LESSON 3

Other Forms of Energy

Guiding Questions

- How can different forms of energy be classified, quantified, and measured?
- How are different forms of energy related to each other?

Connection

Literacy Cite Textual Evidence

MS-PS3-5

HANDS-ON LAB

Investigate Observe the different types of energy at play when you use a flashlight.

Vocabulary

mechanical energy
nuclear energy
thermal energy
chemical energy
electrical energy
electromagnetic radiation

Academic Vocabulary

medium

Connect It!

Circle and label the parts of the drone that are similar to the parts of the hummingbird.

Infer What kinds of energy provide power to the drone and to the hummingbird?

....

....

....

Determining Mechanical Energy

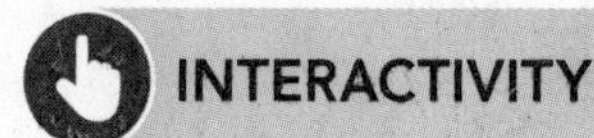

INTERACTIVITY

Discover several different types of energy.

The term *mechanical* may make you think of images of metal machines or a mechanic tinkering under the hood of a car. In science, *mechanical* is an adjective that refers to things that are or can be in motion, which covers just about any object we can think of, from particles all the way up to Earth itself. **Mechanical energy** is the energy an object has due to its motion, shape, position, or a combination of these factors.

An object's mechanical energy equals the total of its kinetic and potential energy. For example, a train chugging uphill has energy, and much of that energy is energy of motion—kinetic energy. But a train that is sitting idle at the top of a hill also has energy—potential energy. By adding these two energy forms together, you can determine the train's mechanical energy:

Mechanical Energy = Potential Energy + Kinetic Energy

READING CHECK **Cite Textual Evidence** What are the three factors that determine an object's mechanical energy?

Inspired by Nature

Figure 1 Engineers often look to nature for inspiration for their machines. This drone has features similar to those of the hummingbird, and they both need energy to function.

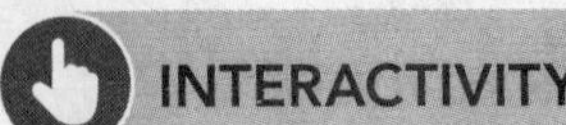

INTERACTIVITY

Investigate forms of energy involved with roller coasters and high divers.

VIDEO

Learn more about nuclear energy.

More Forms of Energy

Much of the energy that you observe is mechanical energy, but energy can take many other forms as well. Some other forms of energy are associated with tiny particles, such as atoms and molecules, that make up objects. These forms include nuclear energy, thermal energy, chemical energy, electric energy, and electromagnetic energy.

Literacy Connection

Cite Textual Evidence
As you read about different forms of energy, underline the types of evidence that can help you identify those different forms.

Nuclear Energy All matter is made of particles called atoms. The center of the atom is called the nucleus (plural: nuclei). **Nuclear energy** is a type of potential energy stored in the nucleus. It can be released through a nuclear reaction. In one type of nuclear reaction, called fission, a nucleus splits into smaller fragments. When it breaks apart, it releases energy (**Figure 2**). If fission reactions are controlled, the release of energy can be used to generate electricity. Nuclear power plants harness nuclear energy for this purpose.

Fusion is another type of nuclear reaction. In fusion, small nuclei combine to form larger nuclei. One place that fusion happens is inside the sun. Some of the energy released by this reaction makes its way to Earth as light. Fusion releases more energy than fission, but the extremely high temperatures that are required to start a fusion reaction make it more difficult to use and control.

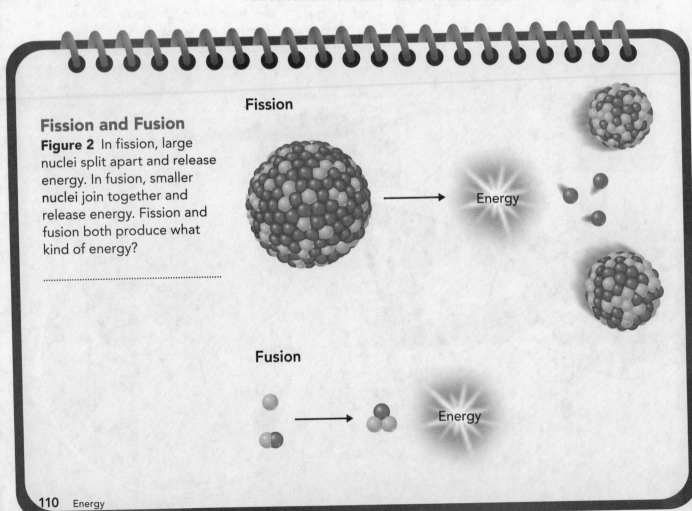

Fission and Fusion

Figure 2 In fission, large nuclei split apart and release energy. In fusion, smaller nuclei join together and release energy. Fission and fusion both produce what kind of energy?

....

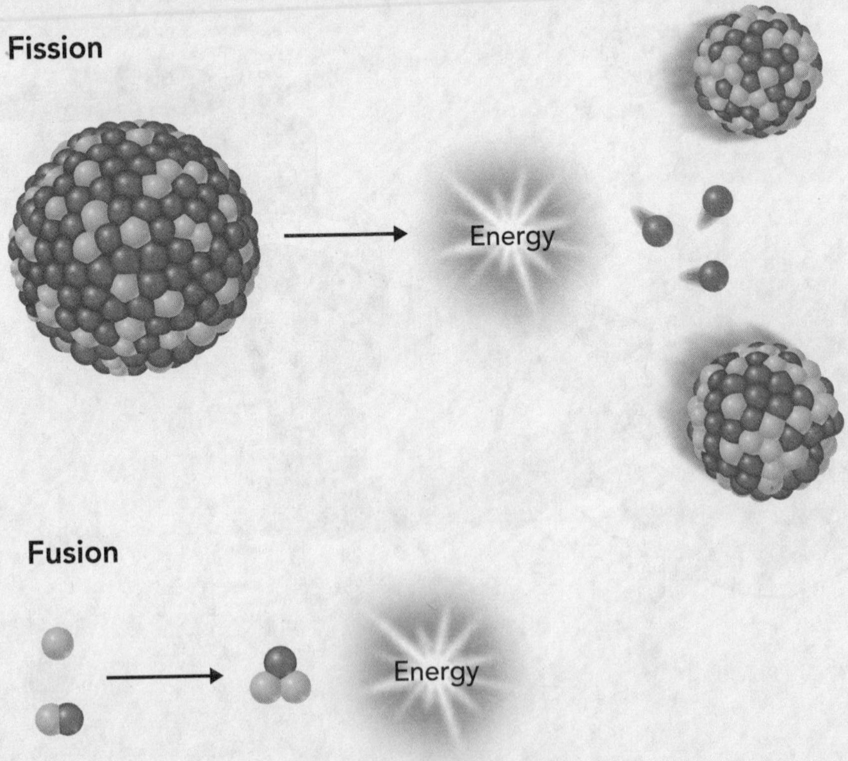

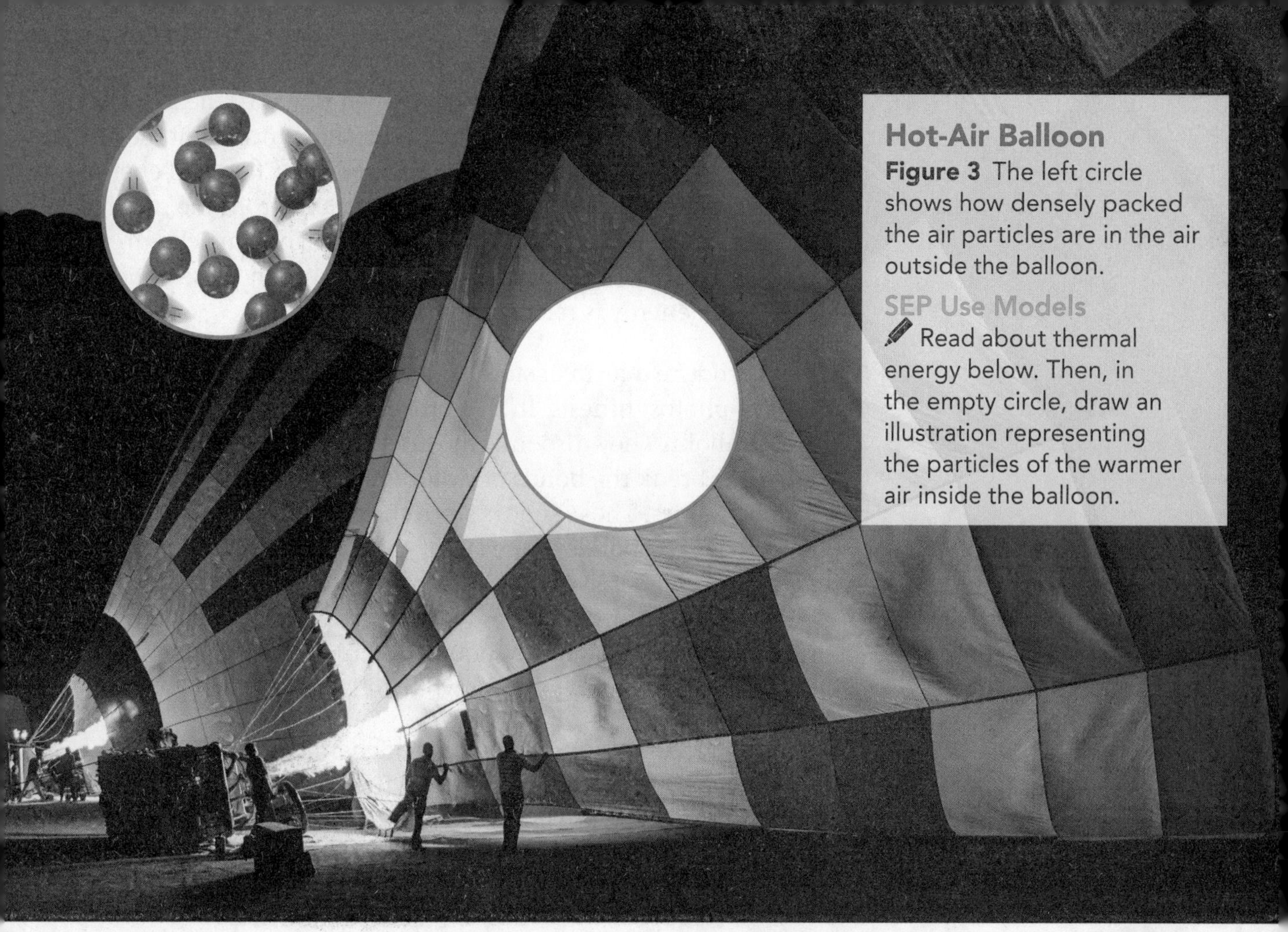

Hot-Air Balloon

Figure 3 The left circle shows how densely packed the air particles are in the air outside the balloon.

SEP Use Models

Read about thermal energy below. Then, in the empty circle, draw an illustration representing the particles of the warmer air inside the balloon.

Thermal Energy The total potential and kinetic energy of particles in an object is called **thermal energy**. Lots of particle movement means lots of kinetic energy, and that means a high temperature. Think of a pot of boiling water. The particles are moving very quickly, which results in a high temperature. This means the water has a lot of thermal energy. If the water is then put in the freezer, its kinetic energy will decrease. When its kinetic energy decreases, its thermal energy and temperature also decrease.

The transfer of energy into the thermal energy of an object is called heat. Heat flows from a hotter object to a cooler one through a combination of processes. These processes are called conduction, convection, and radiation. Most substances expand, or take up more space, when heated. When they lose heat, they contract and take up less space. The effect of heat allows a hot air balloon to rise. A flame heats the air inside the hot-air balloon, giving the particles more thermal energy (**Figure 3**). Since they have more thermal energy, they move faster and spread apart. The air in the balloon is then less dense than the air outside the balloon, so the balloon rises.

HANDS-ON LAB

Investigate Observe the different types of energy at play when you use a flashlight.

Chemical Energy What type of energy is in the food you eat, in the cells of your body, and in the substances that make a lightstick glow? It is called **chemical energy**. Chemical energy is a form of potential energy because it results from the relative positions of the particles within a material. The particles are held in those positions by chemical bonds. When these bonds are broken, energy is released.

Plants produce a form of stored chemical energy when they perform photosynthesis. In this process, plants take in energy from sunlight. They also take in water and carbon dioxide. Plant cells break the bonds of water and carbon dioxide to produce sugars. Those sugars store chemical energy. The plant later breaks the bonds of the sugar to release the chemical energy on which it lives. Similarly, your body breaks bonds of sugar from your food. Energy is released when your body breaks bonds that hold the sugar molecules together. Your body uses that energy to power your cells.

Reflect What have you heard about the pros and cons of using oil for energy? In your science notebook, describe what you have heard, and write down your own conclusions about the burning of oil.

Petroleum, or oil, is another source of chemical energy. Oil is converted into gasoline and diesel fuel, which contain potential energy in the form of chemical bonds. When fuel is burned in engines, the energy in these fuels can be used to makes cars run.

Question It!

1. **Draw Conclusions** Batteries allow us to store energy for when it's needed, such as starting a car engine or jump-starting another car whose battery has lost its charge. But batteries cannot operate without chemical reactions. What kind of energy do you think is stored in the substances within the battery?

2. **Reason Abstractly** When someone jump-starts a car, what do you think happens to the stored energy in the working battery?

Electrical Energy Electrical energy is the form of energy most of us use to power devices such as lights, computers, and audio systems. **Electrical energy** is the energy of electric charges. Different materials, and even particles, can have different charges. These differences in charge can result in the movement of electrical charge—a type of kinetic energy called electricity. When charges are not moving but are near one another, they have electric potential energy. This energy can be converted to electricity.

Electromagnetic Radiation Visible light is one type of electromagnetic radiation. **Electromagnetic radiation** is a form of kinetic energy that travels through space in waves. It does not need a **medium**, such as air or water, to travel through. This is why you can see the stars even though outer space does not contain a medium. Our world has a wide variety of electromagnetic energy, from X-rays that produce images of bones to microwaves that heat leftover food or transmit signals between mobile phones and towers. Other types of electromagnetic radiation include ultraviolet (UV) waves, infrared (or heat) waves, and radio waves. Like other forms of kinetic energy, all types of electromagnetic radiation can transform into thermal energy when heating something.

Academic Vocabulary

In your reading here, the word medium is used to indicate a substance through which a force acts. What are some other meanings of medium that you use or hear in everyday life?

....

....

....

....

....

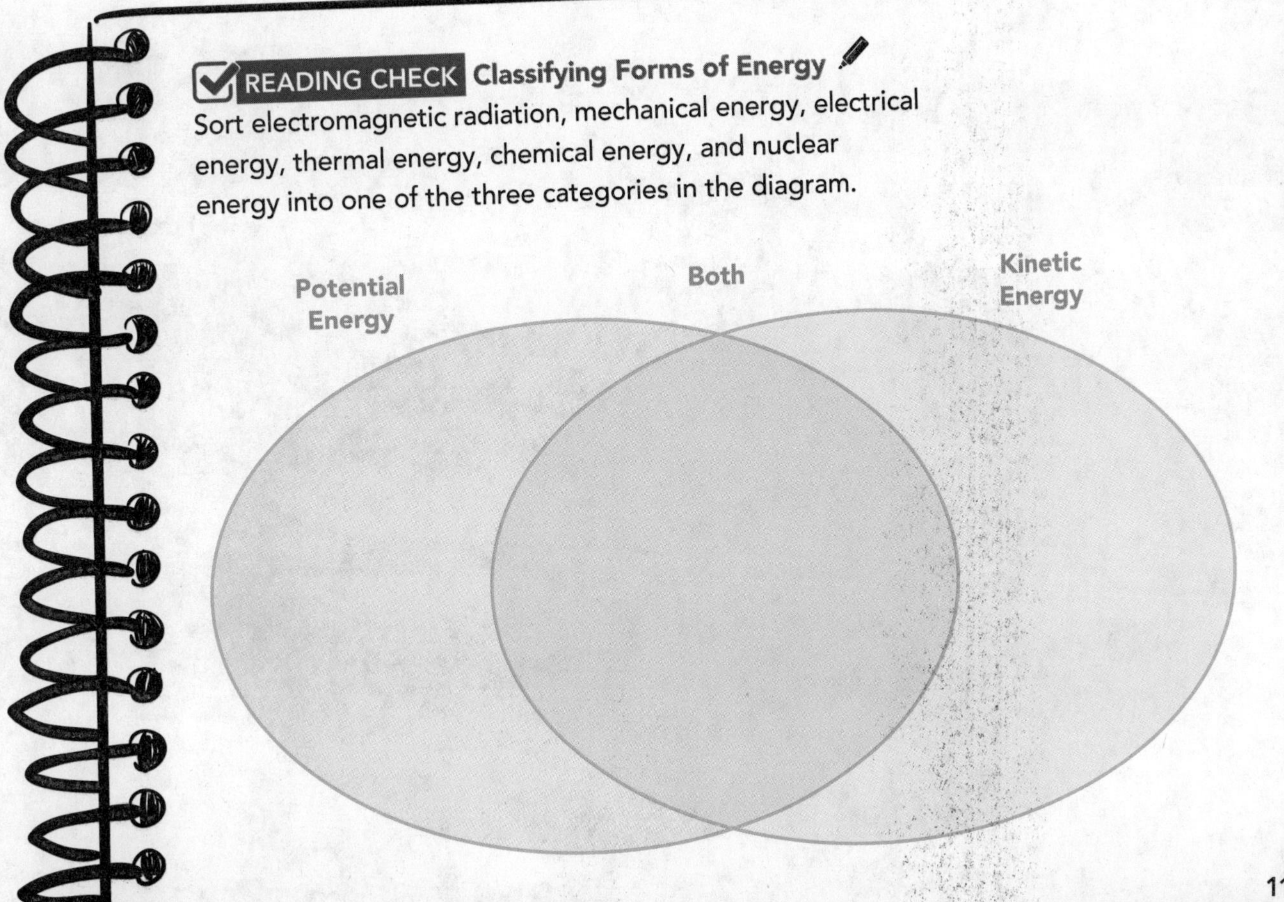

READING CHECK
Classifying Forms of Energy
Sort electromagnetic radiation, mechanical energy, electrical energy, thermal energy, chemical energy, and nuclear energy into one of the three categories in the diagram.
Potential Energy
Both
Kinetic Energy

Energy at the Cookout

Figure 4 Many objects in this scene contain more than one form of energy.

1. **Claim** Label this scene with as many forms of energy as you can find.
2. **Evidence** Draw a star next to an object that contains more than one form of energy and explain your reasoning below.

....

....

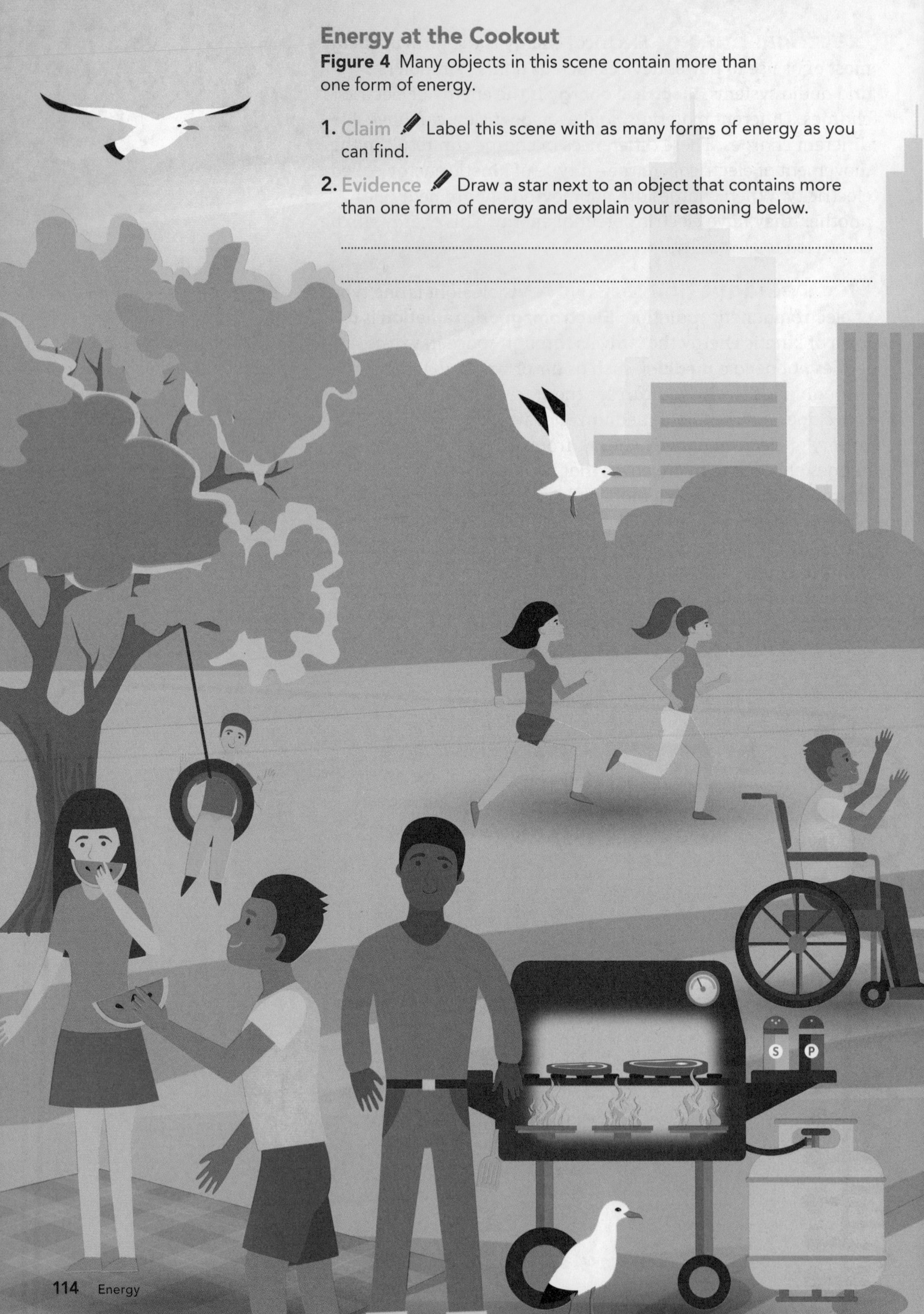

3. Reasoning The grill converts chemical energy from propane into thermal energy that heats food. What is another example of an energy change in this image?

....

....

....

....

....

LESSON 3 Check

MS-PS3-5

1. **SEP Use Mathematics** At a certain point, the kinetic energy of a falling basketball is 30.8 J and its potential energy is 16.0 J. What is its mechanical energy?

2. **Identify** Which type of nuclear energy involves splitting atoms?

3. **Represent Relationships** What are some of the relationships among thermal energy, kinetic energy, particle movement, and temperature?

4. **SEP Construct Explanations** What type(s) of energy do you acquire when you eat a bowl of hot vegetable soup? Explain.

5. **SEP Engage in Argument** Why do we say the particles in a rock lying on the ground have kinetic energy and potential energy?

Quest CHECK-IN

In this lesson, you learned about other forms of energy, such as nuclear energy and electromagnetic radiation. You also started to think about how these forms of energy can change into other forms, and how to tell when such a change has occurred.

Evaluate Why do engineers need to keep track of potential and kinetic energy and energy transformations in prototypes of machines?

HANDS-ON LAB

Test and Evaluate a Chain-Reaction Machine

Go online to download the lab worksheet. Test your chain-reaction machine prototype and evaluate its performance. Then revise your machine's design and retest as needed. Think about energy transformations that are taking place and the roles of potential and kinetic energy.

CAREERS
Energy Engineer

Reinventing ENERGY SYSTEMS

We all use energy every moment of our lives. It lights our classrooms, runs our computers, and powers our industries. For much of the twentieth century, the United States depended largely on fossil fuels for energy. This has been changing in recent decades because the supply of fossil fuels is limited, and excessive use of these fuels has caused environmental damage on a vast scale. Today, people are turning more and more to renewable sources of fuel, such as solar and wind power. This is where the energy engineers play a role.

VIDEO

Learn about the work an energy engineer does.

The purpose of an energy engineer's job is simple: to make the world more energy-efficient. Energy engineers carry out a wide range of work that involves research, design, and construction.

Some energy engineers explore new methods of obtaining energy, while others develop ways to integrate renewable energy sources into the existing power grid. Energy engineers also work with architects to incorporate clean energy sources in new construction. Additionally, some of these engineers help to develop more efficient machinery, such as cars that run on alternative fuels.

This type of work involves mathematics, physics, and chemistry. It offers creative challenges and a wide variety of tasks. If you enjoy these subjects and challenges, this career might be right for you!

MY CAREER

Speak with an energy engineer at a local laboratory or office to learn more about this career.

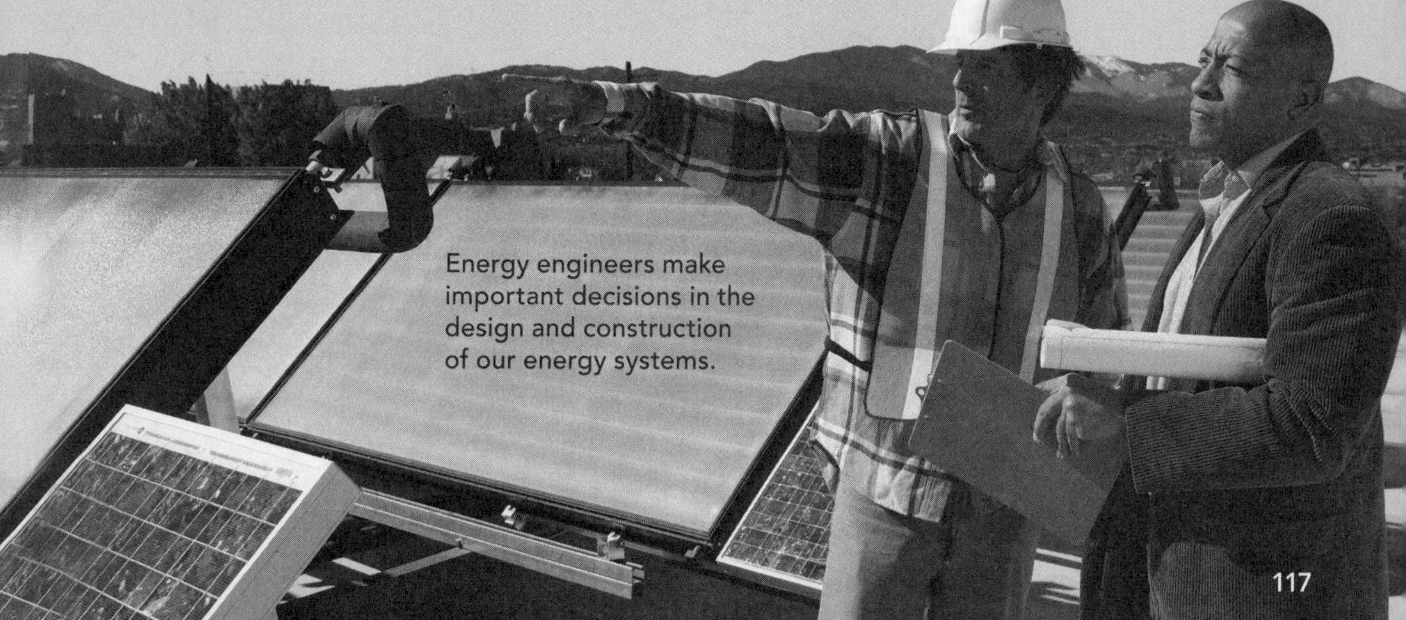

Energy engineers make important decisions in the design and construction of our energy systems.

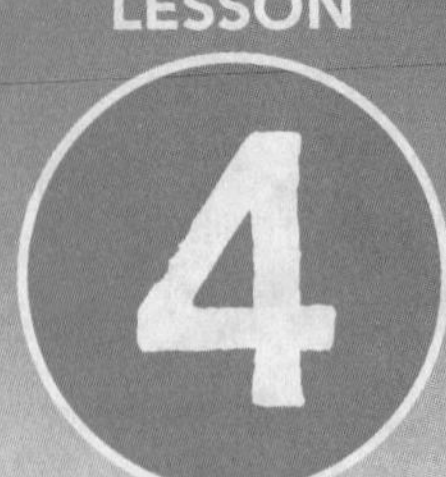

LESSON 4 Energy Change and Conservation

Guiding Questions

- In what ways can energy change from one form to another?
- How is energy transferred?
- How does the law of conservation of energy apply to transformations and transfers?

Connections

Literacy Cite Textual Evidence

Math Use Ratio Relationships

MS-PS3-5

HANDS-ON LAB

uInvestigate Explore how the changing kinetic energy of a bouncing ball is related to conservation of energy.

Vocabulary

law of conservation of energy

Academic Vocabulary

pivot

Connect It!

Trace the movement of the snowboarder.

Infer How is the snowboarder able to soar through the air?

....

....

....

Energy Changes Form

All forms of energy can be transformed into other forms of energy. Energy can transform once (which we call a single transformation) or multiple times. A toaster provides a good example of a single transformation. Electrical energy passes through metal wires and is transformed into thermal energy.

If you eat toast, the resulting process is an example of multiple transformations. Your body transforms chemical energy stored in cells into the kinetic energy that moves your mouth. Your digestive system uses mechanical and chemical energy to digest the bread. Some of the chemical energy in the bread is released as thermal energy that helps your body maintain its temperature. Some of the remaining chemical energy is delivered back to your body's cells. The cells then transform that chemical energy into mechanical energy that allows your body to function.

Multiple transformations also go into the making of the bread. Sunlight, which is a form of electromagnetic radiation, is harnessed by wheat plants to create chemical energy. Mechanical energy is used to grind the wheat into flour. The flour is combined with water and yeast to make dough—more chemical energy. As the dough is baked in the oven, electrical energy is used to increase the thermal energy of the oven. Heat is transferred from the oven to the dough, and the thermal energy of the dough increases as it bakes into bread. Many of the processes that we rely on daily involve multiple transformations.

Literacy Connection

Cite Textual Evidence
What evidence in the text supports the claim that energy changes form? List two examples.

....

....

....

....

....

....

Snowboard Jumping

Figure 1 The snowboarder thrusts up and forward by using her legs. But most of the energy that allows her to travel a great distance through the air is supplied by something else.

Kinetic and Potential Energy

Kinetic and Potential Energy One common energy transformation involves potential energy changing to kinetic energy. The snowboarder on the previous page had potential energy when she stood at the top of the hill. As she pushed herself off the top, gravity transformed the potential energy into kinetic energy. As she accelerated down the hill, the potential energy declined while the kinetic energy increased This is true of any falling object, such as the ball in **Figure 2**. Recall that the weight of an object and its height above the ground are proportionally related to its gravitational potential energy. And so, as the height of the ball decreases, it loses potential energy while gaining kinetic energy. The ball's kinetic energy is greatest right before it hits the ground.

A pendulum also demonstrates the relationship between kinetic and potential energy. A pendulum consists of something with mass suspended on an arm or pole that swings back and forth from a **pivot** point. A swinging boat ride at an amusement park is a kind of pendulum (**Figure 3**). At its highest point, the pendulum has no movement and therefore no kinetic energy. When it begins to swing down, potential energy declines as the kinetic energy increases. The kinetic energy and the speed of the pendulum are greatest at the bottom, or midpoint, of the swing. As the pendulum swings upward, it loses kinetic energy and gains potential energy until it is motionless again and ready to swing back to the other side.

Academic Vocabulary

The term pivot is often used in describing the action of basketball players when they keep one foot firmly in place while moving their other foot. What other things in everyday life might pivot?

....

....

....

Falling Objects

Figure 2 As an object falls, its potential energy decreases while its kinetic energy increases. Circle the location where the ball has the most kinetic energy.

Pendulum Physics

Figure 3 This amusement park ride is basically a pendulum.

Use Models Use the abbreviation *PE* for potential energy and *KE* for kinetic energy to label the positions where the boat has maximum PE, minimum PE, maximum KE, and minimum KE.

Energy Transformation and Transfer Energy transformation and energy transfer sometimes occur in the same process at the same time, but they are not the same thing. Energy transformation occurs when one form of energy changes into another. The potential energy of a pendulum, such as the wrecking ball in **Figure 4**, transforms into kinetic energy as it falls due to the force of gravity. Energy transfer takes place when energy moves from one object to another. When the wrecking ball hits the wall, some of the kinetic energy of the ball transfers to the wall, causing the wall to fall over. As the wrecking ball swings, energy is also transferred from the ball to the air, due to the force of friction. In this case, energy transfers, but it is also transformed. Some of the mechanical energy of the moving wrecking ball is transferred and transformed into thermal energy of the surrounding air. Whenever a moving object experiences friction, some of its mechanical energy is transformed into thermal energy.

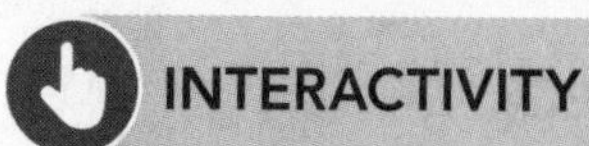

Explore different examples of energy transformations.

READING CHECK **Cite Textual Evidence** Underline the sentences that explain the difference between energy transformation and energy transfer.

Transformation and Transfer in Demolition

Figure 4 Draw pictures in the empty boxes to show what happens as the wrecking ball swings. Describe the energy transformations and transfers that are occurring.

Ball at top of swing	Ball at bottom of swing	Ball hitting the wall

VIDEO

Look into the future and learn about hydrogen fuel cell cars.

Energy Changes and the Law of Conservation

There is a certain amount of energy in the universe, and we cannot make more of it or destroy any that already exists. Another way to state this idea is to say that energy is conserved. When one object loses energy, other objects must gain it. This is known as the **law of conservation of energy**. This law is a factor in both energy transfers and energy transformations. Energy either moves from one place to another or changes forms, but no energy is created or destroyed.

HANDS-ON LAB

Investigate Explore how the changing kinetic energy of a bouncing ball is related to conservation of energy.

When a baseball is hit by a bat, as in **Figure 5**, the ball flies through the air. The law of conservation of energy explains why it does not keep flying forever. The kinetic energy of the ball transfers to the air and transforms into thermal energy due to the force of friction. The more air particles there are, the more transfer there is. So more kinetic energy transfers to the air when the air is dense. That's why baseballs travel farther and faster at a baseball stadium in Denver, Colorado, where the air is thinner, than they do in low-altitude ballparks where the air is denser. You can learn more about this phenomenon in the Math Toolbox activity.

Energy Is Conserved
Figure 5 After the ball is hit, it eventually slows down and falls. As it slows down, where does its kinetic energy go?

....

....

Conservation of Energy in Transfers Think back to the wrecking ball. Most of the kinetic energy in the moving ball is transferred directly to the wall. Any energy not transferred is transformed into thermal energy of the ball and air or the sound energy of the ball hitting the wall. Energy is conserved in this example, as it is in any example. No matter how energy is transformed or transferred, the total amount of energy in a system does not change.

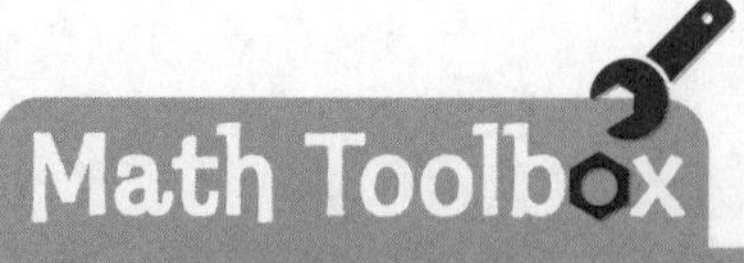

Home Runs and Air Density

For more than 20 years, major league baseball games played in Denver, Colorado, have featured a high percentage of home runs. The high altitude of Denver means the air there is less dense than in lower-altitude locations, so balls flying through the air in Denver do not transfer as much energy to the air. They keep that kinetic energy and travel farther than they do in other ballparks. This table shows how many home runs the Colorado Rockies baseball team hit at home and away over 10 seasons.

Colorado Rockies's Home Runs at Home and Away

	2007	2008	2009	2010	2011	2012	2013	2014	2015	2016
Home	103	92	98	108	94	100	88	119	102	116
Away	68	68	92	65	69	66	71	67	84	88

1. **SEP Use Mathematics** Over the 10-year span, how many more home runs did the Rockies score in their home ballpark in Denver than at other ballparks?

2. **Use Ratio Relationships** What is the ratio of home runs the team hit at home and home runs hit in away games over the 10-year period? Express the ratio in the smallest numbers possible.

3. **Summarize** Describe the high home-run numbers at the Rockies' home ball field in terms of kinetic energy and energy transformation.

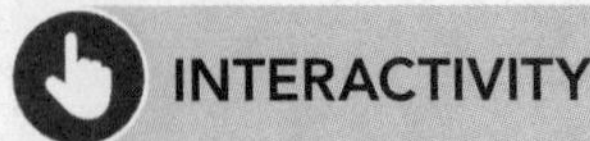

INTERACTIVITY

Explore the role that energy plays in extreme sports.

Conservation of Energy in Waves The vibrations that come from a wrecking ball smashing through a wall travel in sound waves. In a sound wave or any other type of wave, energy passes through matter without moving the matter to a new place. The matter vibrates, meaning it moves temporarily, but ends up back where it was. We can see this on the ocean surface with a floating object (**Figure 6**). An ocean wave passes under the object, lifts it, drops it, and the object ends up back where it was. That's why a surfer cannot catch a wave far out in the ocean. Once a wave breaks, matter is moved and energy is released. A surfer can ride the wave when it breaks (**Figure 7**). Energy is conserved as the breaking wave transfers its energy to the shore.

READING CHECK **Connect to Engineering** Why would the energy industry be interested in developing technologies to transform the kinetic energy in ocean waves to electrical energy?

....

Waves and Matter

Figure 6 A wave's energy passes through matter. Whether the medium is air, water, or some other substance, the matter vibrates but does not end up in a new place. Similarly, a floating ball moves in a circular motion as the wave passes, and the ball ends up back where it started.

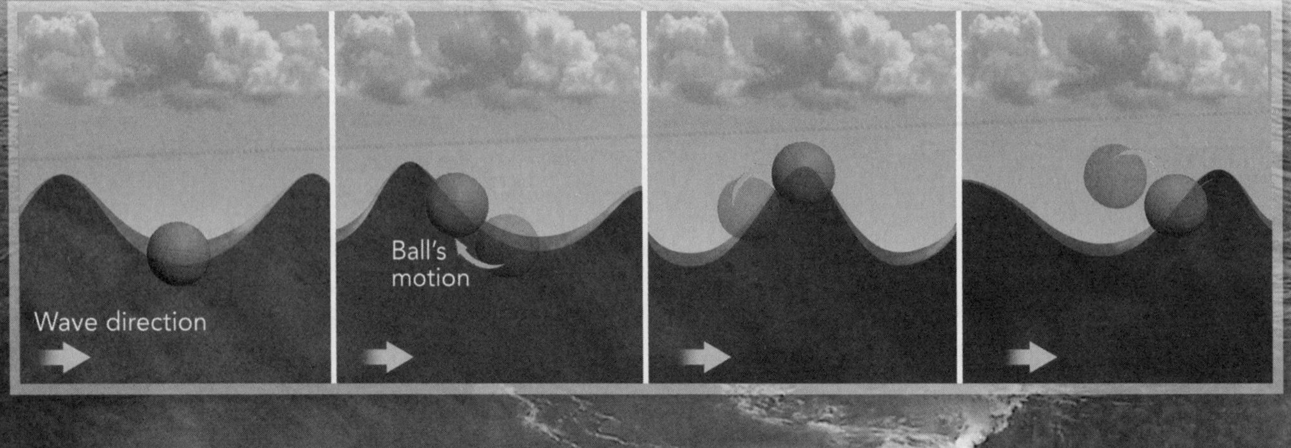

Wave Energy

Figure 7 Ocean waves carry tremendous amounts of energy. When the wave breaks, the energy is released.

LESSON 4 Check

MS-PS3-5

1. **Distinguish Relationships** What does it mean to say that energy is conserved in an energy transformation?

2. **SEP Evaluate Information** A train rumbles along the tracks at high speed. After it passes, the rail feels hot. What kind of energy transformation took place?

3. **Connect to Society** How are pendulums used in society? Give an example of a real-world pendulum that transfers a lot of energy.

4. **SEP Construct Explanations** Explain the changes in kinetic energy (KE) and potential energy (PE) that occur when an apple falls off the table and hits the floor.

5. **SEP Engage in Argument** After a tornado moves through a forest, what kinds of evidence would there be of energy transformations or transfers?

Quest CHECK-IN

In this lesson, you learned about energy transformations and energy transfers and how energy is conserved in both.

CCC Stability and Change Why is it important for engineers to understand and quantify how energy changes as it moves through a machine, or from one object to another?

HANDS-ON LAB

Redesign and Retest a Chain-Reaction Machine

Go online to download the lab worksheet. Modify your chain-reaction machine prototype to include at least one additional energy transformation. Then test, evaluate, and finalize the design, and present it to the class.

Case Study

MS-PS3-5

U.S. ENERGY CONSUMPTION

As we know from the law of conservation of energy, new energy cannot simply be created. Therefore, many people feel that it's important for countries to study how they are using their energy resources. The pie chart shows the sources of energy used in the United States.

Renewable Energy

Light and heat from the sun, energy from wind and water, and heat from wood fires were the major sources of energy until the eighteenth century, when fossil fuels began to dominate. More recently, nations of the world have begun to return to renewable energy sources. These sources exist in an unlimited supply, and they are cleaner and safer for the environment. One disadvantage to renewable energy is the high initial cost involved in switching from fossil fuel systems to renewable energy systems.

Coal

Coal comes from the Earth, and it is easily transported. However, this fossil fuel must be mined from underground. The process damages the environment, and coal miners face some of the most dangerous work there is. Burning coal also releases pollutants into the atmosphere.

Petroleum

The main advantage to petroleum, also called crude oil, is that it is a powerful fuel. However, crude oil exists only in a limited supply. Petroleum also requires drilling to access it. The process is expensive and it damages the environment. Finally, the burning and accidental spilling of petroleum results in air pollution, land pollution, and water pollution on a vast scale.

Natural Gas

Natural gas is cheap and abundant. However, it must be transported through pipelines that often leak. Like petroleum, it requires drilling, which harms the environment. And burning natural gas releases carbon dioxide, which contributes to global warming.

Nuclear Energy

Nuclear energy is the most recently discovered source of power. It is a cleaner form of energy because it does not involve the burning of fossil fuels. The United States can generate its own nuclear power, so there are economic advantages as well. The major drawbacks to nuclear power are its expensive cost, the potential for accidents, and the need to dispose of radioactive wastes that will remain dangerous for thousands of years.

U.S. Energy Consumption by Energy Source, 2014

Based on data from U.S. Energy Information Administration

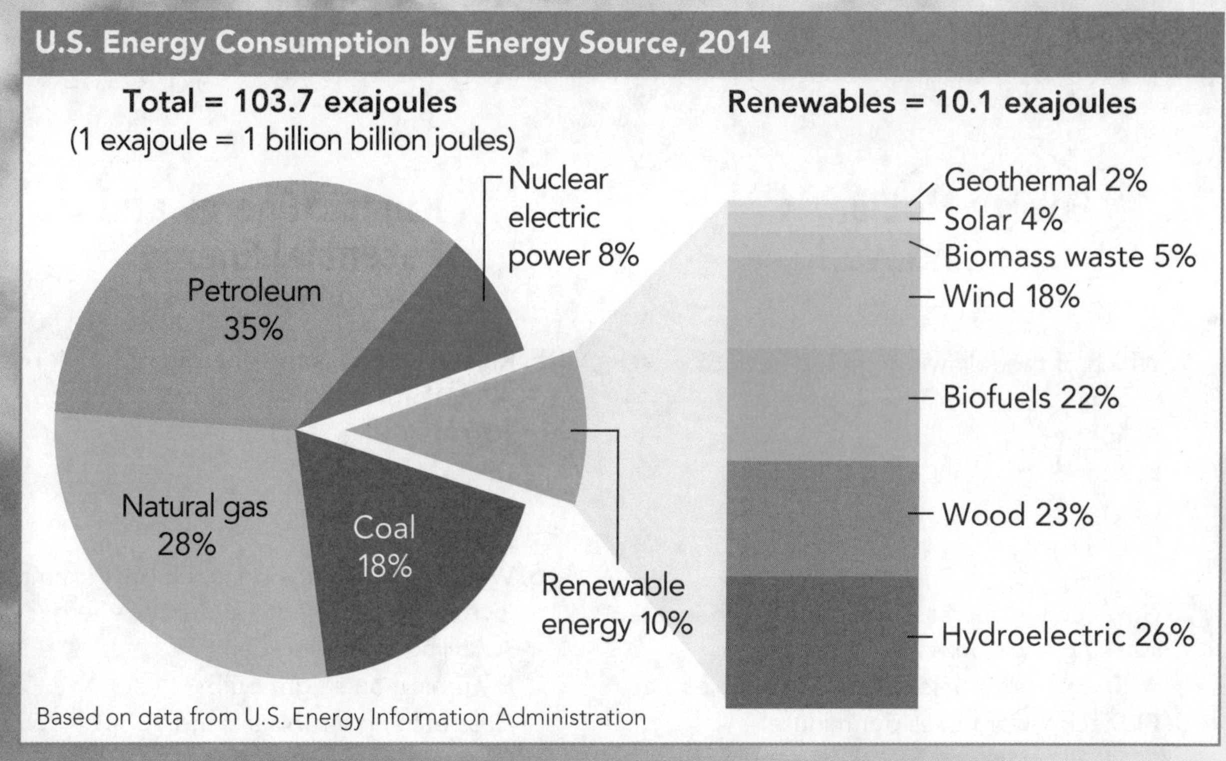

1. **Obtain information** According to the pie chart, which source of energy is used the most in the United States? Which of the five main sources is used the least?

2. **Predict** How do you think the same pie chart might look ten years from now? Why do you think so?

3. **Construct Explanations** Explain why the nations of the world are turning more and more to renewable energy sources.

4. **Solve Problems** Suppose you are in charge of energy policy for the United States. Choose any two sources of fuel in the pie chart and construct an argument for or against the United States expanding its dependence on each.

TOPIC 3 Review and Assess

1 Energy, Motion, Force, and Work

1. Which of the following is not a form of energy?
   A. light
   B. sound
   C. air
   D. electricity

2. How can you increase your power when stacking shoe boxes in a closet?
   A. Spend more time stacking the boxes.
   B. Stack fewer boxes per minute.
   C. Slowly stack the boxes on a lower shelf.
   D. Stack the boxes more quickly.

3. An object is in motion if
   A. its position changes relative to its surroundings.
   B. energy is applied to the object.
   C. a force is applied to it.
   D. it loses energy.

4. **SEP Develop Models** Draw a student carrying textbooks down a hallway. Label the drawing with arrows representing the direction of force on the textbooks and the direction of motion. Explain why no work is done on the textbooks as they are carried.

2 Kinetic Energy and Potential Energy

MS-PS3-1, MS-PS3-2

5. Kinetic energy is the energy of
   A. motion.
   B. potential.
   C. gravity.
   D. distance.

6. Which of the following is the best example of increasing an object's potential energy?
   A. rolling a bowling ball
   B. turning on a light bulb
   C. stretching a rubber band
   D. dropping a pencil

7. Gravitational potential energy is affected by the object's weight and the object's ....

8. **SEP Use Mathematics** A woman is walking at a rate of 0.5 m/s. Her mass is 62 kg. Calculate the woman's kinetic energy in joules.

   ....

   ....

   ....

9. **Reason Quantitatively** What has a greater effect on an object's kinetic energy—increasing its speed by 50 percent or increasing its mass by 75 percent? Explain.

   ....

   ....

   ....

   ....

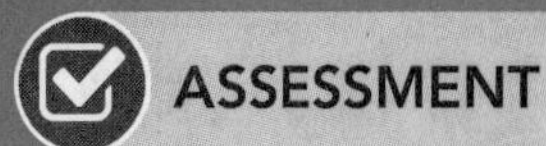

ASSESSMENT

Evaluate your understanding by taking a Topic Test.

3 Other Forms of Energy

MS-PS3-5

10. In the process of fusion, nuclear energy is
    A. absorbed when a nucleus splits.
    B. released when a nucleus splits.
    C. released when nuclei join.
    D. absorbed when nuclei switch places.

11. Which of the following is a type of energy that is *not* involved in the human body's everyday processes?
    A. mechanical energy
    B. nuclear energy
    C. thermal energy
    D. chemical energy

12. An increase in the movement of particles in a substance is associated with an increase in .... energy.

13. Chemical energy is a form of .... energy.

14. **SEP Construct Explanations** A rubber ball that sits motionless near the edge of a tall bookshelf has no kinetic energy. However, it does have mechanical energy. Explain why this is possible.

....

....

....

....

....

4 Energy Change and Conservation

MS-PS3-5

15. Which of the following describes the law of conservation of energy?
    A. Energy cannot be created or destroyed.
    B. Energy can only be released through transformation.
    C. When energy is conserved, it always changes form.
    D. Energy increases when it is transferred from one object to another.

16. An energy .... is the change of energy from one form to another. An energy .... is the movement of energy from one object to another.

17. Draw a circle where the sled rider has the most potential energy. Draw a square where the rider has the most kinetic energy.

18. **SEP Communicate Information** Explain the energy transformation that must occur for your body to participate in a physical activity, such as playing a sport.

....

....

....

MS-PS3-2, MS-PS3-5

Evidence-Based Assessment

Darnell enters a design competition at school. The challenge is to construct a doorbell that works without electricity. The bell must ring loudly enough to be heard in another room of the house.

Darnell's idea is to use the bell, a ball, and gravity. A person would insert the ball into a hole in the wall. The ball would start from rest and fall a short distance to hit a bell. The ball would continue rolling back down and out to where the person could retrieve it in order to ring the bell again. Darnell draws a model of his doorbell design, as shown below.

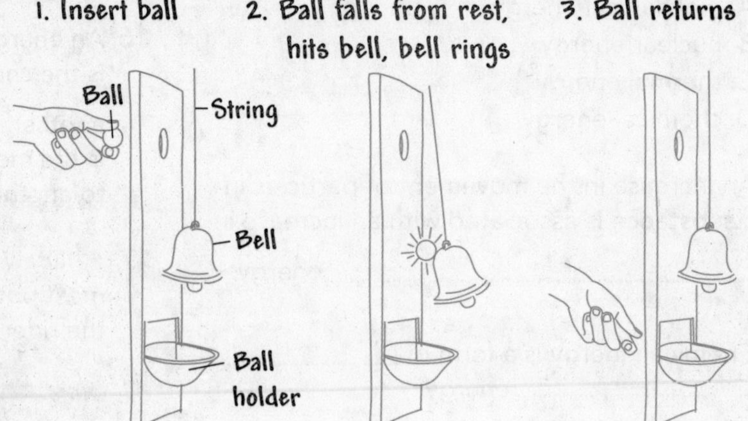

Darnell tests his design. For his first test, he uses a ping-pong ball, places the hole 1 meter above the ground, and hangs the bell 30 centimeters below the hole. He adds labels to his model to show how he set up his first test.

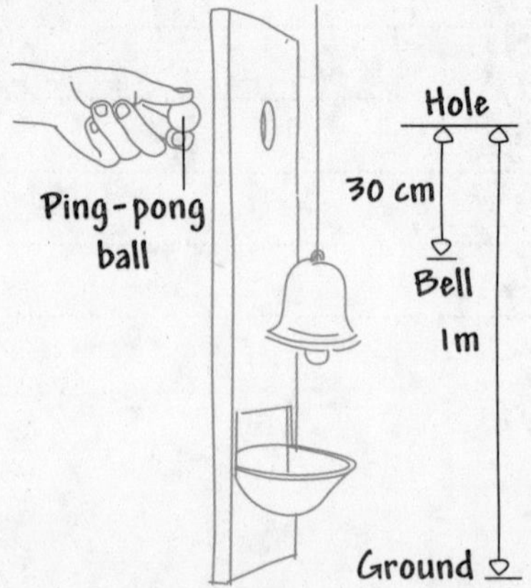

During this first test, Darnell finds that the bell does not ring loudly enough. Answer the following questions to help Darnell improve his design.

1. **CCC System Models** Which of the following two forms of energy are at play in Darnell's design?
   A. chemical energy and nuclear energy
   B. electromagnetic radiation and kinetic energy
   C. electrical energy and gravitational potential energy
   D. gravitational potential energy and kinetic energy

2. **SEP Defining Problems** Based on the results of his first test, Darnell needs to modify his design. What is the problem that Darnell needs to solve in his next doorbell test?

3. **SEP Construct Explanations** Describe the transformations and transfers of energy that are occurring in order for the bell to ring.

4. **SEP Construct Explanations** How could Darnell change his materials or design so that the bell rings more loudly? Provide two options, and explain how they work.

Quest FINDINGS

Complete the Quest!

Phenomenon Determine the best way to demonstrate your chain-reaction machine and show how energy is transformed and transferred from start to finish.

CCC Stability and Change How did energy change form as it made its way through your chain-reaction machine to perform a task?

INTERACTIVITY

Reflect on Your Chain-Reaction Machine

MS-PS3-2, MS-PS3-5

3, 2, 1 . . . Liftoff!

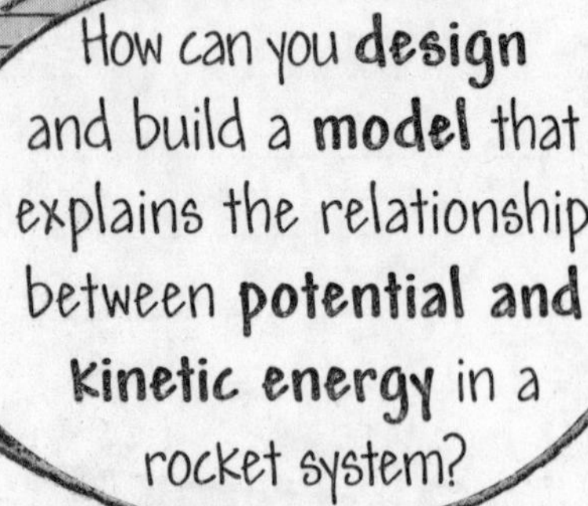
How can you **design** and build a **model** that explains the relationship between **potential and kinetic energy** in a rocket system?

Background

Phenomenon NASA is building a new website devoted to explaining the physics involved in launching rockets. They have asked you to help with a section of the website that deals with energy transfers and transformations. Your task is to design and build a model that explains the relationship between potential and kinetic energy in a rocket system.

Materials

(per group)

- scissors
- rubber bands
- meter stick
- marker
- metric ruler
- stapler
- cardboard tubes of varying diameters (from paper towels or wrapping paper)
- tape
- construction paper

Safety

Be sure to follow all safety guidelines provided by your teacher.

Demonstrate Go online for a downloadable worksheet of this lab.

Design a Model

☐ **1.** Work with your group to develop a model of a rocket and launcher using the rubber bands, cardboard tubes, stapler, and other materials listed. Keep the following criteria in mind:

A. Your rocket must be able to launch vertically into the air. As you work with your group, think about what each of the materials in your model will represent and how the model will operate.

B. You will need to take at least three different measurements of how far the rubber band stretches and how far your rocket travels.

Plan Your Investigation

☐ **2.** As a group, design an investigation to show that the amount of elastic potential energy in the rocket launcher system affects the kinetic energy of the rocket.

As you plan your investigation, consider these questions. Write your ideas in the space below.

- How can you use the meter stick and the ruler in your investigation?
- What tests will you perform?
- How many trials of each test will you perform?
- What variables will you measure?
- What are the dependent and independent variables?

....

....

....

....

....

....

....

....

....

....

☐ **3.** After getting approval from your teacher for your model design and procedure, conduct your experiment. Record the data in your table. See if you can discover a relationship between how far the rubber band stretches and how far the rocket travels.

Sketch of Rocket Launcher Model

Procedure

Data Table

Distance Traveled by Rocket (cm)				
Rubber band stretch (cm)	Trial 1	Trial 2	Trial 3	Average

Analyze and Interpret Data

1. **Analyze Structures** Describe how your rocket launcher works. What might you do to improve it if you could do this experiment again?

2. **CCC Patterns** What is the relationship between the amount of potential energy in the rocket launcher system and the kinetic energy of the rocket? Explain.

3. **CCC Systems** What transfers of energy did you observe in the rocket launcher system? What transformation of energy did you observe? Remember to consider gravity in your answer.

4. **SEP Engage in Arguments** Use evidence from your investigation to support the argument that energy is being transferred and transformed throughout the rocket's travel. Draw a diagram that shows the rocket traveling upward, with different stages (on the ground, midway up, at its peak, and on its way down). Use labels to describe what is happening to the potential and kinetic energy at each stage. Label the position of maximum kinetic energy and the position of maximum potential energy.

TOPIC 4

Thermal Energy

LESSON 1
Thermal Energy, Heat, and Temperature
uInvestigate Lab: Temperature and Thermal Energy

LESSON 2
Heat Transfer
uInvestigate Lab: Visualizing Convection Currents

uEngineer It! STEM Shockwave to the Future

LESSON 3
Heat and Materials
uInvestigate Lab: Comparing How Liquids Cool

NGSS PERFORMANCE EXPECTATIONS

MS-PS3-3 Apply scientific principles to design, construct, and test a device that either minimizes or maximizes thermal energy transfer.

MS-PS3-4 Plan an investigation to determine the relationships among the energy transferred, the type of matter, the mass, and the change in the average kinetic energy of the particles as measured by the temperature of the sample.

MS-PS3-5 Construct, use, and present arguments to support the claim that when the kinetic energy of an object changes, energy is transferred to or from the object.

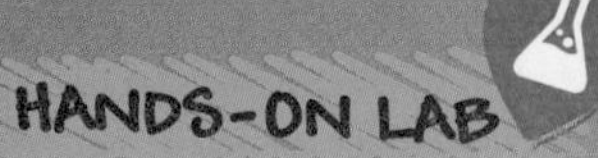

uConnect See how well you can judge temperature differences.

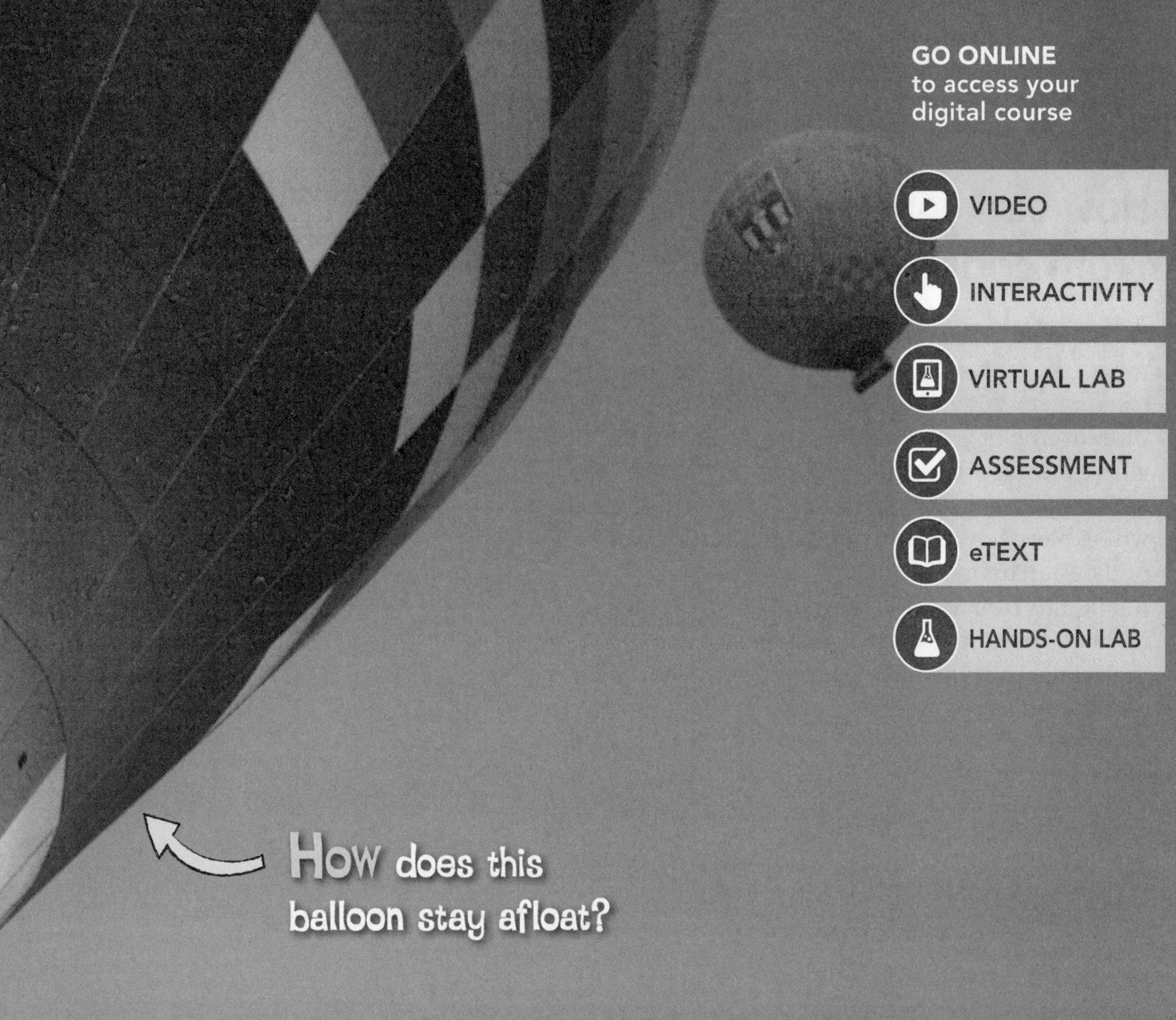

The Essential Question

What happens when heat flows from one object to another?

CCC Cause and Effect An open flame from a burner heats up the air inside the balloon, allowing it to take flight. How is the pilot able to control the altitude of the balloon?

....

....

....

....

....

Quest KICKOFF

How can you keep hot water from cooling down?

STEM **Phenomenon** The Arctic is one of the harshest places on Earth. In the winter, researchers studying the Arctic climate face temperatures averaging –34°C (–30°F). In extremely cold places where it's important to stay warm, having the right gear can be a challenge. In this Quest activity, you will explore how heat is transferred between objects and design an insulating container that will keep hot liquids from cooling down quickly. As you work through the Quest, you will test and evaluate different materials. You will apply what you have learned to design and build a prototype of your container, testing and revising the design as necessary. Then you will reflect on the design process in the Findings activity.

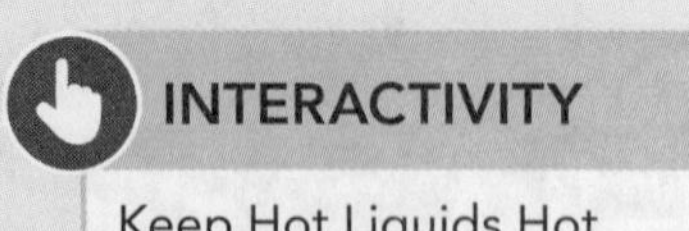

Keep Hot Liquids Hot

MS-PS3-3 Apply scientific principles to design, construct, and test a device that either minimizes or maximizes thermal energy transfer.

NBC LEARN VIDEO

The Quest Kickoff video explores how humans—and even some animals—try to keep themselves warm by controlling the transfer of heat. After watching the video, write three questions you still have about how an insulating device helps limit the transfer of heat.

1 ....

....

2 ....

....

3 ....

....

IN LESSON 1

What happens to hot liquids when exposed to cold temperatures? Think about ways your insulating container can slow the flow of heat.

Quest CHECK-IN

IN LESSON 2

STEM How does heat transfer between objects? Consider how your insulating container must function. Then evaluate different materials you can use to build your container and design a solution.

INTERACTIVITY

Contain the Heat

Researchers in the Arctic work in some of the coldest conditions on Earth.

Quest CHECK-INS

IN LESSON 3

STEM How can you apply what you know about thermal energy and heat transfer to build your container? Consider how different materials affect the flow of heat. Then build, test, and refine your design solution.

HANDS-ON LABS

- Keep the Heat In
- Keep the Cold Out

Quest FINDINGS

Complete the Quest!

Evaluate your work and reflect on the design and engineering process.

INTERACTIVITY

Reflect on Your Insulating Container

uConnect Lab

How Cold Is the Water?

How can you plan an investigation to **explain** whether you can use your senses to accurately determine temperature?

Background

Phenomenon The temperature of an object depends on the average kinetic energy of the particles that make up the object. Temperature can be measured with a thermometer, but how well does your hand work as a tool to judge temperature?

Materials

(per group)

- 3 large bowls
- warm tap water
- cold tap water
- room-temperature water
- markers
- thermometer
- paper

Safety

Be sure to follow all safety procedures provided by your teacher. The Safety Appendix of your textbook provides more details about the safety icons.

Design a Procedure

☐ 1. Fill one of the plastic bowls with cold water, another with warm water, and a third with water at room temperature. Label the bowls 1, 2, and 3 and line them up.

☐ 2. **SEP Plan a Procedure** Write a three-step procedure to make observations about the temperature of the water using your hands. Think about how you could "trick" your hands into perceiving the water at as cooler or warmer than it really is. Include a step that uses a thermometer. Show your plan to your teacher before you begin.

☐ 3. Record your observations in the table.

Observations

HANDS-ON LAB

Connect Go online for a downloadable worksheet of this lab.

Procedure Step	Observations

Analyze and Conclude

1. **SEP Interpret Data** How did the water in the bowls feel when you touched them at the start of the investigation?

....

....

2. **Explain Phenomena** Were you able to "trick" yourself into perceiving the water as cooler or warmer than it was when you began the investigation? Explain.

....

....

....

3. **SEP Construct an Explanation** Use your observations to explain if you can use hands to accurately judge temperature.

....

....

....

....

LESSON 1 Thermal Energy, Heat, and Temperature

Guiding Questions

- What happens to a substance when it is heated?
- What is the difference between thermal energy and temperature?

Connections

Literacy Use Information

Math Convert Measurement Units

MS-PS3-4

HANDS-ON LAB

uInvestigate Measure temperature change as energy is transferred.

Vocabulary

thermal energy
heat
temperature

Academic Vocabulary

transfer
absolute

Connect It!

An ice pop will melt on a hot day. Circle the place on the ice pop where the particles have the most thermal energy.

Explain Phenomena Explain why you circled this place on the ice pop.

....

....

SEP Construct Explanations With enough time, would an ice pop melt on a cool autumn day? Explain.

....

....

Thermal Energy and Heat

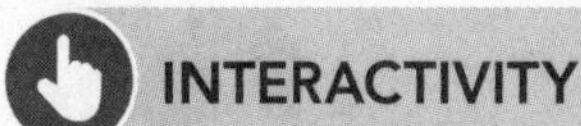

INTERACTIVITY

See how heat flows with examples from the kitchen.

All objects are made up of small particles. These particles are constantly in motion. This means they have kinetic energy. Particles are arranged in specific ways in different objects, so they also have potential energy. The total kinetic and potential energy of all the particles in an object is called **thermal energy**. This total energy can also be called internal energy. Objects contain thermal, or internal, energy even if they do not feel hot. The joule is the SI unit of energy.

The thermal energy of an object changes when heat is **transferred** to or from the object. **Heat** is the energy that is transferred from a warmer object to a cooler object. As the warmer object cools down, the cooler object warms up until the two objects are the same temperature. Once this happens, heat stops transferring between the two objects.

Academic Vocabulary

Heat is energy transferred from one place to another. What other things can you transfer from one place to another?

....

....

....

Heating a substance can cause its particles to move more quickly. For example, when the ice pop in **Figure 1** is held in sunlight, the particles in the ice pop gain kinetic energy. As a result, the temperature of the ice pop increases.

Note that in everyday language, the term *heat* can be used to describe the thermal energy contained in an object. However, when scientists use the term *heat,* they are referring only to energy that is transferred between two objects or systems at different temperatures.

READING CHECK **Compare and Contrast** What is the difference between thermal energy and heat?

....

....

Thermal Energy Changes

Figure 1 An ice pop melts as its thermal energy increases. This thermal energy comes from heat radiated by the sun.

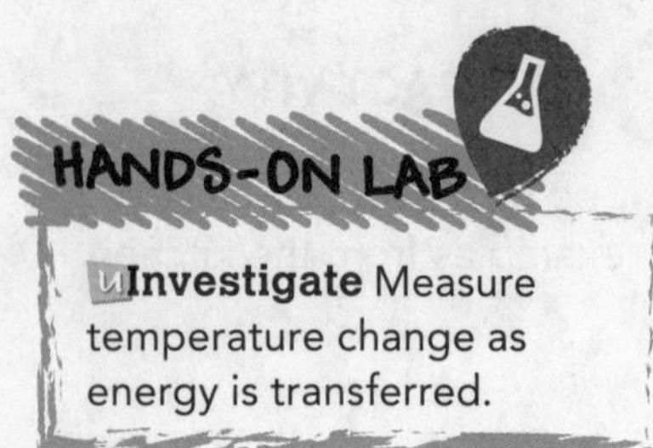

Investigate Measure temperature change as energy is transferred.

Temperature And Its Measurement

We use temperature as a measure of how hot or cold something is. On average, the particles in a substance move faster when the substance is hot than when it is cold. **Temperature** is a measure of the average kinetic energy of the particles in a substance. When a substance is at a higher temperature, the particles move faster and have a greater average kinetic energy than when the substance is at a lower temperature.

Academic Vocabulary

If something is absolute, it is definite or without question. How would you describe absolute silence?

....

....

....

....

Temperature can be measured with a thermometer. Thermometers show how hot or cold something is compared to a reference point. The Celsius scale uses the freezing point of water at sea level as its reference point at zero degrees Celsius (0°C). The United States typically uses the Fahrenheit scale, in which the freezing point of water at sea level is 32 degrees Fahrenheit (32°F). The kelvin is the official SI unit of temperature. On the Kelvin scale, zero kelvins (0 K) refers to **absolute** zero, the lowest temperature possible. At absolute zero, particles theoretically would have no kinetic energy. They would be completely motionless! So, the Kelvin scale only goes up from zero. Units on the Kelvin scale are the same size as units on the Celsius scale. A change of 1 K is the same temperature change as 1°C. Zero K is equal to −273°C.

Temperature Scales

If you have a thermometer with both Celsius and Fahrenheit scales, you can "eyeball" the conversion in temperature. Temperatures that line up on the parallel scales, such as 32°F and 0°C, are equivalent.

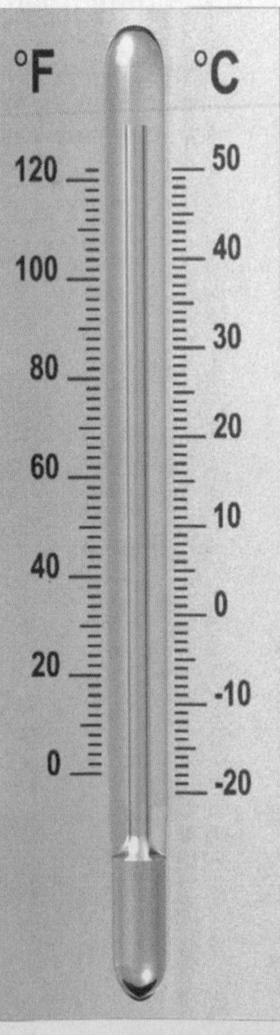

1. Integrate with Visuals A comfortable room temperature is 72°F. Mark the thermometer where approximately 72°F would be. What is the approximate temperature in Celsius? ....

2. Convert Measurement Units Complete the conversion table to compare the temperatures on different scales.

3. SEP Use Mathematics Write a formula for converting temperature to degrees Celsius if you are given the temperature in kelvins.

....

....

°F	°C	K
		263
	0	273
212	100	373

Temperature and Melting

Figure 2 Icicles melt as their thermal energy increases. However, the temperature of the melting icicles remains at 0°C during the change of state.

CCC Stability and Change Think about the difference between thermal energy and temperature. How might the melting icicles gain energy without changing temperature?

How Thermal Energy and Temperature Are Related

Different objects at the same temperature can have different amounts of thermal energy. This is because the thermal energy of an object is the total energy of all the particles in the object. Temperature contributes to an object's thermal energy, but it is not the only factor. Other factors include the potential energy and arrangement of the particles, as well as the states, types, and amounts of matter in the object.

Changing States When thermal energy transfers to another object in the form of heat, it can do work or cause change like all other forms of energy. If enough heat is transferred to or from a substance, the substance can change states. During a change of state, the thermal energy of a substance changes, but its temperature stays the same. For example, as heat is transferred to the melting icicles in **Figure 2**, their thermal energy continues to increase. Since these icicles have already reached their melting point (0°C), the added energy continues to break the rigid arrangement of the water molecules, rather than increase their motion. This means that the average kinetic energy of the molecules themselves does not change during a change of state. Remember, temperature is a measure of the average kinetic energy of the molecules. Therefore, as the ice melts, the thermal energy of the ice increases while the temperature remains the same.

Literacy Connection

Use Information Use the text and an internet source to help you answer the following question: How does thermal energy relate to temperature during condensation?

Model It!

Have you ever broken a piece of ice? You may have noticed that the break has angular edges instead of soft ones. This is because of the rigid, organized arrangement of its particles. The model shows the arrangement of water particles in a piece of solid ice just before it starts to melt.

In the empty circle, draw what the particles would look like after the ice has begun melting. Then write a caption for your drawing that describes what it shows.

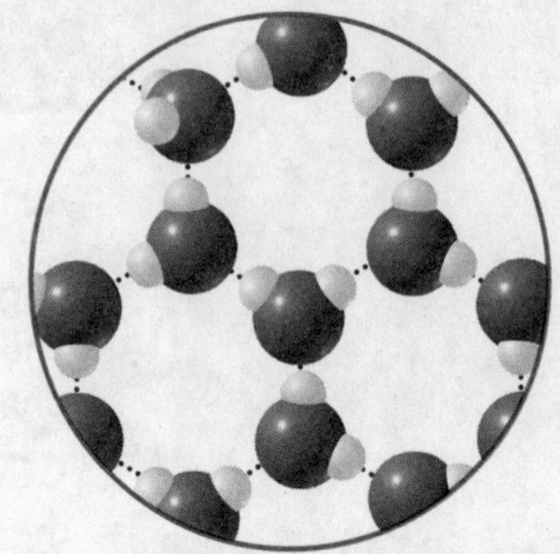

Water particles in solid form have a rigid arrangement.

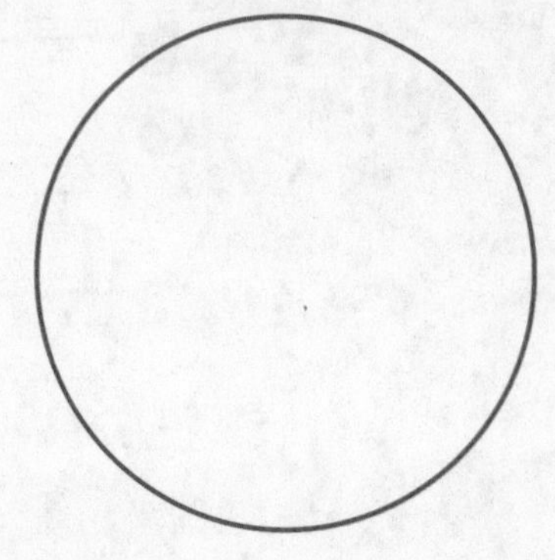

....

....

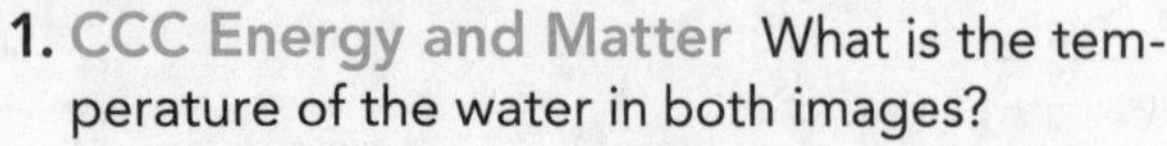

1. **CCC Energy and Matter** What is the temperature of the water in both images?

....

2. **Draw Comparative Inferences** Compare the relative amounts of thermal energy of each model.

....

....

....

VIDEO

Watch a video to help you understand changes of state.

Comparing Thermal Energy The amount of matter in an object affects its thermal energy. This is because more matter means more particles. As you have read, the particles have stored potential energy based on their arrangement. They also have kinetic energy based on their vibration and other movement. Therefore, the more particles an object has at a given temperature, the more thermal energy it has. For example, a 1-liter pot full of tea at 85°C has more thermal energy than a 0.2-liter cup full of tea at 85°C (**Figure 3**), because the pot contains more matter.

What if the objects contain the same amount of matter? The object at the higher temperature has more thermal energy. Remember, temperature is a measure of the average kinetic energy of the particles. If the object has a higher temperature, its particles have a greater average kinetic energy. A greater kinetic energy results in a greater thermal energy. So, if two 1-liter pots of tea have two different temperatures, the pot with the higher temperature has more thermal energy.

Thermal Energy and Amount of Matter

Figure 3 Even though the pot of tea and the cup of tea are at the same temperature, the pot of tea has more thermal energy because it contains more particles.

SEP Interpret Data If you wanted to cool both the pot and the cup of tea to 80°C, which one would take longer to cool down?

....

....

INTERACTIVITY

Discover how a thermometer works.

Changes in Temperature What if we add the same amount of energy to the pot of tea and the cup of tea in **Figure 3**? Will they change to the same temperature? Not necessarily. An object's change in temperature depends on the environment and the types and amounts of matter in the object. Let's say we wanted to raise the temperature of the tea in each container by 1°C. The type of matter is the same, and the environment is the same. But the container with more tea will require more heat. It has more particles, so more energy is needed to get them all moving with the same average kinetic energy as the particles in the smaller cup of tea.

READING CHECK **SEP Construct Explanations** Suppose you heat two bean burritos with the same ingredients in the microwave. One burrito weighs 0.3 pounds, while the other weighs 0.4 pounds. After microwaving each of them for one minute, which burrito will be hotter? Explain your answer.

....

....

....

Write About It Have you ever been served a meal that was not cooked hot enough? Write about the factors that may have contributed to your food being too cold.

LESSON 1 Check

MS-PS3-4

1. **SEP Communicating Information** What is the scientific definition of heat?

2. **Calculate** If the temperature outside is 297 K, what is this temperature in degrees Celsius?

3. **CCC Energy and Matter** What is the minimum value for the Kelvin temperature scale, and what would happen at that temperature?

4. **Identify** What are the factors that determine an object's thermal energy?

5. **Apply Concepts** Suppose that you have 0.5 liters of tomato soup and 0.5 liters of split pea soup in your kitchen. Can you tell for certain which one will require more thermal energy to heat up to 60°C? Why or why not?

6. **SEP Construct Explanations** Ice is melting at 0°C. Explain how the temperature of the melting ice stays the same while its thermal energy increases.

7. **Apply Scientific Reasoning** Object A has less thermal energy than Object B, but heat flows from Object A to Object B. What conditions would make this possible?

8. **CCC Cause and Effect** Jamie heats a pot of water on the stove. When the water boils, she turns the stove off and the water begins to cool. Draw a diagram with before and after pictures—before the stove is turned off, and after the stove is turned off. Add arrows to show the direction that heat flows in each picture.

MS-PS3-4

Glassblowing:

Not Just a Bunch of Hot Air

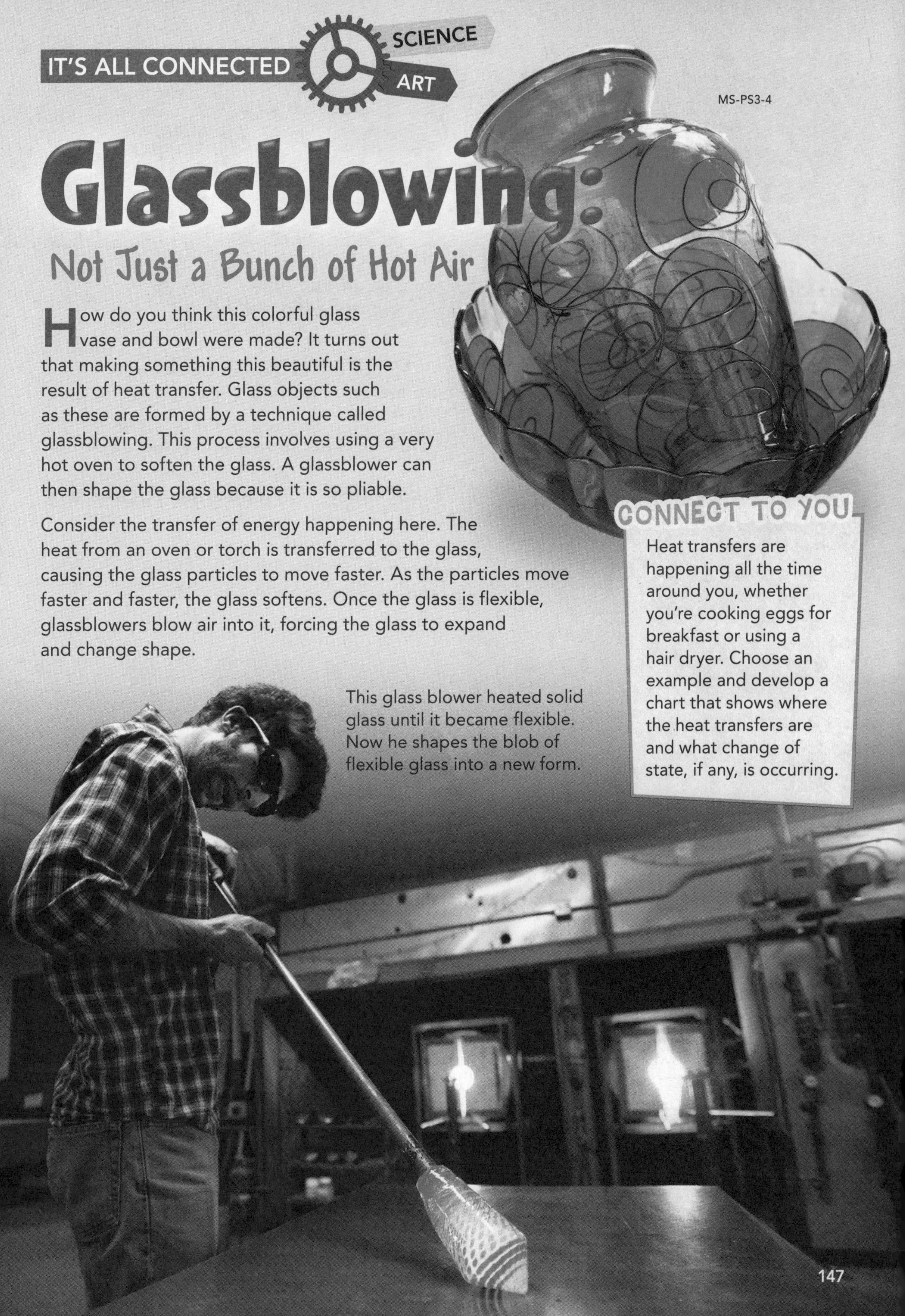

How do you think this colorful glass vase and bowl were made? It turns out that making something this beautiful is the result of heat transfer. Glass objects such as these are formed by a technique called glassblowing. This process involves using a very hot oven to soften the glass. A glassblower can then shape the glass because it is so pliable.

Consider the transfer of energy happening here. The heat from an oven or torch is transferred to the glass, causing the glass particles to move faster. As the particles move faster and faster, the glass softens. Once the glass is flexible, glassblowers blow air into it, forcing the glass to expand and change shape.

This glass blower heated solid glass until it became flexible. Now he shapes the blob of flexible glass into a new form.

CONNECT TO YOU

Heat transfers are happening all the time around you, whether you're cooking eggs for breakfast or using a hair dryer. Choose an example and develop a chart that shows where the heat transfers are and what change of state, if any, is occurring.

LESSON

2 Heat Transfer

Guiding Questions

- How is heat transferred?
- How is energy conserved during transformations?

Connections

Literacy Conduct Research Projects

Math Reason Quantitatively

MS-PS3-4, MS-PS3-5

HANDS-ON LAB

uInvestigate Observe convection currents with colored hot and cold water.

Vocabulary

conduction
convection
convection current
radiation

Academic Vocabulary

transform

Connect It!

When you're outside on a cold day, it's nice to stay warm near a fire. Draw an arrow on Figure 1 to show the direction of heat flow between the fire and the person's hands.

Predict What happens in terms of heat transfer the longer you sit near the fire?

....

....

Infer Why would you rather have hot cocoa than lemonade on a cold day?

....

....

Types of Heat Transfer

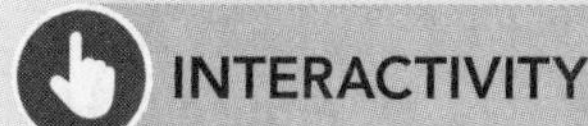

Watch this visual summary of conduction, convection, and radiation.

Heat is transferring around you all the time. Heat doesn't transfer in random directions, though. It is transferred from warmer areas to cooler areas by conduction, convection, and radiation.

Conduction is the transfer of energy from one particle of matter to another within an object or between two objects that are in direct contact. Conduction occurs when you place your head on a cool pillow. The fast-moving particles in your skin collide with the slow-moving particles in the pillow. This causes the particles in the pillow to move faster. The pillow becomes warmer, while your skin becomes cooler.

Convection is a type of heat transfer that occurs through the movement of fluids, which can be solid, liquid, or gas. Fluids are materials that flow. When air is heated, its particles speed up and move farther apart. This makes the heated air less dense. The heated air rises to float on top of the denser, cooler air. Cooler air flows into its place, heats up, and rises. Previously heated air cools down, sinks, and the cycle repeats. This flow creates a circular motion known as a **convection current**. Convection currents in air cause wind and changes in the weather.

Radiation is the transfer of energy by electromagnetic waves. Radiation is the only form of heat transfer that does not require matter. You can feel the radiation from a fire without touching the flames, as in **Figure 1**. The sun's transfer of energy to Earth is another example of radiation. Sunlight travels 150 million kilometers through empty space before it warms Earth.

Warming Up

Figure 1 A fire feels especially warm to your hands on a cold day, when heat from your body quickly transfers to the frigid air.

Heat Flow

Figure 2 Heat transfer goes on all around you all the time.

READING CHECK **Translate Information** In this lake scene, name each type of heat transfer shown and explain what it means. Then, draw arrows to show how heat is being transferred in each situation.

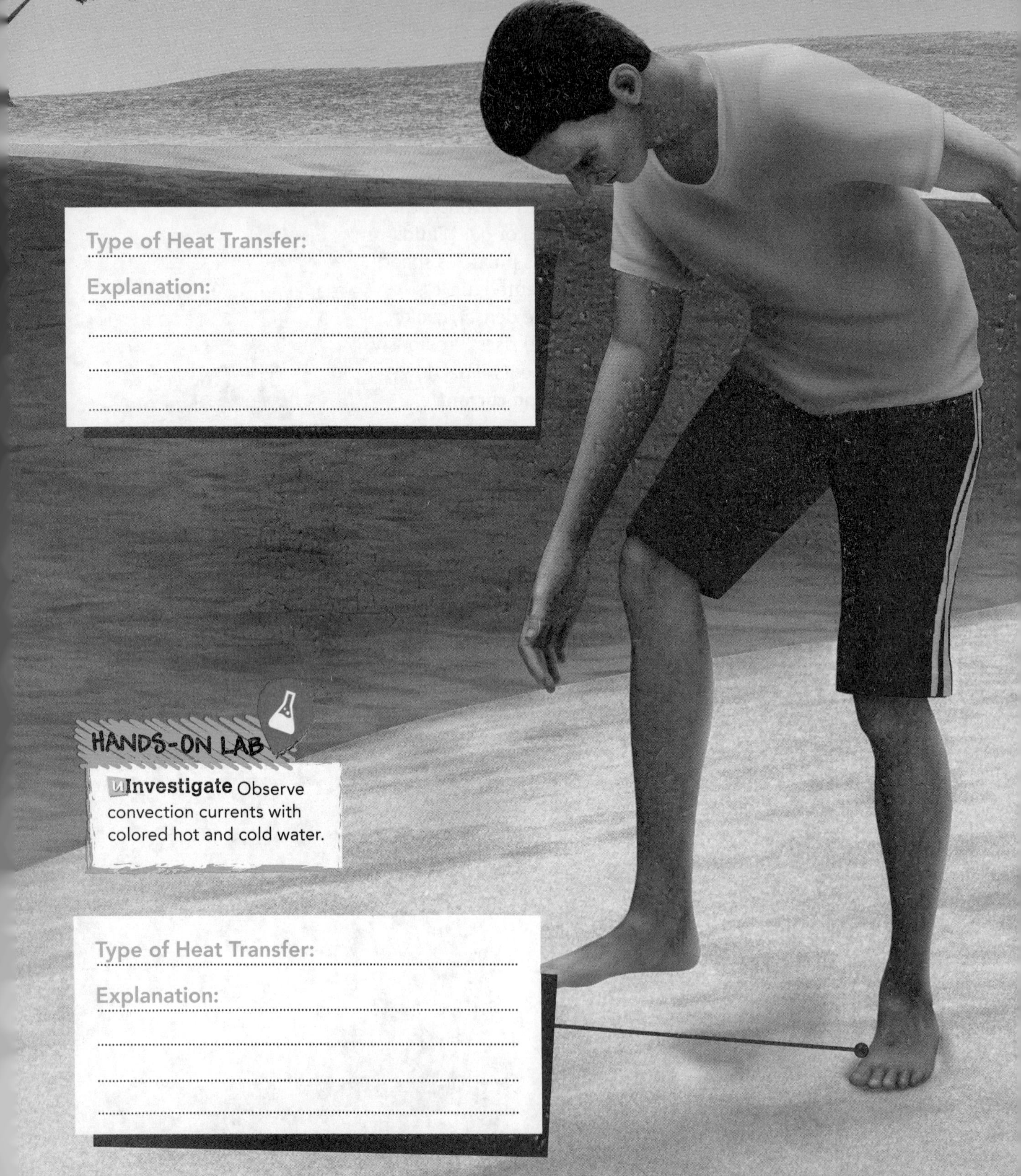

Type of Heat Transfer: ....

Explanation: ....

....

....

....

HANDS-ON LAB

Investigate Observe convection currents with colored hot and cold water.

Type of Heat Transfer: ....

Explanation: ....

....

....

....

Type of Heat Transfer:

Explanation:

Math Toolbox

Graphing Changes in Temperature

It's a hot day at the lake, with an air temperature of 30°C (86°F). Jeremy has two cups of water—one at 10°C and the other at 50°C. He places them on a picnic table where they receive the same amount of sunlight and no wind for a half an hour. The air temperature does not change during this time.

1. Reason Quantitatively Sketch two trend lines on the graph showing how the temperature of the water in the two cups would change over the 30 minutes. Create a legend to distinguish which line represents which cup (for example, the warmer cup = dotted line).

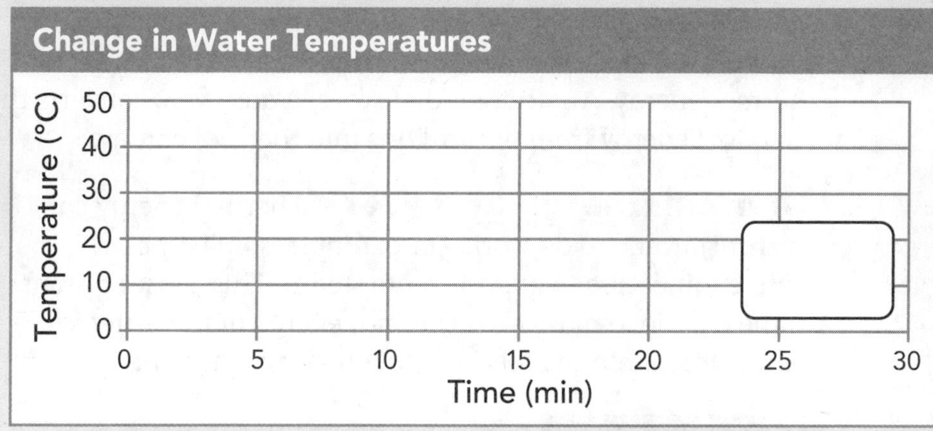

2. SEP Construct Explanations Describe the method(s) of heat transfer involved in causing the change in temperature of the two cups.

Heat Transfer

Figure 3 A wood-fired pizza oven demonstrates all three types of heat transfer: conduction, convection, and radiation.

SEP Construct Explanations Draw arrows to show the direction of heat transfer. How is energy conserved in the system of the pizza and the wood-fired oven?

....

....

....

....

....

VIDEO

See what it's like to become a firefighter.

Energy Conservation

In conduction, convection, and radiation, energy is transferred from one place to another. Even though the energy moves, it is always conserved within a system. For instance, in the pizza oven shown in **Figure 3**, the oven loses energy, but the pizza gains that energy. So the total energy of the oven-pizza system is conserved. By the law of conservation of energy, energy cannot be created or destroyed.

Energy Transformations The law of conservation of energy applies to everything—even when energy **transforms**. Many energy transformations involve thermal energy. For example, an electric stove transforms electrical energy into thermal energy. Another kind of stove, a gas oven, converts the chemical energy from natural gas into thermal energy.

Academic Vocabulary

What is another way of saying that energy can transform?

....

....

....

Thermal Energy and Work Thermal energy can be transformed to do work. For example, some types of train engines heat water to create steam. This causes pistons in the engine to move. The thermal energy of the water is transformed into the mechanical energy of the train.

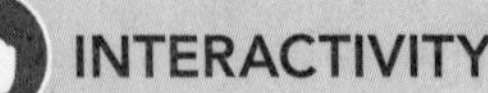

INTERACTIVITY

Figure out the best method for reheating a pizza.

READING CHECK **Determine Conclusions** Is there a type of energy transformation in which the system destroys or creates energy? What conclusion can you draw?

....

....

Question It!

Alicia performed an experiment on squash soup. She wanted to see whether stirring the soup would really help it cool down faster. She heated two 10-ounce bowls of soup in a microwave for 120 seconds. Then, she stirred one bowl of soup with a spoon for 60 seconds and let the other sit for 60 seconds. She used two thermometers to make measurements, and she recorded her data in the chart below.

Temp of soup after heating (°F)	Stir or let sit for 60 seconds?	Temp after 60 seconds (°F)
150	Stir	137
150	Let sit	145

1. **SEP Construct Explanations** Describe the energy transformations involved in heating the soup in the microwave. Which method of heat transfer is involved in heating the soup?

2. **Summarize Data Sets** Based on the data, summarize Alicia's results. Describe how stirring the soup affects heat transfer.

Literacy Connection

Conduct Research Projects Perform the experiment, and think about what you've learned about heat transfer in this lesson. Then, write a new question that would explore these concepts further. Discuss the possible answers to your question with a partner or teacher.

Write About It Think about how your breakfast or lunch was prepared. How did thermal energy come into play?

LESSON 2 Check

MS-PS3-4, MS-PS3-5

1. **Classify** What type of heat transfer occurs when eggs fry in a hot pan?

2. **Identify** What type of heat transfer occurs when you roast a marshmallow by holding it over a campfire?

3. **CCC Energy and Matter** Name a type of food in which convection helps the cooking process. Explain your answer.

4. **Explain Phenomena** When you touch a warm picnic table, your hand becomes warmer. Explain how energy conservation applies to this situation.

5. **SEP Develop Models** Draw a picture that shows a convection current in a real-life situation. Use arrows to represent the convection current.

6. **SEP Construct Explanations** Give a real-world example of how energy is transformed from electrical energy to thermal energy. Describe how the heat can be transferred to other objects through conduction, convection, or radiation.

Quest CHECK-IN

So far, you have learned how energy can be transferred by means of conduction, convection, and radiation.

SEP Define Problems Why is it important to consider the types of materials that are available and how those materials interact with cold exterior temperatures and warm interior temperatures of a food container?

INTERACTIVITY

Contain the Heat

Go online to apply what you've learned about thermal energy and heat transfer. How can you use this knowledge to design your insulating container? Brainstorm possible solutions with a group, and record your work in a graphic organizer. Then select the best method and materials to use in your design.

uEngineer It! Prototype to Product STEM

MS-PS3-5

SHOCKWAVE TO THE FUTURE

VIDEO

See how engineers use energy transformations to develop a real-world solution.

How do you make car engines more efficient?

You engineer them! The new shockwave engine offers a better way to get where you are going.

The Challenge: To build a more efficient engine.

Phenomenon Most cars on the road today still contain combustion engines. These engines use pistons to run. The pistons make the car heavier, and they also cause friction that wastes energy.

The shockwave engine does not contain pistons. It is more like a fan, circular in shape and ringed with blades. The shockwave engine converts the chemical energy of fuel into heat, and pressure increases within the engine. The thermal energy is converted to mechanical energy when the blades begin to spin. These spinning blades cause a crankshaft to turn, which causes the wheels of the car to spin.

The shockwave engine has fewer moving parts, and it is lighter than combustion engines. It can improve fuel economy by about 60 percent!

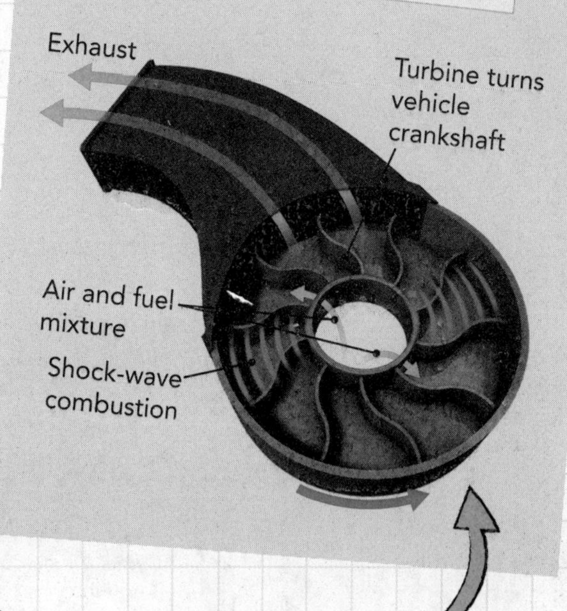

The shockwave engine works with thermal energy and pressure, causing a simple spinning motion. No pistons required!

DESIGN CHALLENGE

How can you build a simple heat engine? Go to the Engineering Design Notebook to find out!

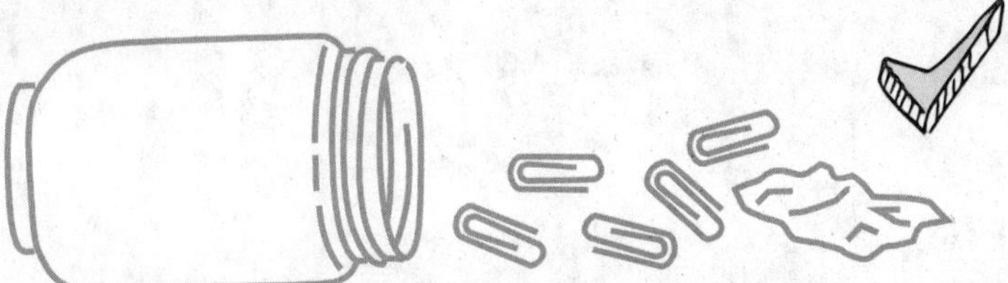

Case Study

MS-PS3-4, MS-PS3-5

Earth Power

Electricity is the largest form of energy used in the United States. Power plants generate this energy using a variety of sources. These sources include fossil fuels (such as natural gas and coal), nuclear power, hydroelectric, wind, and solar.

Coal used to be the major source of electricity, but it is one of the most expensive sources. It is also harmful to human health and the environment. Many coal plants, which produce soot and toxic gases, are now changing to natural gas, which is cheaper and cleaner. The burning of all fossil fuels releases carbon dioxide, which is a greenhouse gas that affects the climate.

Geothermal energy can also be used to generate electricity. In this process, warm water deep underground is pumped to the surface. The thermal energy of the water is transformed into electricity within a power plant. Review the steps in the diagram.

How a Geothermal POWER PLANT Works

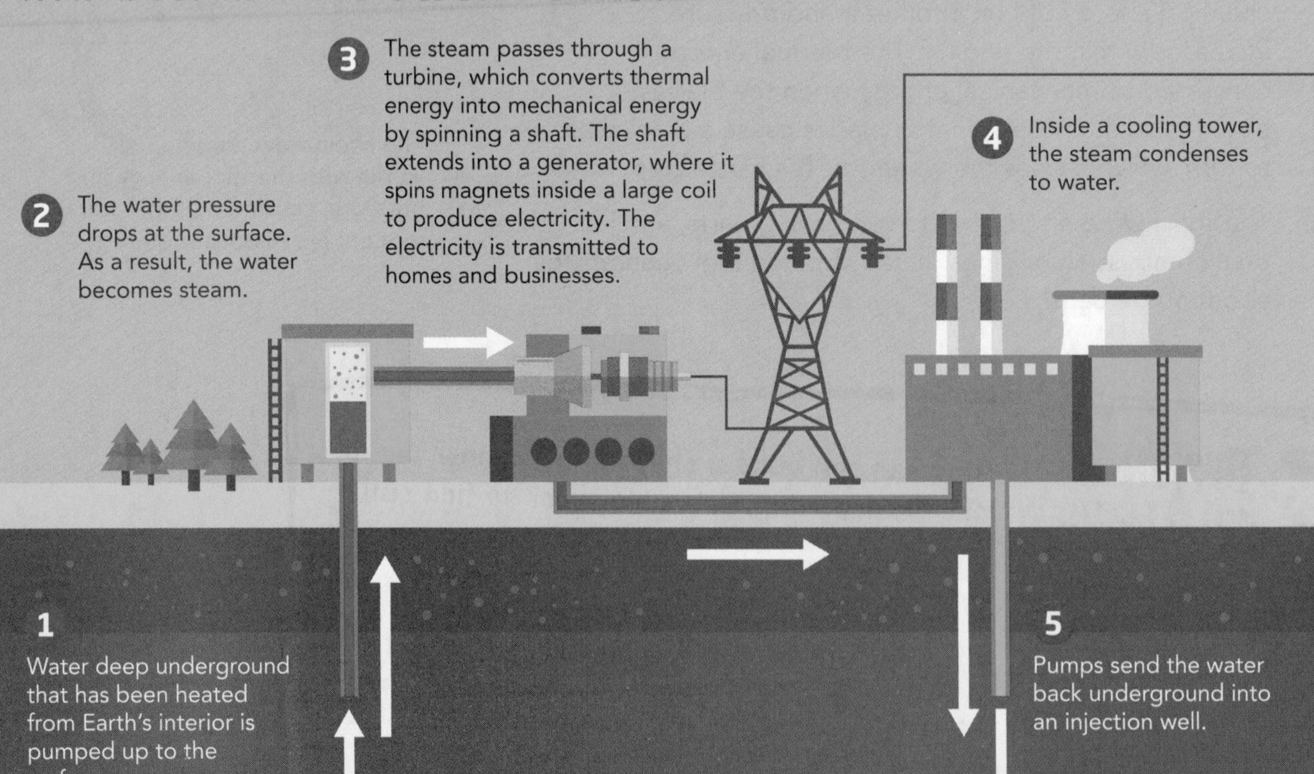

3 The steam passes through a turbine, which converts thermal energy into mechanical energy by spinning a shaft. The shaft extends into a generator, where it spins magnets inside a large coil to produce electricity. The electricity is transmitted to homes and businesses.
4 Inside a cooling tower, the steam condenses to water.
2 The water pressure drops at the surface. As a result, the water becomes steam.
1 Water deep underground that has been heated from Earth's interior is pumped up to the surface.
5 Pumps send the water back underground into an injection well.

Geothermal on the Rise

Over the past 10 years, the demand for geothermal energy has increased greatly. While it is still one of the less common ways to generate electricity, it is a much cleaner method than burning coal, and it has garnered public support. A disadvantage to using geothermal energy is that it is very expensive to generate and transmit, and the number of sites where geothermal energy is accessible from Earth's surface is not as high as the number of sites where natural gas, oil, and coal can be found. Still, there are significant efforts to increase demand for renewable energy resources, such as geothermal, solar, and wind, to reduce our impact on the environment.

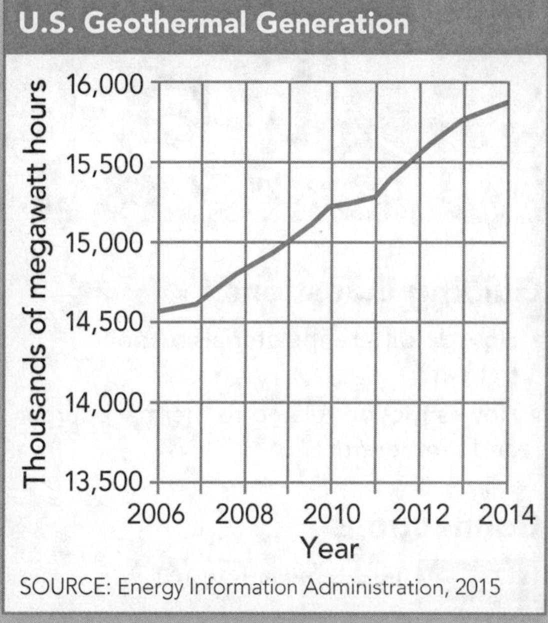

Use the graph to answer the following questions.

1. Patterns Describe any patterns you see in the graph.

2. Predict What do you think the data will look like for the generation of geothermal energy through the year 2040 in the United States? Why?

3. Construct Explanations The country of Iceland resides in a very volcanically active location. Geothermal plants provide 25 percent of Iceland's electricity. What factors do you think contribute to the high percentage of energy supplied by geothermal sources in Iceland?

4. Communicate What do you think could be done to encourage more people to use geothermal energy?

LESSON 3

Heat and Materials

Guiding Questions

- How do different materials respond to heat?
- How is friction related to thermal energy and temperature?

Connections

Literacy Integrate with Visuals

Math Analyze Proportional Relationships

MS-PS3-4, MS-PS3-5

HANDS-ON LAB

uInvestigate Explore how different amounts of liquid change temperature.

Vocabulary

conductor
insulator
specific heat
thermal expansion

Academic Vocabulary

contract

Connect It!

When divers explore deep ocean waters, the temperatures they encounter are very cold. In the space provided, describe how you think the wetsuit keeps the diver warm in cold water.

Communicate You also use special clothing to stay warm and perform different functions. What items of clothing do you use for specific activities?

....

....

Relate Structure and Function What materials are those items made of?

....

Thermal Properties of Materials

INTERACTIVITY

Determine what kind of container to use when taking lunch to the beach.

When you bake something in the oven, you use dishes made of glass, ceramic, or metal instead of plastic. Some materials can stand up to the heat of an oven better than others. Materials respond to heat in different ways. The thermal properties of an object determine how it will respond to heat.

Conductors and Insulators If you walk barefoot from your living room rug to the tile floor of your kitchen, you will notice that the tile feels colder than the rug. But the temperature of the rug and the tile are the same—room temperature! The difference has to do with how materials conduct heat, which is another way of saying how well they absorb or transmit heat.

Reflect Conductors and insulators are all around you. In your science notebook, write one conductor and one insulator that you see. Describe their materials and why you believe they are conductors or insulators.

A material that conducts heat well is called a **conductor**. Metals such as silver are good conductors. Some materials are good conductors because of the particles they contain and how those particles are arranged. A good conductor, such as the tile floor, feels cold to the touch because heat easily transfers out of your skin and into the tile. However, heat also transfers out of conductors easily. A metal flagpole feels much hotter on a summer day than a wooden pole would in the same place because heat easily conducts out of the metal pole and into your hand.

A wooden pole and your living room rug are good insulators. **Insulators** are materials that do not conduct heat well. Other good insulators include air and wool. For example, wool blankets slow the transfer of heat out of your body.

Surviving the Cold Water

Figure 1 A diver stays warm in a special wetsuit.

Investigate Explore how different amounts of liquid change temperature.

VIRTUAL LAB

Explore energy changes with a calorimeter and investigate the amount of calories in different foods.

Specific Heat Imagine running across hot sand toward the ocean. You run to the water's edge, but you don't go any farther— the water is too cold. How can the sand be so hot and the water so cold? After all, the sun heats both of them. The answer is that water requires more heat to raise its temperature than sand does.

When a substance or material is heated, its temperature rises. But the temperature does not rise at the same rate for all materials. The amount of heat required to raise the temperature of a material depends on the material's chemical makeup. Different materials require different amounts of energy to have the same temperature increase.

The amount of energy required to raise the temperature of 1 kilogram of a material by 1 kelvin is called its **specific heat**. It is measured in joules per kilogram-kelvin, or J/(kg·K), where kelvin is a measure of temperature. A material with a high specific heat can absorb a great deal of energy without a great change in temperature.

If a material's temperature changes, you can calculate how its energy changes with a formula.

Energy Change = Mass × Specific Heat × Temperature Change

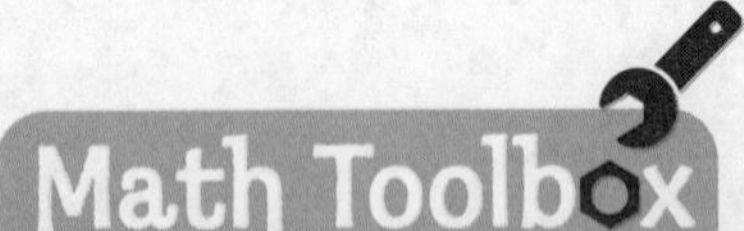

Math Toolbox

Energy Change, Specific Heat, and Mass

A chef is preparing vegetables in two pans. The pans are the same mass, but one is made of aluminum and the other is made of iron. She heats both pans to the same temperature before adding the vegetables.

Material	Specific Heat (J/(kg·K))
Aluminum	900
Water	4,180
Silver	235
Iron	450

1. **Analyze Proportional Relationships** The ratio of the specific heat of aluminum to the specific heat of iron is 2:1. How much energy must be transferred to the aluminum pan, compared with the amount of energy transferred to the iron pan?

2. **CCC Energy and Matter** If the chef used an aluminum pan and a silver pan of equal mass, which would undergo a greater energy change?

3. **Predict** Suppose the chef used two silver pans instead, but one was three times the mass of the other. How would the energy change of the two pans compare?

Pop!

Figure 2 When you make popcorn, heat flows to a tiny droplet of water inside the kernel. This causes the liquid water to change into vapor. The expanding water vapor builds up pressure inside the kernel. Finally, the kernel explodes, turning into a piece of popcorn!

Thermal Expansion Have you ever tried to open a jar, but the lid was firmly stuck? Thermal expansion could help you in this situation. To loosen a jar lid, you can hold it under a stream of hot water. This works because the metal lid expands more than the glass does as it gets hotter.

As the thermal energy of matter increases, its particles usually spread out, causing the substance to expand. This is true for almost all types of matter. The expansion of matter when it is heated is known as **thermal expansion**. When matter is cooled, the opposite happens. Thermal energy is released. This causes the particles to slow down and move closer together. As matter cools, it usually decreases in volume, or **contracts**. Different materials expand and contract at different rates and to different volumes.

Academic Vocabulary

In this context, the verb *contract* means to decrease in size. Write a sentence using the word *contract*.

....

....

Expansion Joints

Figure 3 Bridge joints allow room for the bridge to expand in the heat.

READING CHECK **Write Informative Texts**
What might happen if thermal expansion had not been considered in the building of this bridge?

....

....

....

....

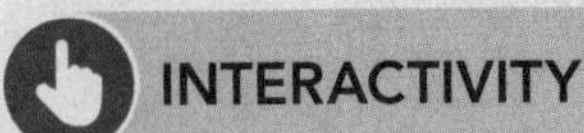

INTERACTIVITY

Design and build your own solar oven.

Temperature, Energy, and Friction

The kinetic energy of particles can change, as in thermal expansion, but an entire object's kinetic energy can change as well. A change in an object's kinetic energy indicates that a transfer of energy to or from the object is happening. If the kinetic energy of the object increases, then some form of energy is being transferred to the object. If the kinetic energy decreases, then the object is transferring kinetic energy to something else. This is true because energy is always conserved. The kinetic energy is not created or destroyed—it is transferred and sometimes transformed to other forms of energy in the process.

From Fast to Warm

Figure 4 As this bike skids to a stop, the tires and the ground become warmer.

Friction and Energy Transformation

Some objects lose kinetic energy because of friction. The law of conservation of energy accounts for this change in energy. For example, when a bike skids to a stop, as in **Figure 4**, the tires experience friction with the ground. When this happens, the kinetic energy of the entire bike changes—the bike slows down. Where does that kinetic energy go? If you could feel the bike tire or the ground, you would observe the answer. They both become hot. As friction slows the bike, the kinetic energy transforms into thermal energy of the tire and the ground. As the tire and the ground cool down, that thermal energy transfers to the surrounding air.

Literacy Connection

Integrate With Visuals
How does friction between the bike tires and the ground relate to thermal energy and temperature?

....

....

....

....

Model It!

Friction and Energy Transformation
In the space provided, draw an example in which friction causes kinetic energy to transfer and transform. Describe the transfers or transformations that are occurring.

....

....

....

Space Shuttle Entering Atmosphere

Figure 5 This NASA illustration shows how a space shuttle burns through the atmosphere as it returns to Earth.

Materials for Space Shuttles

When space shuttles were used for various missions, friction occurred between the space shuttles and the air in Earth's atmosphere. When a shuttle returned from space and re-entered the atmosphere, as in **Figure 5**, it experienced compression and friction from the atmospheric gas. Even though the upper atmosphere is cold, the space shuttle experienced high temperatures due to friction. Some of the kinetic energy of the moving space shuttle transformed into thermal energy.

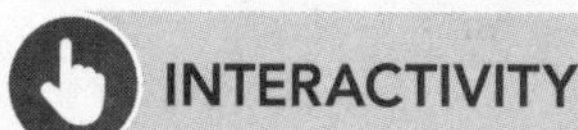

INTERACTIVITY

Evaluate and recommend materials in the design of a playhouse for a park.

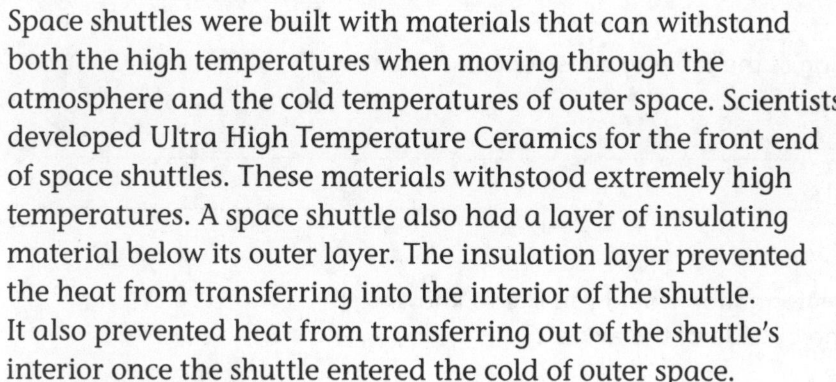

Space shuttles were built with materials that can withstand both the high temperatures when moving through the atmosphere and the cold temperatures of outer space. Scientists developed Ultra High Temperature Ceramics for the front end of space shuttles. These materials withstood extremely high temperatures. A space shuttle also had a layer of insulating material below its outer layer. The insulation layer prevented the heat from transferring into the interior of the shuttle. It also prevented heat from transferring out of the shuttle's interior once the shuttle entered the cold of outer space.

READING CHECK **Infer** Which type of material, an insulator or a conductor, should be used to keep an airplane warm inside? Why?

....

....

Plan It!

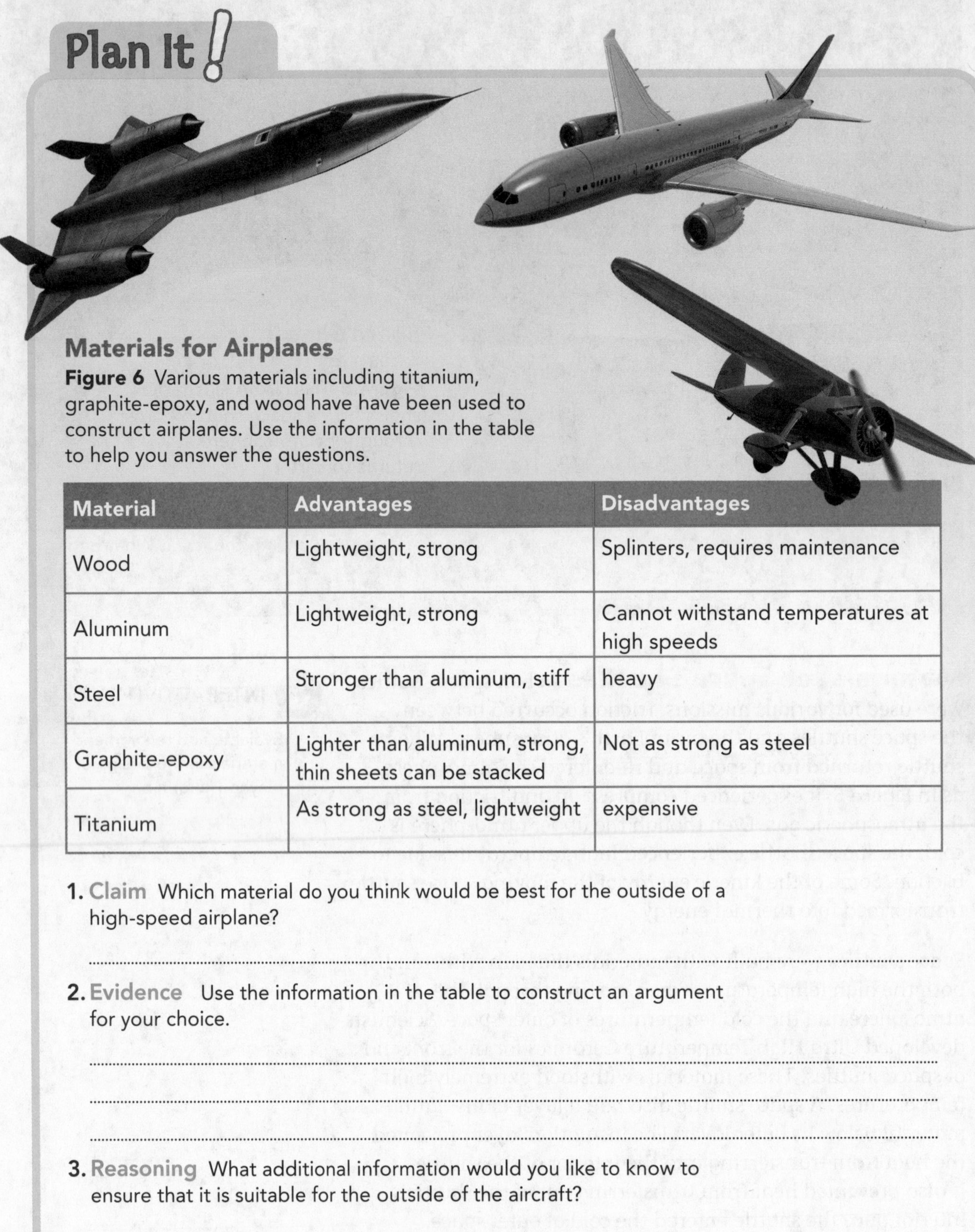

Materials for Airplanes

Figure 6 Various materials including titanium, graphite-epoxy, and wood have have been used to construct airplanes. Use the information in the table to help you answer the questions.

Material	Advantages	Disadvantages
Wood	Lightweight, strong	Splinters, requires maintenance
Aluminum	Lightweight, strong	Cannot withstand temperatures at high speeds
Steel	Stronger than aluminum, stiff	heavy
Graphite-epoxy	Lighter than aluminum, strong, thin sheets can be stacked	Not as strong as steel
Titanium	As strong as steel, lightweight	expensive

1. **Claim** Which material do you think would be best for the outside of a high-speed airplane?

   ....

2. **Evidence** Use the information in the table to construct an argument for your choice.

   ....

   ....

   ....

3. **Reasoning** What additional information would you like to know to ensure that it is suitable for the outside of the aircraft?

   ....

   ....

   ....

LESSON 3 Check

MS-PS3-4, MS-PS3-5

1. **SEP Construct Explanations** Why do some materials feel hotter than others, even if the two materials are at the same temperature?

2. **Classify** Foam picnic coolers keep food cool on a hot day. Is foam a conductor or an insulator? Explain.

3. **Calculate** Suppose you have two slices of cheese. They have the same specific heat, but one is twice the mass of the other. How much energy is needed to melt the larger slice compared to the amount of energy needed to melt the smaller slice?

4. **SEP Communicate Information** Why do objects tend to expand when they are heated?

5. **SEP Engage in Argument** The driver of a car slams on the brakes so that his car does not crash into a deer in the road. What happens to the thermal energy of the tires as the car skids to a stop? What causes this change in thermal energy?

Quest CHECK-INS

In this lesson, you learned how the specific heat of different substances affects how they transfer heat and whether they're likely to be classified as insulators or conductors.

Evaluate How could the specific heat of the substance your container will hold affect the performance of the container?

HANDS-ON LABS

- Keep the Heat In
- Keep the Cold Out

Go online to download the lab worksheets. You will finalize the design of your container, and then build, test, and evaluate the finished product.

TOPIC 4 Review and Assess

1 Thermal Energy, Heat, and Temperature

MS-PS3-4

1. What is the total energy of all of the particles in an object called?
   A. chemical energy
   B. thermal energy
   C. potential energy
   D. nuclear energy

2. Energy that is transferred from a warmer object to a cooler object is called
   A. temperature.
   B. substance.
   C. heat.
   D. mechanical energy.

3. When the kinetic energy of the particles in an object increases, the temperature of the object
   A. increases.
   B. decreases.
   C. remains the same.
   D. becomes fixed at 100°C.

4. A/an .... is an instrument that can be used to measure temperature.

5. **CCC Stability and Change** What happens to the state of liquid water if enough heat is added?

   ....

   ....

6. **Draw Comparative Inferences** A 2-ounce apple and a 4-ounce apple are at the same temperature. Which requires more thermal energy to raise its temperature by 1°F? Why?

   ....

   ....

   ....

   ....

Use the illustration to answer questions 7 and 8.

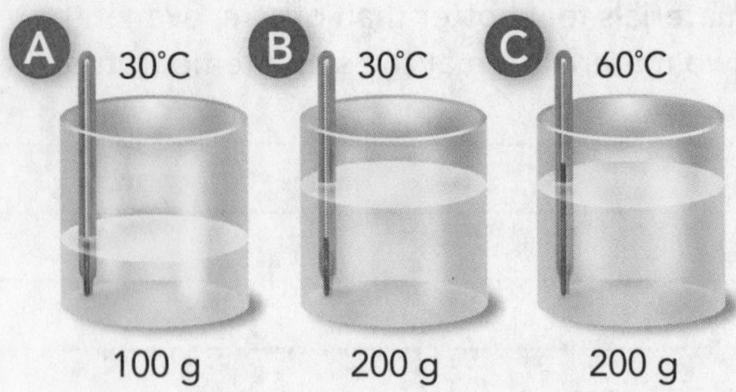

7. **SEP Interpret Data** Compare the average motion of the particles in the three containers of water. Explain your answer. (Note: The same substance is in each container.)

   ....

   ....

   ....

   ....

8. **SEP Analyze Data** Compare the amount of thermal energy in containers A and B. Explain your answer.

   ....

   ....

   ....

2 Heat Transfer

MS-PS3-4, MS-PS3-5

9. What is the process by which heat transfers from one particle of matter to another when the particles collide?
   A. conduction B. convection
   C. expansion D. radiation

10. When energy transforms from one form to another, the total amount of energy in the system
    A. decreases. B. increases.
    C. is conserved. D. drops to zero.

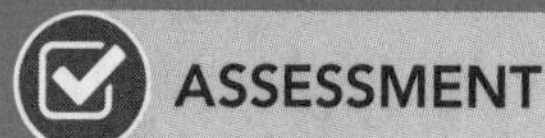

Evaluate your understanding by taking a Topic Test.

11. Air currents transfer energy by the method of heat transfer called ....

12. Identify each example of heat transfer as conduction, convection, or radiation.

A.

B.

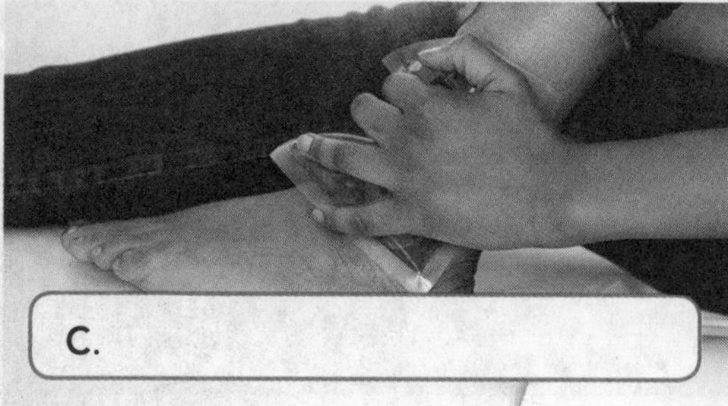

C.

13. **Explain** How can heat be transferred across empty space? Explain your answer.

....

....

14. **Make Judgments** Suppose you try to heat up your home using a fireplace in one of the rooms. Would a fan be helpful? Explain.

....

....

....

3 Heat and Materials

MS-PS3-4, MS-PS3-5

15. Which kinds of materials do not conduct heat well?
A. insulators
B. conductors
C. metals
D. radiators

16. The amount of energy per kilogram needed to increase the temperature of a material by 1 K is called the
A. specific heat.
B. heat sensitivity.
C. heat resistance.
D. thermal heat.

17. The speeds of two bumper cars decrease as their bumpers rub against each other. What happens to the temperatures of the bumpers due to the force of friction?
A. Both bumpers cool down.
B. Both bumpers warm up.
C. One bumper cools down while the other warms up.
D. Both bumpers remain the same temperature.

18. **SEP Develop Models** Draw before and after diagrams of the particles in a log that is heated. Does the log expand or contract?

TOPIC 4 Review and Assess

MS-PS3-4, MS-PS3-5

Evidence-Based Assessment

Out in space, sand-sized particles of rock approach Earth every single day. However, they do not reach Earth's surface because they burn up in the atmosphere. Sometimes, larger space rocks called meteoroids also travel through the atmosphere. Once the meteoroid enters the atmosphere, it appears as a bright light moving through the sky, called a meteor. A meteoroid typically enters the atmosphere with an average speed in the range of 10–70 km/s. The rock burns as it travels, losing mass and speed in the process. The burning is due to friction between the meteoroid and the air particles in the atmosphere. The density of the air particles in the atmosphere is greater closer to Earth's surface. Some meteoroids do not burn up completely, and they reach Earth's surface as meteorites.

The following data provides information about three meteoroids traveling towards Earth's surface. The meteoroids are all roughly spherical and of the same density.

Meteoroid	Initial Mass (kg)	Surface temperature of meteoroid in space, before entering atmosphere (°C)	Surface temperature of meteoroid in atmosphere, 150 km above Earth's surface (°C)
1	0.52	90	1730
2	3.24	92	1727
3	1.05	91	1735

1. **CCC Cause and Effect** Which statement describes what happens to the kinetic energy of the particles in the atmosphere as they come into contact with the meteoroid?
   - A. The kinetic energy of the surrounding air particles is converted to electrical energy.
   - B. The average kinetic energy of the surrounding air particles increases.
   - C. The kinetic energy of the surrounding air particles is converted to potential energy.
   - D. The average kinetic energy of the surrounding air particles decreases.

2. **Cite Evidence** What happens to the kinetic energy of a meteoroid as it travels farther through the atmosphere toward Earth's surface? Support your claim with evidence from the information provided.

3. **Infer** Explain how two methods of heat transfer are involved as the meteoroid burns.

4. **SEP Construct Explanations** Which meteoroid is most likely to reach Earth's surface? Explain why this is so, in terms of heat transfer. Use data from the table to support your response.

Quest FINDINGS

Complete the Quest!

Phenomenon After applying what you learned to the design and construction of an insulating container, reflect on the use of models and scientific principles in the design of your containers.

SEP Design Solutions How did concepts related to thermal energy and heat transfer guide your design process?

INTERACTIVITY

Reflect on Your Insulating Container

uDemonstrate Lab STEM

MS-PS3-3, MS-PS3-4

Testing Thermal Conductivity

How can you **design** an experiment to determine the best **metal** to use for a **heat sink**?

Background

Phenomenon Electronics manufacturers use heat sinks to draw heat away from components that can overheat. Engineers for a new tablet company have designed a super-fast processor. The problem is, the processor gets very hot, causing the tablet to shut down. The company has asked you to design an experiment to provide evidence for the best metal to use for a heat sink in their new tablet.

Materials

(per group)

- 3 metal conducting strips (10 cm x 2 cm each): copper, aluminum, and brass
- 6 insulating foam cups (5 cm tall)
- aluminum foil
- 2 plastic-backed thermometers
- boiling water (75 mL)
- room-temperature water (40 mL)
- graduated cylinder
- scissors
- stopwatch

Safety

Be sure to follow all safety procedures provided by your teacher. Appendix B of your textbook provides additional details about the safety icons.

Develop Possible Solutions

☐ You will conduct an experiment to investigate how each of the three metals conducts heat from a cup of hot water to a cup of room-temperature water. Design an experiment using the materials provided. Write out a procedure below, and then conduct the experiment. Construct a data table to record the results of your experiment, and note any important observations you make.

Demonstrate Go online for a downloadable worksheet of this lab.

Data and Observations

Analyze and Interpret Data

1. **Apply Scientific Reasoning** What roles did the metal strips and the foam cups play in terms of heat transfer?

2. **SEP Use Mathematics** Determine the temperature change of the room temperature water after 10 minutes for each metal used.

   Copper: ....

   Aluminum: ....

   Brass: ....

3. **SEP Use Mathematics** Determine the average rate of temperature change of the room temperature water for each metal used.

   Copper: ....

   Aluminum: ....

   Brass: ....

4. **SEP Engage in Argument** Brass costs about $0.90 per pound, copper costs $2.15 per pound, and aluminum costs $0.75 per pound. Which metal would you recommend be used for for use as a heat sink in the tablet? Explain your choice.

5. **Provide Critique** Examine the setup and procedure for another group's experiment. Make recommendations to the group for improving the design of its experiment.

TOPIC 5

Waves and Electromagnetic Radiation

NGSS PERFORMANCE EXPECTATIONS

MS-PS4-1 Use mathematical representations to describe a simple model for waves that includes how the amplitude of a wave is related to the energy in a wave.

MS-PS4-2 Develop and use a model to describe that waves are reflected, absorbed, or transmitted through various materials.

HANDS-ON LAB

uConnect See how particles on a wave move in this rope experiment.

GO ONLINE
to access your
digital course

VIDEO

INTERACTIVITY

VIRTUAL LAB

ASSESSMENT

eTEXT

HANDS-ON LABS

How are these laser beams made?

The Essential Question

What are the properties of mechanical and electromagnetic waves?

SEP Construct Explanations The boats in this harbor bob gently up and down due to the motion of water waves. But the laser light show is also made of waves—light waves! What do you think these two types of waves have in common?

....

....

....

....

Quest KICKOFF

How can you design a system to stop a thief?

STEM **Phenomenon** It may seem like something out of the movies, but some security systems use lasers to help prevent the theft of priceless objects. Engineers apply their knowledge of light and how it behaves to design these security systems. In this Quest activity, you will explore how light waves interact with lenses and mirrors. You will design possible solutions for a security demonstration and then test and evaluate your solutions to determine the optimal design. After making any additional modifications, you will demonstrate your expertise by directing a beam of light around an obstacle to reach a target.

INTERACTIVITY

Design to Stop a Thief

MS-PS4-1 Use mathematical representations to describe a simple model for waves that includes how the amplitude of a wave is related to the energy in a wave. **MS-PS4-2** Develop and use a model to describe that waves are reflected, absorbed, or transmitted through various materials.

After watching the Quest Kickoff video, think about a problem in your community that might be solved with the use of lasers. Record your solutions. Then share your ideas with a partner and discuss how lasers are important to our daily lives.

....

....

....

....

....

....

....

....

Quest CHECK-IN

IN LESSON 1

What effects do lenses and mirrors have on a beam of light? Explore models to observe how light interacts with different objects.

INTERACTIVITY

Light Behavior

Quest CHECK-IN

IN LESSON 2

What happens when light waves are reflected or transmitted? Experiment with mirrors and lenses to observe how they affect light waves.

INTERACTIVITY

Virtual Optics

IN LESSON 3

How do the properties of sound waves differ from light waves? Consider the properties of waves in your solution.

Museums use high-tech security systems to protect priceless works of art.

Quest CHECK-IN

IN LESSON 4

How can you make a beam of light bend around an object? Develop and evaluate possible solutions to the challenge.

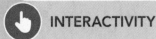

INTERACTIVITY

Optical Demonstration

Quest CHECK-IN

IN LESSON 5

STEM How can you apply your knowledge of lenses and mirrors to your solution? Build and test a solution, using lenses and mirrors. Then communicate your solution in a presentation or visual display.

HANDS-ON LAB

An Optimal Optical Solution

Quest FINDINGS

Complete the Quest!

Evaluate your security system designs and reflect on the design and engineering process.

INTERACTIVITY

Reflect on Your Demonstration

uConnect Lab

What Are Waves?

How can you **use a model** to understand waves?

Background

Phenomenon You've seen waves before, but do you know what waves really are? In this activity, you will observe waves and draw a conclusion about what waves are.

Materials

(per group)

- 5-meter length of rope or clothesline
- colored tape

Safety

Be sure to follow all safety procedures provided by your teacher. The Safety Appendix of your textbook provides more details about the safety icons.

Design a Procedure

☐ **1.** Wrap a piece of tape around the rope at approximately the halfway point.

☐ **2.** You will send waves along the rope. Predict how the waves will change the position of the piece of tape.

☐ **3. SEP Plan an Investigation** Write a procedure that uses the rope and tape to model waves.

☐ **4.** Show your plan to your teacher before you begin. Then, use your materials to model a wave. Draw a sketch of your model and describe it.

Sketch

Connect Go online for a downloadable worksheet of this lab.

Analyze and Interpret Data

1. **Explain Phenomena** What happened to the rope and tape? Was your prediction correct?

2. **SEP Construct an Explanation** Without using the word "wave," describe what you think moved from one end of the rope to the other end.

LESSON

1 Wave Properties

Guiding Questions

- How can you use a simple model to describe a wave and its features?
- How can you observe the properties of waves?
- What kinds of patterns can you predict based on wave properties?

Connections

Literacy Integrate Information

Math Use Proportional Relationships

MS-PS4-1

uInvestigate Model the three different types of mechanical waves.

Vocabulary

wave
mechanical wave
medium
electromagnetic radiation
transverse wave
amplitude
longitudinal wave
wavelength
frequency

Academic Vocabulary

vacuum

Connect It!

Read the caption, and then label the photos with different types of waves that are indicated in some way by the photos.

SEP Engage in Argument How is Earth dependent on the sun for energy?

....

....

....

Connect to Society How is a tsunami warning system a benefit to society?

....

....

Types of Waves

When you think of a wave, you probably picture a surface wave on the ocean. Actually, a **wave** is any disturbance that transfers energy from place to place. An ocean wave is one type of wave called a **mechanical wave**, meaning it moves through some type of matter. The matter a wave travels through is called a **medium**. A mechanical wave cannot travel through a **vacuum**, such as space.

Sound waves are another type of mechanical wave. Sound can travel through the ocean, but it can also travel through a solid object, such as a piece of metal, or a gas, such as the air. It cannot travel through a vacuum such as space.

Another type of wave is an electromagnetic wave. This type of wave transfers **electromagnetic radiation**, a type of energy. Examples of electromagnetic radiation include visible light, radio waves, X-rays, and microwaves. Like a mechanical wave, electromagnetic waves transfer energy. However, electromagnetic waves are unique in that they can travel without a medium.

Both types of waves involve a transfer of energy without a transfer of matter. While mechanical waves travel *through* matter, the waves themselves do not move the matter to a new place. The waves are disturbances in matter that transfer energy.

Figure 1 shows several different types of waves at work. Ocean waves cause the buoy to bob in the water. If a seafloor sensor detects a wave called a tsunami (soo NAH mee), it sends a signal to the buoy, which then sends a radio signal to a satellite orbiting Earth. The signal gets relayed to scientists, who can then warn coastal communities. The sunlight that lights this scene is also made of waves.

Academic Vocabulary

A vacuum is completely empty. Why is the space around you not considered a vacuum?

....

....

Reflect Write down some examples of waves that you are familiar with from everyday life. Can you classify them as mechanical or electromagnetic?

World of Waves

Figure 1 A tsunameter is a buoy anchored to the ocean floor. It detects extremely large waves called tsunamis and sends a radio signal to warn people.

INTERACTIVITY

See how the energy and amplitude of a wave are related.

Transverse Waves Waves can be classified by how energy is transmitted. Energy is transmitted through a medium by mechanical waves. Electromagnetic waves are capable of transmitting energy through empty space.

Waves can also be classified by how the particles in a disturbance vibrate. A mechanical wave begins when a source of energy causes a medium to vibrate. The direction of the vibration determines what type of mechanical wave is produced. A **transverse wave** travels perpendicular (at right angles) to the direction of the source's motion. The person in **Figure 2** is using his arms to make up-and-down vibrations in two ropes. Each particle of the rope moves up and down. The direction of the waves he's producing, though, is perpendicular to that up-and-down motion. The energy travels toward the far ends of the ropes.

The curved shape of the rope indicates the main features of a transverse wave. The high point of a wave is its crest, and the low point is the trough. Halfway between the crest and trough is the wave's resting position. The distance between the highest crest and the resting position marks the wave's **amplitude**. In general, the amplitude of a wave is the maximum distance the medium vibrates from the rest position.

Electromagnetic waves, such as sunlight, are also transverse waves. In their case, however, there is no motion of particles, even when light travels through a liquid, such as water, or a solid, such as glass.

Transverse Waves

Figure 2 Use arrows to indicate the direction the rope is vibrating and the direction energy is flowing. Label a crest and a trough, and indicate the amplitude.

Longitudinal Waves A wave that travels in the same direction as the vibrations that produce it is called a **longitudinal wave**. Sound is a longitudinal wave. Sound travels from speakers when flat surfaces inside the speakers vibrate in and out, compressing and expanding the air next to them.

Figure 3 shows a longitudinal wave in a spring toy. When the left hand pulls on the toy, the result is a series of stretches and compressions. Gaps between compressions are called rarefactions. Energy moves to the right along the toy.

While the wave travels, the spring particles do not move all the way to the right like the wave does. Each spring particle moves back and forth, like the hand. The small piece of ribbon on the spring moves the same way the particles in the spring move.

Literacy Connection

Integrate Information As you learn about waves, take notes that summarize and categorize the different motions that waves produce.

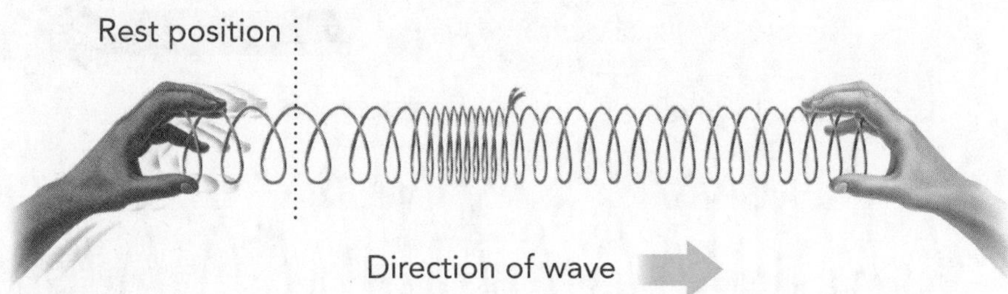

Longitudinal Wave
Figure 3 Label a compression and a rarefaction.

Surface Waves Combinations of transverse and longitudinal waves are called surface waves. For example, an ocean wave travels at the surface of water. When a wave passes through water, the water (and anything on it) vibrates up and down. The water also moves back and forth slightly in the direction that the wave is traveling. The up-and-down and back-and-forth movements combine to make each particle of water move in a circle, as shown in **Figure 4**.

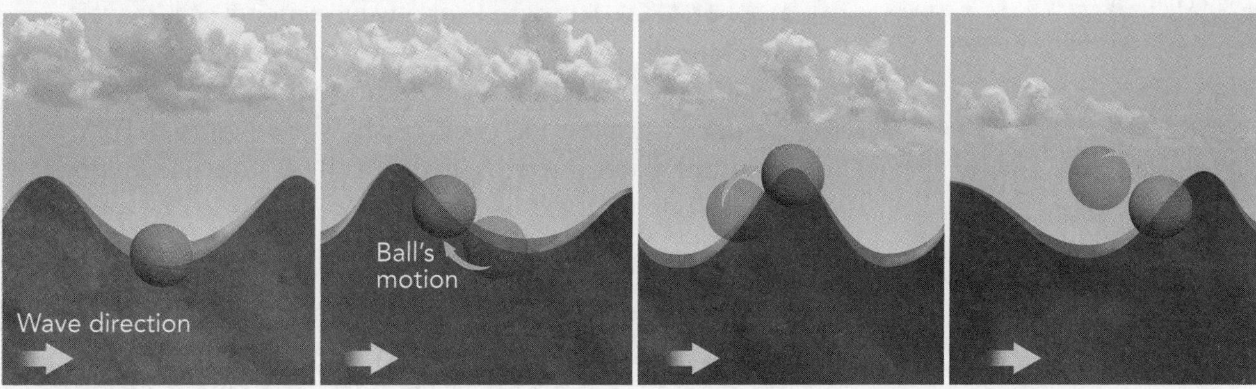

Surface Wave
Figure 4 As waves move from left to right, they cause the ball to move in a circle.

READING CHECK **Compare and Contrast** What is the main difference between a surface wave and a longitudinal wave?

....

....

Properties of Waves

Figure 5 All waves have amplitude, wavelength, frequency, and speed. After you read about these properties, answer the questions on the image.

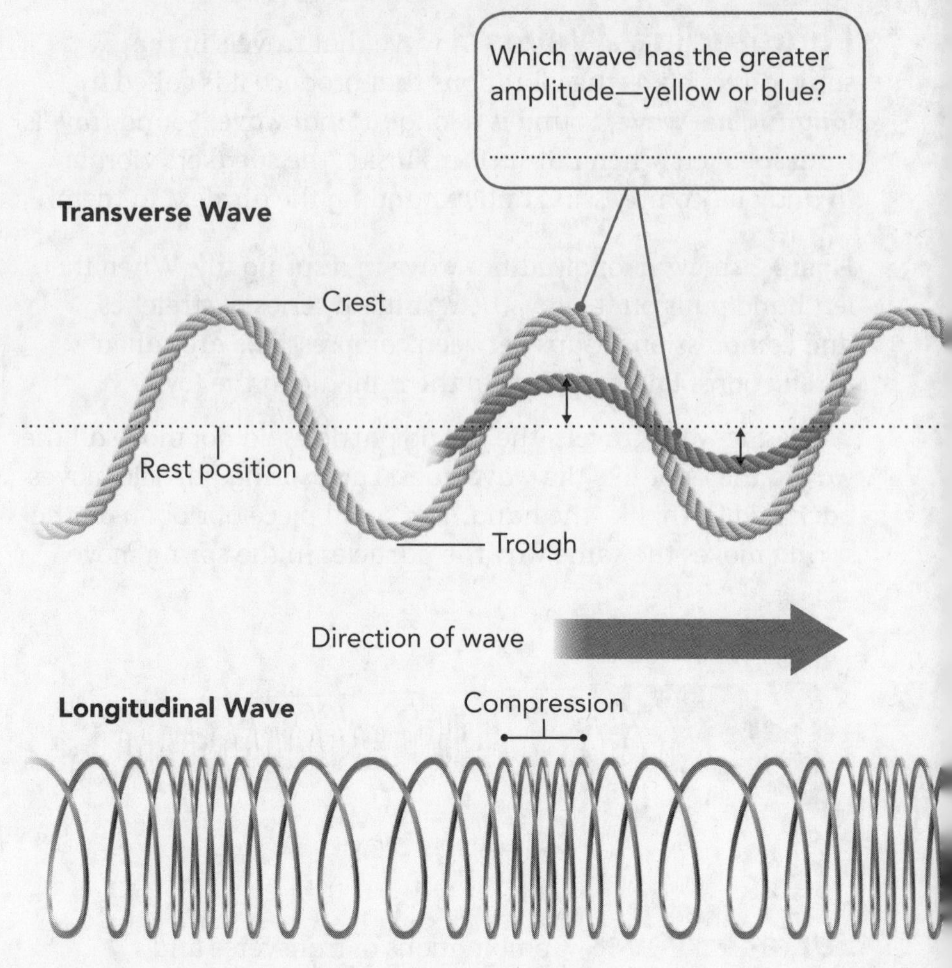

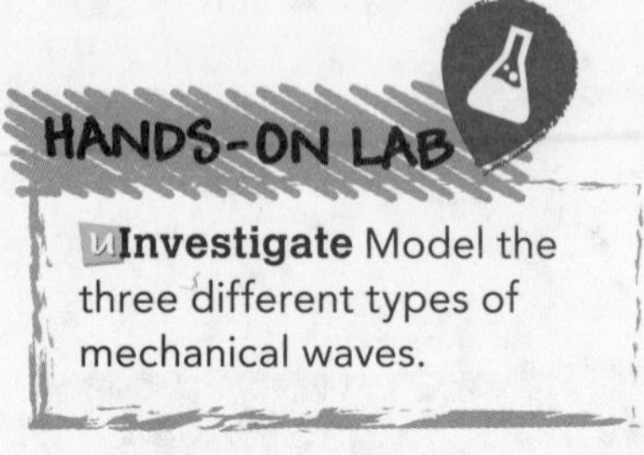

Investigate Model the three different types of mechanical waves.

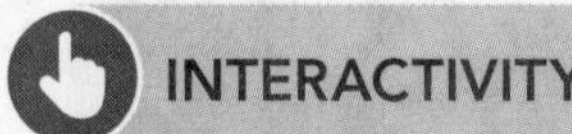

See how a wave travels through a coil.

Properties of Waves

In addition to amplitude, all waves have three other properties: wavelength, frequency, and speed. These properties are all related to one another.

Wavelength Suppose that a wave repeats as it travels. Its **wavelength** is determined by the distance it travels before it starts to repeat. The wavelength of a transverse wave is the distance from crest to crest, as shown in **Figure 5**. For a longitudinal wave, the wavelength is the distance from one compression to the next.

Frequency The number of times a wave repeats in a given amount of time is called its **frequency**. You can also think of frequency as the number of waves that pass a given point in a certain amount of time. For example, if you make waves on a rope so that one wave passes by a point every second, the frequency is 1 wave per second. Frequency is measured in units called hertz (Hz). A wave that occurs every second has a frequency of 1 Hz. If two waves pass by in a second, the frequency is 2 Hz.

One yellow wave passes by this point each second, so the frequency of the yellow wave is ....

Two green waves pass by this point each second, so the frequency of the green wave is ....

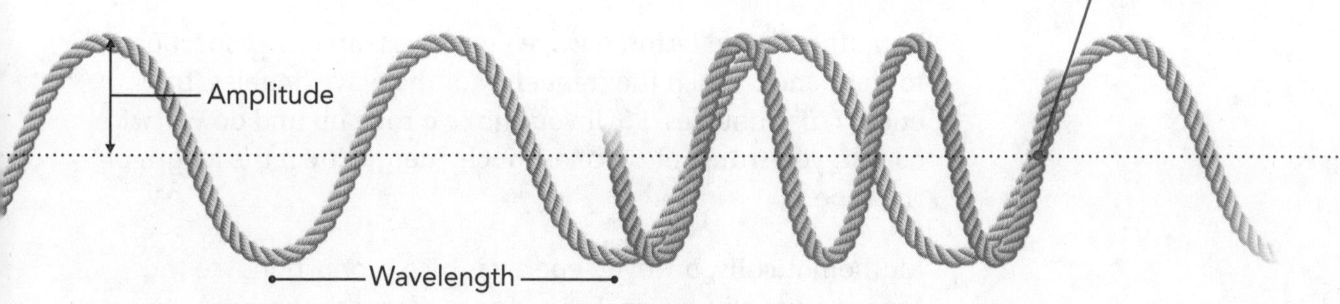

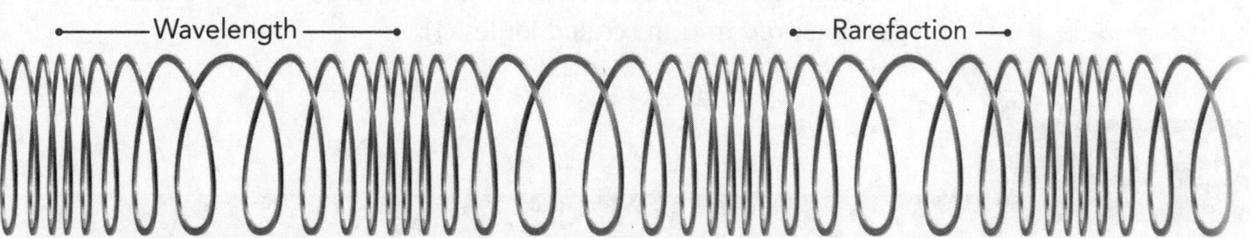

Speed The speed of a wave is determined by the distance it travels in a certain amount of time. Different waves have different speeds. For instance, a light wave travels almost a million times faster than a sound wave travels through air! Waves also travel at different speeds through different materials. For example, light travels faster through water than through glass. Sound travels more than three times faster through water than through air.

To calculate a wave's speed, divide the distance it travels by the time it takes to travel that distance. You can also find a wave's speed if you know its wavelength and frequency—just multiply wavelength times frequency.

Wave speed = Wavelength × Frequency

INTERACTIVITY

Generate virtual waves in a wave pool.

READING CHECK **Predict** If you and a friend are standing at opposite ends of a gymnasium and one of you claps, will the other person hear the clap at the same time she sees it happen? Why or why not?

....

....

See what happens when balls of different masses are dropped in water.

Wave Energy

Waves transmit energy from place to place. The amount of energy they transmit depends on how much energy was input by the original source of the vibration. Faster vibrations transmit more energy. Larger amplitude vibrations also transmit more energy.

In mathematical terms, a wave's energy is directly proportional to frequency. When the frequency of the wave doubles, the energy also doubles. So, if you shake a rope up and down twice as fast, you transmit twice as much energy down the length of the rope.

Mathematically, a wave's energy is also proportional to the square of its amplitude. For instance, if you shake a rope to make waves and then move your hand three times as high with each shake, the wave energy increases by a factor of 3 times 3, or nine! Like other forms of energy, a wave's energy is measured in units called joules (J).

Wave Properties

The table shows the properties of waves near the beach on one summer day. Use the relationship between speed, wavelength, and frequency to complete the table. Then answer the questions.

Waves at a Beach

Time	Amplitude	Wavelength	Frequency	Speed
10 AM	0.4 m	10 m	2 Hz	
2 PM	0.2 m		4 Hz	32 m/s
6 PM	0.3 m	12 m		36 m/s

1. **Use Tables** What would happen to the energy of the 10 AM wave if the frequency increased to 6 Hz?

2. **Apply Mathematics** If the amplitude of the 6 PM wave increases to 0.6 m, how many times greater would the energy become?

3. **Use Proportional Relationships** Recall that speed = wavelength × frequency. Assuming that the wavelength of a wave stays the same, would the energy of the wave increase or decrease if the speed of the wave increases? Why?

LESSON 1 Check

MS-PS4-1

1. **Explain** How can you measure the wavelength of a longitudinal wave?

2. **SEP Use Mathematics** A sound wave's frequency is 4 Hz and its wavelength is 8 meters. What is the wave's speed?

3. **SEP Use Models** Draw a model of a transverse wave. Use lines and labels to show the amplitude and wavelength of the wave.

4. **Use Proportional Relationships** During high tide, ocean waves often become larger. If the amplitude of a wave increases by a factor of 4, by how much does the energy increase?

5. **CCC Cause and Effect** If a musician increases the wavelength of the sound waves she produces without changing their speed, what must be happening to the frequency? Explain your answer.

Quest CHECK-IN

In this lesson, you learned about the difference between electromagnetic and mechanical waves, including the three different types of mechanical waves that move through and affect the matter around us. You also learned how the properties of waves such as amplitude, frequency, energy, and speed are related.

SEP Define Problems If you were designing a security system that uses light to detect an intruder, why would it be important to know about the different media and materials that would be parts of the system?

INTERACTIVITY

Light Behavior

Go online to learn more about the behavior of light, including how a mirror affects a laser beam.

Case Study

MS-PS4-2

SOUND AND LIGHT AT THE Ballpark

It's baseball season! The lights illuminate the field. As the batter swings, there is a whoosh of the bat through the air, and a satisfying CRACK! as he hits a long ball to the outfield.

Fans are yelling and cheering. "PEANUTS! Get your PEANUTS!" shout the vendors as they move through the packed stands. "Take Me Out to the Ball Game" blares over the speakers, and everyone stands up and sings.

A baseball game is a sporting event. But everything that happens there obeys the laws of physics. How do light and sound waves behave at the ball park? Take a look—and listen!

There are runners on all the bases, and the batter hits the ball. It's a ground ball to the shortstop. He throws it to the third baseman, who has his foot on third base. The umpire at third base watches the runner's foot touch the base while listening for the sound of the ball striking the third baseman's glove.

The next batter comes up to the plate and misses the first pitch. You see the catcher catch the ball before you hear the thwack of the ball hitting his glove.

You see the umpire signal a strike before you hear him call "STRIKE ONE!"

On the next pitch, you hear the crack of the bat hitting the ball after you see the batter hit the ball. It's a home run!

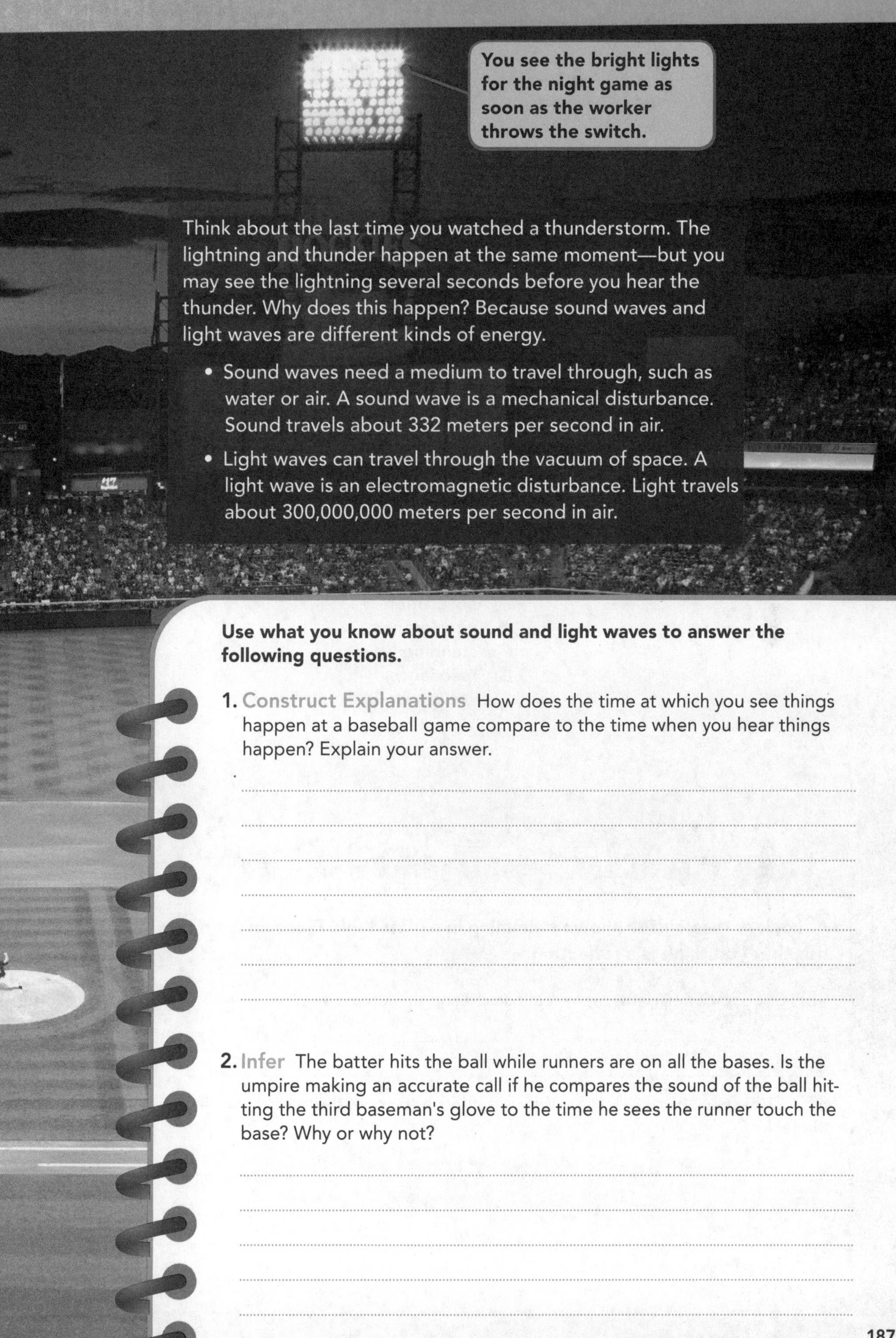

You see the bright lights for the night game as soon as the worker throws the switch.

Think about the last time you watched a thunderstorm. The lightning and thunder happen at the same moment—but you may see the lightning several seconds before you hear the thunder. Why does this happen? Because sound waves and light waves are different kinds of energy.

- Sound waves need a medium to travel through, such as water or air. A sound wave is a mechanical disturbance. Sound travels about 332 meters per second in air.
- Light waves can travel through the vacuum of space. A light wave is an electromagnetic disturbance. Light travels about 300,000,000 meters per second in air.

Use what you know about sound and light waves to answer the following questions.

1. Construct Explanations How does the time at which you see things happen at a baseball game compare to the time when you hear things happen? Explain your answer.

2. Infer The batter hits the ball while runners are on all the bases. Is the umpire making an accurate call if he compares the sound of the ball hitting the third baseman's glove to the time he sees the runner touch the base? Why or why not?

LESSON 2

Wave Interactions

Guiding Questions

- How do waves interact with different materials?
- How do waves interact with each other?

Connection

Literacy Integrate Information

MS-PS4-2

HANDS-ON LAB

uInvestigate See what type of interference you get when you send waves down a coil.

Vocabulary

reflection
refraction
diffraction
absorption
interference
standing wave
resonance

Academic Vocabulary

transmitted

Connect It!

Look at the goldfish shown swimming in a glass tank. Place an X on any fish that you think is a reflection.

SEP Use Evidence How many real fish do you think there are?

SEP Construct Explanations Why is it difficult to count the number of fish in the tank?

Reflection, Refraction, and Absorption

If you've ever been to the beach, you've seen how different kinds of waves move. Some ocean waves crash into rocks or piers, while others reach the shore smoothly. Rays of sunlight hit the surface of the water, and some bounce off while others pass through. In general, when waves encounter different media, they are either reflected, transmitted, or absorbed.

Reflection Some waves are completely blocked by an obstruction, but their energy is not absorbed or converted to another form of energy. These types of waves bounce off, or reflect from, those obstructions. In a **reflection**, the wave bounces off and heads in a different direction. The law of reflection states that the angle of incidence equals the angle of reflection. This means that the angle at which the wave strikes the material will match the angle at which the reflected wave bounces off that material, as shown in **Figure 2**. Light reflecting from a mirror is the most familiar example of reflection. The echo of a voice from the walls of a canyon is another example.

Reflection

Figure 2 A flashlight beam reflects off of a mirror at the same angle it strikes.

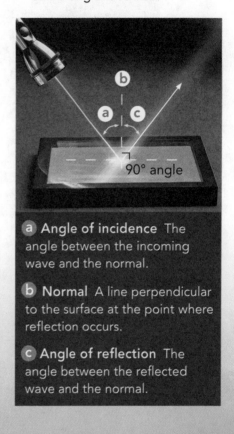

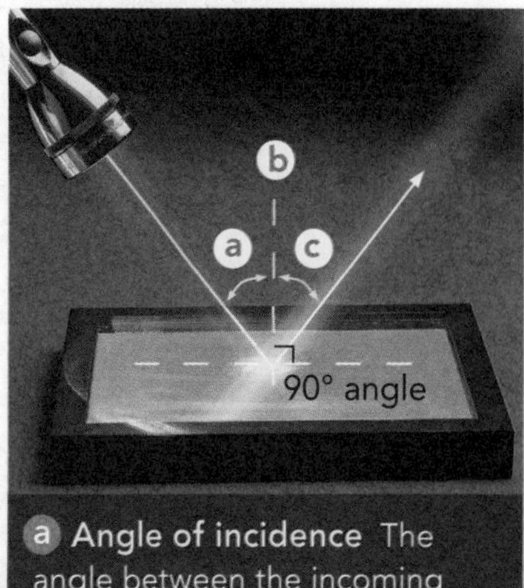

ⓐ **Angle of incidence** The angle between the incoming wave and the normal.

ⓑ **Normal** A line perpendicular to the surface at the point where reflection occurs.

ⓒ **Angle of reflection** The angle between the reflected wave and the normal.

Fish Reflection and Refraction

Figure 1 Light waves reflecting off the walls of a tank can create multiple images of the same fish.

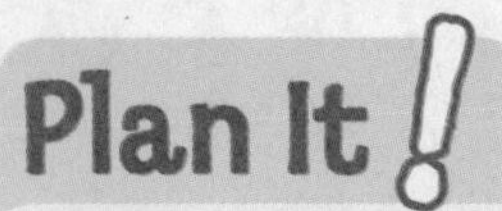

SEP Develop Models Have you ever seen a movie scene in which a character appears to be looking at a mirror, yet the camera is not visible in the mirror? Think about how the director sets up this scene. Draw a set up that shows the position of the actor, the camera, and the mirror, and demonstrate why the camera's image is not visible to the camera.

Refraction

Figure 3 Light rays bend as they enter water because one side of the wave fronts slows down in water while the other side continues at the same speed in air.

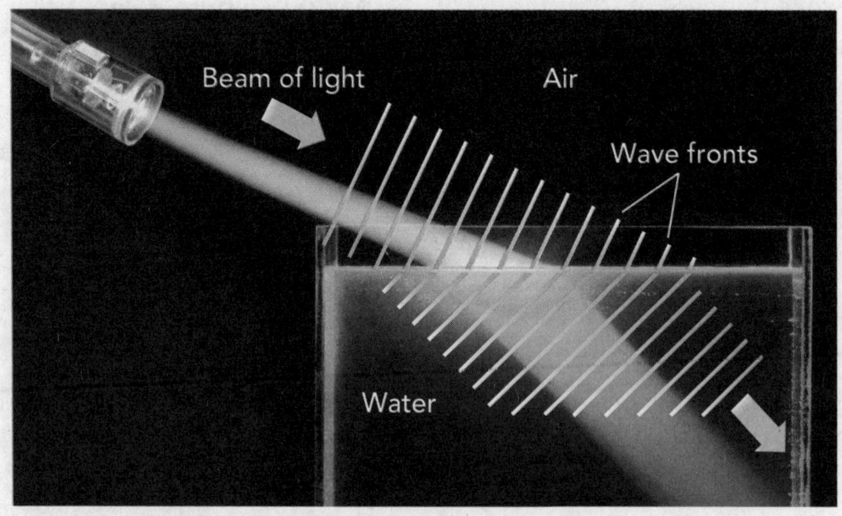

Academic Vocabulary

What is another way for saying that a wave is "transmitted" through a medium?

....

....

....

Refraction

Imagine riding a bike down a smooth asphalt road. When you turn off the road onto a dirt path, the transition can be jarring. You might have to grip the handlebars hard to keep the bike going straight as each wheel is on a different surface.

When light waves are **transmitted** from one medium into another, they also bend in different directions. This bending is due to **refraction**, or the bending of waves due to a change in speed.

When a wave enters a new medium at an angle other than perpendicular, it changes direction. For instance, when light is directed at water at an angle, as in **Figure 3**, the light slows down and bends downward. The wave bends toward the normal, the imaginary line that runs perpendicular from the boundary between the two media.

Diffraction Did you ever wonder how you can hear someone speaking even if they are around the corner of a building or doorway? This is an example of **diffraction**. Waves don't only travel in straight lines. They are also bend around objects.

You can observe diffraction with water waves as well as sound waves. Water waves can diffract around a rock or an island in the ocean. Because tsunami waves can diffract all the way around an island, people on the shores of the entire island are at risk.

Absorption When you think of something being absorbed, you might think of how a paper towel soaks up water. Waves can be absorbed by certain materials, too. In **absorption**, the energy of a wave is transferred to the material it encounters. When ocean waves reach a shoreline, most of their energy is absorbed by the shore.

When light waves encounter the surface of a different medium or material, the light waves may be reflected, refracted, or absorbed. What happens to the waves depends on the type of material they hit. Light is mostly absorbed by dark materials, such as the surface of a parking lot, and mostly reflected by light materials, such as snow.

Literacy Connection

Integrate Information
As you read, classify the phenomena you learn about as either interactions between waves and media or interactions among waves.

Reflect What are some ways in which you use reflection in your everyday life? Are there things you have to keep in mind when you use reflective devices, such as mirrors?

VIDEO

Discover how reflection and absorption create echoes.

Question It!

Classify Identify each picture as being an example of reflection, refraction, or absorption.

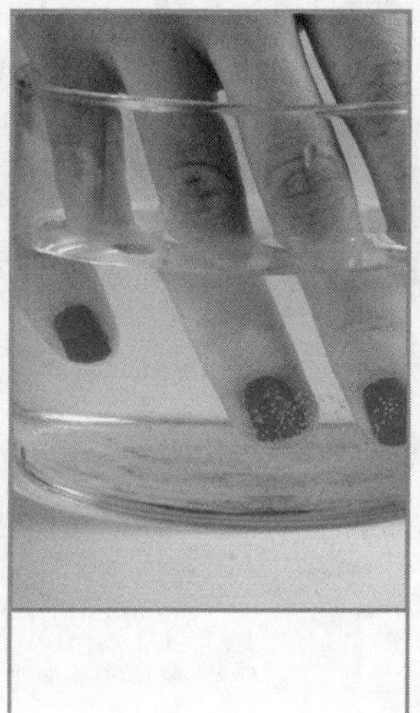

Investigate See what type of interference you get when you send waves down a coil.

Wave Interference

Have you ever seen two ocean waves collide from opposite directions so they momentarily form a bigger, hill-like shape before continuing in their original directions? This is an example of wave **interference**. There are two types.

Constructive Interference The example of two waves of similar sizes colliding and forming a wave with an amplitude greater than either of the original waves is called constructive interference. You can think of it as waves "helping each other," or adding their energies together. As shown in **Figure 4**, when the crests of two waves overlap, they make a higher crest. If two troughs overlap, they make a deeper trough. In both cases, the amplitude of the combined crests or troughs increases.

Types of Interference

Figure 4 Write captions to describe three parts of destructive interference. Complete the key to explain what the different arrows mean in the images.

Constructive Interference

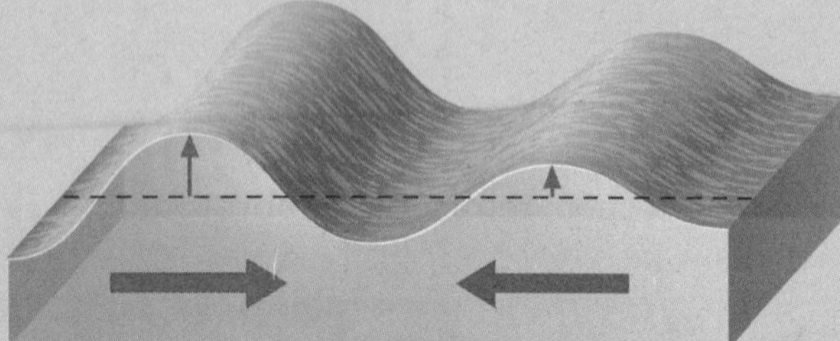

1 Two waves approach each other. The wave on the left has a greater amplitude.

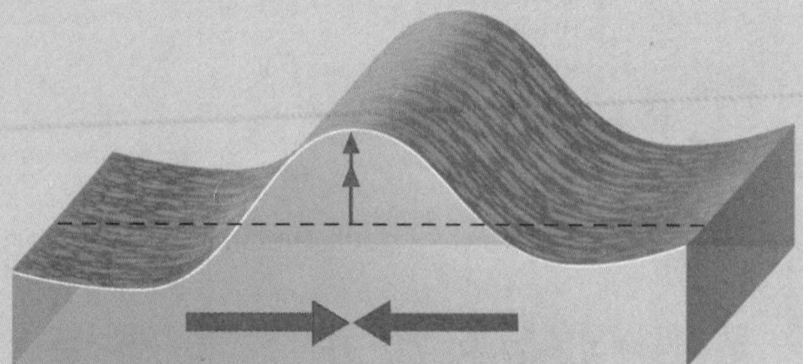

2 The new crest's amplitude is the sum of the amplitudes of the original crests.

Destructive Interference

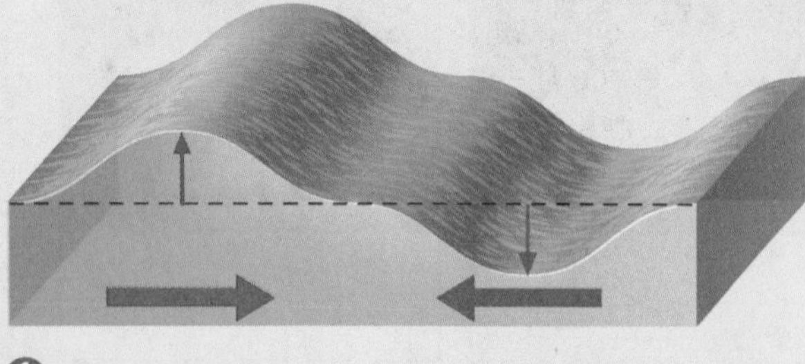

1 ....

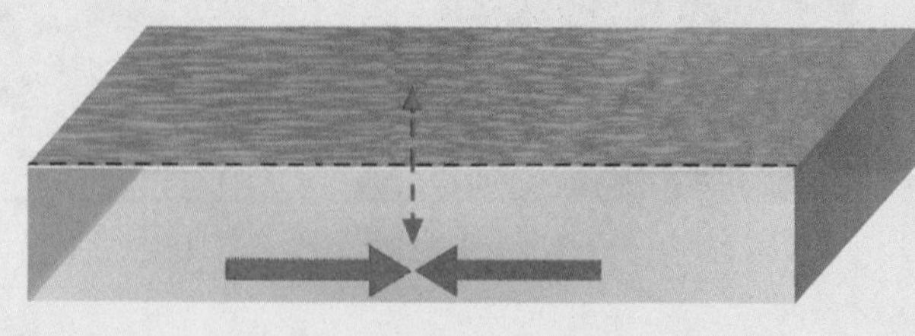

2 ....

Destructive Interference When two waves combine to form a wave with a smaller amplitude than either original wave had, this is called destructive interference. Destructive interference occurs when the crest of one wave overlaps the trough of another wave. If the crest has a larger amplitude than the trough of the other wave, the crest "wins," and part of it remains. If the original trough has a larger amplitude than the crest of the other wave, the result is a trough. If a crest and trough have equal amplitudes, they cancel each other out, as shown in **Figure 4**. Destructive interference is used in noise-canceling headphones to block out distracting noises in a listener's surroundings.

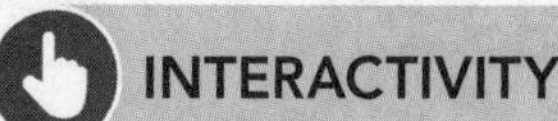

Observe wave interference in a rope and in surface waves.

READING CHECK **Infer** Which type of wave interference could cause sound to become louder? Explain your answer.

....

....

....

Interfering Waves

Figure 5 Ripples created by rain water on a pond interfere with one another in a pattern that exhibits both constructive and destructive interference.

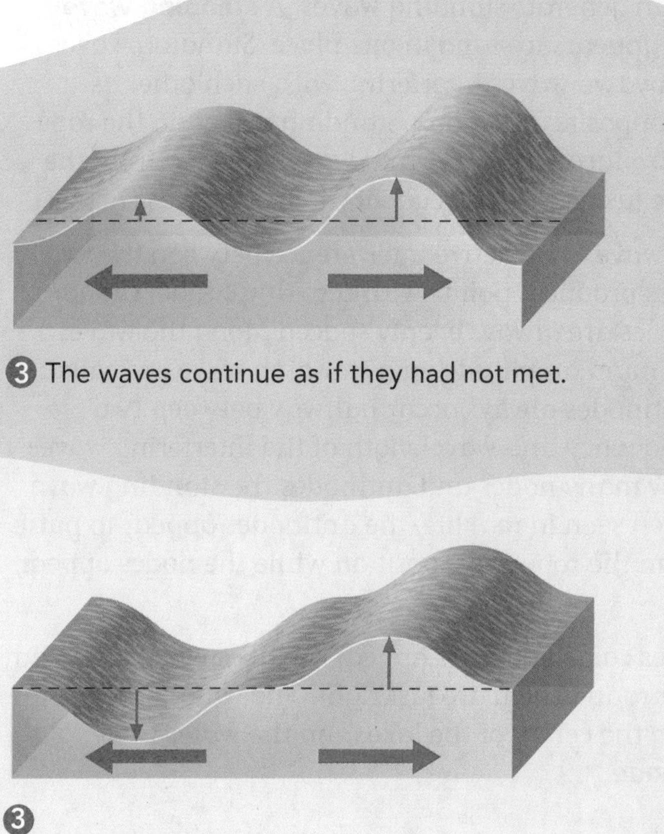

❸ The waves continue as if they had not met.

❸ ....

....

Standing Waves

Figure 6 As the hand shown at left increases the frequency, the number of wavelengths present in the standing wave will increase. In a standing wave, it looks like there's a mirror image of both the crest and trough. Label the rest of the nodes and antinodes.

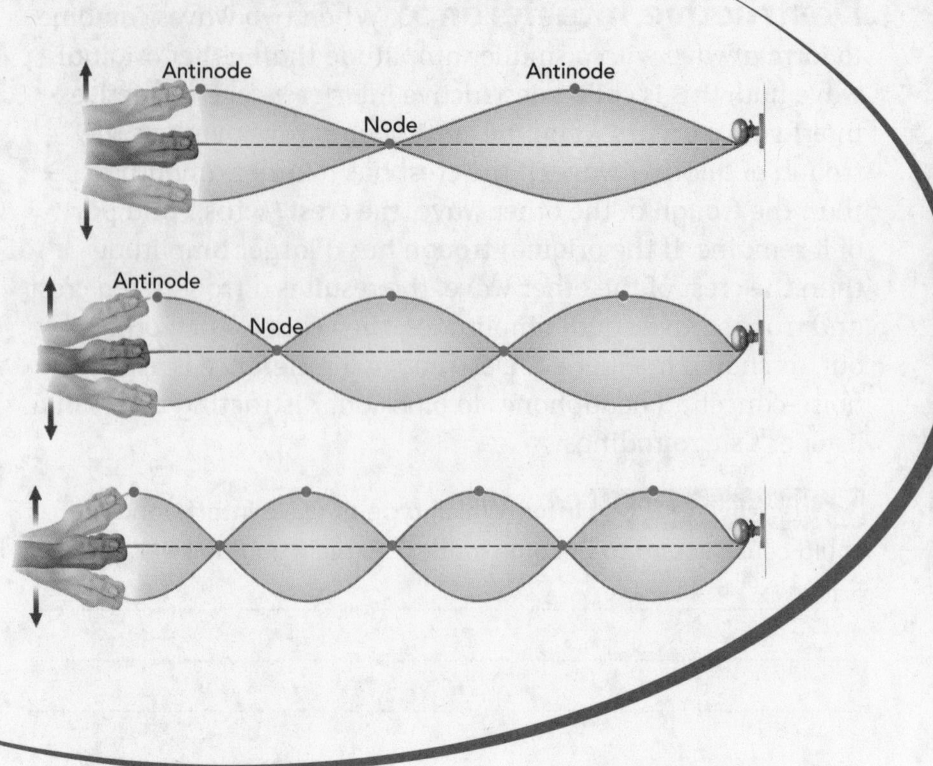

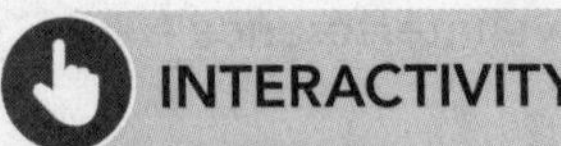

INTERACTIVITY

Describe how waves behave when they interact with a barrier or boundary.

Standing Waves Look at the rope setup in **Figure 6.** The rope is tied to a doorknob, and someone shakes the free end. This motion can generate standing waves. A **standing wave** is a wave that appears to stand in one place. Standing waves are produced by two waves interfering with each other as they travel in opposite directions. Standing waves on the rope appear when an incoming wave and wave reflected from the doorknob have just the right frequency to interfere as shown.

In a standing wave, destructive interference between the two colliding waves produces points with zero amplitude, called nodes. The nodes are always evenly spaced along the wave. Points of maximum amplitude on a standing wave are called antinodes. Antinodes always occur halfway between two nodes. The frequency and wavelength of the interfering waves determine how many nodes and antinodes the standing wave will have. When seen in real life, the antinodes appear to pulse in and out from the rope's rest position while the nodes appear motionless.

Standing waves can sometimes appear on lakes when the wind and pressure around them are just right. The water appears to have a node in the center of the lake, and the water wave rolls around that node.

Resonance Think about the last time you swung on a swing at a playground. You may have noticed that it is difficult to get yourself going. Once you are in motion, you can pull on the chains of the swing and pump your legs at the right time to keep yourself swinging. The swing has a natural frequency, and your actions match that frequency to create greater amplitudes in your motion.

Most objects have at least one natural frequency of vibration. Standing waves occur in an object when it vibrates at one of these natural frequencies. If a nearby object vibrates at the same frequency, it can cause resonance. **Resonance** is an increase in the amplitude of a vibration that occurs when external vibrations match an object's natural frequency.

When engineers build a bridge, they have to make sure that bridge supports are not placed at potential nodes for a standing wave. Otherwise, wind could cause the bridge to swing wildly like the rope in **Figure 6** and collapse.

Understanding the resonance of different materials is also useful for people who build guitars, violins, or other wood-based stringed instruments. If the wood in a guitar, such as the one in **Figure 7**, resonates too much with a certain note, it may sound too loud when that particular note is struck. Likewise, if the wood does not resonate with any particular note, the instrument may lack volume or "presence" and sound dull.

Make Meaning Make a two-column chart in your notebook. Use it to record descriptions of constructive interference, destructive interference, standing waves, and resonance.

READING CHECK **Summarize** In general, why is it risky to build something whose natural frequency can be matched by external vibrations?

....

....

....

Musical Resonance

Figure 7 The types of wood and construction techniques used to make a guitar affect aspects of its sound, including its resonance.

LESSON 2 Check

MS-PS4-2

1. **CCC Cause and Effect** Explain what happens to light when it is refracted at the surface of water.

2. **SEP Interpret Data** The diagrams below show two waves interfering to form a dark blue result. Which of the diagrams depicts constructive interference? Explain your choice using the term *amplitude*.

A. B.

3. **Explain** What does it mean for waves to be absorbed by a certain medium? Make sure to include energy in your explanation.

4. **SEP Construct Explanations** Why does the transition of light waves from water to air make it seem as if fish and other things in a pond are shallower than they actually are?

Quest CHECK-IN

In this lesson, you learned how waves interact with their surroundings and with each other. Waves can reflect, refract, and be absorbed depending on the media they travel through and the materials they strike. They can also interfere with each other in ways that are destructive or constructive, resulting in phenomena such as standings waves and resonance.

SEP Design Solutions Think about the ways that light can change direction. What are two ways that you could change the path of light? What materials would you need to do it?

INTERACTIVITY

Virtual Optics

Go online to experiment with light and its transmission or reflection.

littleBits CHALLENGE

MS-PS4-2

Say "CHEESE!"

VIDEO

Find out how cameras work.

For hundreds of years, people who traveled took sketch pads and pencils to record their memories. This all changed in the nineteenth century with the invention of photography.

The Challenge To continue to improve the ways in which people can record images.

Phenomenon Early cameras were large and clumsy objects that printed images on glass. In the twentieth century, engineers experimented with smaller and lighter cameras that used film. Today we have digital cameras. But they all use the same process to create images.

Cameras have changed a lot over the years!

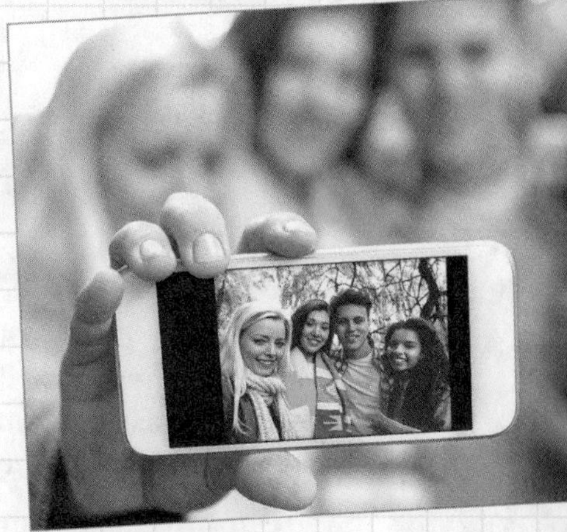

Today, cameras all have three main parts for capturing light:

- The **lens** is the camera's eye. It detects the light reflected off of what you want to photograph.
- The **aperture** lets light in through the lens. The wider the aperture, the more light is let in.
- The **shutter** is like a curtain that opens when you take the photo.

In a film camera, the light changes the film both physically and chemically to create an image. In a *digital* camera, the light reaches photosensors, which convert the image to a string of numbers.

Can you build your own simple camera using just a box? Go to the Engineering Design Notebook to find out!

LESSON

3 Sound Waves

Guiding Questions

- How are sound waves reflected, transmitted, or absorbed by materials?
- What factors affect the speed of sound waves?

Connections

Literacy Integrate With Visuals

Math Reason Quantitatively

MS-PS4-2

HANDS-ON LAB

uInvestigate Use models to examine how sound waves travel through different media.

Vocabulary

loudness
intensity
decibel
pitch
Doppler effect

Academic Vocabulary

differentiate

Connect It!

When someone strikes a cymbal, the cymbal vibrates to produce sound. Draw compressions and rarefactions of the air particles as the sound waves travel away from the cymbal.

SEP Engage in Argument Is sound a mechanical wave or an electromagnetic wave? Explain your answer.

....

CCC Cause and Effect What do you think happens to a sound wave when the volume of sound increases?

....

The Behavior of Sound

HANDS-ON LAB
Discover how the amplitude of a guitar string affects its loudness.

All sound waves begin with a vibration. Look at the woman in **Figure 1.** When she hits a drum or a cymbal with her drumstick, the drum or cymbal vibrates rapidly, disturbing the air particles around the drum set. When the drum or cymbal moves away from its rest position, it creates a compression by pushing air particles together. When it moves back toward its rest position, it creates a rarefaction by causing air particles to spread out.

Recall that sound waves are mechanical waves that require a medium through which to travel. In the case of the drummer and the drum set, the compressions and rarefactions that are created travel through the air. Sound waves, however, travel more easily through liquids and solids. When you set a glass down on a table, for example, the sound waves that are generated travel first through the glass and the table and then are released into the air.

Sound waves are also longitudinal—they travel in the same direction as the vibrations that produce them. Like other types of mechanical waves, sound waves can be reflected, transmitted, absorbed, and diffracted.

Making Waves

Figure 1 The vibrations caused by hitting drums and cymbals generate sound waves.

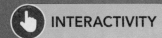

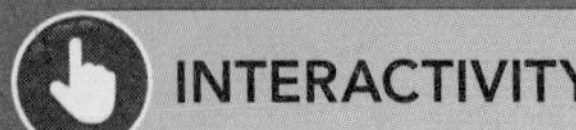

Observe and analyze sound waves in a variety of everyday situations.

Reflection and Transmission Like other mechanical waves, sound waves that pass through a surface are called transmitted waves, and sound waves that bounce off a surface are called reflected waves. When a sound wave travels through the air and comes into contact with a solid surface, such as a wall, a portion of the wave passes through the surface. Most of the wave, however, is reflected away from the surface.

Absorption Have you ever been to a concert in a large indoor theater? If so, you may have noticed panels on the walls. Most large theaters have acoustic panels to help with sound absorption. Sound absorption describes the process of sound waves striking a surface and quickly losing energy. The energy is converted to thermal energy in the surface. Acoustic panels in theaters are porous, meaning they are full of small holes, and they absorb a portion of the sound waves. In the case of a theater, absorption of sound waves improves the listening experience for people at the concert. More sound energy is absorbed than reflected, so the audience does not experience as much interference from reflected sound waves. See **Figure 2** for another example of absorption. Any material with a porous surface can act as a sound absorber.

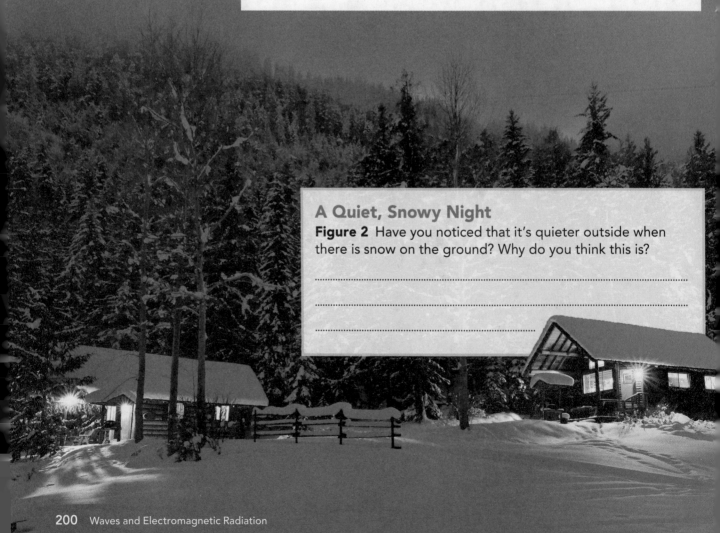

A Quiet, Snowy Night

Figure 2 Have you noticed that it's quieter outside when there is snow on the ground? Why do you think this is?

....

....

....

Model It!

If you've ever yelled loudly into an open space, such as a canyon or a courtyard, then you may have heard an echo. An echo occurs when sound waves are reflected off a hard surface, such as the wall of a rocky mountain. The sound you hear is delayed because it takes time for the sound waves to reflect off the surface and reach your ears.

SEP Develop Models Draw a picture of sound waves when an echo is created. In addition to reflected waves, your model should also indicate waves that are transmitted or absorbed.

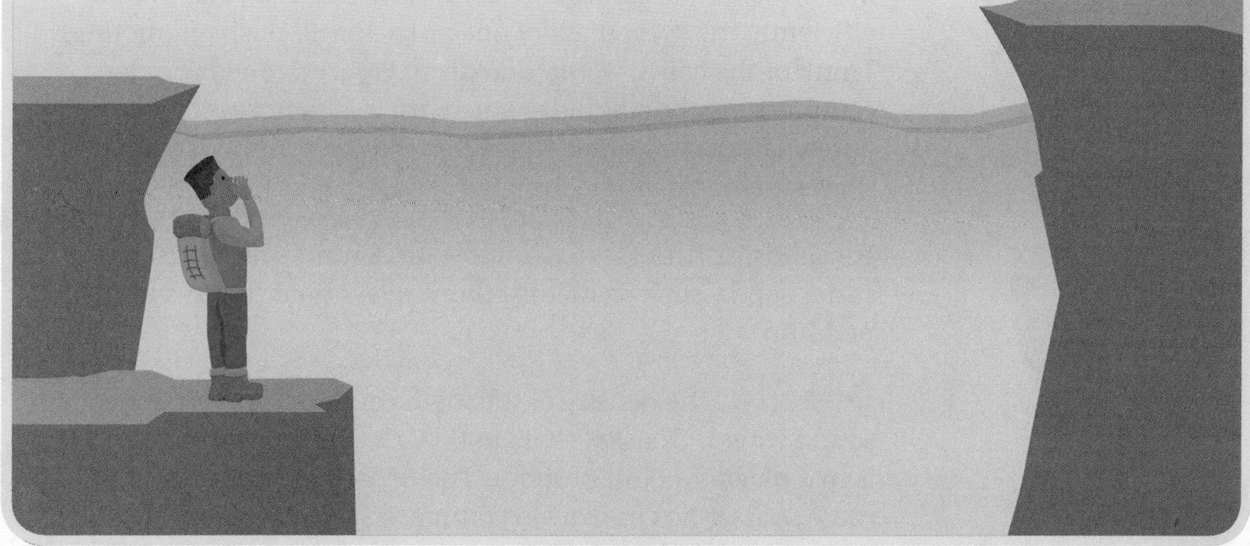

Diffraction It is usually easy to hear someone talking if they are in the same room as you, but you can also hear people in other rooms nearby. Why is this? You can hear them because sound waves can bend around the edges of an opening, such as a doorway. This is called sound diffraction. Sound waves, like water waves, spread out after passing through an opening.

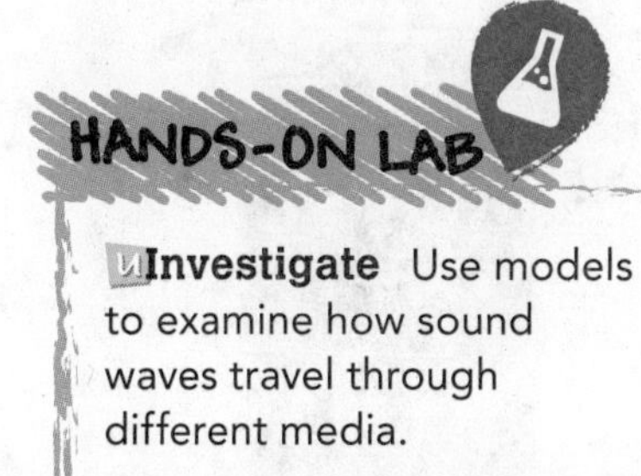

Investigate Use models to examine how sound waves travel through different media.

How much sound waves are transmitted, reflected, absorbed, or diffracted depends greatly upon the medium through which they travel. If sound waves travel through air and hit a solid surface, such as a concrete wall, much of the energy in the waves is reflected back toward the source. If the surfaces they hit are softer or more porous, then more sound waves will be absorbed. Sound waves will be diffracted around corners and through passageways between hard surfaces.

READING CHECK **Summarize** What are four things that can happen to sound waves when they reach a barrier?

....

....

VIDEO

Explore what thunder is and how to determine your distance from an approaching storm.

Factors Affecting the Speed of Sound

As you have read, sound waves are mechanical waves that require a medium through which to travel. The characteristics of the medium have an effect on the speed of the sound waves traveling through them. The main factors that affect the speed of sound are compressibility, stiffness, density, and temperature.

Stiffness In general, sound waves travel faster in materials that are harder to compress. This is because of how efficiently the movement of one particle will push on another. Think of the coins, water, and air in **Figure 3**. Solids are less compressible than liquids, which are less compressible than gases. Therefore, sound waves travel fastest in solids and slowest in gases.

For solids, stiffness is also important. Sound travels faster in stiffer solids, such as metals, than in less rigid solids, such as pudding.

Density The density of the medium also affects the speed of sound waves. Density refers to how much matter or mass there is in a given amount of space. The denser the material, the more mass it has in a given volume, so the greater its inertia. Objects with greater inertia accelerate less from an energy disturbance than objects with less inertia, or less massive objects. Therefore, in materials of the same stiffness, sound travels more slowly in the denser material.

Temperature The temperature of a medium also affects the speed at which sound waves travel through it, though in more complicated ways. For solids, an increase in temperature reduces the stiffness, so the sound speed decreases. For fluids, such as air, the increase in temperature reduces the density, so the sound speed generally increases.

READING CHECK **Hypothesize** Would sound waves travel slower through air at the North Pole or at the equator? Explain.

....

....

....

....

....

Speed of Sound

Figure 3 Rate the speed of sound through the medium in each container, with "1" being the fastest and "3" being the slowest.

Loudness and Pitch

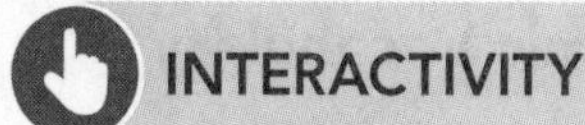

INTERACTIVITY

Explore how the frequency and intensity of a sound wave affect the sound you hear through headphones.

How might you describe a sound? You might call it loud or soft, high or low. When you turn up the volume of your speakers, you increase the loudness of a sound. When you sing higher and higher notes, you increase the pitch of your voice. Loudness and pitch depend on different properties of sound waves.

Factors Affecting Loudness You use the term **loudness** to describe your awareness of the energy of a sound. How loud a sound is depends on the energy and intensity of the sound waves. If someone knocks lightly on your front door, then you might hear a quiet sound. If they pound on your door, then you hear a much louder sound. Why? The pounding transfers much more energy through the door than a light knock does. That's because a hard knock on a door produces a much greater amplitude in the sound waves than a softer knock does. Increased energy results in greater intensity of the waves. **Intensity** is the amount of energy a sound wave carries per second through a unit area. The closer the sound wave is to its source, the more energy it has in a given area. As the sound wave moves away from the source, the wave spreads out and the intensity decreases.

Intensity of Sound

Figure 4 Sound waves spread out as they travel away from the source producing the sound. For each of the locations in the image, rank the intensity of the sound waves coming from the band on a scale of 1 to 3, with 1 being the greatest intensity.

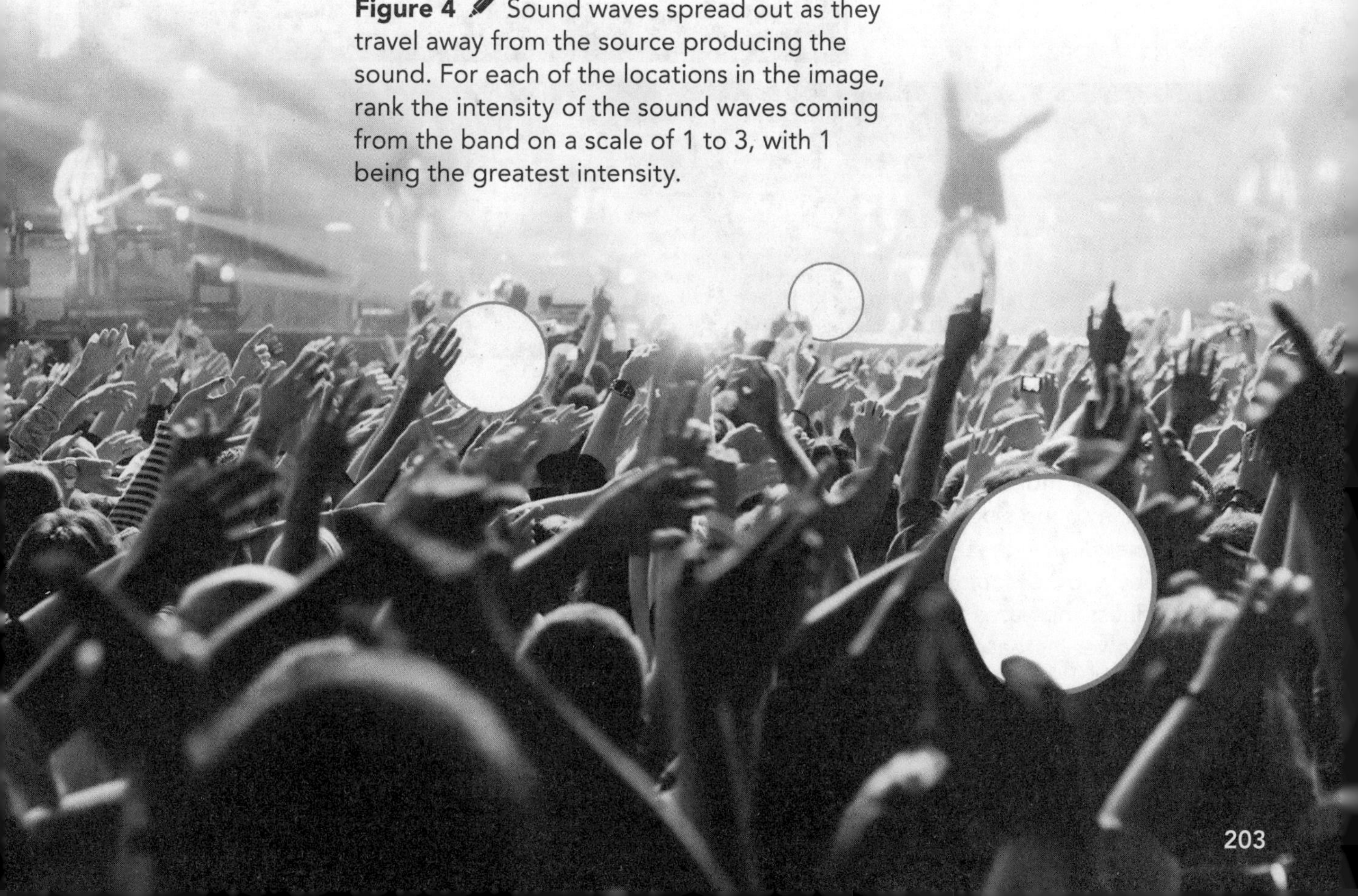

Academic Vocabulary

What is the root word in *differentiate*? How does this help you figure out the word's meaning?

Measuring Loudness So, how do our ears **differentiate** between a light knock and a hard knock on a door? Loudness can be measured by a unit called a **decibel** (dB). The greater the decibels of the sound, the louder that sound seems to a listener. The loudness of a sound you can barely hear, such as a pin dropping to the floor, is about 0 dB. When someone lightly taps on your door, the loudness is about 30 dB. But if someone pounds on your door, that loudness might increase to 80 dB! Sounds louder than 100 dB, such as the sound of a chainsaw, can cause damage to people's ears, especially if they are exposed to the sounds for long periods of time. Music technicians use equalizers to change the loudness levels of different frequencies of sound, as in **Figure 5.**

Using an Equalizer

Figure 5 You can use an equalizer to adjust the loudness of sound waves at different frequencies. Raising the decibel level of low frequencies increases the bass tones of music. How might you increase the high-pitched tones of music?

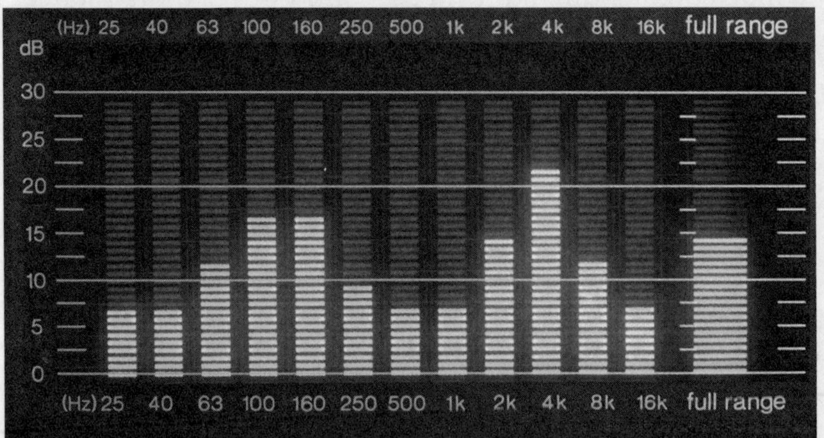

Math Toolbox

Decibel Levels

Every 10-decibel increase represents a tenfold increase in intensity and power. For example, when loudness increases from 20 to 30 decibels, a sound's power is multiplied by 10. If loudness increases by 10 again, power increases by another factor of 10. Therefore, when loudness increases from 20 to 40 decibels, power increases by a factor of 100!

1. **Use Ratio Reasoning** If a sound's power level increases from 20 decibels to 50 decibels, by what factor does its power increase?

2. **Reason Quantitatively** If you want to lower the loudness of the bass tones in your music by 20 decibels, by how much does the intensity need to decrease?

Thickness Affects Pitch

Figure 6 On a standard 6-string guitar, the strings range in thickness.
✏ On the photo, draw an X on the guitar string that has the lowest pitch.

Factors Affecting Pitch Have you ever heard someone describe a note on a piano as "high-pitched" or "low-pitched"? The **pitch** of a sound refers to how high or low the sound seems. Pitch depends upon the frequency of the sound waves. Sound waves with a high frequency have a high pitch, and waves with a low frequency have a low pitch.

The frequency of a sound wave depends upon how fast the source of the sound is vibrating. For example, when people speak or sing, the air from their lungs moves past their vocal cords and makes the cords vibrate, producing sound waves. When vocal cords vibrate more quickly, they produce higher-frequency sound waves with higher pitches. When vocal cords vibrate more slowly, they produce lower-frequency sound waves with lower pitches.

This phenomenon happens with all things that vibrate and produce sound waves. Guitars produce sound when someone strums or plucks their strings. If you've ever studied a guitar, then you may have noticed that its strings vary in thickness. The thicker strings of a guitar vibrate more slowly than the thinner strings do, and so the thicker strings have a lower frequency, and therefore a lower pitch, than the thinner strings (**Figure 6**).

INTERACTIVITY

Explain how sounds from moving objects can change in pitch.

The Doppler Effect

Have you ever had a loud motorcycle drive by you and heard the pitch of the engine noise change? Change in pitch occurs because the movement of the source of the sound causes a sound wave to either compress or stretch. As the motorcycle approaches, the peaks of the emitted sound waves are scrunched together. When the peaks are closer together, the sound waves have a higher frequency. As the motorcycle moves away, the peaks of the emitted sound waves are spread out. The sound waves then have a lower frequency.

A change in frequency is perceived by a listener as a change in pitch. This change in frequency (and therefore, in pitch) of the sound wave in relation to an observer is called the **Doppler effect. Figure 7** shows the Doppler effect when a firetruck rushes by a person on the sidewalk.

READING CHECK **Summarize** What property of a sound wave determines the pitch of a sound?

....

Literacy Connection

Integrate With Visuals Do you think the motorcyclist would hear a change in pitch of the motorcycle's sound as he passes by you? Why or why not?

....

....

....

....

The Doppler Effect

Figure 7 As a firetruck speeds by, an observer detects changes in the pitch of the truck's siren. The firetruck approaches the observer in the first image. It then passes her and continues on.

CCC Cause and Effect Draw the sound waves as the truck moves away.

LESSON 3 Check

MS-PS4-2

1. **Identify** What is the cause of any sound wave?

2. **SEP Construct Explanations** Explain why sound waves are mechanical waves rather than electromagnetic waves.

3. **SEP Communicate Information** Why does sound travel more quickly through a solid than through a liquid or a gas?

4. **Form a Hypothesis** Dogs can hear higher-pitched whistles that humans do. How do you think the sound frequencies that dogs can hear compare to the frequencies that humans can hear?

5. **CCC Cause and Effect** What effect might spending years working on a construction site have on a person's hearing? Why?

6. **Apply Concepts** Ultrasound, also known as sonography, is a technology that uses high-frequency sound waves to produce images. It is used in medical applications to help doctors see inside patients' bodies. How do you think the sound waves can be used to image bones, muscles, and other internal structures?

7. **SEP Develop Models** Imagine a person is sitting on a beach, and a speedboat passes by on the water. Draw a model of this situation, and indicate how the Doppler effect would influence how the sound waves coming from the boat would be perceived by the person on shore.

LESSON 4

Electromagnetic Waves

Guiding Questions

- What makes up an electromagnetic wave?
- How can you model electromagnetic wave behavior?
- What kinds of waves make up the electromagnetic spectrum?

Connections

Literacy Translate Information

Math Draw Comparative Inferences

MS-PS4-2

HANDS-ON LAB

uInvestigate Develop a model of a wave.

Vocabulary

electromagnetic wave
electromagnetic spectrum
radio waves
microwaves
visible light
ultraviolet rays
infrared rays
X-rays
gamma rays

Academic Vocabulary

transverse

Connect It!

Look at the image of this ship. Imagine that an airplane some 25 kilometers in front of the ship is sending out radar waves to detect vessels. Recall the law of reflection from Lesson 2. Draw arrows to represent the radar waves and to show how they would reflect off this unusually angular ship.

SEP Construct Explanations Do you think the reflected waves would ever return to the airplane that transmitted them? Explain.

Characteristics of Electromagnetic Waves

As you read this book, you are surrounded by waves. There are radio waves, microwaves, infrared rays, visible light, ultraviolet rays, and tiny amounts of X-rays and gamma rays. These waves are all electromagnetic waves. An **electromagnetic wave** is made up of vibrating electric and magnetic fields that can move through space at the speed of light. The energy that electromagnetic waves transfer through matter or space is called electromagnetic radiation.

Electromagnetic waves do not require a medium such as air, so they can transfer energy through a vacuum. This property makes them different from mechanical waves, which do require a medium. Mechanical waves are caused by a disturbance or vibration in the medium, while electromagnetic waves are caused by a source of electric and magnetic fields. Those fields are produced by the movement of charged particles.

Radar is a technology that uses microwaves, a type of electromagnetic wave, to detect objects in the atmosphere. The vessel in **Figure 1** is the U.S. Navy's attempt at using stealth technology to deflect radar. Its angular surface causes the microwaves to deflect away from the radar source.

Reflect Think about the devices you use every day. What are some examples of technology that use electromagnetic waves?

Stealth Ship

Figure 1 *The U.S.S. Zumwalt* is the first in a class of "stealth" destroyers. Much of its hull and other structures have surfaces that are angled upward. This means radar waves will be deflected away from the source of the radar.

Academic Vocabulary

The term *transverse* means "situated across." It is always applied to something that has a specific orientation or direction. Is there a part of the term *transverse* that signals this meaning?

....

....

....

....

Models of Electromagnetic Wave Behavior

Light is mysterious in that it can behave as either a wave or a particle depending on the situation. A wave model can explain most of the behaviors, but a particle model best explains others. Light is an electromagnetic wave, which is a transverse wave. Light has many properties of **transverse** waves, but it can sometimes act as though it is a stream of particles.

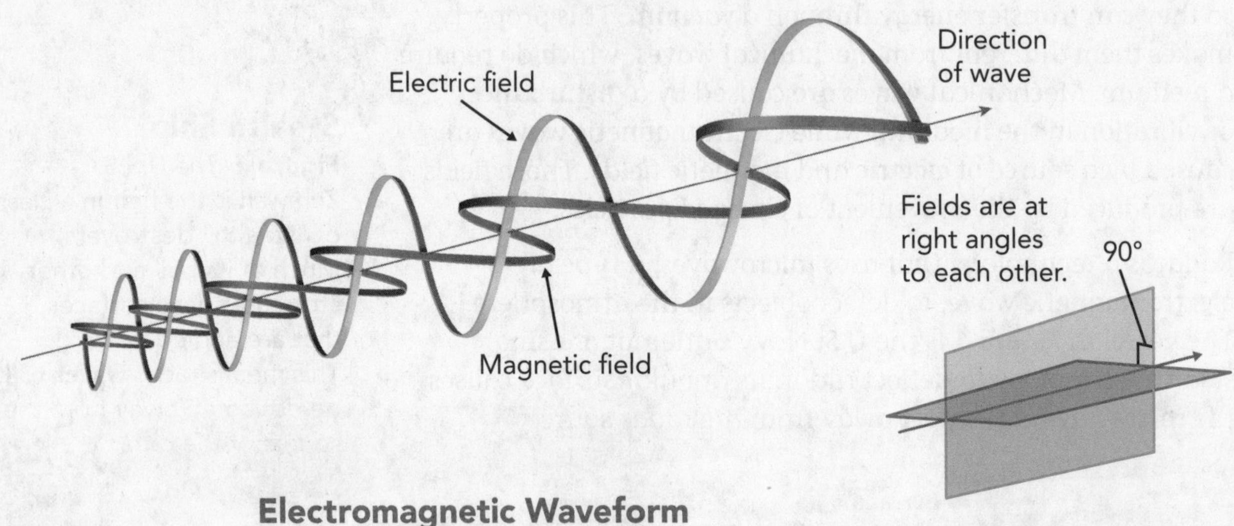

Electromagnetic Waveform

Figure 2 An electromagnetic wave consists of vibrating electric and magnetic fields.

INTERACTIVITY

Find out more about the differences between light waves and sound waves.

Wave Model of Light One way to visualize light is using a wave model. The wave originates due to a disturbance of a charged particle. The disturbance results in vibrating electric and magnetic fields, which are oriented perpendicular to each other as shown in **Figure 2.** The two vibrating fields reinforce each other, causing energy to travel as light through space or through a medium. A ray of light consists of many of these traveling disturbances, vibrating in all directions.

A polarizing filter acts as though it has tiny slits aligned in only one direction. The slits can be horizontal or vertical. When light enters the filter, only waves whose vibrating electric fields are oriented in the same direction as the slits can pass through it. The light that passes through is called polarized light. Polarized sunglasses block out some waves of light so that your eyes are not exposed to as much radiation.

Model It

Polarizing Glasses

SEP Develop Models These sunglasses allow light through only if the light waves are oriented vertically. Draw the light wave that passes through each lens.

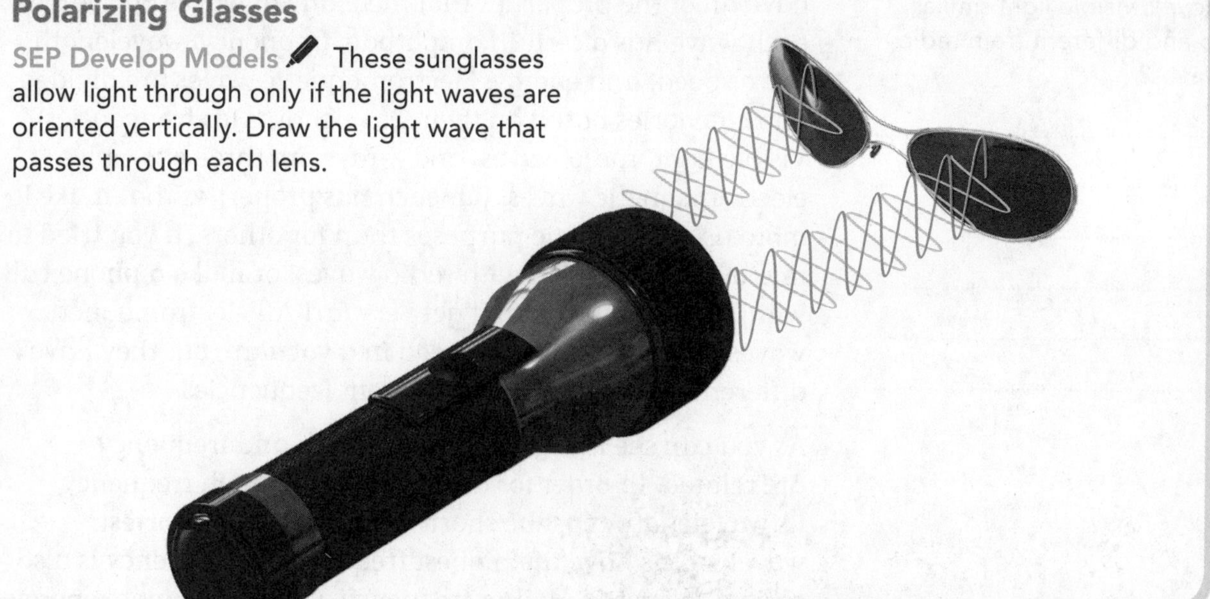

Particle Model of Light The wave model of light does not explain all of its properties. For example, when a beam of high-frequency light shines on some metals, it knocks some tiny particles called electrons out of the metal. This is called the photoelectric effect. However, lower-frequency light such as red light doesn't have enough energy to knock the electrons out.

VIDEO

Watch this video to compare the wave and particle models of light.

The photoelectric effect can be explained by thinking of light as a stream of tiny packets, of energy instead of as a wave. Each packet of light energy is called a photon. For the effect to occur, each photon must contain enough energy to knock an electron free from the metal.

INTERACTIVITY

Explore the particle model of light yourself.

One property of light that the wave model explains but the particle model does not is diffraction. When light passes through a narrow enough slit, instead of forming one image of the slit on a screen, it spreads out and produces a striped pattern of light and dark areas. This is similar to a water wave passing through a narrow channel and then spreading out on the other side.

READING CHECK **Summarize** Light is described as what two things in the two models you just read about?

....

....

Literacy Connection

Translate Information
How is visible light similar to and different from radio waves?

Wavelength and Frequency

If you use a wave model for electromagnetic waves, the waves have all of the properties that mechanical waves do. Namely, each wave has a certain amplitude, frequency, wavelength, wave speed, and energy. Electromagnetic waves are divided into categories based on their wavelengths (or frequencies). Visible light, radio waves, and X-rays are three examples of electromagnetic waves. But each has properties that make it more useful for some purposes than for others. If you tried to microwave your food with radio waves, or make a phone call with X-rays, you wouldn't get very far! All electromagnetic waves travel at the same speed in a vacuum, but they have different wavelengths and different frequencies.

As you can see in **Figure 3**, wavelength and frequency are related. In order for a wave to have a high frequency, its wavelength must be short. Waves with the shortest wavelengths have the highest frequencies. Frequency is also related to energy. Higher frequency waves have more energy, while lower frequency waves have less energy.

Visible light is the only range of wavelengths your eyes can see. A radio detects radio waves, which have much longer wavelengths than visible light. X-rays, on the other hand, have much shorter wavelengths than visible light.

READING CHECK **Draw Conclusions** Of X-rays, radio waves, and visible light, which wave type has the most energy? Explain.

Wavelengths and Frequencies

Figure 3 Use the information from the text to label the three wavelength ranges shown in the diagram as either X-rays, radio waves, or visible light.

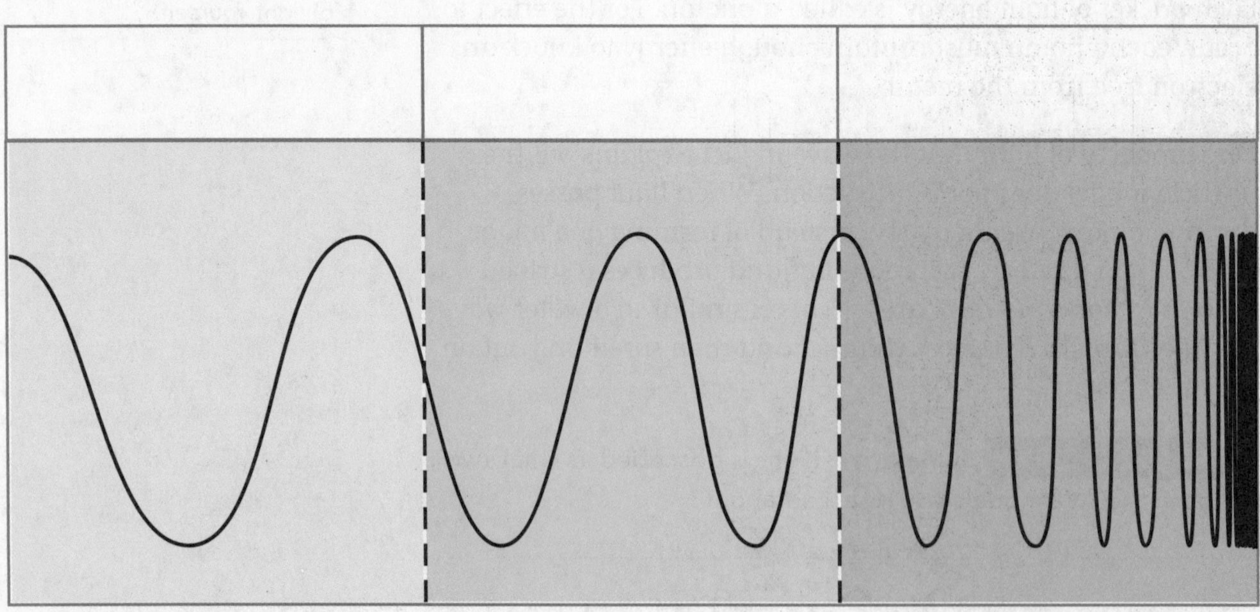

The Electromagnetic Spectrum

There are many different types of electromagnetic waves. The complete range of electromagnetic waves placed in order of increasing frequency is called the **electromagnetic spectrum**. The electromagnetic spectrum is made up of radio waves, microwaves, infrared rays, visible light, ultraviolet rays, X-rays, and gamma rays. The full spectrum is shown in the Math Toolbox.

Mobile Phones

Figure 4 Mobile phones depend on a network of towers to transmit, receive, and relay radio signals.

Radio Waves Electromagnetic waves with the longest wavelengths and the lowest frequencies are **radio waves**. Radio waves are used in mobile phones. Towers, such as the one in **Figure 4**, receive and transmit radio waves along a network that connects mobile phones to each other, to the Internet, and to other networks.

Frequencies and Wavelengths of Light

Electromagnetic Spectrum

Visible spectrum

Radio waves — Microwaves — Infrared — Ultraviolet — X-rays — Gamma-rays

LONGER WAVELENGTH — Wavelength (m) decreases → — SHORTER WAVELENGTH

10^{3} 10^{2} 10^{1} 1 10^{-1} 10^{-2} 10^{-3} 10^{-4} 10^{-5} 10^{-6} 10^{-7} 10^{-8} 10^{-9} 10^{-10} 10^{-11} 10^{-12} 10^{-13} 10^{-14} 10^{-15}

10^{6} 10^{7} 10^{8} 10^{9} 10^{10} 10^{11} 10^{12} 10^{13} 10^{14} 10^{15} 10^{16} 10^{17} 10^{18} 10^{19} 10^{20} 10^{21} 10^{22} 10^{23}

Lower Frequency — Frequency (Hz) increases → — Higher Frequency

Use the electromagnetic spectrum to answer the following questions.

1. **Draw Comparative Inferences** Which has a higher frequency: microwaves or blue light? How do you know?

2. **SEP Use Models** If a certain electromagnetic wave has a wavelength of 100 m, what type of electromagnetic wave is it? How do you know?

Lighting Up the Radar Gun

Figure 5 Radar guns are used in law enforcement to stop speeding drivers, but they are also used to measure the speeds of pitches in a game of baseball. Some pitchers' fastballs have been clocked at 105 miles per hour!

Microwaves

Microwaves have shorter wavelengths and higher frequencies than radio waves. When you think about microwaves, you probably think of microwave ovens. But microwaves have many other uses, including radar. Radar is a system that uses reflected microwaves to detect objects and measure their distance and speed. Radar guns, such as the one in **Figure 5**, are used to measure the speed of a baseball pitch. Police also use them to detect cars that are traveling over the speed limit.

Infrared Rays

If you turn on an electric stove's burner, you can feel it warm up before the heating element starts to glow. The invisible heat you feel is infrared radiation, or infrared rays. **Infrared rays** are electromagnetic waves with wavelengths shorter than those of microwaves. An infrared camera uses infrared rays instead of visible light to take pictures called thermograms, such as the one in **Figure 6.**

Visible Light

Electromagnetic waves that you can see are called **visible light**. Visible light waves have shorter wavelengths and higher frequencies than infrared rays.

Recall that light waves bend, or refract, when they enter a new medium, such as water or glass. Light from the sun contains electromagnetic waves of many frequencies, both visible and invisible. Sunlight passing through a prism splits into its different frequencies, forming a rainbow pattern. After rainy conditions, rainbows such as the one in **Figure 7** can also form in the sky.

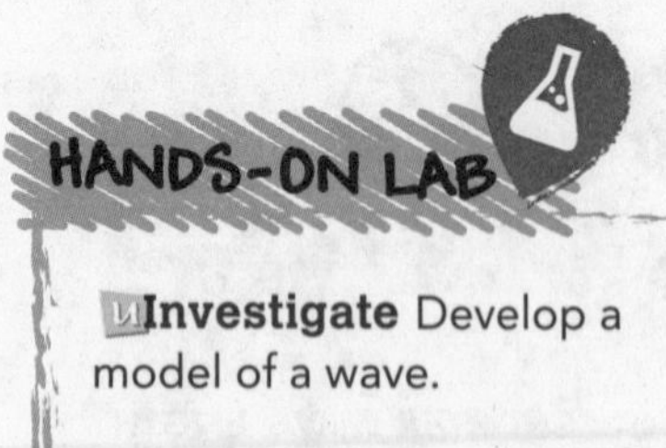

Investigate Develop a model of a wave.

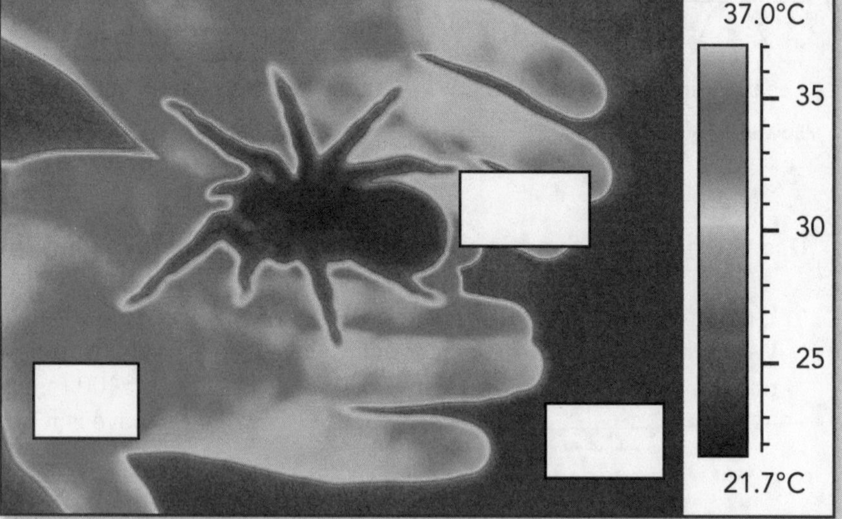

Thermogram

Figure 6 Label the blank spaces rectangles on the thermogram with temperatures in degrees Celsius.

Ultraviolet Rays Electromagnetic waves with wavelengths just shorter than those of visible light are called **ultraviolet rays**, or UV rays for short. UV rays have higher frequencies than visible light, and carry more energy. Sunscreen helps protect your skin from some of the sun's harmful UV rays.

X-rays Electromagnetic waves with wavelengths shorter than those of ultraviolet rays are **X-rays**. Because of their high frequencies, X-rays carry more energy than ultraviolet rays and can penetrate most matter. However, dense matter, such as bone, absorbs X-rays. Therefore, X-rays are used to make images of bones and teeth in humans and animals.

Gamma Rays Electromagnetic waves with the shortest wavelengths and highest frequencies are **gamma rays**. They have the greatest amount of energy of all the electromagnetic waves. Gamma rays are dangerous, but they do have beneficial uses. Radiosurgery shown in **Figure 8,** is a tool that uses several hundred precisely focused gamma rays to target tumors, especially in the brain. The blast of radiation at the point where the beams cross destroys the targeted tumor cells.

Rainbow

Figure 7 Label the rainbow to show which colors have the highest frequency and which have the lowest frequency.

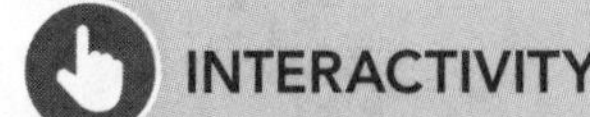

Observe how electromagnetic and mechanical waves differ.

Radiosurgery

Figure 8 The combination of 200 beams of gamma rays can leave tumor cells unable to reproduce, which can stop tumors from growing.

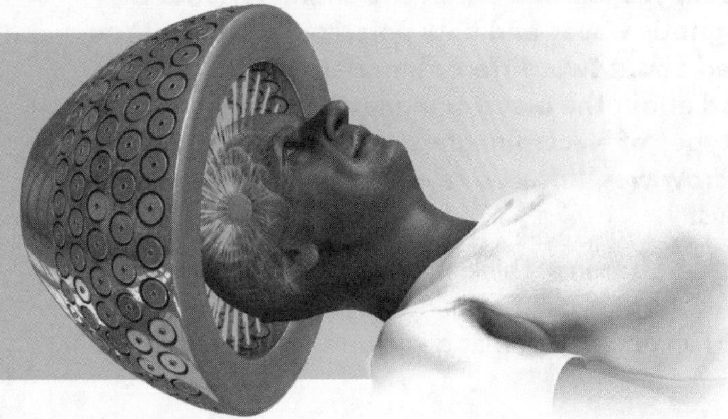

READING CHECK **Draw Conclusions** Can radio waves be used to form images of your bones like x-rays are? Why or why not?

....

....

LESSON 4 Check

MS-PS4-2

1. **Organize Information** In order from lowest to highest frequency, list the different waves along the electromagnetic spectrum.

2. **SEP Communicate Information** Describe the electromagnetic spectrum in a few sentences.

3. **SEP Construct Explanations** Compare the particle model of light to the wave model of light.

4. **Connect to Society** How would you describe the connection between the amount of energy a type of electromagnetic wave has and how that wave is used in technology and society?

Quest CHECK-IN

In this lesson, you learned about the characteristics of electromagnetic waves and how polarization works. You also learned about two different models of light. Finally, you learned about the electromagnetic spectrum and the different types of electromagnetic waves, including radio waves, microwaves, infrared rays, ultraviolet rays, x-rays, and gamma rays.

SEP Design Solutions Think about the properties of visible light and how its path can be changed. How might you move light around an obstacle? What devices might you use in your design?

INTERACTIVITY

Optical Demonstration

Go online to plan your demonstration.

CAREERS

Lighting Designer

Lights! Camera! ACTION!

A lighting designer plans how to light a stage or performance space. The designer uses three factors—color, intensity, and motion—to light a show in the most striking and effective way possible.

There are three primary, or basic colors. For pigments, the primary colors are red, yellow, and blue. In lighting, the primary colors are red, green, and blue. When the three primary colors are mixed in equal amounts, a painter ends up with black paint, but a lighting designer creates white light!

Lighting designers use gels to change the colors of stage lights. A gel is a thin sheet of plastic polymer that slides into grooves at the front of the light. Gels come in every color of the rainbow.

Lighting designers can use lots of instruments and a variety of gels to light the stage. By mixing gels, the designer creates new colors. Red and purple gels, used together, make magenta light.

Lighting designers need a good understanding of physics and engineering, as well as dramatic performance, to create effective displays. Lighting designers are called on to illuminate many kinds of spectacles and events. Ice shows, movie sets, political appearances, and concerts are only a few examples of situations in which lighting designers create the right mood and appearance.

VIDEO

Explore how lighting designers use and manipulate light to communicate with an audience.

MY CAREER

What kinds of decisions do you think lighting designers have to make? Write down your thoughts and think about whether lighting design might be a good career for you.

A lighting designer shines lights at different angles all around the stage to set a bright and lively mood for this concert.

LESSON 5 Light

Guiding Questions

- How are the transmission, reflection, and absorption of light related to the transparency and color of objects?
- What happens to light when it is strikes different types of mirrors?
- What happens to light when it passes through different types of lenses?

Connection

Literacy Evaluate Media

MS-PS4-2

HANDS-ON LAB

uInvestigate Discover how light is reflected, refracted, and transmitted.

Vocabulary

transparent
translucent
opaque
diffuse reflection
convex
focal point
concave

Academic Vocabulary

compare

Connect It!

Shadows are made by different objects in the picture. Label two shadows with the names of the objects that made them.

SEP Construct Explanations Why do some objects make shadows, while others do not?

Light, Color, and Objects

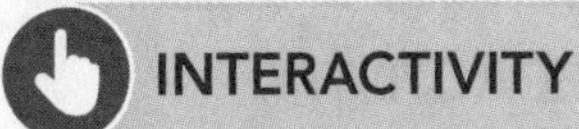

INTERACTIVITY

Write about the appearance of your own reflection on several materials.

When people talk about light, they are usually referring to the part of the electromagnetic spectrum that is visible to humans. This light interacts with the world around us to determine what we see and how it appears.

Materials can be classified based on how much light transmits through them. A material that transmits most of the light that strikes it is **transparent**. You can see through a transparent object, such as a window pane or the plastic wrap on a package.

A **translucent** material scatters the light that passes through it. You might be able to see through a translucent material, but the image will look blurred. Waxed paper and gelatin dessert are examples of translucent materials.

Reflect Explain why you have a shadow, but a window pane does not.

A material that reflects or absorbs all of the light that strikes it is called **opaque**. A book, a marshmallow, and a hippopotamus are all opaque—you can't see through them because light does not transmit through them. **Figure 1** shows an example of what happens when light strikes transparent and opaque objects.

Shadows

Figure 1 You can see shadows of both the person and the window frame. There is no shadow of the panes of glass in the window because light passes through them.

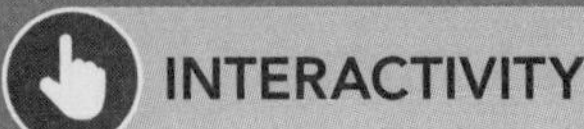

INTERACTIVITY

Observe and describe the behavior of light in various situations.

The Color of Objects Recall that white light is a mixture of all of the colors in the rainbow. When white light shines on an object, some of the colors of light are reflected and some are absorbed.

The color of an opaque object is the color of light that the object reflects. It absorbs all other colors. Under white light, the soccer ball in **Figure 2** appears blue and red. It reflects blue and red wavelengths of light and absorbs all other colors. Other objects, such as a brown tree trunk, do not appear as basic colors of light. These objects reflect more than one color of light. Brown is a combination of red and green, so a brown object reflects both red and green light, and it absorbs all other colors. If an object appears black, then it absorbs all colors of light. A white object reflects all light.

The color of a transparent or a translucent object is the color of light that passes through it. For example, the color of a clear, green drinking glass is green because green light is the only color of light that passes through it.

READING CHECK **Determine Central Ideas** Why does snow appear white?

....

Light and Color

Figure 2 When light shines on an object, some wavelengths of light are reflected and some are absorbed. Circle the answers that correctly complete the sentences. The color of an opaque object is the color of light it (absorbs / reflects). If the object (absorbs / reflects) all of the light, the object appears black.

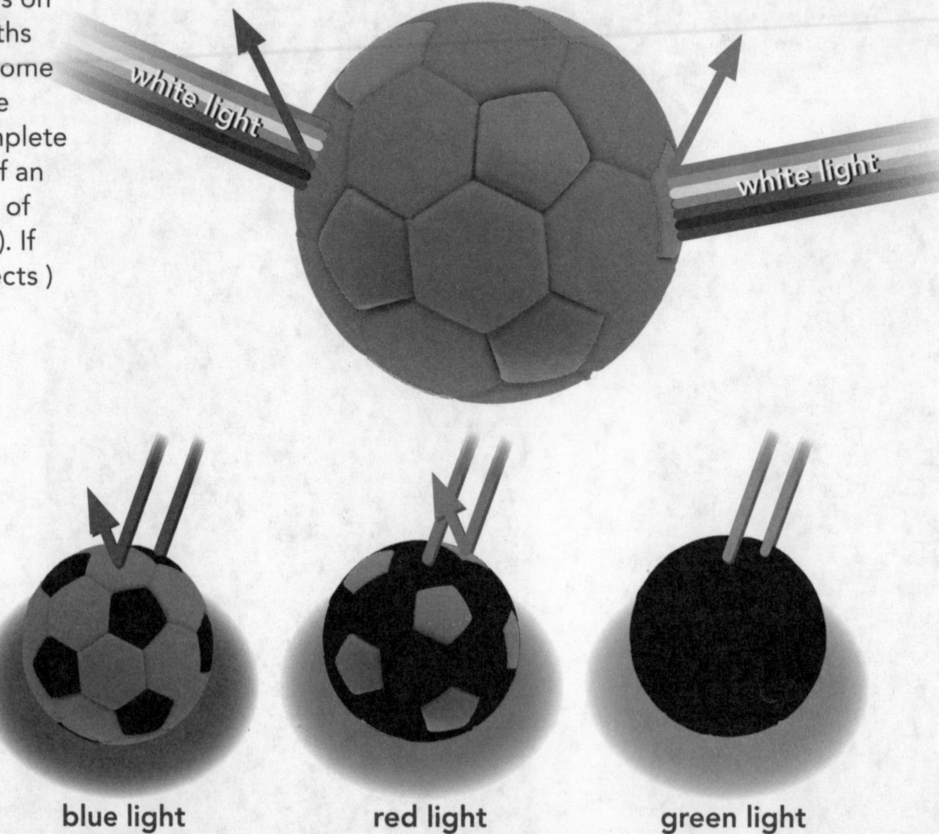

Color Filters Perhaps you have looked at an object that has a colored light shining on it. You might have noticed that the color of the object looks different than it does when white light shines on it. The color of the light might come from white light shining through a colored filter—a tinted piece of glass or plastic. A red filter, for example, transmits only red light. When light shines through a red filter onto an object, any part of the object that is red, looks red. Any other color looks black. **Figure 3** shows several different color filters and what happens when white light shines on them.

Color filters are often used in photography and movies. They are part of the special effects that create different moods for scenes. Use what you know about filters to complete the activity in **Figure 3**.

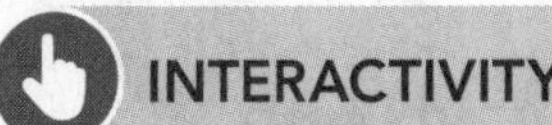

INTERACTIVITY

Explore how color filters affect the appearance of different objects.

Literacy Connection

Evaluate Media Describe an image you've seen with a filter on it, and write about how the filter altered the image.

Photography and Color Filters

Figure 3 Color filters can be used in photography to bring out certain colors or create dramatic moods. For each of the inset images, write the color of the filter that produced the altered images.

Investigate Discover how light is reflected, refracted, and transmitted.

Reflecting Light

You have seen that sometimes light is transmitted through materials. Like other electromagnetic radiation, light can also be reflected. The reflection of light occurs when parallel rays of light bounce off a surface. Reflected light is how you see your image in a mirror, but reflected light is also why you see a distorted image or no image at all in the surface of rippling water on a lake. The difference lies in whether the light undergoes regular reflection or diffuse reflection.

Regular reflection occurs when parallel rays of light hit a smooth surface. As shown in **Figure 4**, the trees are reflected because light hits the smooth surface of the water, and the rays all reflect at the same angle. As a result, the reflection is a clear image.

In **diffuse reflection**, parallel rays of light hit an uneven surface. The angle at which each ray hits the surface equals the angle at which it reflects. The rays, however, don't bounce off in the same direction because the light rays hit different parts of the surface at different angles. **Figure 4** shows why light undergoes diffuse reflection when it hits choppy water on a lake.

Regular and Diffuse Reflection

Figure 4 Light reflects off the surface of water.

For each type of reflection, circle the terms that correctly complete the sentence.

You (can / cannot) see an image in the still water because the light undergoes (regular / diffuse) reflection.

You (can / cannot) see an image in the choppy water because the light undergoes (regular / diffuse) reflection.

Mirror Images The most common way to form a clear image using reflected light is with a mirror. There are three different types of mirrors—plane, convex, and concave. The types of mirrors are distinguished by the shape of the surface of the mirror.

The mirror you have hanging on a wall in your home probably is a flat mirror, also known as a plane mirror. The image you see in the mirror is called a virtual image, which is an image that forms where light seems to come from. **Figure 5** shows an example of a virtual image in a plane mirror. This image is upright and the same size as the object that formed the image, but the right and left sides of the image are reversed.

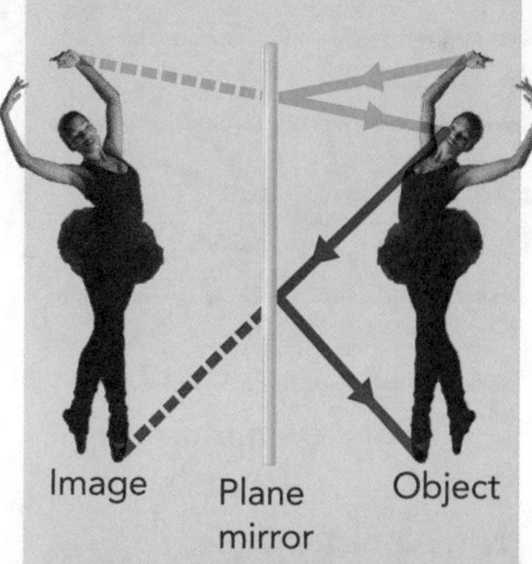

Plane Mirror Image

Figure 5 In this virtual image, the reflected light rays appear to come from behind the mirror, where the image forms. The distance from the image to the mirror is the same as the distance from the object to the mirror.

Convex Mirrors To visualize a convex mirror, think about a metal bowl. A **convex** mirror is like the outside of the bowl because it is a mirror with a surface that curves outward. If you look at an image in the outside of the bowl, it is smaller than the image in a plane mirror. **Figure 6** shows an example of an image in a convex mirror. To understand how these images form, look at the optical axis and the focal point of the mirror. The optical axis is an imaginary line that divides a mirror in half. The **focal point** is the location at which rays parallel to the optical axis reflect and meet. The light reflects off the curved surface such that the image appears to come from a focal point behind the mirror.

Convex Mirror Image

Figure 6 Most rear-view mirrors are convex. Light rays bend when they hit the surface of the mirror in such a way that the object appears smaller than it is.

Optical axis

Focal point

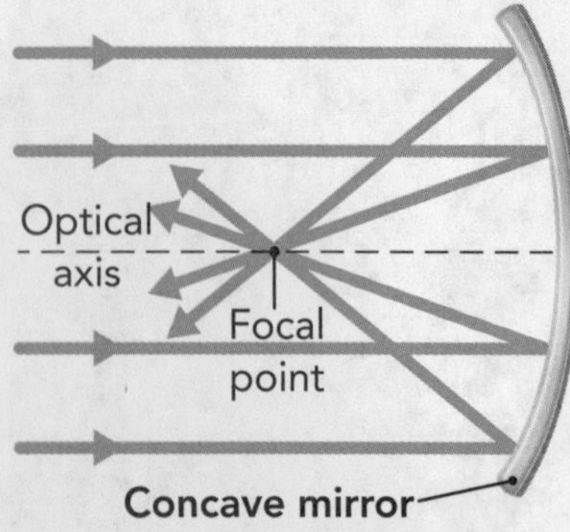

Mirror Images

Figure 7 The images formed by mirrors depend upon the shape of the mirror. Examine the diagram, and then identify the type of image in each example.

The object is located farther from the mirror than the focal point is. It forms a .... image.

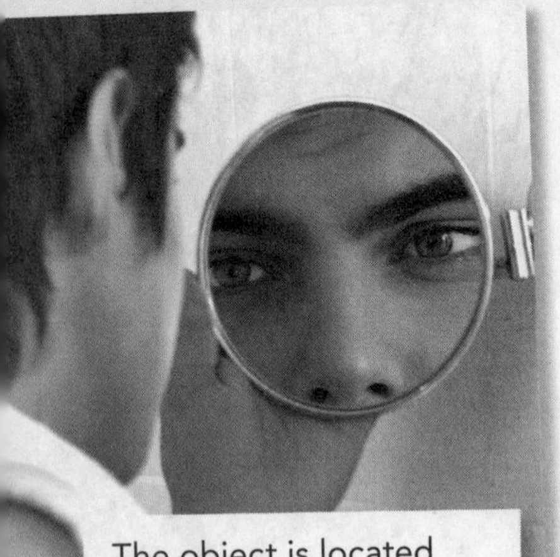

The object is located between the mirror and the focal point. It forms a .... image.

Concave Mirrors Just as a convex mirror is like the outside of a shiny bowl, a concave mirror is like the inside of the bowl. The surface of a **concave** mirror curves inward. **Figure 7** shows that the focal point of a concave mirror is on the reflecting side of the mirror. The image that forms from a concave mirror depends on whether the object is between the focal point and the mirror or farther away from the mirror than the focal point. If the object is farther from the mirror than the focal point is, then reflected light rays cross past one another, and the image is inverted. This image is called a real image. If the object is between the focal point and the mirror, then the image is not inverted and is larger than the actual object. This image is a virtual image.

READING CHECK **Classify** If a mirrored image is inverted, what type of image is it?

....

Model It!

Fun with Mirrors

In a fun house, mirrors are often used to change the appearance of objects.

SEP Develop Models Suppose you want to use a mirror to make a door look smaller and rounder. In the space below, draw the mirror and the door, along with the focal point. Label the mirror with the type of mirror it is.

Lenses

Light not only reflects, as it does with a mirror, but it also bends, or refracts. A lens is a curved piece of transparent material that refracts light. Every time you look through a telescope, a microscope, or a pair of eyeglasses, you are looking through a lens. Just like a mirror, a lens is either convex or concave, based on its shape.

VIDEO

Explore the effects of different lenses and filters in cameras.

Convex Lenses Look at **Figure 8** to see what convex lenses look like, how they refract light, and what type of image is produced. You can see that convex lenses are thicker in the middle and thinner at the edges. As light passes through the lens, it refracts toward the center of the lens. The more curved the lens is, the more the light refracts.

A convex lens can produce either a virtual image or a real image depending on where the object is located relative to the focal point of the lens. If the object is between the lens and the focal point, then a virtual image forms. This image is larger than the actual object. You may have observed this when using a magnifying glass. If the object is farther away from the lens than the focal point is, then a real image forms. This image can be larger, smaller, or the same size as the object.

Does this description of a convex lens sound familiar? **Compare** a convex lens and a concave mirror. Both a convex lens and a concave mirror focus light, and the type of image formed depends on the location of the object compared to the location of the focal point.

Academic Vocabulary

How does comparing items differ from contrasting them?

....

....

....

....

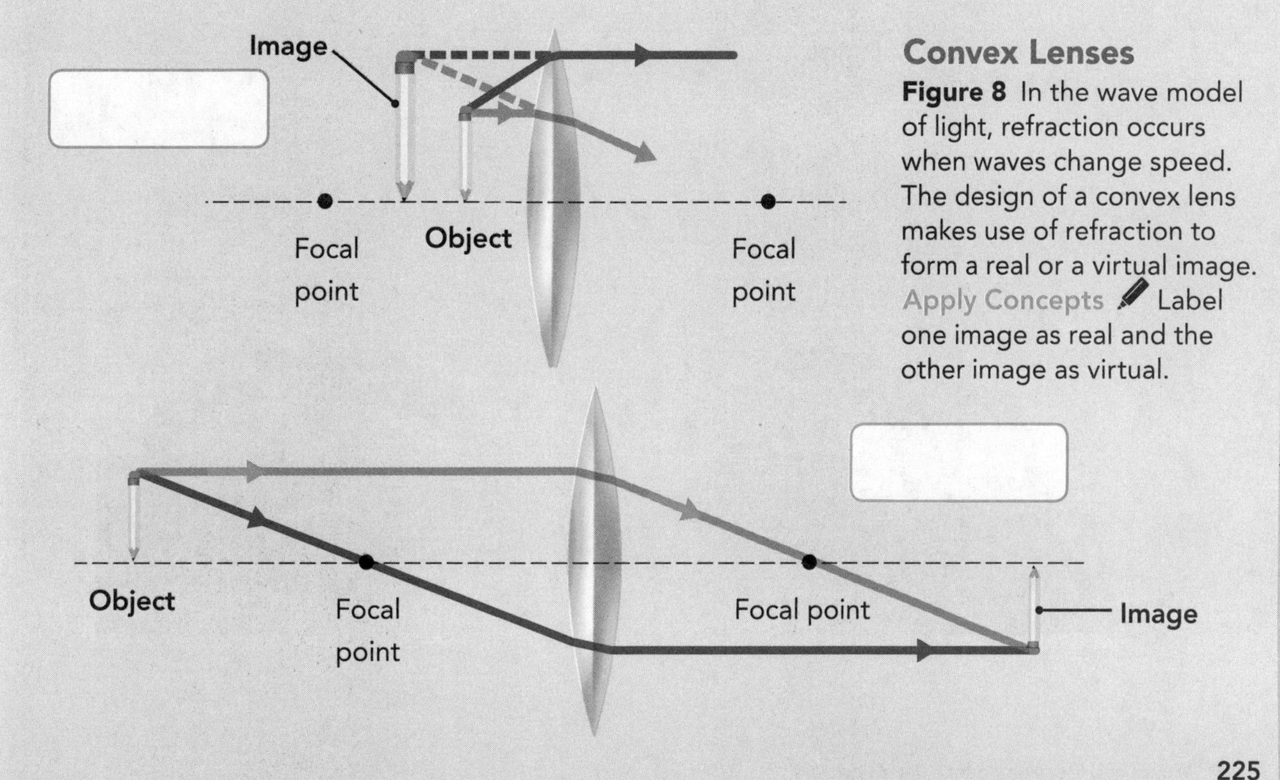

Convex Lenses

Figure 8 In the wave model of light, refraction occurs when waves change speed. The design of a convex lens makes use of refraction to form a real or a virtual image. Apply Concepts Label one image as real and the other image as virtual.

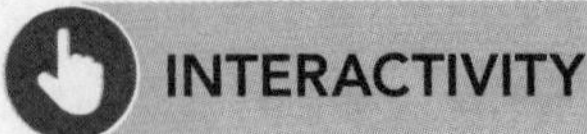

INTERACTIVITY

Predict the behavior of light rays as they encounter different objects and substances.

Concave Lenses Concave lenses are thinner at the center than they are at the edges. When light rays travel through the lens, the rays are bent away from the optical axis, so the rays never meet. Because the rays never meet, concave lenses form only virtual images, and these images are upright and smaller than the objects. **Figure 9** shows how concave lenses form images.

READING CHECK **Compare and Contrast** In what ways is a convex lens like a concave mirror? In what ways are they different?

....

....

....

....

Concave Lenses

Figure 9 When looking through a concave lens, a virtual image forms which is always smaller than the object itself.

Apply Concepts After examining the diagrams, circle the photo in which the image is formed by using a concave lens.

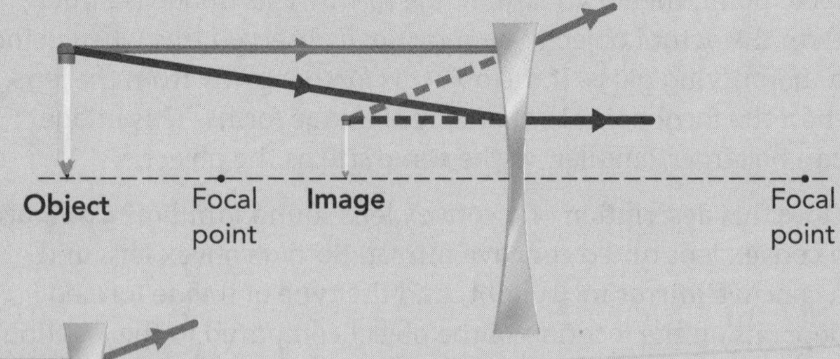

Focal point Object Image

Focal point

LESSON 5 Check

MS-PS4-2

1. **Classify** What kind of material transmits some light, making objects behind it appear blurry?

2. **Identify** A bird runs into the window of a building because it sees the reflection of the sky in the window. The sky does not appear distorted in this window. What type of mirror or lens is the window acting as? Explain your answer.

3. **SEP Design Solutions** When a person is nearsighted, an eyeglass lens is needed to bend light entering the eye away from the optical axis. What type of lens will do this?

4. **CCC Cause and Effect** Why might some rear-view mirrors in a car state, "Objects are closer than they appear"?

5. **SEP Construct Explanations** Suppose a movie director is filming on a set that should look like a hot desert. He wants the scene to appear warmer, such that the red and yellow tones are the most apparent. What color filters should he use? What color will the blue sky appear when he uses those filters, and why?

Quest CHECK-IN

In this lesson, you observed how light behaves when it encounters transparent, translucent, and opaque objects. You saw how the color of light or filters affects the color of objects. You also discovered the ways that light can reflect from mirrors or refract through lenses.

CCC Structure and Function How might you apply this knowledge to choose the objects and their placement in your quest?

HANDS-ON LAB

An Optimal Optical Solution

Go online to download the lab worksheet. Build and test your optical security system.

TOPIC 5 Review and Assess

1 Wave Properties

MS-PS4-1

1. Which of the following is a property of a mechanical wave?
   A. amplitude B. weight
   C. incidence D. color

2. The sound wave frequency of an F-sharp in music is 370 Hz, and its wavelength is 0.93 m. What is the wave's speed?
   A. 34.4 m/s B. 397.9 m/s
   C. 344.1 m/s D. 300,000 km/s

3. Which statement about the speed of sound is correct?
   A. Sound travels faster through water than air.
   B. Sound travels at the same speed through water and air.
   C. Sound travels faster through space than air.
   D. Sound travels at the same speed through space and air.

4. If the amplitude or frequency of a wave increases, the energy of the wave ....

5. **SEP Construct Explanations** It's been said that you can estimate how far away a lightning bolt is by counting the number of seconds that elapse between seeing the flash and hearing the thunderclap, and then dividing that number by five to get a distance in miles. In terms of the physics of light and sound waves, does this method make sense?

....

....

....

....

....

....

....

2 Wave Interactions

MS-PS4-2

6. Refraction is the bending of waves that occurs due to a change in
   A. speed. B. frequency.
   C. height. D. amplitude.

7. Which of the following pairs of terms describes the two different wave interactions depicted below?

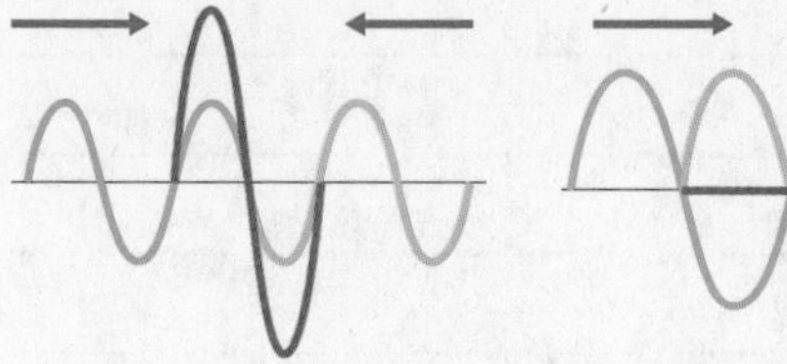

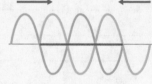

   A. constructive and destructive interference
   B. moving and standing waves
   C. mechanical and electromagnetic waves
   D. sound waves and light waves

8. When a ray of light strikes a surface, it can be ...., ..., or ....

9. **SEP Engage in Argument** Why is it important for engineers to understand the natural frequency of vibrations in building materials when planning to build a bridge in an area with high winds or frequent earthquakes?

....

....

....

....

....

....

....

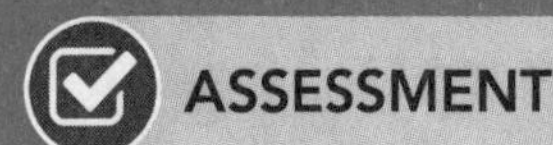

ASSESSMENT

Evaluate your understanding by taking a Topic Test.

3 Sound Waves

MS-PS4-2

10. When a sound wave is absorbed by an object,
- **A.** it quickly gains energy.
- **B.** it quickly loses energy.
- **C.** it slowly gains energy.
- **D.** its energy does not change.

11. **CCC Cause and Effect** How do stiffness, density, and temperature affect sound waves?

....

....

....

....

....

4 Electromagnetic Waves

MS-PS4-2

12. Which electromagnetic wave type has the highest frequency?
- **A.** visible light
- **B.** infrared rays
- **C.** gamma rays
- **D.** microwaves

13. Of all of the colors in the visible part of the electromagnetic spectum, red light has the lowest frequency, the .... wavelength, and the .... energy.

14. **SEP Use Models** Describe how you could use a simple rope to teach someone about the different waves along the electromagnetic spectrum.

....

....

....

....

....

5 Electromagnetic Radiation

MS-PS4-2

15. Which statement is correct?
- **A.** A red apple reflects green light.
- **B.** A blue ball absorbs blue light.
- **C.** A green leaf reflects green light.
- **D.** A black shirt reflects all colors of light.

16. What happens when light rays encounter a concave lens?
- **A.** The light rays are reflected back.
- **B.** The light rays travel through the lens and refract away from the center of the lens.
- **C.** The light rays travel through the lens and refract toward the center of the lens.
- **D.** The light rays travel through the lens without bending.

17. When an object is located between a concave mirror and the focal point, a .... image is produced.

18. **SEP Develop Models** Draw a model to show what happens to light when it meets a convex mirror.

TOPIC 5 Review and Assess

MS-PS4-1, MS-PS4-2

Evidence-Based Assessment

Bianca is helping the theater director at her school with lighting, sound, and set design for a school play. She will be choosing the materials that will be used on stage and on the walls of the theater. After she reads the script and makes observations inside the theater, she makes the following list of the factors to consider in her design.

- The echoes throughout the theater need to be reduced.
- The set should not reflect too much light into the audience's eyes.
- The only lights available are white, purple, and yellow. The filters available are red and blue.
- The blue sky on the set should appear black for Act 2.

Bianca draws a detailed illustration of her plan to show the theater director. She labels it with the materials she plans to use.

1. **Apply Scientific Reasoning** Bianca plans to shine a few spotlights on the sky for Act 2 and use a filter to change the color. Which filter should Bianca use on the white light to make the blue sky appear black?
   A. a red filter
   B. a blue filter
   C. a white filter
   D. no filter at all

2. **Identify Criteria** Which of the following considerations does Bianca need to take into account as she works on the set and lighting design? Select all that apply.
   - ☐ Two different sets are needed for Act 2.
   - ☐ The set materials should not be too shiny or glossy.
   - ☐ Only the colors white, purple, and yellow can be used to paint the sets.
   - ☐ The walls have hard surfaces that reflect sound waves.
   - ☐ Only the white lights can be used for Act 2.

3. **SEP Use Models** Based on Bianca's illustration, did she choose the appropriate material on the walls for reducing echoes? Why or why not?

4. **SEP Develop Models** As sound waves travel away from the speaker, their amplitudes and energy decrease. Where will the sound be the most quiet? If you were to move the speaker, where would you place it and why?

5. **SEP Design Solutions** Based on Bianca's criteria and model, which materials would you change on stage? Explain your reasoning.

Quest FINDINGS

Complete the Quest!

Phenomenon Reflect on your demonstration and answer questions about modifying and improving your design. List some other kinds of jobs that may require a good knowledge of light and its behavior.

Apply Concepts You've seen how light can bend and move. How might a grocery store manager use the properties of light and set up objects to make sure the entire store can be visible from one location without using cameras?

INTERACTIVITY

Reflect on Your Demonstration

uDemonstrate Lab

MS-PS4-2

Making Waves

How can you use a **model** to demonstrate what happens when **waves interact** with barriers or other waves?

Background

Phenomenon A wave breaker is a large wall made of rocks or concrete objects that extends into the ocean. Breakers often are built near beaches to make the water calmer for swimmers. These barriers help to diminish the force of incoming waves by scattering them and interfering with their movements.

In this lab, you will model the behavior of water waves and explain how the waves interact with each other and with objects in their paths. You will then decide on the best method and materials for diminishing waves.

Materials

(per group)

- water
- plastic dropper
- metric ruler
- paper towels
- modeling clay
- plastic knife
- cork or other small floating object
- ripple tank (aluminum foil lasagna pan with mirror on the bottom)

Safety

Be sure to follow all safety guidelines provided by your teacher.

This rock barrier helps to block big waves and make the beach more enjoyable for swimmers.

Design an Investigation

☐ One way to generate waves is to squeeze drops of water from an eyedropper into a pan of water. How can you use the dropper to control how forceful the waves are?

....

....

....

☐ What questions will you explore in your investigation? Some questions to explore include:

- What happens when waves hit a solid surface?
- What happens when waves travel through a gap between two solid objects?
- How does a floating object react to waves?
- What happens when one wave meets another wave?

☐ Record any additional questions you hope to answer in your investigation.

....

....

....

☐ Design an experiment to show how waves behave when they interact with different objects or with each other. Write out a procedure. Then decide what information to record and design a data table to record your observations.

HANDS-ON LAB

Demonstrate Go online for a downloadable worksheet of this lab.

uDemonstrate Lab

Procedure

Data

Analyze and Interpret Data

1. **Identify** Are the waves in water mechanical waves or electromagnetic waves? How do you know?

2. **CCC Cause and Effect** In what situations did you observe waves interfering with one another? How did it affect the amplitude of the waves?

3. **Claim** Which material and set-up was best for reducing waves? Which was worst?

4. **Evidence** What evidence led you to your conclusions?

5. **Reasoning** Repetition is when you repeat a step of the procedure a few times to see if you get the same results. Did you use repetition in your experiment? Why or why not?

6. **SEP Design Solutions** Share your results with members of another group. What did they do differently? In what ways would you suggest that the other group members revise their procedure?

TOPIC

6

Electricity and Magnetism

NGSS PERFORMANCE EXPECTATIONS

MS-PS2-3 Ask questions about data to determine the factors that affect the strength of electric and magnetic forces.

MS-PS2-5 Conduct an investigation and evaluate the experimental design to provide evidence that fields exist between objects exerting forces on each other even though the objects are not in contact.

MS-PS3-2 Develop a model to describe that when the arrangement of objects interacting at a distance changes, different amounts of potential energy are stored in the system.

HANDS-ON LAB

uConnect Make observations to determine the north and south poles of a magnet.

GO ONLINE
to access your
digital course

VIDEO

INTERACTIVITY

VIRTUAL LAB

ASSESSMENT

eTEXT

HANDS-ON LABS

How does pedaling generate electricity for the lights?

The Essential Question

What factors affect the strength of electric and magnetic forces?

CCC Energy and Matter When the rider pedals this bicycle, he generates electricity for the lights on the carousel. The process uses electromagnets. As the cyclist pedals faster, the lights become brighter. How do you think the action of pedaling produces light?

....

....

....

....

....

Quest KICKOFF

How can you lift an object without making contact?

STEM **Phenomenon** In Japan, South Korea, and China, you can hop on a train that uses electromagnets to levitate above a rail and travel at incredibly high speeds. The technology is the result of years of research and testing by electric and mechanical engineers. In this STEM Quest, you will explore how you can use electromagnetism to lift or raise objects without coming into contact with them. In digital activities, you will investigate electric and magnetic forces. By applying what you have learned, you will design, build, and test a device that can levitate objects.

INTERACTIVITY

Light as a Feather?

MS-PS2-3 Ask questions about data to determine the factors that affect the strength of electric and magnetic forces.
MS-PS2-5 Conduct an investigation and evaluate the experimental design to provide evidence that fields exist between objects exerting forces on each other even though the objects are not in contact.
MS-PS3-2 Develop a model to describe that when the arrangement of objects interacting at a distance changes, different amounts of potential energy are stored in the system.

NBC LEARN VIDEO

After watching the video, which examines some industrial applications of magnets and electromagnets, list two examples of objects that you use every day that rely on magnets or electromagnets.

Example 1

....

....

....

Example 2

....

....

....

Quest CHECK-IN

IN LESSON 1

STEM What kinds of forces are exerted by positive and negative charges? Think about how charged objects interact and apply what you have learned to your levitating device.

INTERACTIVITY

Apply Electrical Forces

Quest CHECK-IN

IN LESSON 2

STEM How can you use magnets to build a levitation device? Develop possible design solutions by exploring magnetic forces.

HANDS-ON LAB

Tracking Levitation

Quest CHECK-IN

IN LESSON 3

STEM How can you control the strength of your device? Build an electromagnet and explore how you can incorporate the technology into your device.

HANDS-ON LAB

Building an Electromagnet

Magnetism is used to elevate this "maglev" train several centimeters above the tracks and also to propel it forward. The absence of friction between the train and the track allows the maglev train to achieve speeds up to 600 kilometers per hour!

Quest CHECK-IN

IN LESSON 4

STEM How can you refine your levitating device to improve your results? Redesign and retest your device using electromagnets.

HANDS-ON LAB

Electrifying Levitation

Quest FINDINGS

Complete the Quest!

Apply what you've learned by describing other scenarios in your daily life in which electromagnets could be used to make a task easier.

INTERACTIVITY

Reflect on Your Levitating Device

uConnect Lab

Magnetic Poles

How can you **gather evidence** about magnetic forces and poles?

Background

Phenomenon A magnet has a north and a south pole. Two magnets will behave differently depending on how their poles are aligned. In this activity, you will design a procedure to observe how magnets behave in the presence of other magnets.

Materials

(per group)

- toy cars
- tape
- bar magnets, with ends labeled "A" and "B"
- bar magnet without labels
- ruler

Safety

Be sure to follow all safety procedures provided by your teacher. The Safety Appendix of your textbook provides more details about the safety icons.

Design a Procedure

☐ 1. **Plan an Investigation** Design a procedure with at least two steps that uses the labeled magnets, tape, toy cars, and ruler to observe how magnets behave when different ends are forced to interact.

☐ 2. Show your plan to your teacher before you begin. Then, carry out your experiment and record your data.

☐ 3. Add at least one more step to determine how to label the bar magnet without labels. Show your teacher before you begin. Record your observations.

Observations

Step	Observations

Analyze and Interpret Data

Connect Go online for a downloadable worksheet of this lab.

1. **CCC Cause and Effect** Based on your observations, determine the cause-and-effect relationship between different combinations of magnetic poles.

2. **SEP Interpret Data** Explain how you used your observations from your experiment to correctly label the sides of a blank magnet.

LESSON

1 Electric Force

Guiding Questions

- What causes electric fields and electric forces?
- How is potential energy affected by positions of charges?
- How is static electricity different from current?

Connection

Literacy Integrate with Visuals

MS-PS2-5, MS-PS3-2

HANDS-ON LAB

uInvestigate Use a device to detect electric charges.

Vocabulary

electron
electric force
electric field
electric current
conductor
static electricity

Academic Vocabulary

charge
neutral

Connect It!

Identify the parts of this picture that you think show the transfer of electric charges. Draw dots to indicate the paths of the moving electric charges from a cloud to the ground.

Explain Why do you think lightning is so dangerous if it comes in contact with a person?

Electric Force, Fields, and Energy

Did you know that there are electric **charges**, forces, and fields inside your body? You might not see them or feel them, but they are in every atom, everywhere!

Atoms are made up of protons, neutrons, and electrons, as shown in **Figure 1**. Protons are positively charged particles, and **electrons** are negatively charged particles. Neutrons are **neutral**, meaning that they do not have a charge. Most objects are made of atoms in which the number of protons is equal to the number of electrons. As a result, the positive and negative charges cancel out and the atoms are neutral. However, electrons can move from one atom or object to another. If an object loses electrons, it is left with more protons than electrons. It has an overall positive charge. If an object gains electrons, it will have an overall negative charge.

If you have ever watched a lightning storm, as in **Figure 2**, you have seen a dramatic display of electric charges. The lightning bolts are made up of moving electrons.

READING CHECK **Summarize Text** How can a neutral object become negatively charged?

....

....

Academic Vocabulary

Charge is a basic property of matter that creates a force and accounts for electric interactions. Some particles and atoms have no charge, so they are neutral. Is the atom in **Figure 1** neutral or charged?

....

Model of an Atom

Figure 1 Charged particles make up atoms.

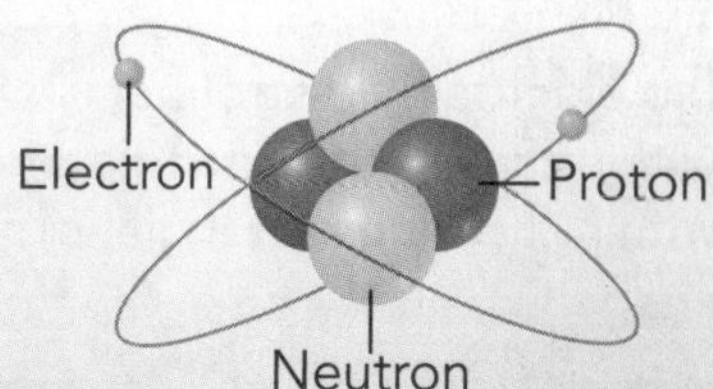

Lightning Storm

Figure 2 Lightning bolts can travel from clouds to the ground. They can also travel within a cloud and between clouds. These streaks of light are the result of the movement of electric charges.

Electric Force

Electric Force The force between charged particles or objects is called **electric force**. If a proton and an electron come close together, the opposition of their positive and negative forces creates an attraction that draws them together. On the other hand, if two electrons come close together, they repel each other because they both are negatively charged. The electric force causes them to move apart. In general, opposite charges attract, and like charges repel.

The strength of the electric force depends on the distance between the charges. For example, when a positively-charged particle or object is close another positively-charged particle, a strong force between them pushes them away from each other. As they move apart, the force between them becomes weaker. The strength of the electric force also depends on the amount of charge present. When more charge is involved, the electric force is stronger. For instance, three protons attract an electron more strongly than one proton alone.

Electric Fields Two charged particles will experience electric forces between them without even touching. How is this possible? An electric charge has an invisible **electric field** around it—a region around the charged particle or object where the electric force is exerted on other charged particles or objects. Electric fields can be represented by field lines, as in **Figure 3**. They point in the direction that the force would push a positive charge. Field lines around a positively charged object point away from the object. They indicate that the object would repel a positive charge. Field lines around a negatively charged object point toward the object. The negatively charged object would attract a positive charge. When multiple charges are in the same area, the field lines show a slightly more complicated combination of the two fields.

Electric Field Lines

Figure 3 Images A and B show the field lines around single charges. Image C shows the field lines around a positive charge and a negative charge next to each other. Where field lines are closer together, the electric field is stronger.

1. SEP Use Models Is the electric field stronger within the white rectangle or within the blue rectangle in image C?

....

2. Draw Conclusions Is the electric field stronger close to the charges or further away from the charges?

....

READING CHECK In which direction would a positive charge move if it were placed in between the positive and negative charges in image C?

....

....

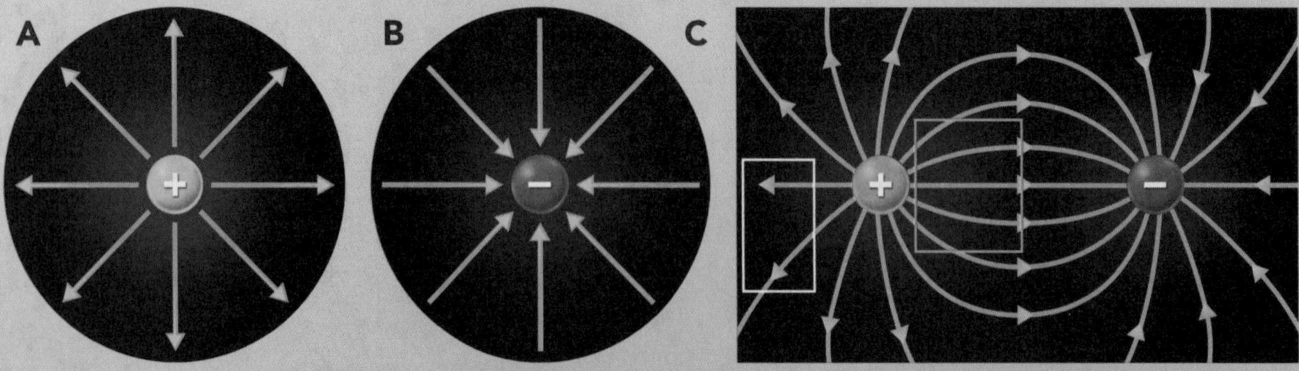

Charges and Potential Energy When forces are in action, you can be sure that energy is also involved. Suppose you have a system that consists of two opposite charges and their interaction. If you pull the opposite charges away from each other, the potential energy of the system increases. You can understand this by comparing it to gravitational potential energy. Gravity is an attractive force. When you lift an object higher above the ground, you apply a force and transfer energy to it. The object's gravitational potential energy increases. When you drop the object, the force of gravity pulls the object to the ground and its gravitational potential energy decreases. The force between opposite charges is also an attractive force. As you apply a force to move opposite charges away from each other, the electric potential energy of the system increases. When the electric force between opposite charges pulls them together naturally, the potential energy of the system decreases, as shown in **Figure 4**.

Potential energy changes in a different way between two like charges. Two like charges naturally repel each other. An outside force is not needed to move them apart. Therefore, as the electric force between two like charges pushes them away from each other, the potential energy of the system decreases.

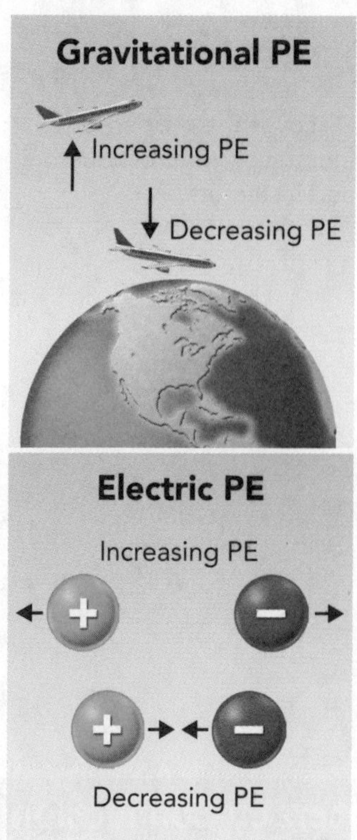

Potential Energy
Figure 4 Electric potential energy behaves a lot like gravitational potential energy.

Question It!

Students are conducting an experiment to provide evidence that electric fields exert forces on objects even when the objects are not in contact. They use pith balls hanging from strings. Pith balls are small balls that pick up charge easily. These pith balls have been charged by touching another charged object. The students drew this diagram to show the result of their experiment.

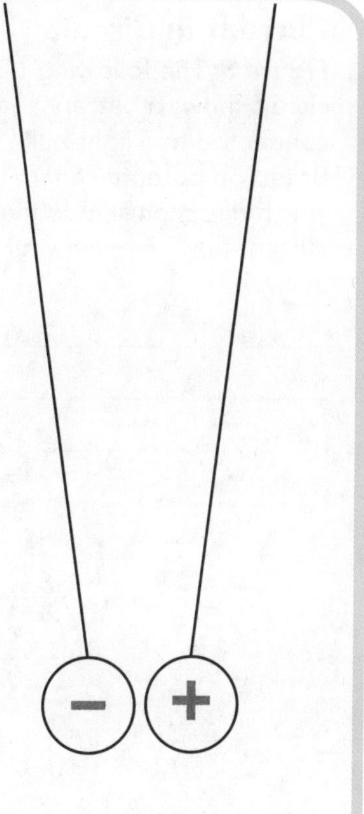

1. CCC Cause and Effect When the two pith balls have opposite charges, they are naturally pulled together due to the attractive electric force between them. If you pull the two pith balls away from each other, what happens to the potential energy of the system? Explain.

....

....

....

2. Cite Textual Evidence How do the results of this experiment provide evidence that electric fields exert forces on the pith balls, even when they are not in contact?

....

....

Discover the properties of electric current, conductors, and insulators.

Electric Current and Circuits

Electric charges play a major role in daily life. Any time you use electricity, you are using energy from electric charges that are in motion. The charges flow through materials like water flows down a stream. The continuous flow of charge is known as **electric current**. Current is measured as a rate in units called amperes. The abbreviation for this unit is A. The number of amperes describes the amount of charge that passes by a given point each second.

Current flows through paths known as circuits. A circuit is a path that runs in a loop. A basic electric circuit contains a source of energy connected with wires to a device that runs on electricity. Current flows from the source of energy, through the wires, through the electric device, and back to the source.

Voltage Why do charges flow through a circuit? They move because of differences in potential energy. Current flows from a point of higher potential energy to a point of lower potential energy in the circuit. For instance, a battery, like the one shown in **Figure 5**, has one end where current has a higher potential energy per charge than it has at the other end of the battery. This difference in electric potential energy per charge is called voltage. The voltage acts like a force that causes current to flow. Voltage is measured in units of volts. The abbreviation for this unit is V.

Literacy Connection

Integrate with Visuals

Draw dots and arrows to represent current flowing through the circuit.

Current in Circuits

Figure 5 The following circuit shows a battery connected to a light bulb. Based on potential energy, which direction should the current flow? Explain your answer.

....

....

....

....

....

....

....

....

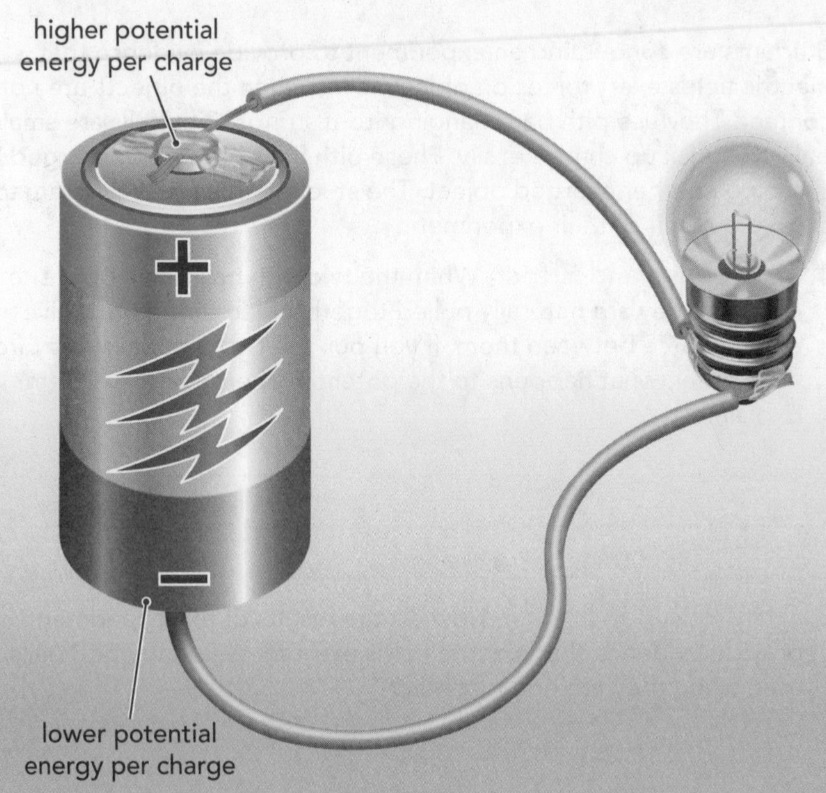

Energy in Circuits You can compare a charge in a circuit to an object in the gravitational field of Earth. When an object falls, the force of gravity pulls the object from a position of higher potential energy to a position of lower potential energy. You give that potential energy back when you lift the object up to its initial position. A battery gives energy back to charges as well. Inside the battery, the energy from chemical substances is converted to electric energy. That electric energy becomes the potential energy of the charges. They return to a position of higher potential energy, from which they flow through the circuit.

Current and Resistance What are the charges that flow through a circuit? They are electrons. Historically, the current is described as flowing in the direction in which positive charges would move. However, electrons are negatively charged. So the direction of current is opposite to the direction of electron flow.

Some materials have electrons that are tightly bound to their atoms. Their electrons are difficult to move. Those materials, called insulators, do not allow charge to flow. Therefore, they have a high resistance to electric current. On the other hand, some materials have electrons that are more loosely bound to their atoms. Those materials are **conductors**—they allow charge to flow more freely (**Figure 6**). Just as there are insulators and conductors of heat, there are insulators and conductors of charge. Insulators of charge are materials such as rubber, wood, and glass, while conductors include materials such as silver, copper, and gold.

READING CHECK **Explain** Describe why current flows through a circuit, and explain why some materials allow charges to flow more easily than others.

....

....

....

....

Conductors and Insulators of Charge

Figure 6 Conductors and insulators of charge are all around you. Label each of these common items as a conductor or an insulator.

SEP Construct Explanations Which of the materials used to make these objects would you use in a circuit? Explain why.

....

....

....

....

Investigate Use a device to detect electric charges.

Static Electricity

Recall that most objects are made of atoms in which the number of protons is equal to the number of electrons. As a result, these atoms are neutral. By the law of conservation of charge, charge cannot be created or destroyed, but it can be transferred. The transfer of charge happens by moving electrons from one object to another or from one part of an object to another. When charges build up on an object, they do not flow like current. Instead, they remain static, meaning they stay in place. This buildup of charge on an object is called **static electricity**.

Charging by Induction

Figure 7 If your finger has a build-up of charge, it may induce a charge in a doorknob. Electrons in the doorknob move away from your finger to the opposite side of the doorknob.

Methods of Charging

Objects can become charged by four methods: conduction, friction, induction, and polarization. Charging by conduction is simply the movement of charge by direct contact between objects. The object that is more negatively charged transfers electrons to the other object. Charging by friction occurs when two objects rub against each other and electrons move from one object to the other. Objects become charged by induction without even touching. The electric field of one charged object repels the electrons of the other object. So the second object ends up with a buildup of charge on its opposite side, as in **Figure 7**. Polarization is similar except the electrons only move to the opposite side of their atoms rather than to the opposite side of the entire object. See if you can identify the methods of charging in **Figure 8**.

Interactions with Static Electricity

Figure 8 Label the method of charging in each image as conduction, friction, induction, or polarization.

The broom becomes charged as it sweeps across the floor.

Bits of paper are attracted to the broom's negative charge. In the paper, electrons of the atoms move to the opposite side of each atom, away from the broom.

Balloon and Paper

Figure 9 CCC Energy and Matter  The balloon attracts the paper because of static electricity. Draw the charges on the balloon and on the bits of paper. Then, describe what happens to potential energy as you pull the bits of paper off of the balloon.

VIDEO

Watch and learn how lightning works.

INTERACTIVITY

Develop a model to show the potential energy of a system involving electric forces.

Reflect Describe a time when you experienced a shock from static electricity. Explain what happened in terms of electric charges.

Potential Energy and Static Electricity If you rub a balloon, you might be surprised that it can pick up bits of paper. The balloon attracts the paper because of static electricity. Rubbing the balloon causes electrons to transfer to it. The charged balloon polarizes the bits of paper. Because the surface of the balloon is negatively charged and the surface of the paper is positively charged, they attract each other as in **Figure 9**. As the bits of paper move toward the balloon, the potential energy between the balloon and paper decreases. When you pull the bits of paper off of the balloon, you apply a force to them. The potential energy between the balloon and the paper increases the further you move them apart.

Static Discharge Most objects that become charged eventually lose their charge to the air. Charge transfers to or from the air until the charged object is neutral. The process of discharging can sometimes cause a spark or shock when the electrons transfer. If you have ever reached to pet a cat and experienced a shock, it was the result of static discharge.

Lightning is also the result of static discharge. Water droplets in the clouds become charged due to all of the motion within the air during a storm. Electrons then move from areas of negative charge to areas of positive charge. The movement of charge produces the intense spark that we see as a lightning bolt.

READING CHECK **Describe** What happens to charges during static discharge?

LESSON 1 Check

MS-PS2-5, MS-PS3-2

1. **Describe** Why are conductors better than insulators for the flow of electric current?

2. **Explain** A proton is placed next to an negatively charged object. In which direction would the proton move? Explain why.

3. **CCC Cause and Effect** If you move two objects with opposite charges apart, what happens to the potential energy between them? Explain your response.

4. **SEP Develop Models** After Sandra combs her hair, she notices that her hair moves toward the comb. Draw a model of the comb and Sandra's hair. Show the charges on both the comb and the hair. Describe the types of charges that you think occurred to charge the comb and then to charge the hair.

Quest CHECK-IN

In this lesson, you learned about the interactions of electric charges through forces and fields. You also discovered how potential energy plays a role in the flow of current. Additionally, you explored how charges behave in static electricity.

SEP Design Solutions How might electric fields become involved in your levitation device?

INTERACTIVITY

Apply Electrical Forces

Go online to explore how the interaction between charged particles could be used to develop a design for a levitation device.

MS-PS2-5, MS-PS3-2

Bumblebees and Electric Flowers

Most people assume that bumblebees are attracted to certain flowers only because of their colors and scents. As it turns out, there's more to it!

Bumblebees also respond to flowers' electric fields! While the bee has a positive electric charge, the flower and its pollen usually have a negative charge. The opposite charges make the pollen cling to the bee's body.

Scientists believe that bumblebees can use the strength of a flower's electric field to tell how much pollen is there. If they can sense that the field has changed and another bee has already taken all the pollen, then they will move to another flower. Given the number of flowers a bee visits, this information would be really useful!

Bumblebees may use this electric sense for many things, such as recognizing landmarks or identifying which bees have been in a garden before them. Although the bumblebee population is declining, perhaps scientists can find a way to use the bees' electric sense to help save them.

MY DISCOVERY

With a classmate, come up with some questions you have about the relationship between bees and flowers. How might this information be helpful in restoring the bumblebee population? What sources might you investigate to find answers?

LESSON

2 Magnetic Force

Guiding Questions

- How can you change the magnetic force and potential energy between objects?
- How can you detect and describe a magnetic field?

Connection

Literacy Verify

MS-PS2-5, MS-PS3-2

HANDS-ON LAB

uInvestigate Discover how you can use a magnet to tell the difference between real and fake coins.

Vocabulary

magnet
magnetism
magnetic force
magnetic pole
magnetic field

Academic Vocabulary

interaction

Connect It!

Magnetic field lines are drawings that represent the invisible force around a magnet. Trace one of the magnetic field lines on this page.

Translate Information How can you describe the shape of Earth's magnetic field?

SEP Use Models What does the model show about Earth's magnetic field?

SEP Define Problems What is a limitation of this two-dimensional model?

Magnetic Force and Energy

You may use magnets to display notes or pictures on the door of the refrigerator. A **magnet** attracts iron and materials that contain iron. Magnets can be any size, from the ones you use in the kitchen to the entire Earth and beyond. People can use magnetic compasses in navigation because the whole planet acts as a magnet (**Figure 1**).

Magnets attract iron and some other materials—usually metals. They attract or repel other magnets. This attraction or repulsion is called **magnetism**. The **interaction** between a magnet and a substance containing iron is always an attraction. Magnets themselves can either attract or repel one another, depending on how they are placed.

Magnetism can be a permanent or temporary property of a material. Some materials, containing iron or certain other metals, can become permanent magnets after interacting with other magnets. On the other hand, temporary magnetism can occur in different ways. An iron or steel object that is touching a magnet can become a magnet itself as long as the contact exists. For example, you can make a chain of paper clips that hangs from a permanent magnet. Another type of temporary magnet is created when an electric current flows through a conductor. This kind of magnet exists as long as the current is flowing.

Academic Vocabulary

The term *interaction* comes from words meaning *action* and *between two* things. Describe an interaction that you had today.

....

....

....

Magnetic Force

Figure 1 Lines and arrows show the direction of the magnetic field around Earth.

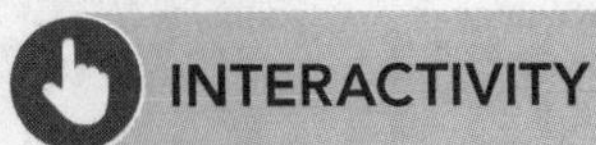

Examine magnetic objects and their fields.

Magnetic Force Magnetism is caused by a force that can act at a distance. This **magnetic force** is a push or pull that occurs when a magnet interacts with another object. Some large magnets can attract objects from many meters away and are powerful enough to lift a car or truck.

How do you know if the magnetic force between two objects will be a push or a pull? A magnet always exerts a pull on a magnetic object that is not itself a magnet. If you place the ends of the horseshoe magnet in **Figure 2** near a pile of paper clips, the paper clips always move toward the magnet. They never move away. Every magnet has two ends, called **magnetic poles**, where the magnetic force is strongest. One pole is known as the north pole and the other is known as the south pole.

The arrangement of magnets determines which type of force exists between them. If you bring two magnets together so that *like* poles—either both north or both south—are near one another, the magnets repel. If you bring the magnets together so that opposite poles are close to one another, the magnets attract. **Figure 2** shows two ways in which bar magnets can interact.

Push or Pull
Figure 2 SEP Develop Models ✏ Magnets can either push or pull. Draw arrows on the paperclips and on the bar magnets to show the direction of the magnetic force.

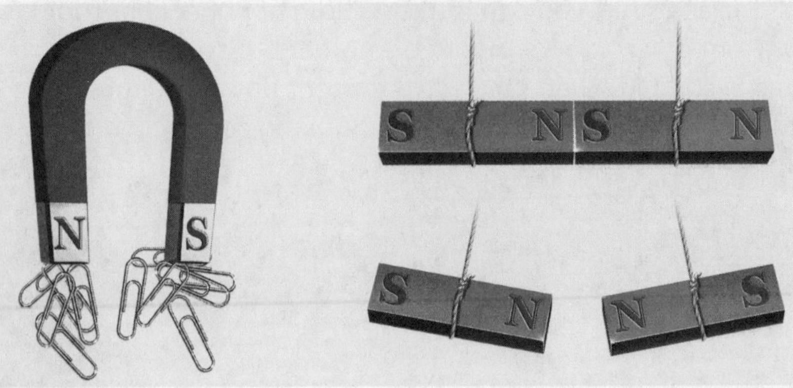

Magnets and Potential Energy Recall the ways in which the potential energy of a system of electrical charges can change. As you apply a force to move opposite charges away from each other, the electric potential energy of the system increases. The same is true of magnets. Opposite poles naturally attract each other, so you must put energy into the system to pull them apart. As you apply a force to separate the two opposite poles, the potential energy of the system increases. When the magnetic force between opposite poles pulls them together the potential energy of the system decreases. On the other hand, like poles repel each other. To push them together, you have to transfer energy to the system. This increases the potential energy of the system. Use the **Figure 3** activity to summarize these changes in potential energy.

HANDS-ON LAB

Investigate Discover how you can use a magnet to tell the difference between real and fake coins.

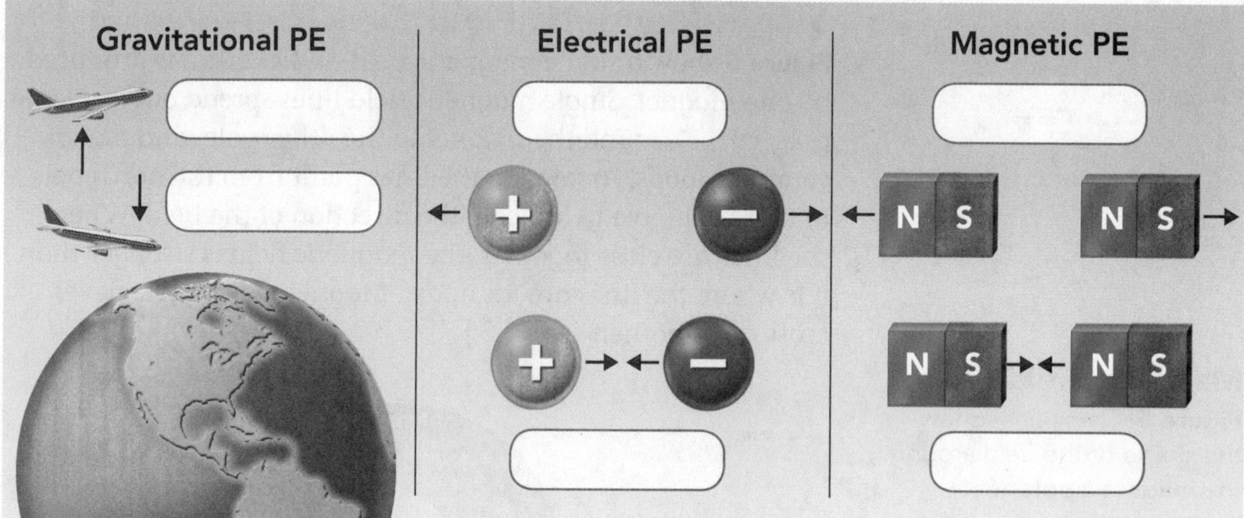

Magnetic Fields

The magnetic force is strongest at a magnet's poles. That is why the paper clips tend to stick to the horseshoe magnet at its ends. There is an area of magnetic force that surrounds a magnet. This area of force is the **magnetic field** of the magnet. This field is the source of magnetic energy. It allows magnets to attract objects at a distance. The magnetic field extends from one pole to the other pole of the magnet. You cannot see a magnetic field, but if you place tiny pieces of iron near a magnet, they will arrange themselves along the magnetic field. Their arrangement looks a lot like lines, so illustrations of magnetic fields are drawn with lines, as shown in **Figure 4**.

Objects containing iron, such as steel paper clips, experience a force when they are in a magnetic field. These objects line up with the field around them. Particles inside the objects can also line up with the field. When the particles in an object line up with the field, the object becomes a temporary magnet.

Potential Energy

Figure 3 The gravitational force between the plane and Earth is an attractive force. The forces between opposite charges and opposite magnetic poles are also attractive. Label the locations of increasing and decreasing potential energy in the images.

Visualizing Magnetic Fields

Figure 4 The magnetic field around a bar magnet causes iron filings to form the arrangement shown. This arrangement can also be represented by magnetic field lines. The field is strongest where the lines are closest together.

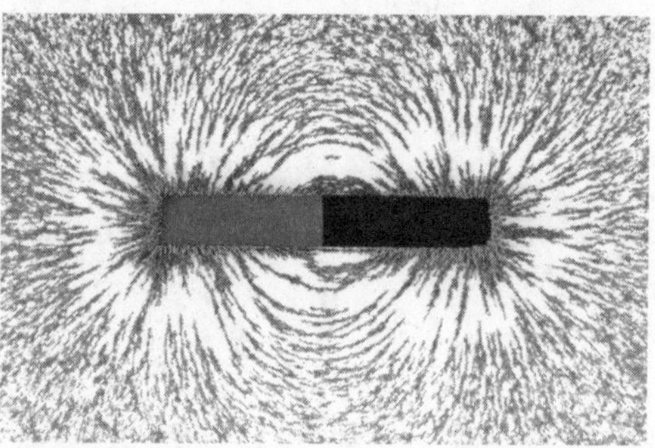

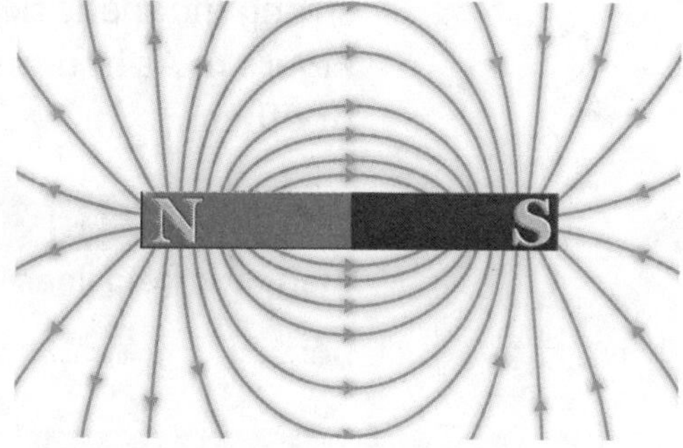

Single Magnetic Field The lines in **Figure 4** and **Figure 5** show a single magnetic field—a field that is produced by one magnet. Single magnetic field lines spread out from one pole, curve around the magnet to the other pole, and make complete loops. Arrows on the lines point from the north pole to the south pole to indicate the direction of the field. When the lines are close together, the magnetic field is stronger than it is where the lines are far apart. Magnetic field lines never cross one another.

Magnetic Field Lines

Figure 5 These lines show the shape of the field around the magnetic poles of a horseshoe magnet.

1. Claim Add labels to the illustration to show where the magnetic field is strongest and where it is weakest.

2. Evidence What is the relationship between distance from the magnet and the strength of its magnetic field?

....

....

....

3. Reasoning Could you pick up a nail using the curved part of the horseshoe magnet farthest from the poles? Explain your answer.

....

....

....

....

....

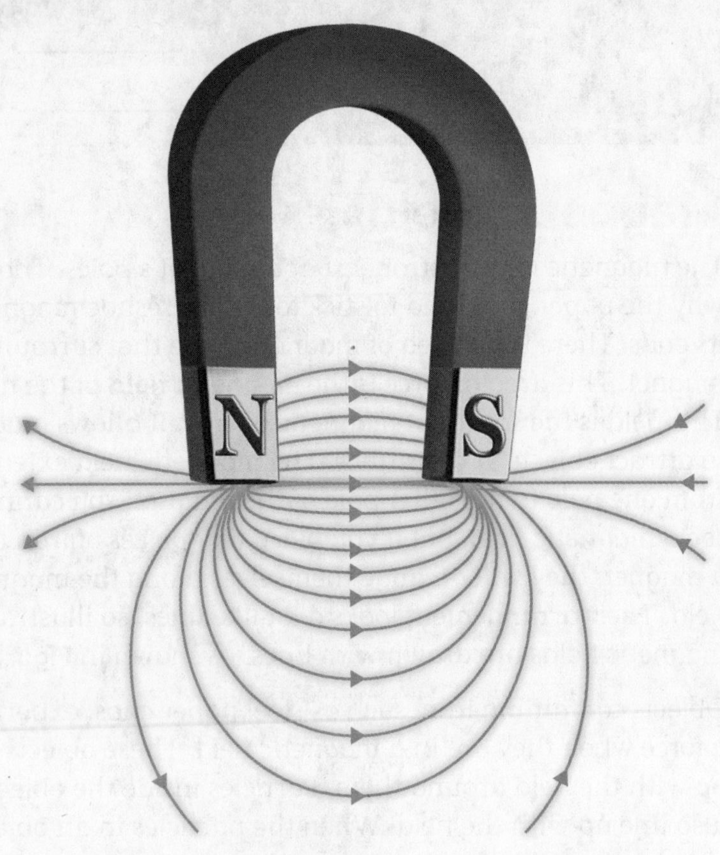

Combined Magnetic Field The magnetic fields of two magnets placed near each other will interact with one another. When two like poles are close together, the poles and the magnetic fields around them repel one another. When two opposite poles are close together, the fields combine to form a strong magnetic field between the two magnets, as shown in **Figure 6**. As in a single magnetic field, the lines never cross one another.

READING CHECK **Identify** What does the distance between magnetic field lines indicate?

....

....

Combined Magnetic Field Lines

Figure 6 The image on the left shows the combined magnetic field when opposite poles of bar magnets face each other.

SEP Develop Models What would the magnetic field look like if like poles faced each other?

Draw a model of the magnetic field lines in the image on the right.

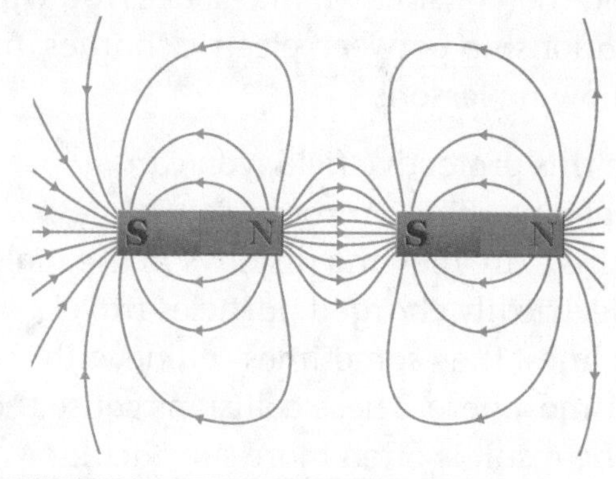

Earth's Magnetic Field Earth itself acts as a very large magnet. Materials in the core of the planet generate a magnetic field that surrounds the planet. This magnetic field is very similar to the field that surrounds a bar magnet. The magnetic poles of Earth are located near the geographic poles. These are the points where the magnetic field is strongest. The magnetic field lines pass out of the core and through the rocky mantle. They also loop through the space surrounding Earth. The magnetic field is three-dimensional and it is shaped like a donut, as shown in **Figure 7**.

VIDEO

See how magnetic fields interact.

People have used this magnetic field for many centuries for navigation. A compass, shown in **Figure 7**, is a magnetized needle that can turn easily. The needle interacts with Earth's magnetic field. One end is attracted to the north magnetic pole and the other end to the south magnetic pole. People can use a compass to determine the direction in which they are traveling.

Compass

Figure 7 Sailors and hikers use a compass to determine direction. The needle always points toward the geographic north pole. This is the pole that we call the North Pole, but because it is actually a south magnetic pole, the magnetic field lines point toward it.

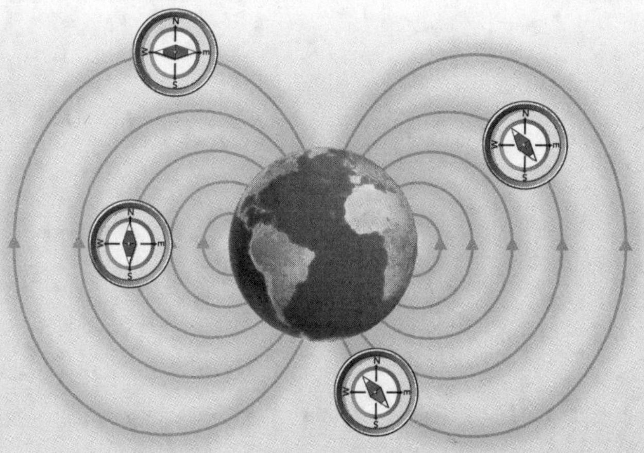

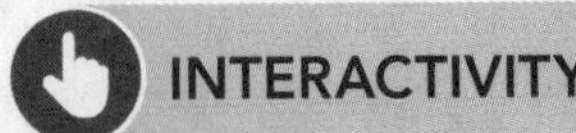

INTERACTIVITY

Explore magnetic forces and potential energy using models.

Literacy Connection

Verify Use a reliable Internet source to verify that Earth's magnetic field is caused by substances inside the planet. Which source did you use? How do you know that it's reliable?

....

....

....

....

Protecting Life on Earth There is a constant stream of particles that flows from the sun toward Earth. This stream is known as the solar wind. These particles have electric charges and they have a lot of energy as they move very rapidly through space. If they were to reach the surface of Earth, the particles in the stream could harm living things. Fortunately, Earth's magnetic field protects us. Electrically charged particles interact with magnetic forces. Earth's magnetic field changes the motion of the charged particles. They flow toward the north and south poles and then past Earth into space. You will learn more about the relationship between electric charges and magnetic fields in the following lessons.

Although you cannot see this protective field, you can sometimes see evidence of it working. Auroras, sometimes called the "Northern Lights," are glowing displays in the night sky. As these energetic electrically charged particles travel along the magnetic field lines, they sometimes collide with gas atoms in the upper atmosphere. These collisions cause the atoms to give off light. The result is often more spectacular than a fireworks show (**Figure 8**).

READING CHECK **Use Evidence** Describe how the Aurora Borealis is evidence that the Earth has a magnetic field.

....

....

....

Aurora Borealis

Figure 8 Auroras form when Earth's magnetic field pushes charged particles toward the poles. The high-energy particles interact with molecules in the atmosphere.

LESSON 2 Check

MS-PS2-5, MS-PS3-2

1. **Identify** How can you identify the magnetic north pole of an unlabeled magnet by using a labeled magnet?

2. **CCC Patterns** How would increasing the magnetic force of a magnet change the pattern of magnetic field lines between its poles?

3. **Apply Concepts** Explain how potential energy changes when you pull a magnet off a refrigerator door.

4. **SEP Construct Explanations** Why is the electrical charge on particles in the solar wind an important element of the protection that Earth's magnetic field provides?

5. **SEP Develop Models** Draw the magnetic field lines around a nail which has its head as its north pole and its point as its south pole.

Quest CHECK-IN

In this lesson, you discovered magnetic fields and how to draw the lines that represent them. You also learned how potential energy changes when a magnet is present.

SEP Design Solutions Describe how you could orient two magnets so that they repel each other. How might this apply to your levitation device?

HANDS-ON LAB

Tracking Levitation

Go online to download the lab worksheet. You will consider how a stable train and section of track can be built using permanent magnets.

LESSON 3

Electromagnetic Force

Guiding Questions

- How does electricity relate to magnetism?
- How can you describe the magnetic field produced by a current?
- What are the properties of solenoids and electromagnets?

Connections

Literacy Cite Textual Evidence

Math Draw Comparative Inferences

MS-PS2-3

HANDS-ON LAB

uInvestigate Explore the relationship between electricity and magnetism.

Vocabulary

electromagnetism
solenoid
electromagnet

Academic Vocabulary

produce

Connect It!

Circle the magnet in the photo.

SEP Interpret Data How do you know that the object picking up the metal beams is a magnet?

....

....

SEP Construct Explanations What material do you think makes up this magnet?

....

Electromagnetic Principles

Have a look at **Figure 1**. How is this crane's magnet strong enough to lift these heavy metal beams? The answer may surprise you. The magnetic field of this crane is actually generated by an electric current! The relationship between electricity and magnetism is called **electromagnetism**.

Electromagnetism was first discovered by a scientist named Hans Christian Ørsted. During a class he was teaching, he brought a compass near a wire that had an electric current running through it. He noticed that the compass needle changed direction when it was near the wire. He placed several different compasses near a wire and found out that the compass needles changed direction when a current passed through the wire. The compass needles did not change direction when no current flowed. Ørsted concluded that an electric current produces a magnetic field, so electricity and magnetism are related.

Literacy Connection

Cite Textual Evidence What evidence did Ørsted use to conclude that an electric current produces a magnetic field?

....

....

....

....

....

Write About It In your science notebook, describe a time that you drew a new conclusion from your observations.

Magnetic Strength

Figure 1 A regular magnet is not strong enough to pick up these heavy beams. This special type of magnet, called an electromagnet, has the strength to do it.

Magnetism from Electricity

Figure 2 Predict Phenomena This figure shows how the direction of a current in a straight wire affects the magnetic field that forms. In the image on the left, the current flows upward. Draw your predicted magnetic field lines in the image on the right, in which the current flows downward.

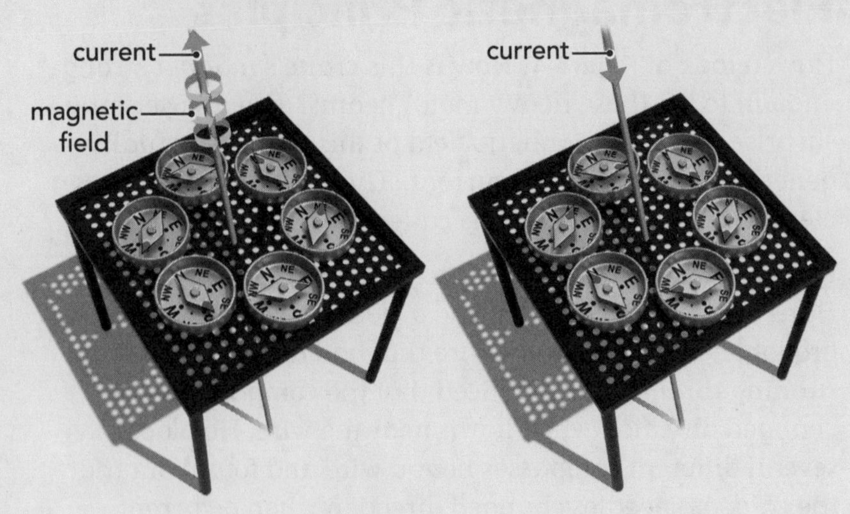

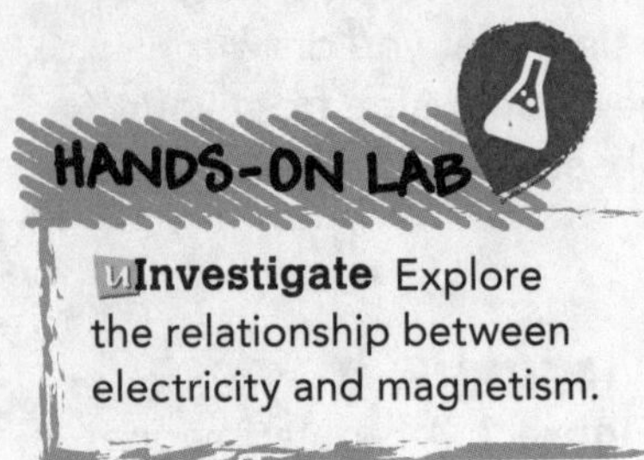

Magnetic Fields and Current

When you examine **Figure 2**, you can see that the magnetic field produced by a current has a certain direction. This field also has a certain strength. How can the field change? It can change in direction and strength, and it can be turned off or on. To turn the magnetic field off or on, simply turn the current off or on.

Magnetic Fields Around Straight Wires In a straight wire, the field's direction depends on the direction of the current. How do you determine the direction of a magnetic field based on the direction of current through a straight wire? You can use what is known as the right-hand rule, as shown in **Figure 3**.

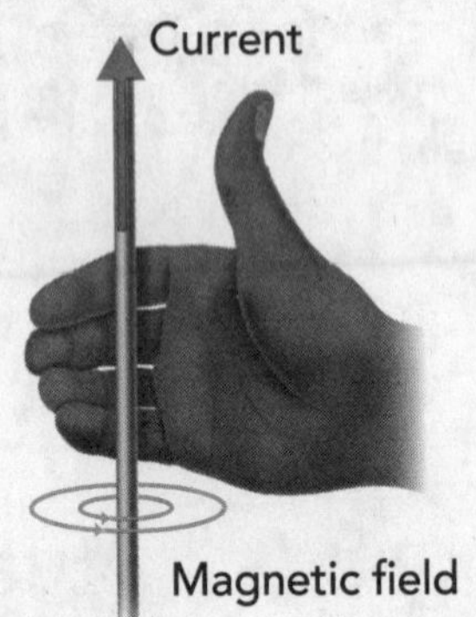

The Right-Hand Rule

Figure 3 Imagine that you are holding the wire in your right hand with your thumb pointing in the direction the current flows. The direction of the magnetic field is the same as the direction that your fingers curl.

To change the strength of a magnetic field around a current-carrying straight wire, change the amount of current running through the wire. If current is increased, the magnetic field becomes stronger. If the current is decreased, the strength of the magnetic field decreases.

READING CHECK **Determine Central Ideas** How do electric currents relate to magnetic fields?

....

....

Magnetic Fields Around Wire Loops

Suppose you have a loop of wire rather than a straight wire. The magnetic field formed around the loop of wire is in many ways like the field formed when a current flows through a straight wire. The direction of the field depends on the direction of the current and can be determined by using the right-hand rule. The field can be turned off or on by turning the current off or on. The strength of the field depends on the strength of the current.

There is one main difference, however, when a current flows through a loop of wire. Look at **Figure 4**, which shows a current flowing through a loop of wire and the magnetic field it produces. Shaping a wire into a loop can increase the strength of the magnetic field within the loop.

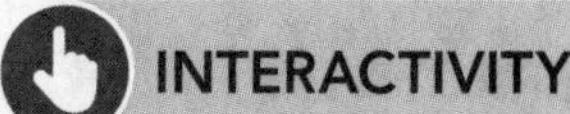

Predict the direction of magnetic field lines around a current-carrying wire.

READING CHECK **Cause and Effect** You have a straight wire with a current running through it. What effect will looping the wire have on the magnetic field?

....

Model It!

Magnetic Field Strength

Figure 4 The overhead view of a magnetic field formed by a current flowing through a single wire is shown. The magnetic field lines are closest together in the center of the loop, where the magnetic field is stronger. The number of loops in a wire can control the strength of a magnetic field.

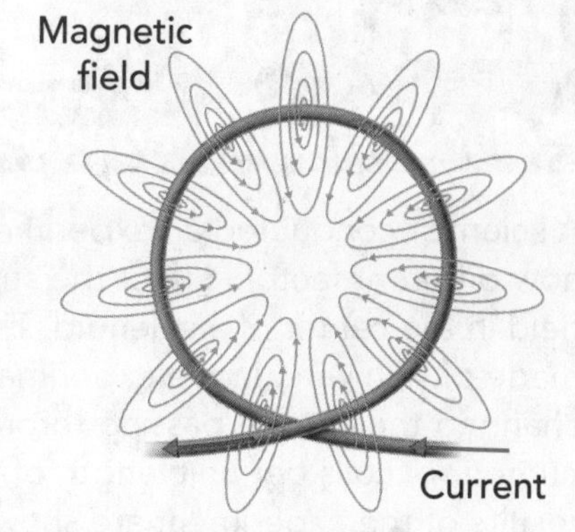

1. SEP Develop Models Draw the magnetic field lines around the two stacked loops of wire.

2. SEP Use Models Is the strength of the magnetic field inside the loop greater or less than the strength when there was just one loop of wire? Justify your answer.

....

....

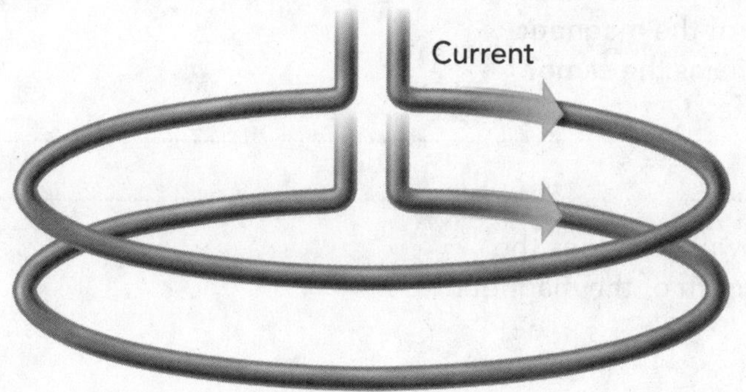

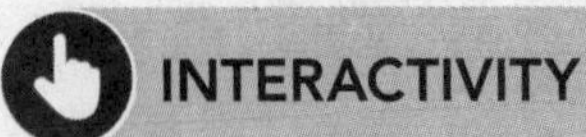

INTERACTIVITY

Design and build a virtual electromagnet that can pick up objects.

Solenoids and Electromagnets

There are many practical uses of coiling a current-carrying wire to make a strong magnetic field. Two devices that strengthen a magnetic field by running a current through coiled wire are solenoids and electromagnets. A **solenoid** is a coil of wire with a current running through it, as shown in **Figure 5**. It is similar to stacked loops of wire. In a solenoid, the magnetic field is strengthened in the center of the coil when a current runs through the coil. One end of a solenoid acts like the north pole of a magnet, and the other end acts like the south pole.

Solenoids

Figure 5 The image shows the magnetic field lines around a solenoid.

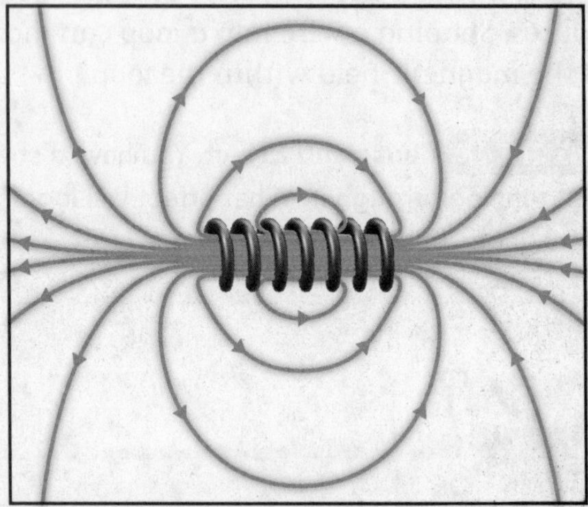

Reason Abstractly The diagram shows that field lines spread out as you move away from the magnet. Do the spreading lines show that the magnetic force gets stronger or gets weaker with increasing distance?

....

Math Toolbox

Solenoids and Magnetic Fields

A scientist conducted an experiment to investigate how different factors affect the strength of a magnetic field in the center of a solenoid. The solenoid was made of iron wire. In the experiment, the scientist changed the current passing through the wire and the number of coils per unit length of the solenoid. The results of the experiment are shown in the table. Tesla is the SI unit for the strength of a magnetic field.

Number of Coils per meter	Current (amps)	Magnetic Field Strength (Tesla)
100	1	20,000
200	1	40,000
100	2	40,000
200	2	80,000

1. **Draw Comparative Inferences** From the data shown, how does the current affect the strength of the magnetic field, if the number of coils per meter remains the same?

....

....

2. **SEP Interpret Data** From the data shown, how does the number of coils per meter affect the strength of the magnetic field, if current is constant?

....

....

Field Strength and Solenoids You can increase the strength of the magnetic field inside a solenoid by increasing the number of coils or loops of wire. Winding the coils closer together also produces a stronger magnetic field. As in a straight wire, increasing the current through the solenoid wire will also increase the magnetic field.

INTERACTIVITY

Apply your knowledge of electromagnets and factors that affect electromagnetic force.

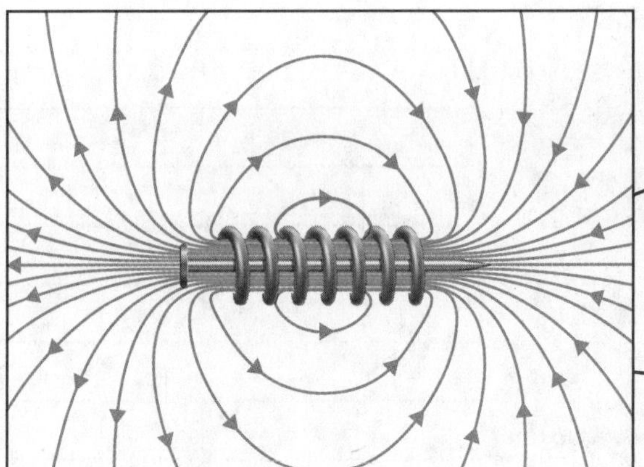

Electromagnets

Figure 6 A solenoid with a nail in the core is a simple electromagnet. More advanced electromagnets have many practical uses.

Some doors are locked with electromagnets and can only be unlocked electronically.

Electromagnets are used both to lift this train off the track and to propel it forward.

An electromagnet helps to produce the vibrations in these earphones. These vibrations carry sound to your ears.

Electromagnets What else can you do to a solenoid to make the magnetic field even stronger? You add a ferromagnetic material to it. A ferromagnetic material is a substance that becomes a magnet when exposed to a magnetic field. The elements iron, nickel and cobalt are ferromagnetic. As shown in **Figure 6**, a solenoid with a ferromagnetic core is called an **electromagnet**. When a ferromagnetic material is placed within a solenoid, both the current and the magnetized material **produce** a magnetic field. This combination produces a magnetic field that is stronger than that produced by the solenoid alone. As in a solenoid, the magnetic field of an electromagnet increases when the number of coils , the closeness of the coils, or the current increases.

Think back to the electromagnet you saw in **Figure 1**. How might you get the electromagnet to drop the metal beams? Just as with other magnetic fields caused by currents, you turn off the current. The magnetic field no longer exists, and the beams drop. Some other uses for electromagnets are shown in **Figure 6**.

Academic Vocabulary

The term *produce* has several meanings. What does it mean in the text on this page?

READING CHECK **Summarize** What is the structural difference between a solenoid and an electromagnet?

LESSON 3 Check

MS-PS2-3

1. **Explain** What did Ørsted discover about electricity and magnetism?

2. **CCC Cause and Effect** Suppose that an electric current flows in a straight wire. The current changes so that it flows in the opposite direction. What changes occur in the magnetic field, and what stays the same?

3. **SEP Develop Models** A straight wire has a current running through it. Draw the current-carrying wire and the magnetic field that it produces.

4. **Compare and Contrast** Compare and contrast a solenoid and an electromagnet. What do they have in common? How are they different?

5. **SEP Engage in Argument** An MRI machine uses an electromagnet to obtain scans of the human body. It uses these scans to generate images. What advantage is there in using an electromagnet instead of a solenoid in an MRI machine?

Quest CHECK-IN

In this lesson, you learned about electromagnetism and how electric currents generate magnetic fields. You also discovered how solenoids and electromagnets increase the strength of the magnetic fields.

SEP Evaluate Information How might you apply the principles of electromagnetism when building your levitating device?

HANDS-ON LAB

Building an Electromagnet

Go online to download the lab worksheet. Build an electromagnetic and determine how to control the strength of the electromagnetic force.

uEngineer It! Impact on Society STEM

MS-PS2-3

ELECTROMAGNETISM In Action

VIDEO

Explore examples of electromagnetism.

How can you combine electric and magnetic forces to play a game or accomplish a task? You engineer it!

The Challenge: To engineer devices that rely on elecromagnetic force.

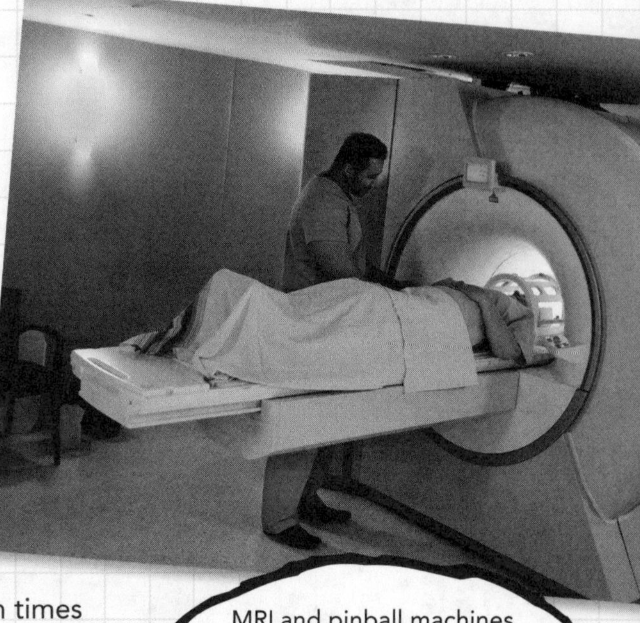

Phenomenon People have known for centuries that electricity sparks and that magnets attract. The magnetic compass, for example, has been around since at least the 13th century, and possibly a great deal longer. But it was only in modern times that scientists and engineers began to understand that electricity and magnetism could affect each other.

MRI and pinball machines are just two examples of the many devices that use electromagnets!

Electromagnets differ from ordinary magnets because they only attract or repel when an electric current runs through them. An engineer can control an electromagnet, making it useful in industrial applications.

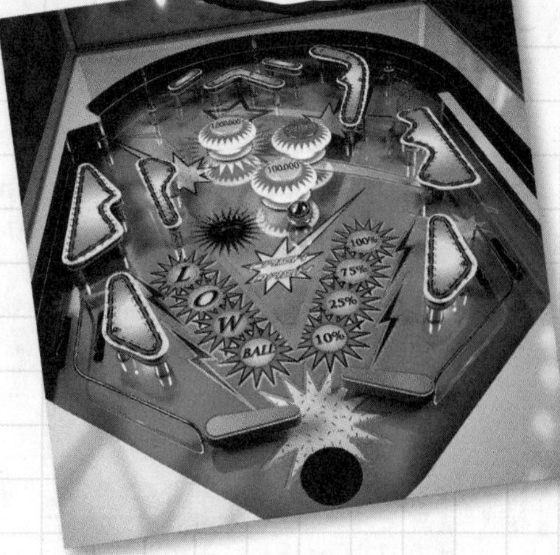

Electromagnetics govern a wide variety of devices and games, from a simple pinball machine to the Large Hadron Collider, an underground experimental facility that physicists are using to study particles. Hospitals use electromagnetics in procedures such as Magnetic Resonance Imaging (MRI). The music industry has found many uses for electromagnets—in speakers, headphones, complex percussion instruments, and recording equipment. Transportation is another field that makes extensive use of electromagnetic technology. The high-speed maglev trains use electromagnetic force to hover above the train tracks and whisk passengers to their destinations at speeds up to 600 kilometers per hour.

DESIGN CHALLENGE

What can you design and build with an electromagnet? Go to the Engineering Design Notebook to find out!

LESSON

4 Electric and Magnetic Interactions

Guiding Questions

- How do magnetic fields affect moving charges?
- How can current be produced in a conductor?
- How do generators and transformers work?

Connections

Literacy Draw Evidence

Math Understand Ratio Concepts

MS-PS2-3

HANDS-ON LAB

uInvestigate Discover the factors that affect the strength of electric and magnetic forces in a motor.

Vocabulary

galvanometer
electric motor
electromagnetic induction
generator
transformer

Academic Vocabulary

source

Connect It!

Circle the part of the image that shows that electrical energy has been transformed into mechanical energy.

SEP Construct Explanations Explain how you think the fan works.

....

....

....

Identify List two other examples in which electrical energy transforms into mechanical energy.

....

....

Magnetic Force on Moving Charges

If a charged particle is at rest in a magnetic field, it is not affected by the field. But if the charged particle moves, it experiences a magnetic force. Why does this happen?

Recall that electric current is charged particles in motion. Suppose you have a wire with a current flowing through it, and you place it at rest in a magnetic field between two magnets. In this situation, there are two magnetic fields at play. The first field is caused by the magnets. The second field is caused by the current flowing through the wire. The magnetic field of the magnets interacts with the magnetic field around the wire. This interaction results in a force on the wire and causes the wire to move in the same direction as the force. The resulting force on the wire is perpendicular to the magnetic field, as given by another right-hand rule. This right-hand rule explains the direction a current-carrying wire moves in a magnetic field, as shown in **Figure 1**.

How does the fan in **Figure 2** work? Inside the fan is an electric motor. The motor uses interactions between magnetic fields around loops of wire and magnetic fields between magnets. To understand how the motor works, take a look at how a current-carrying loop of wire is affected by a magnetic field.

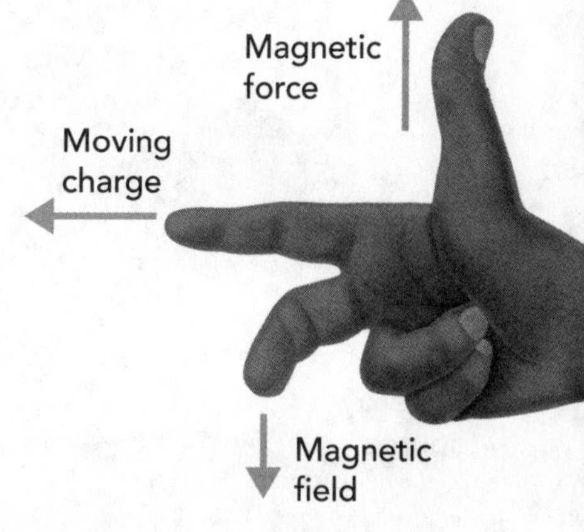

Right-Hand Rule #2

Figure 1 Point your index finger in the direction of the current, and bend your middle finger so that it points in the direction of the magnetic field. Your thumb points in the direction of the magnetic force on the moving charges.

Transforming into Mechanical Energy

Figure 2 The blades of this fan start moving when current flows into the fan.

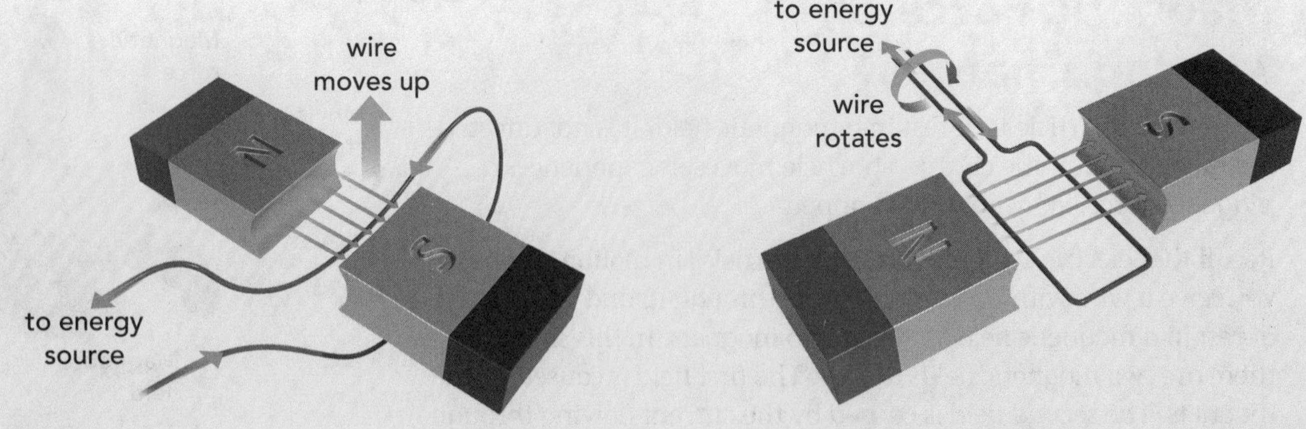

Current in a Magnetic Field

Figure 3 A straight wire moves in one direction in a magnetic field. A loop of wire rotates.

Loop of Current in a Magnetic Field

If a straight wire with a current through it moves in the direction of the force on it, what happens when that wire forms a loop? Compare the two situations in **Figure 3**. When a single wire of current is placed in a magnetic field, it moves in one direction. But when a loop of current is placed in that same field, it rotates. In the loop, the current flows in one direction on one side of the loop. On the other side of the loop, the current flows in the opposite direction. As a result, the magnetic force on one side of the loop points up, and on the other side, the force points down. Because of the directions of these forces, the loop does not rotate in a complete circle. It rotates only half a turn, moving from horizontal to vertical.

INTERACTIVITY

Design and build a virtual motor for a model airplane.

Galvanometers

This type of rotation is the basis of a **galvanometer**, which is a device that measures small currents. Showing how much current is flowing has many uses, such as in fuel gauges or even lie detectors. **Figure 4** shows a galvanometer. In this device, an electromagnet is suspended between two permanent magnets and is attached to the needle of the galvanometer. Recall that one way the strength of an electromagnet is determined is by the amount of current supplied to it. In a galvanometer, the current supplied to the electromagnet is the current that is being measured. If the current is extremely small, the force created is also small, and the needle rotates only a small amount. For a larger current, the force is greater, and the needle moves more.

Galvanometer

Figure 4 An electromagnet in the galvanometer turns the pointer to indicate the amount of current present. Why does an electromagnet act like a loop of wire in a magnetic field?

....

....

....

Electric Motors

Recall the fan you saw in **Figure 1**, which contains a motor. An **electric motor** is a device that uses an electric current to turn an axle. In doing that, it transforms electrical energy into mechanical energy.

VIDEO

See what it's like to be an electrical engineer.

Examine **Figure 5** to learn the parts that make up an electric motor and how they work together to produce mechanical energy. Recall that a simple loop of wire in a magnetic field can only rotate half a turn because the current flows in only one direction. However, the brushes and the commutator enable the current that flows through the armature to change direction. Each time the commutator moves to a different brush, the current flows in the opposite direction. Thus, the side of the armature that just moved up will now move down, and the armature rotates continuously in one direction. Just picture the armature of a motor attached to an axle to which the blades of a fan are connected. Start the current, and feel the breeze!

Investigate Discover the factors that affect the strength of electric and magnetic forces in a motor.

READING CHECK **Determine Differences** What is the only part of a motor through which a current does not flow?

....

How a Motor Works

Figure 5 A motor is made of several basic parts, each of which is described below. Study the information about each part. Then, write the number of each description in the appropriate circle on the image.

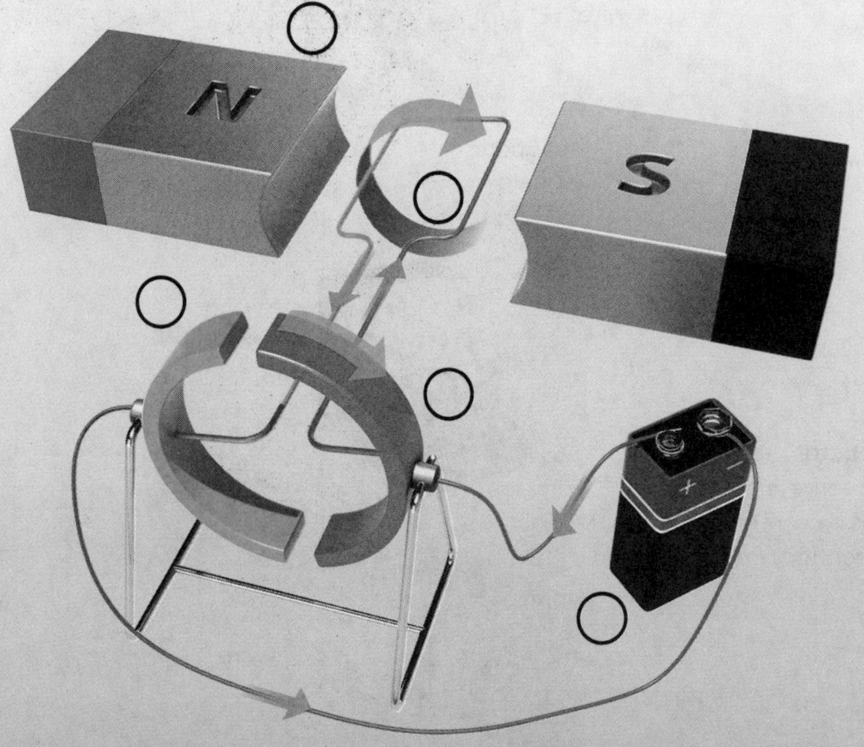

1. **Permanent magnets** produce a magnetic field. This causes the armature to turn.
2. The **commutator** consists of two semicircular pieces of metal. It conducts current from the brushes to the armature.
3. **Brushes,** which do not move, conduct current to the rest of the commutator.
4. The **armature** is a loop of wire that current flows through.
5. The **battery** is the energy source that supplies the current to the brushes.

VIDEO

Watch electromagnetic induction in action.

Literacy Connection

Draw Evidence Underline the sentence in the text which identifies the transformation of energy that occurs during electromagnetic induction.

Electromagnetic Induction

You've seen how a current flowing through a wire produces a magnetic field, and how electrical energy can be transformed into mechanical energy. In fact, the opposite is also possible. A magnetic field can be used to produce a current. If a conductor is moving through a magnetic field, a current is generated in the conductor. **Electromagnetic induction** is the process of generating an electric current from the motion of a conductor through a magnetic field. In this case, mechanical energy is transformed into electrical energy. The resulting current is called an induced current.

Induced Current and Moving Conductors By experimentation, scientists discovered that when a conductor is moved in a magnetic field, a current flows through the conductor. Current can be induced if the conductor is a straight wire, as shown in **Figure 6**. The same principle applies if the conductor is a coil of wire. Induced current is present any time that a conductor moves through a magnetic field.

Induction from a Moving Wire

Figure 6 When a conductor (such as a metal wire) moves through a magnetic field, current will be induced in the conductor.

SEP Interpret Data

Examine the image. Then, use the term *clockwise* or *counterclockwise* to complete each sentence correctly.

When the conductor moves upward through the magnetic field, the induced current flows ________________.
When the conductor moves downward, the induced current is ____________________.

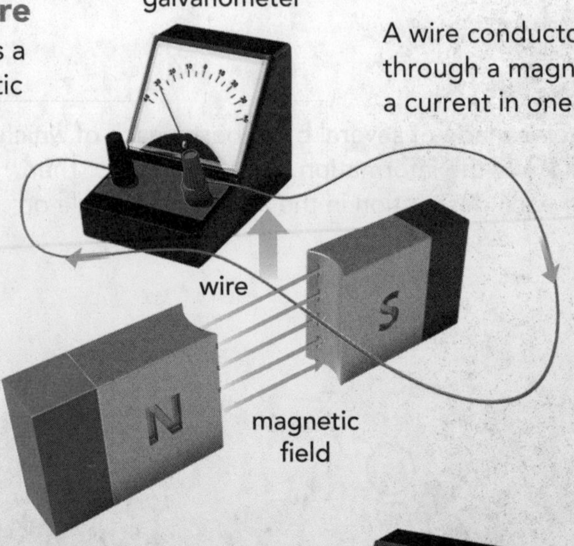

A wire conductor moving up through a magnetic field induces a current in one direction.

A wire conductor moving down through the same magnetic field induces a current in the opposite direction.

Induced Current and Moving Magnets As you have read, an electric current is induced when a conductor moves through a magnetic field. A current also is induced when a magnet moves through a loop of conductive wire. Examine **Figure 7**, which shows what happens when a magnet moves through a loop of wire.

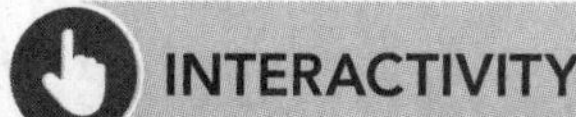

Predict the direction of a current through a wire near a moving magnet.

In summary, electric current is induced in a conductor whenever the magnetic field around the conductor is changing. When a conductor is in a magnetic field, a current is induced in the conductor whenever either the conductor or the magnetic field is moving.

READING CHECK **Integrate with Visuals** Based on Figure 6 and Figure 7, what are the two ways that a magnetic field can change, relative to a conductor?

....

....

....

Induction from a Moving Magnet

Figure 7 Current will be induced in a conductor in a magnetic field when the magnetic field moves in relation to the conductor.

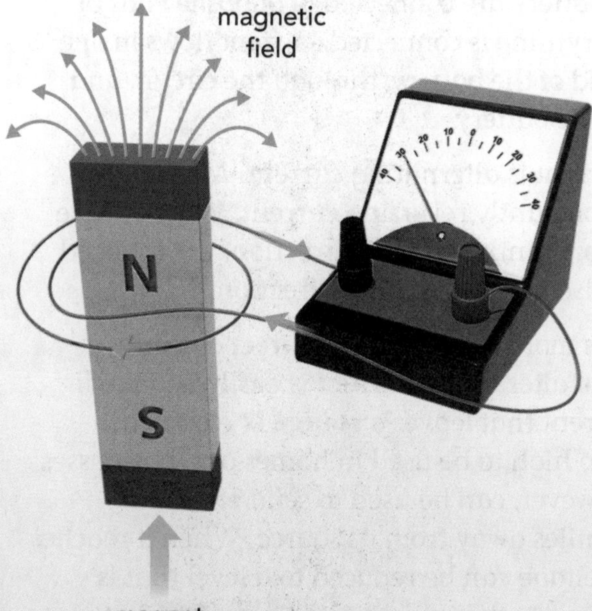

A magnetic field moving up through a wire conductor induces a current in one direction.

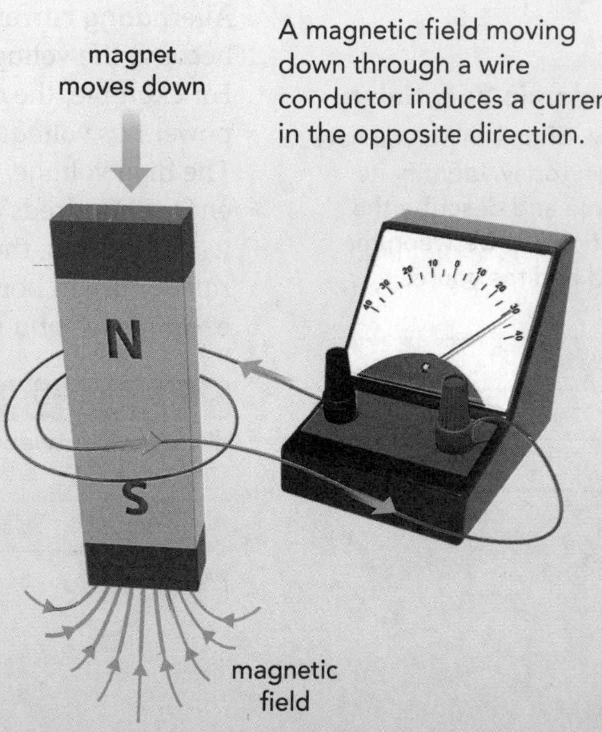

A magnetic field moving down through a wire conductor induces a current in the opposite direction.

Types of Current

Figure 8 It is not uncommon for one object to require both direct and alternating currents to operate.

SEP Ask Questions An electric car is one item that requires both AC and DC. Write a question about the use of AC and DC in the car.

....

....

....

Alternating and Direct Current You have probably noticed that not all electrical currents are alike. The type of current that comes from a battery is direct current. Direct current, or DC, has charges that flow in only one direction. Objects that run on batteries use direct current. In these objects, opposite ends of the battery are connected to opposite ends of the circuit. When everything is connected, current flows in one direction from one end of the battery, through the circuit, and into the other end of the battery.

The other type of current is alternating current. Alternating current, or AC, is a constantly reversing current. When a wire in a magnetic field constantly changes direction, the induced current it produces also keeps changing direction.

Alternating current is more common than direct current because the voltage of alternating current is easily changed. For example, the current that leaves a **source** of electrical power has voltage too high to be used in homes and businesses. The high voltage, however, can be used to send electrical energy hundreds of miles away from its source. When it reaches its destination, the voltage can be reduced to a level that is safe for use in homes and other places. Use **Figure 8** to further examine AC and DC.

Academic Vocabulary

Think of one thing you have eaten today. Identify its source and describe the relationship between the food and the source.

....

....

....

....

READING CHECK **Determine Central Ideas** What is the main difference between AC and DC?

....

....

Generators and Transformers

Two common and important devices that use induced current are generators and transformers. Generators and transformers are alike in that an electrical current leaves both of them. They differ in that generators produce electricity, and transformers change the voltage to make the electricity useful.

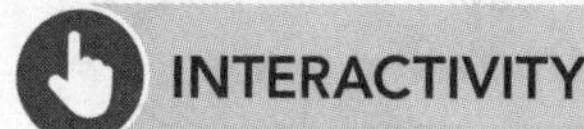

INTERACTIVITY

Construct a virtual generator that can charge a cell phone.

INTERACTIVITY

Explore how electricity and magnetism affect the motion of various materials.

How Generators Work

An electric **generator** transforms mechanical energy into an electric current. The movement of a conductor within a magnetic field produces a current. The essential parts of a generator are the armature, slip rings, magnets, brushes, and a crank. **Figure 9** shows what these parts are and how they all work together to produce an alternating electric current. The basic operation of a small home generator is the same as that of a large generator that provides current to many homes and businesses.

Although a generator contains some of the same parts as an electric motor, the two devices work in reverse. In an electric motor, an existing current produces a magnetic field, and electrical energy is transformed into mechanical energy. In a generator, the motion of a coil of wire through a magnetic field produces a current and mechanical energy is transformed into electrical energy.

How a Generator Works

Figure 9 A generator works when its component parts operate in the correct order. Number the part names in the correct order to show the operation of a generator from the magnets to the moment when the current is produced. Then, circle the names of the parts of the generator that you would also find in an electric motor.

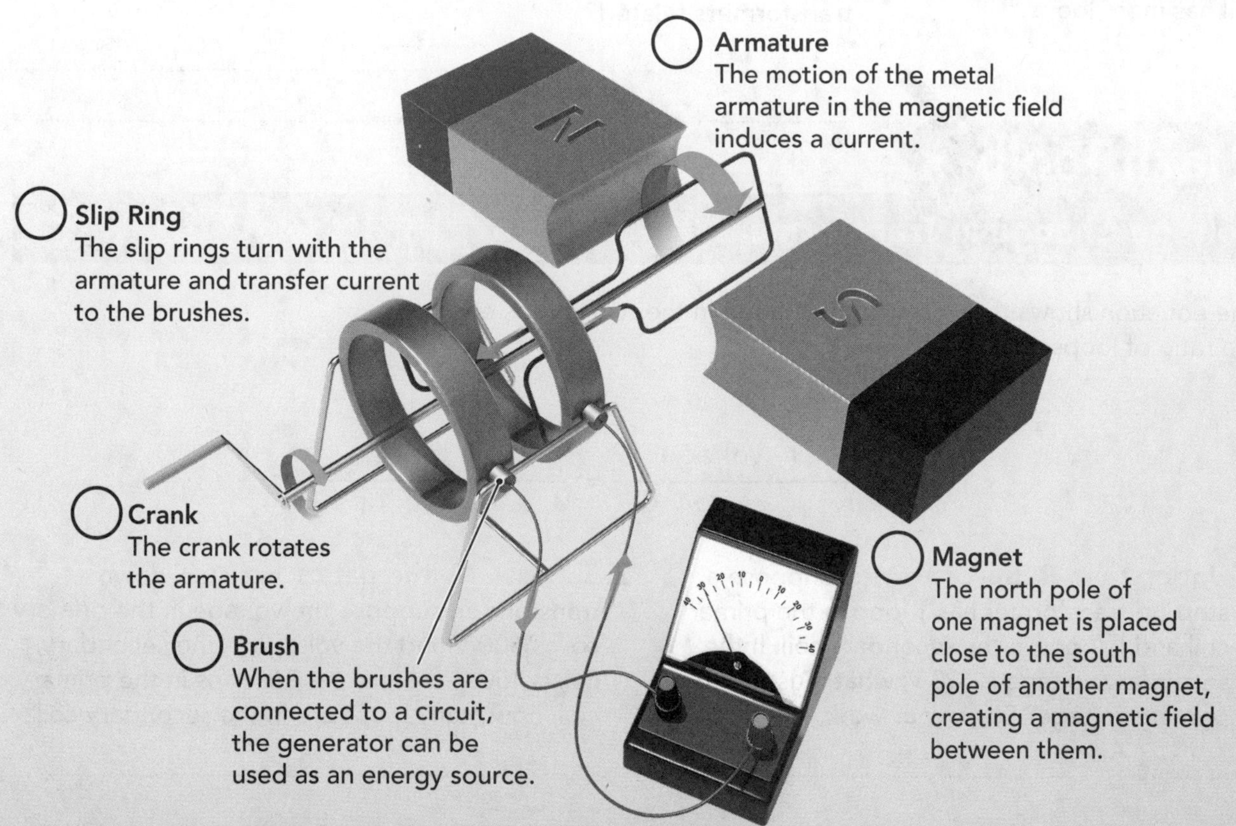

Armature
The motion of the metal armature in the magnetic field induces a current.
N
S
Slip Ring
The slip rings turn with the armature and transfer current to the brushes.
Crank
The crank rotates the armature.
Brush
When the brushes are connected to a circuit, the generator can be used as an energy source.
Magnet
The north pole of one magnet is placed close to the south pole of another magnet, creating a magnetic field between them.

Step-Up Transformer

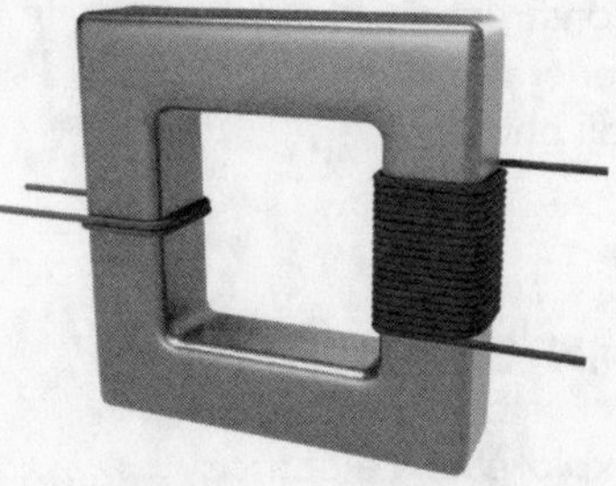

Step-Down Transformer

Types of Transformers

Figure 10 In step-up transformers, the primary coil has fewer loops than the secondary coil. In step-down transformers, the primary coil has more loops.

How Transformers Work You have probably heard the word *transformer* before. What does it mean when a transformer refers to electric current? This type of **transformer** is a device that increases or decreases voltage using two separate coils of insulated wire that are wrapped around an iron core.

The first coil that the current goes through is called the primary coil. This coil is connected to a circuit with a voltage source and alternating current. The other coil is called the secondary coil. It is connected to a circuit, but it does not have a voltage source. The coils share an iron core. Because the primary coil is connected to alternating current, the direction of the current constantly changes. As a result, the magnetic field around it also changes, and it induces a current in the secondary coil.

There are two types of transformers. As shown in **Figure 10**, the type depends on which coil has more loops. Step-up transformers, such as those used to help transmit electricity from generating plants, increase voltage. Step-down transformers, such as those used in phone chargers, decrease voltage. The phone charger plugs into an outlet and reduces the voltage to what is needed to charge a cell phone. The greater the difference between the number of loops in the primary and secondary coils in a transformer, the more the voltage will change.

READING CHECK **Summarize Text** How are generators and transformers related?

....

....

Math Toolbox

Voltage Change in Transformers

The equation shows that the ratio of voltage in the two coils is equal to the ratio of loops.

$$\frac{\text{primary voltage}}{\text{secondary voltage}} = \frac{\text{primary loops}}{\text{secondary loops}}$$

1. **Understand Ratio Concepts** Suppose a step-up transformer has 1 loop in the primary coil and 8 loops in the secondary coil. If the secondary voltage is 120 V, what must be the primary voltage? Show your work.

....

....

2. **SEP Use Mathematics** In a step-down transformer, suppose the voltage in the primary coil is 600 V and the voltage in the secondary coil is 150 V. If there are 36 loops in the primary coil, how many loops are in the secondary coil?

....

....

LESSON 4 Check

MS-PS2-3

1. **SEP Use Mathematics** What will be the primary voltage of a transformer if the secondary voltage is 60 V and there are 40 loops on the primary coil and 120 loops on the secondary coil? Show your work.

2. **Compare and Contrast** How are electric motors and generators similar? How are they different?

3. **SEP Construct Explanations** In many areas electricity is produced by big generators within dams. What function does large volumes of moving water have in generating electricity?

4. **SEP Develop Models** Suppose you build model airplanes. Use what you know from this lesson to draw a model of a device that would keep a propeller turning as the plane flew.

Quest CHECK-IN

In this lesson, you discovered how an electric charge in motion experiences a magnetic force in a magnetic field. You also learned how charges can be set in motion within a conductor by moving the conductor through a magnetic field. A moving magnetic field can also induce a current through a wire. Additionally, you discovered how motors, generators, and transformers work.

Apply Concepts How might a motor, generator, or transformer be used as part of your levitation device?

HANDS-ON LAB

Electrifying Levitation

Go online to download the lab worksheet. Test your levitation device and see how an optimal design can be achieved.

Case Study

MS-PS2-3

This is an artist's conception of the X-57 Maxwell, showing the electric motors on the extra-thin wings.

THE X-57 Maxwell

Airplanes fly people, mail, and cargo all over the world. Fossil fuels supply the power that planes need in order to fly. With the reserves of fossil fuels dropping, engineers and scientists continue to look for alternative sources of power for planes and other forms of transportation.

NASA's X-57 Maxwell, which is nearing the completion of a long development process, has proved that a battery-powered plane is a possibility. NASA engineers nicknamed the plane "Maxwell" in honor of Scottish physicist James Clerk Maxwell, whose discoveries in physics rank him right behind Einstein and Newton.

The X-57 won't just have electric motors instead of engines; it will have many design features that distinguish it from a traditional plane. The wings will be much smaller, which will reduce the plane's weight and wind resistance. The electric motors will weigh about half as much as traditional combustion engines, and there will be fourteen of them instead of one or two. Twelve of the motors will shut down once the plane is at cruising altitude. There will be special design elements to reduce drag while the plane is aloft.

There are disadvantages to the battery-propelled plane, however. Because the batteries are heavy, the plane won't be able to carry much weight, or many passengers. The plane would also fly more slowly than fuel-power planes, and have a flight distance of about 160 kilometers before its batteries would have to be recharged.

Still, a battery-propelled plane would have many advantages over one that is powered by fossil fuels. Generating the electricity to power the batteries could release less carbon dioxide, which is good news for the climate. Electric motors would also make far less noise than traditional combustion engines.

	X-57 Maxwell	Combustion-Engine Version of Same Plane
Aircraft Weight	1360 kg	819 kg
Cruising Speed	277 km/h	278 km/h
Takeoff Speed	109 km/h	65 km/h
Range	160 km	1240 km

Use the text and the data table to answer the following questions.

1. **Summarize** Describe the physical features that will make the X-57 Maxwell unique.

2. **Calculate** What fraction of the plane's full speed would be needed for the plane to get off the ground?

3. **Evaluate** What factor, aside from the reliance on a battery, do you think makes the range of the X-57 Maxwell shorter than the range of the combustion-engine version of the same plane?

4. **Apply Concepts** Suppose that the technology pioneered by the X-57 were applied to passenger airliners. What is one advantage that passengers would experience by flying on an X-57 instead of a traditional combustion-engine plane? What would be one disadvantage of passengers flying on an X-57?

TOPIC 6 Review and Assess

1 Electric Force

MS-PS2-5, MS-PS3-2

1. The area around a charge in which the electric force is experienced by other charged objects is the
   A. electric charge. B. electric field.
   C. electric force. D. electric current.

2. Charges flow through a circuit due to differences in
   A. resistance. B. potential energy.
   C. conductivity. D. insulation.

3. Why would two electrons repel each other if they were close together?
   A. They have like charges, so they experience an attractive force.
   B. They have opposite charges, so they experience a repulsive force.
   C. They have like charges, so they experience a repulsive force.
   D. They have opposite charges, so they experience an attractive force.

4. In ...., current flows more easily because electrons are more loosely bound to their atoms than they are in insulators.

5. **SEP Construct Explanations** Suppose a blanket has a sock stuck to it due to static electricity. When you pull the sock off of the blanket, what happens to the potential energy between them? Explain your response.

2 Magnetic Force

MS-PS2-5, MS-PS3-2

6. The push or pull that occurs when a magnet interacts with another object is known as the
   A. magnetic force. B. magnetic field.
   C. magnetism. D. magnet.

7. How is a magnet able to pick up bits of metal without actually touching them?
   A. The magnet is surrounded by an electric field that attracts the metal.
   B. The metal exerts a repulsive force on the magnet.
   C. There is an invisible magnetic field around the magnet where it exerts magnetic force.
   D. The electric force from the magnet attracts the bits of metal.

8. **Explain Phenomena** A magnet is placed on a refrigerator to hold up a calendar. As the magnet approaches the refrigerator, the potential energy between the magnet and the refrigerator decreases. Explain why.

9. **SEP Develop Models** ✎ Draw the magnetic field lines around a bar magnet, and label the places where the magnetic field is the strongest.

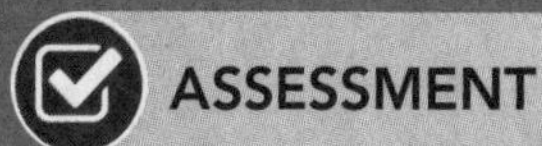

Evaluate your understanding by taking a Topic Test.

3 Electromagnetic Force

MS-PS2-3

10. What do you call the relationship between electricity and magnetism?

A. static electricity **B.** magnetic current
C. electric force **D.** electromagnetism

11. A(n) .... is a coil of wire with a current running through it. If you wrap the coil around a ferromagnetic material, it becomes a(n) ....

12. SEP Use Models In the diagram, the direction of a current and the magnetic field around it are shown. Describe what would happen to the magnetic field if you increased the number of turns in the coil and reversed the direction of the current.

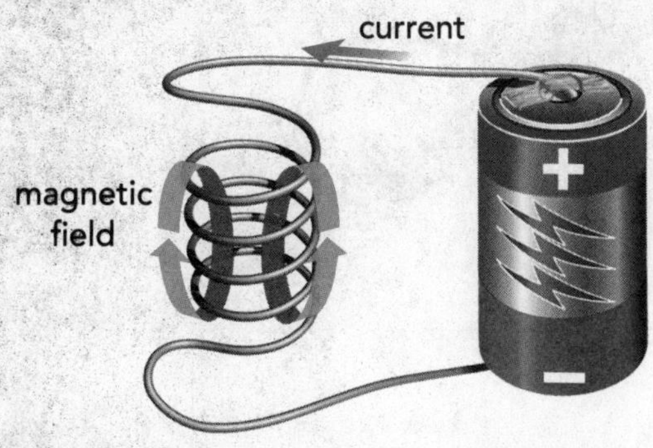

....
....
....
....
....
....
....
....
....
....

4 Electric and Magnetic interactions

MS-PS2-3

13. Which of the following descriptions describes electromagnetic induction?

A. Current running through a wire creates a magnetic field.
B. Moving a conductor through a magnetic field generates a current through the conductor.
C. Connecting a conductive wire to both ends of a battery allows current to flow.
D. Moving north poles of two magnets away from each other decreases potential energy.

14. A step-down transformer has a voltage of 400 V through the primary coil and 200 V through the secondary coil. There are 5 loops in the secondary coil. How many loops are in the primary coil?

A. 2 loops **B.** 5 loops
C. 10 loops **D.** 20 loops

15. Increasing the number of magnets within an electric motor will .... (increase/decrease) the speed of the motor.

16. CCC Structure and Function Electric motors and generators have similar parts but are considered to be opposites. Describe how they are different in terms of electromagnetism and the transformations of energy involved.

....
....
....
....
....
....
....

MS-PS2-3, MS-PS2-5, MS-PS3-2

Evidence-Based Assessment

Manny is investigating factors that affect electric and magnetic forces. He needs to design an experiment to show that objects can exert forces on each other even when they are not in direct contact.

After doing some additional research, Manny decides to make an electromagnet with a battery, some wire, an iron nail, and a switch. He uses a rubber eraser as an insulator to open and close the switch. He uses the electromagnet to see if he can pick up some paperclips.

The diagram shows the setup of Manny's experiment.

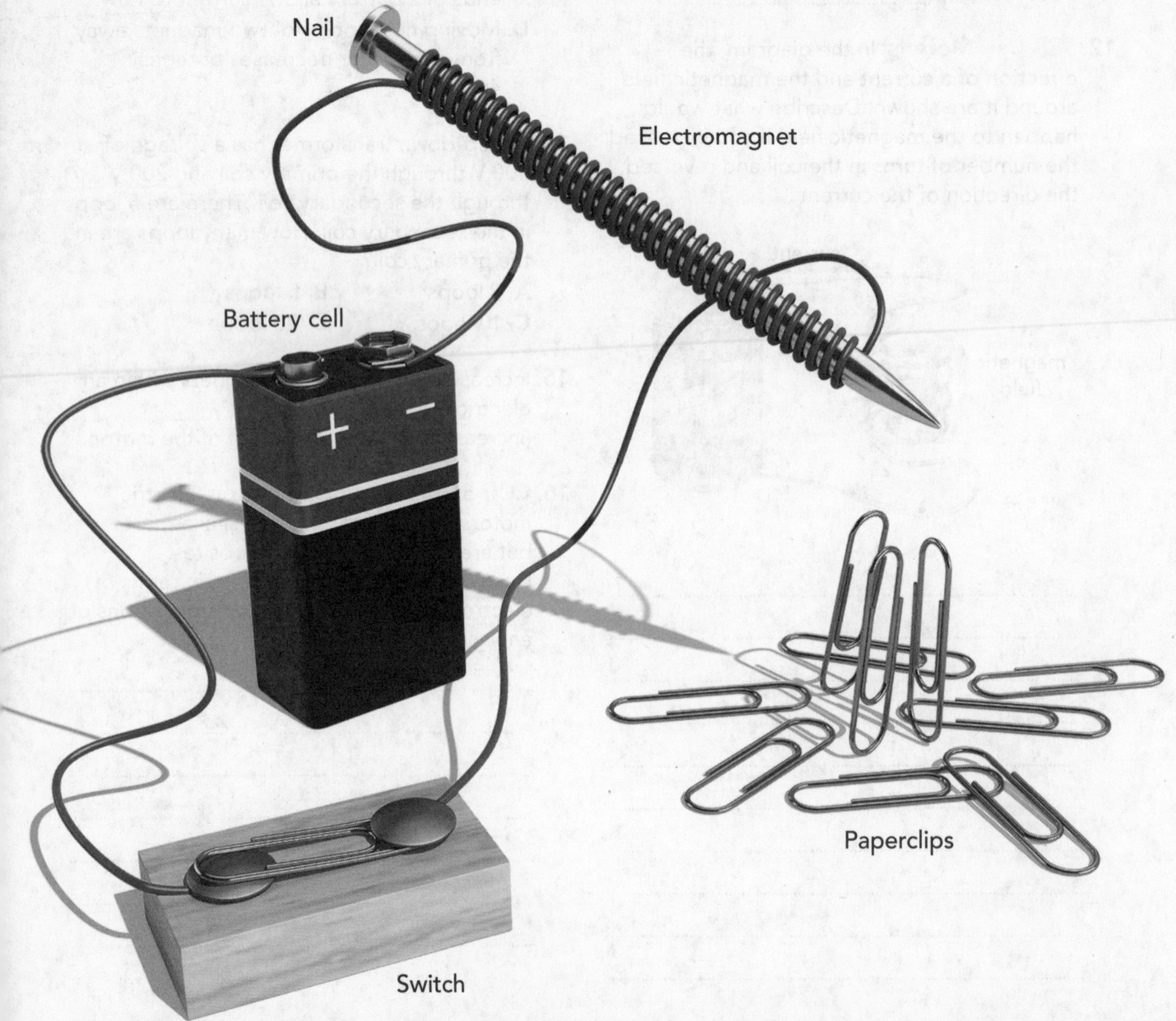

1. **SEP Analyze Data** What is one of the benefits of Manny's electromagnet?
   A. It can only repel objects.
   B. It produces a current through electromagnetic induction.
   C. The magnetic field can be turned on and off.
   D. Its strength cannot be changed.

2. **CCC Cause and Effect** What could Manny do to increase the strength of the electromagnetic force? Select all that apply.
   - ☐ Increase the number of coils around the nail.
   - ☐ Increase the current by using a battery with a greater voltage.
   - ☐ Decrease the number of coils around the nail.
   - ☐ Decrease the current by using a battery with a smaller voltage.

3. **Cite Evidence** What evidence is there that the electromagnet exerts a force on the paper clips, even though they are not touching each other?

4. **CCC Analyze Systems** Manny detaches the two wires from the battery and reattaches them to the opposite terminals. Explain how this changes the current and magnetic field.

5. **Explain Phenomena** Suppose you pull the paperclips away from the nail. Explain how the potential energy between the paperclips and the nail changes.

Quest FINDINGS

Complete the Quest!

Phenomenon Reflect on the engineering and design work you did building your levitating device.

SEP Design Solutions Magnets are used in a variety of industrial and medical applications. How do you think magnet technology might be applied to sports?

INTERACTIVITY

Reflect on Your Levitating Device

MS-PS2-5, MS-PS3-2

Planetary Detective

How can you **build** a device to **detect** magnetic fields on distant planets?

Background

A group of astronomers has approached you for assistance. They are studying three exoplanets, or planets that orbit a star outside our solar system. The three planets orbit in the habitable zone of the star. This means that liquid water can potentially exist on the planets, which is one requirement for life as we know it. The astronomers want to know whether or not the planets have magnetic fields, which will help them determine each planet's capacity for supporting life.

In this investigation, you will build a simple magnetometer, a device that detects magnetic fields, to test models of the three planets. Using evidence from your investigation, you will decide which of the planets have magnetic fields and which one most likely could support life.

Materials

(per group)

- 3 planet models
- iron filings, 50 mL
- paper cups, 2–3
- pieces of cardboard or small cardboard box
- string, 60 cm
- clear tape
- scissors
- plastic wrap, 2–3 sheets
- copy paper, 3–4 sheets
- small bar magnet

Earth's magnetic field helps to deflect charged particles in dangerous solar wind. Without this magnetic field, life would not be possible on our planet.

Safety

Be sure to follow all safety guidelines provided by your teacher. The Safety Appendix of your textbook provides more details about the safety icons.

Design Your Investigation

☐ 1. In your investigation, you must build a magnetometer and use it to look for evidence of magnetic fields for models of the three exoplanets, provided by your teacher. Space probes and satellites use this technology to look for evidence of magnetic fields and metals on planets throughout our solar system without coming into contact with the planets.

☐ 2. Think about how you can use the available materials to build a magnetometer. Consider the following questions as you work with your group to design your device:

- How can you use the iron filings to help you detect and observe magnetic forces?
- How can you use the cups or cardboard along with paper or plastic wrap to design a device that keep the iron filings contained and allows you to safely observe them?
- How can you make sure that your device's design allows it to detect magnetic fields without coming into contact with the model?
- How can you use the magnet to test your device?

☐ 3. Sketch your design in the space provided and be sure to label the materials you are using to construct the magnetometer. Then build your device.

☐ 4. Plan your investigation by determining how you will use the magnetometer to test the models. Record your plan in the space provided. Consider the following questions as you develop your plan:

- How can you determine whether or not the planet you are studying has a magnetic field?
- If you detect magnetic fields, how can you compare the strength of the planets' magnetic forces?

☐ 5. After getting your teacher's approval, carry out your investigation. Make a table to record your observations and data in the space provided.

Sketch and Procedure

Data Table and Observations

Analyze and Interpret Data

1. **Apply Concepts** What characteristics do you think a planet needs in order to generate a magnetic field?

2. **SEP Use Models** Look at your data and observations for the planet with the strongest magnetic field. The iron filings in your magnetometer were attracted to the magnetic material inside the model. Where does the greatest amount of potential energy exist—when the magnetometer is 10 cm from the surface of the planet or when the magnetometer is 3 cm the surface of the planet? Explain.

3. **CCC Cause and Effect** How do the results of your investigation provide evidence that the magnetic force inside the planet interacts with the iron filings in the magnetometer even though they do not come into contact with each other?

4. **SEP Construct Arguments** Which of the three planets most likely could support life? Support your response with evidence from your investigation.

TOPIC 7

Information Technologies

NGSS PERFORMANCE EXPECTATIONS

MS-PS4-3 Integrate qualitative scientific and technical information to support the claim that digitized signals are a more reliable way to encode and transmit information than analog signals.

What do these tiny circuits do?

HANDS-ON LAB

uConnect Consider ways to represent the terms *continuous* and *discrete*.

The Essential Question

Why are digital signals a reliable way to produce, store, and transmit information?

SEP Construct Explanations Circuit boards are found in all kinds of electronics devices, from toasters to televisions. How is information transmitted through these boards?

....

....

....

....

....

....

Quest KICKOFF

What is the best way to record sound for my scenario?

STEM **Phenomenon** Sound engineers work on all kinds of audio recordings, from television shows and movies to music albums. If you wanted to record people's voices and manipulate them to use as sound effects, then how would you do it? In this Quest activity, you will identify the most reliable way to encode and transmit an audio recording. You will explore differences between analog and digital technologies with a hands-on lab and digital activities. By applying what you have learned, you will create a multimedia display that communicates your findings.

INTERACTIVITY

Testing, Testing . . . 1, 2, 3

MS-PS4-3 Integrate qualitative scientific and technical information to support the claim that digitized signals are a more reliable way to encode and transmit information than analog signals.

NBC LEARN VIDEO

After watching the video, which looks at how an audio engineer records sound, describe how attending a live concert is different than listening to an album recorded in a studio.

....

....

....

....

....

....

....

....

....

Quest CHECK-IN

IN LESSON 1

STEM How does a microphone convert sound waves into electrical signals? Design and build a model of a microphone to learn how.

HANDS-ON LAB

Constructing a Microphone

Quest CHECK-IN

IN LESSON 2

How has recording technology changed? Consider the advantages and disadvantages of analog and digital recording technologies.

INTERACTIVITY

Analog and Digital Recordings

Microphones are just one of the many kinds of technology used to record sound.

Quest CHECK-IN

IN LESSON 3

What type of recording technology would best suit your scenario? Design a multimedia presentation that communicates your choices and reasons.

INTERACTIVITY

Evaluate Recording Technologies

Quest FINDINGS

Complete the Quest!

Reflect on your work and identify fields or careers that require knowledge of analog and digital signals.

INTERACTIVITY

Reflect on Your Recording Method

Continuous or Discrete?

How can you **use patterns** to distinguish between continuous and discrete data?

Background

Phenomenon Scientists use data to identify patterns and make predictions. Some data is considered to be continuous, while other data is considered to be discrete. In this lab, you will investigate how you can determine whether data is continuous or discrete.

Materials

(per pair)

- graph paper

Safety

Be sure to follow all safety procedures provided by your teacher. The Safety Appendix of your textbook provides more details about the safety icons.

Design a Procedure

☐ **1.** Consider these four scenarios.

a. A botanist is studying plant growth. She measures the height of a tree each year for 10 years.

b. An astronomer records the number of stars in the sky on one particular night that fit into each category: giant stars, white dwarfs, supergiant stars.

c. A scientist records the temperature of a glass of hot water for 60 minutes as it cools down in a classroom.

d. A geneticist records the number of people in a classroom that have one of the following genetic traits: brown hair, blue eyes, curly hair, left-handedness. *(note: the geneticist records the number of people for each separate trait).*

☐ **2. SEP Plan an Investigation** Develop a plan for how you can use these four scenarios to determine if a data set is continuous or discrete.

....

....

....

....

☐ **3.** Show your plan to a teacher before you begin. Record your observations.

Observations

Connect Go online for a downloadable worksheet of this lab.

Analyze and Interpret Data

1. **CCC Patterns** Based on your observations, what patterns did you notice between the data sets?

2. **SEP Construct Arguments** For which scenarios was the data continuous? For which scenarios was the data discrete? Use evidence to support your argument.

3. **SEP Evaluate Claims** A friend is observing sparrows in his neighborhood. Each day, he records the number of sparrows he sees. He says that a graph of the data will be a continuous line that rises and falls. Is he correct? Explain.

LESSON

1 Electric Circuits

Guiding Questions

- What are the components of a circuit?
- How does Ohm's law apply to circuits?
- What is the difference between a series circuit and a parallel circuit?

Connections

Literacy Determine Central Ideas

Math Use Proportional Relationships

MS-PS4-3

HANDS-ON LAB

uInvestigate Explore Ohm's law in action with your own circuit.

Vocabulary

electrical circuit
voltage
resistance
Ohm's law
series circuit
parallel circuit

Academic Vocabulary

diameter

Connect It!

Circle an object in the image that you think contains a circuit.

Analyze Systems What provides the energy for the circuit?

....

....

Explain Phenomena Describe any transformations of energy that occur in the circuit.

....

....

Parts of a Circuit

The wall clock in **Figure 1** is part of an electrical circuit. An **electrical circuit** is a complete, unbroken path that electric charges can flow through.

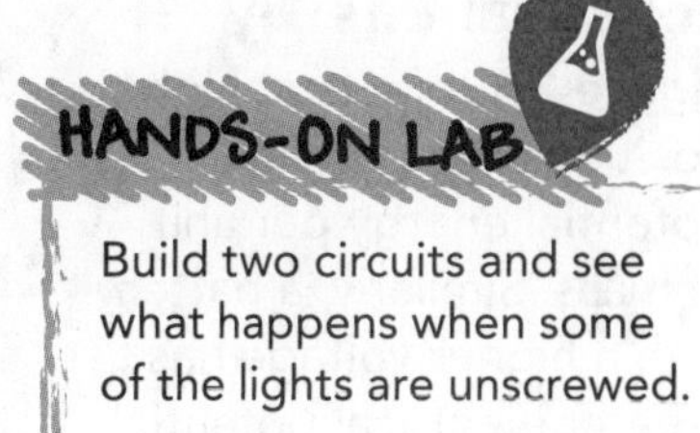

HANDS-ON LAB

Build two circuits and see what happens when some of the lights are unscrewed.

A circuit consists of a few basic parts: a source of electrical energy, conducting wires, and a device that runs on the electrical energy. In a wall clock batteries are the source of electrical energy. Conducting wires connect the batteries to a motor attached to the clock's arms. The motor runs on electrical energy—converting the batteries' energy to the clock's motions. Circuits sometimes also contain switches. When a switch is closed, charges can flow through the circuit. When a switch is open, the circuit is broken and charges cannot flow. A light switch in your home is used to open and close the circuit that sends electrical energy from a power plant to your light bulb.

Even though energy in circuits is used to power devices, the energy is always conserved. The electrical energy does not get used up—instead, it is transformed from one form to another. For example, in a table lamp, the electrical energy is transformed into light and heat.

Electric Circuits in a Home

Figure 1 Many devices in a typical home contain circuits and use electricity.

Potential Energy

Figure 2 Objects at higher positions have greater potential energy per unit of mass. Similarly, a battery with a higher voltage has greater electrical potential energy per charge.

SEP Develop Models

Draw an X on the water slide where a person would have the greatest gravitational potential energy per unit of mass. Draw an X on the circuit where it has the greatest electric potential energy per charge.

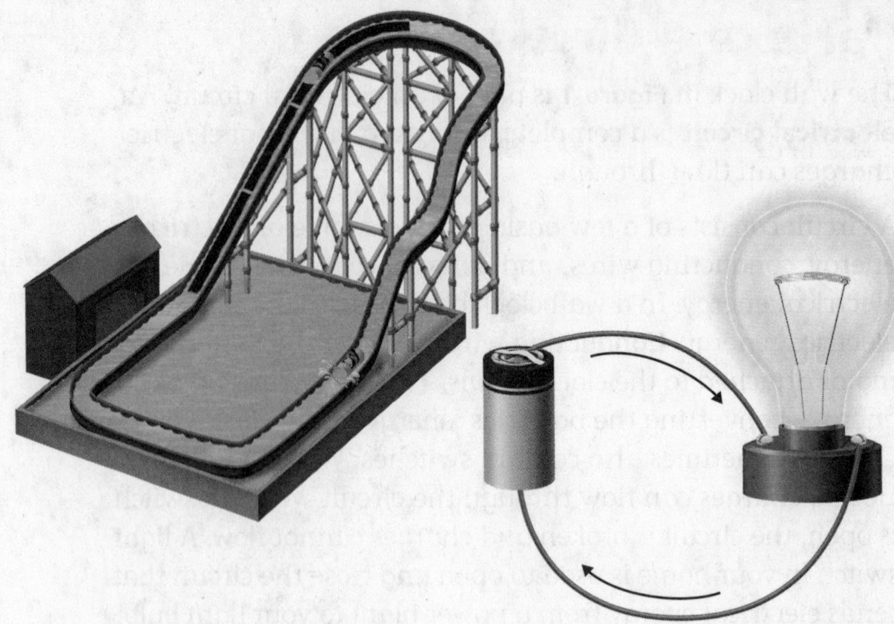

Literacy Connection

Determine Central Ideas What does voltage measure?

....

....

....

....

....

Voltage Electric current flows through a circuit because of differences in electric potential energy in the electric charges. In circuits, it is helpful to think about the electric potential energy per charge, or electric potential, at different points in a circuit. **Voltage** is the difference in electric potential energy per charge between two points in a circuit. So, voltage is the difference in electric potential. Voltage is measured in volts (V).

A typical battery has two ends. One end has a higher electric potential than the other. The end with higher electric potential is called the positive end, and the end with lower electric potential is the negative end. The difference in electric potential is the battery's voltage. For example, the positive end of a 12-volt battery has an electric potential 12 volts higher than the negative end. When the battery is connected within a circuit, this voltage causes current to flow. The current moves from the positive end through the circuit and back to the negative end. The current flows naturally, much like water on a water slide (**Figure 2**).

As the current flows through the circuit, the electric potential energy is converted to other forms of energy. As a result, the electric potential drops as the charges move through the circuit. When the charges reach the battery, they need to regain potential energy if the current is going to continue. The battery supplies the charges with energy by converting chemical energy (from chemicals within the battery) to electrical energy.

The directions of current and voltage were originally defined for positive charges. It was later discovered that negatively-charged electrons flow through a wire circuit. It can be confusing, but remember that what we call electric current goes in the opposite direction of the actual flow of electrons.

Resistance Objects that run on electricity act as resistance to the flow of current. **Resistance** is a measure of how difficult it is for current to flow through an object. It takes more energy for charges to move through objects with higher resistance. Therefore, there is a greater drop in electric potential as the current flows through the circuit. Objects that provide resistance are called resistors. A light bulb, for example, acts as a resistor (**Figure 3**).

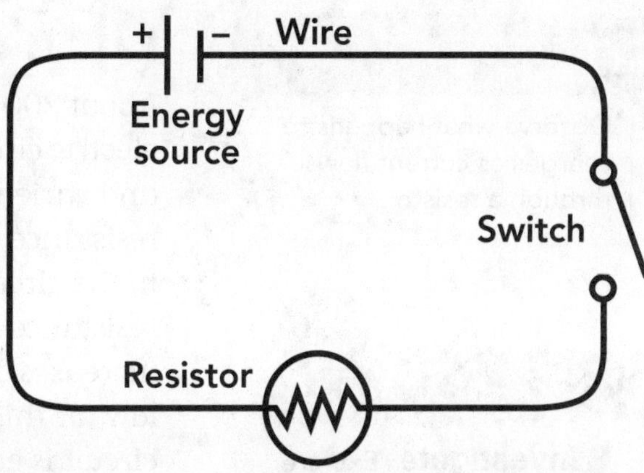

The resistance of an object depends on its **diameter**, length, temperature, and material. Objects with a smaller diameter and longer length are more difficult to flow through. In the same way, it is more difficult to sip a drink through a narrow and long straw than a wide and short straw. Current also flows more easily through an object when it is cold than when it is hot. Warmer particles vibrate more and obstruct the flow of current. Current also flows more easily through materials that are good conductors. The conductors have electrons that are more loosely bound, so the charges can move more easily.

Potential Energy

Figure 3 The diagrams show a circuit with a battery, conducting wires, a switch, and a light bulb.

READING CHECK **Summarize** What kind of device in a circuit supplies voltage? What kind of device acts as a resistor?

....

....

....

....

Academic Vocabulary

Student Discourse

Discuss with a classmate how you would describe the diameter of a round wire. Record your response here.

....

....

....

Model It!

Drawing Circuit Diagrams

As shown in **Figure 3**, symbols are used in a diagram to show the parts of a circuit.

1. **SEP Develop Models** In the space provided, draw what the circuit in **Figure 3** would look like if another battery and another light bulb were added.
2. **CCC Cause and Effect** Will the total resistance in the circuit increase or decrease when more light bulbs are added? Explain.

....

....

....

Observe what happens to charges as current flows through a resistor.

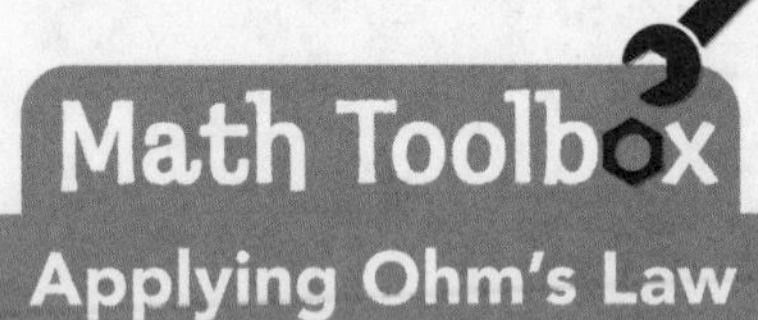

HANDS-ON LAB

Investigate Explore Ohm's law in action with your own circuit.

Ohm's Law

About 200 years ago, scientist Georg Ohm experimented with electric circuits. He measured the resistance of a conductor and varied the voltage to find the relationship between resistance and voltage. He found that changing the voltage in the circuit changes the current but does not change the resistance of the conductor. When voltage increases, current increases but resistance does not change. Ohm came up with a law for this relationship. **Ohm's law** states that resistance in a circuit is equal to voltage divided by current.

$$\text{Resistance} = \frac{\text{Voltage}}{\text{Current}}$$

Resistance is measured in ohms (Ω). This means that one ohm of resistance is equal to one volt (V) divided by one amp (A). If you increase voltage without changing resistance, then current must increase as well.

Solving this equation for voltage, you obtain:

$$\text{Voltage} = \text{Current} \times \text{Resistance}$$

If you increase the resistance of a circuit without changing the voltage, then the current must decrease.

Math Toolbox

Applying Ohm's Law

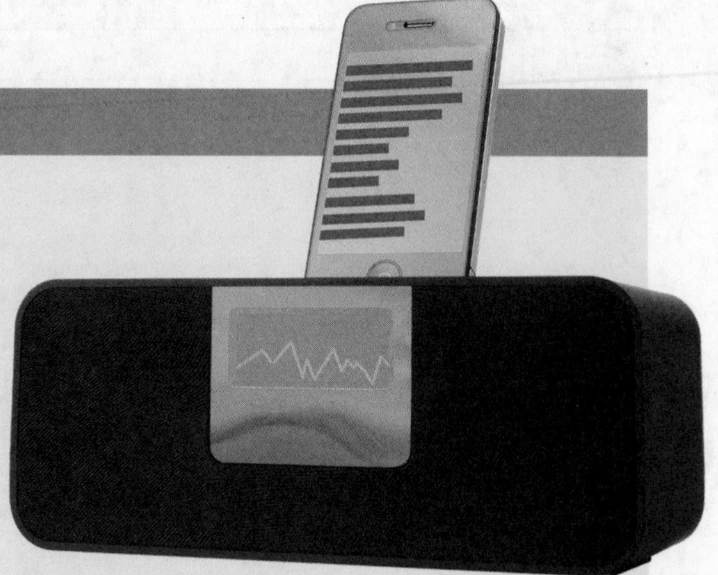

A stereo converts electrical energy into sound energy. The stereo is plugged into a wall outlet. The voltage is supplied by a power plant, and the current is carried through electrical wires to the stereo.

1. **Use Proportional Relationships** When you turn up the volume on a stereo, the voltage increases. Assuming the resistance of the stereo remains the same, what happens to the current?

   ....

2. **SEP Use Mathematics** Suppose you turn up the volume on a stereo so that the voltage increases to 110 V while the resistance remains at 55 Ω. Calculate the current after this voltage increase.

   ....

   ....

Series and Parallel Circuits

Different situations may call for different types of circuits. Suppose a factory uses multiple machines in an assembly line to recycle glass bottles. If the glass-melting machine breaks down but the bottles keep moving, there could be a major safety hazard as the bottles pile up! To prevent this problem, the machines can be wired so that if one machine breaks, then the circuit is broken and all other machines stop working as well. This is called a series circuit.

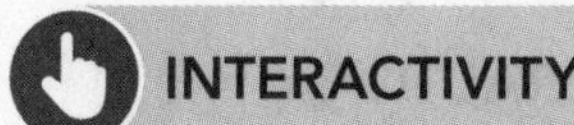

Explore the similarities and differences between series and parallel circuits.

Write About It Give one example of a situation in your life in which a series circuit is an advantage, and another example in which it could be a disadvantage.

Series Circuits In a **series circuit**, all parts of the circuit are connected one after another along one path (**Figure 4**). There are advantages to setting up a circuit this way, as in the example of the recycling factory. However, it can sometimes be a disadvantage. The more devices you add to the circuit, the more resistance there is. As you learned with Ohm's law, if voltage remains the same and resistance increases, then current decreases. Adding more light bulbs to a string of lights causes them to shine less brightly. The circuit would have more resistance and the current would decrease, causing the bulbs to appear dimmer.

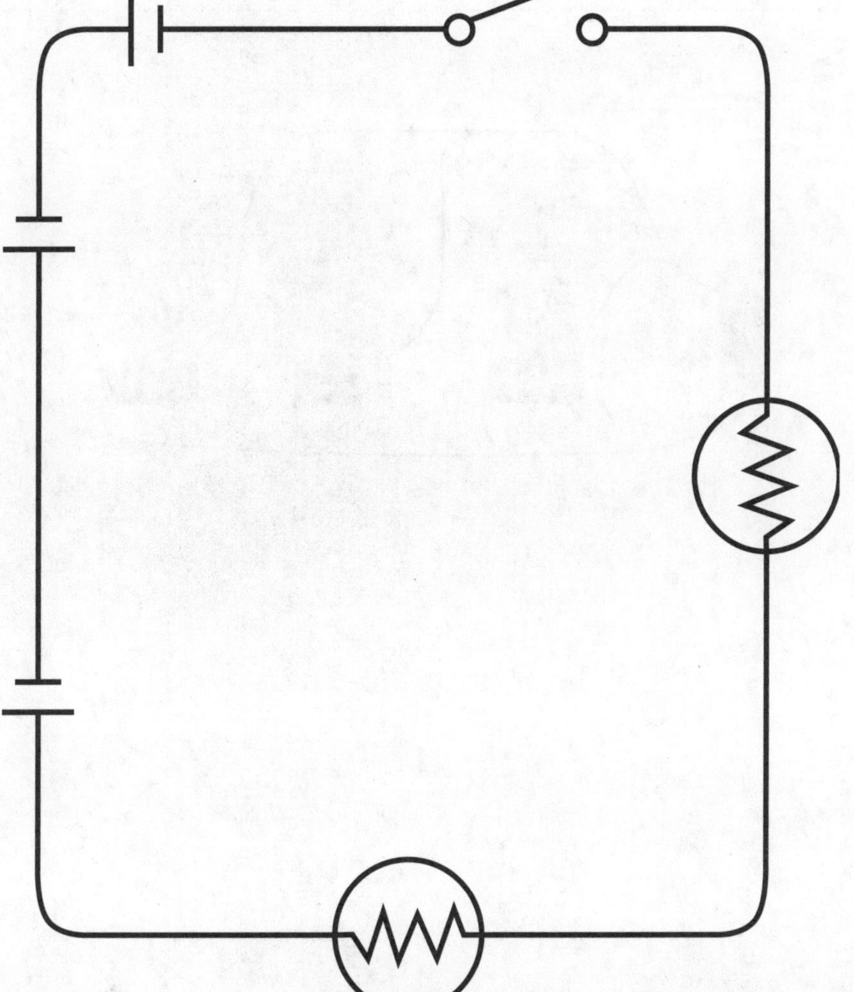

Correcting Circuit Diagrams

Figure 4 An electrical engineer draws a circuit diagram of a series circuit that includes three resistors, two batteries, and a switch. **SEP Develop Models** Find the engineer's mistake, and mark the drawing with your correction.

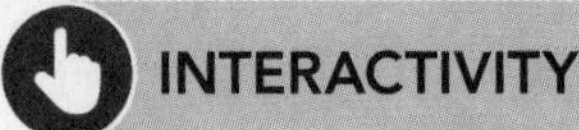

INTERACTIVITY

Review the parts of a circuit and fix a set of broken lights.

Parallel Circuits In other situations, you may want each device in a circuit to be wired so that if one device breaks, the others still work. For instance, when one overhead light burns out in the kitchen, you don't expect the other lights to go out, leaving you in the dark. In situations like this, you should use a **parallel circuit**, in which different parts of the circuit are on separate branches. As shown in **Figure 5**, there are several paths for the current to take in a parallel circuit.

Surprisingly, adding resistors in parallel to the circuit actually causes resistance to decrease. How is this possible? Adding a branch opens up another path for current to flow. This is similar to adding another pipe for water to flow through. Therefore, resistance in the circuit decreases and current increases. However, the additional current flows down the new path, so it does not affect the other devices. If a string of lights is set up along a parallel circuit, then each new bulb you add will glow as brightly as those originally on the strand.

READING CHECK **Determine Central Ideas** Describe the main difference between a series circuit and a parallel circuit.

Light Bulbs in Parallel
Figure 5 The circuit diagram shows three light bulbs in parallel.

1. **CCC Cause and Effect** What happens to the other two light bulbs when one light bulb goes out? Explain.

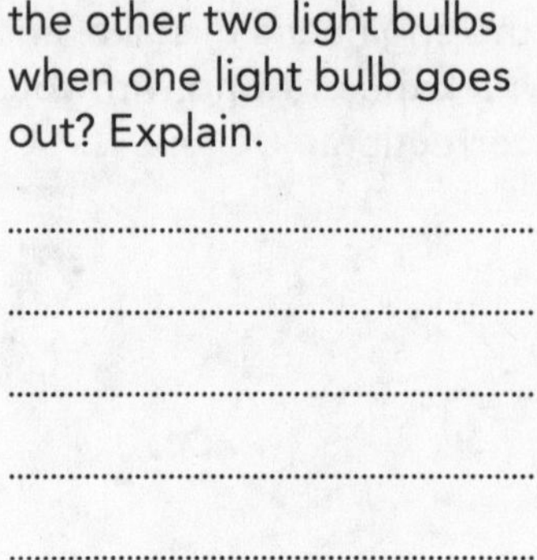

2. **SEP Develop Models** Draw the circuit again, adding one switch to each branch so that the bulbs can be controlled separately.

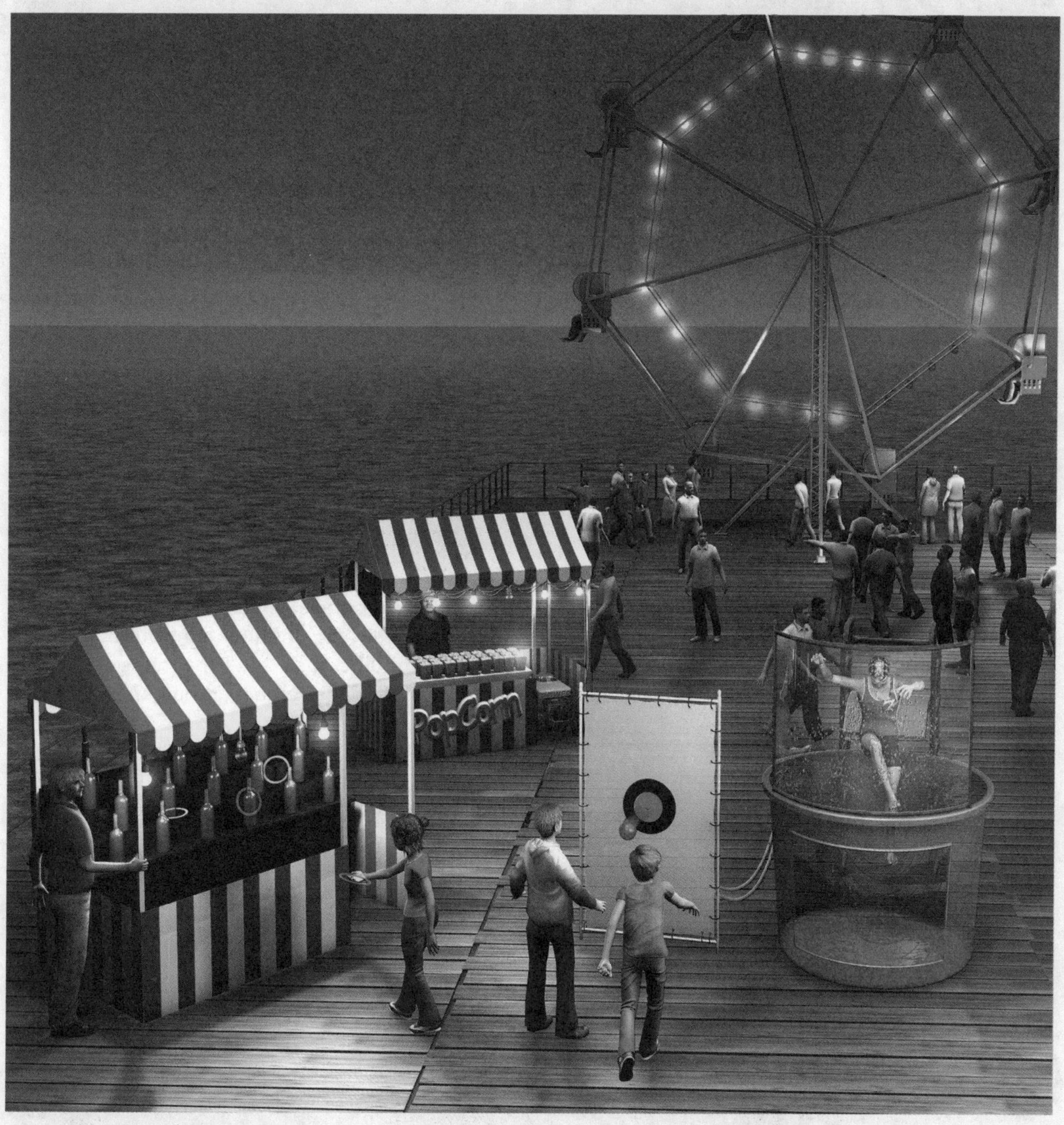

At the Boardwalk

Figure 6 Many activities at the boardwalk involve circuits. Circle the places where circuits would be.

SEP Construct Explanations Why do you think five of the last lights on the Ferris wheel have gone out?

LESSON 1 Check

MS-PS4-3

1. **Identify** What are the three main parts that must be present to make up a circuit?

2. **Define** How is voltage related to electric potential energy?

3. **SEP Develop Models** Draw a series circuit diagram that contains a battery, a switch, and three resistors. Label the parts of the circuit.

4. **CCC Structure and Function** A long, narrow resistor is placed in a series circuit along with a short, wide resistor made of the same material. Which will have a greater electric potential drop across it? Explain your reasoning.

5. **CCC Cause and Effect** Suppose you construct a parallel circuit consisting of a battery, a switch, and four light bulbs. One of the light bulbs goes out. What happens to the brightness of the remaining bulbs? Explain.

Quest CHECK-IN

You have discovered the meaning of voltage and resistance and how they relate to current as described by Ohm's law. You've also read about the different parts of a circuit and how to connect them in series or in parallel.

SEP Communicate Information How might your understanding of circuits help you decide what type of recording device to use?

HANDS-ON LAB

Constructing a Microphone

Go online to download the lab worksheet. Develop and use a model that shows how a simple microphone converts sound waves into electrical signals.

MS-PS4-3

A LIFE-SAVING Mistake

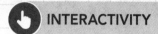

INTERACTIVITY

Explore what makes up a pacemaker and how it works.

How do you create a tiny device that saves hundreds of thousands of lives? You engineer it! The story of Wilson Greatbatch shows us how.

The Challenge: To develop the first successful cardiac pacemaker.

Phenomenon In 1956, Greatbatch was working at the University of Buffalo, in New York, as an assistant professor in electrical engineering. He was building an electronic device to record the heart rhythms of cardiac patients. While tinkering with the circuitry, he made a mistake and put a resistor into the circuit that was the wrong size.

When Greatbatch added the resistor, he did not get the outcome he expected. The circuit periodically buzzed with electrical pulses that reminded the engineer of a human heartbeat.

Greatbatch's error turned out to be a happy accident. He realized that the device could help cardiac patients whose hearts beat irregularly. He used the idea to develop the first successful pacemaker, a device that delivers small electrical shocks to the heart muscle to keep it beating regularly and pumping blood normally.

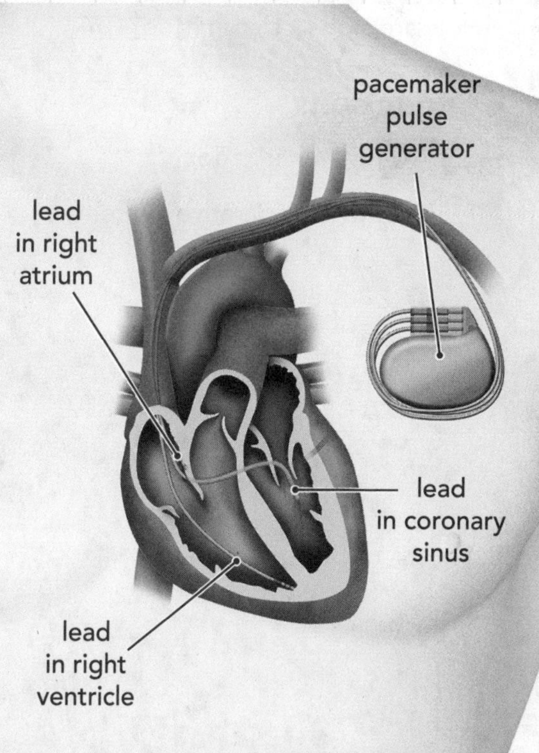

A pacemaker uses a pulse generator implanted below a patient's skin to send electric pulses to the heart. The pulses travel through wires called leads.

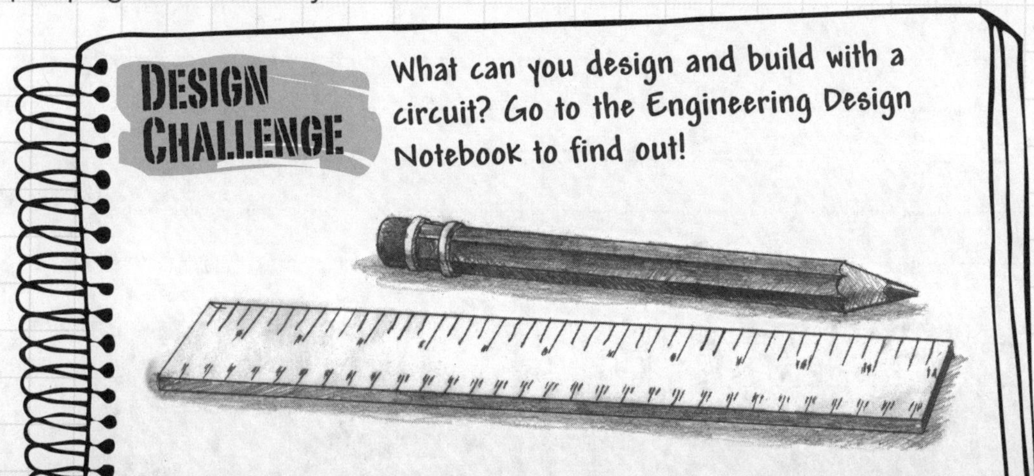

DESIGN CHALLENGE
What can you design and build with a circuit? Go to the Engineering Design Notebook to find out!

LESSON

2 Signals

Guiding Questions

- How is information sent as signals?
- What are digital and analog signals?
- How are signals transmitted?

Connections

Literacy Summarize Text

Math Draw Comparative Inferences

MS-PS4-3

HANDS-ON LAB

uInvestigate Explore how analog signals can be converted to digital information.

Vocabulary

wave pulse
electronic signal
electromagnetic signal
digital signal
analog signal
pixel

Academic Vocabulary

transmission

Connect It!

Circle the visual signal that is being used to communicate information.

SEP Construct Explanations Why do you think hand signals are useful for communicating with a dog?

Signals and Information

Compare and contrast analog and digital clocks.

An electric circuit can be used to power a device like a light bulb. However, circuits can also be used to send information. Think about a doorbell, which is usually a circuit. When someone presses a button outside a door, the circuit is complete and the electricity powers a bell that chimes. If you understand the meaning of the chime (a signal that someone is at the door), then you can respond by going to the door. For any signal to be understood, there needs to be agreement between the sender and the receiver about what the signal means. In some cases, the signal can be simple, such as a doorbell or basic hand signals, like the one the pet owner is using in **Figure 1**. Others are more complex. For example, you are reading a specific sequence of letters and spaces on this page to learn about signals.

For much of the 1800s, people communicated with each other over great distances using electrical signals. Samuel Morse patented a version of the electrical telegraph in 1837, and by the Civil War in 1861, there were telegraph lines that carried Morse code from one side of the United States to the other.

Signaling

Figure 1 A human can teach a dog to respond to visual signals.

Morse Code

Figure 2 In Morse code, combinations of short (dot) and long (dash) wave pulses are sent and each combination is translated into a letter.

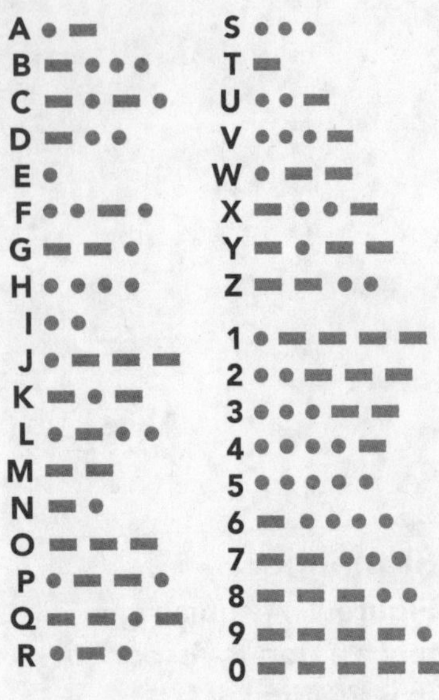

Electronic Signals An electrical telegraph is used to send Morse code as an **electronic signal**, information that is sent as a pattern in a controlled flow of current through a circuit. The telegraph turns the current on and off as the operator taps a device to close and open the circuit, as shown in **Figure 2**. In Morse code, combinations of short (dot) and long (dash) wave pulses stand for the letters of the alphabet and punctuation marks. A **wave pulse** is a pulse of energy that travels through the circuit when it is closed. In Morse code, the letter *A* is sent and received as "•—", *B* is "—•••", and so on. This code can be used to send messages, but it is very slow.

Electronic signaling became more useful and widespread when inventors developed ways to transmit information without translating them into code. In 1876, Alexander Graham Bell patented the first telephone. In Bell's telephone, two people spoke into devices that were part of the same circuit. A microphone converted soundwaves in the air—a caller's voice—into electronic signals that would be carried to the receiver somewhere else. At the time, switchboard operators manually connected two telephones into the same circuit. Eventually, switchboards became fully automated.

Model It!

Be a Telegraph Operator

1. **CCC Patterns** Use the Morse code chart in **Figure 2** to decode the following four lines of code.

   •—— •••• •— — ....

   •• ••• ....

   ••—• ——— •—• ....

   •—•• ••— —• —•—• •••• ....

2. **SEP Use Models** Use Morse code to provide an answer to the message you decoded.

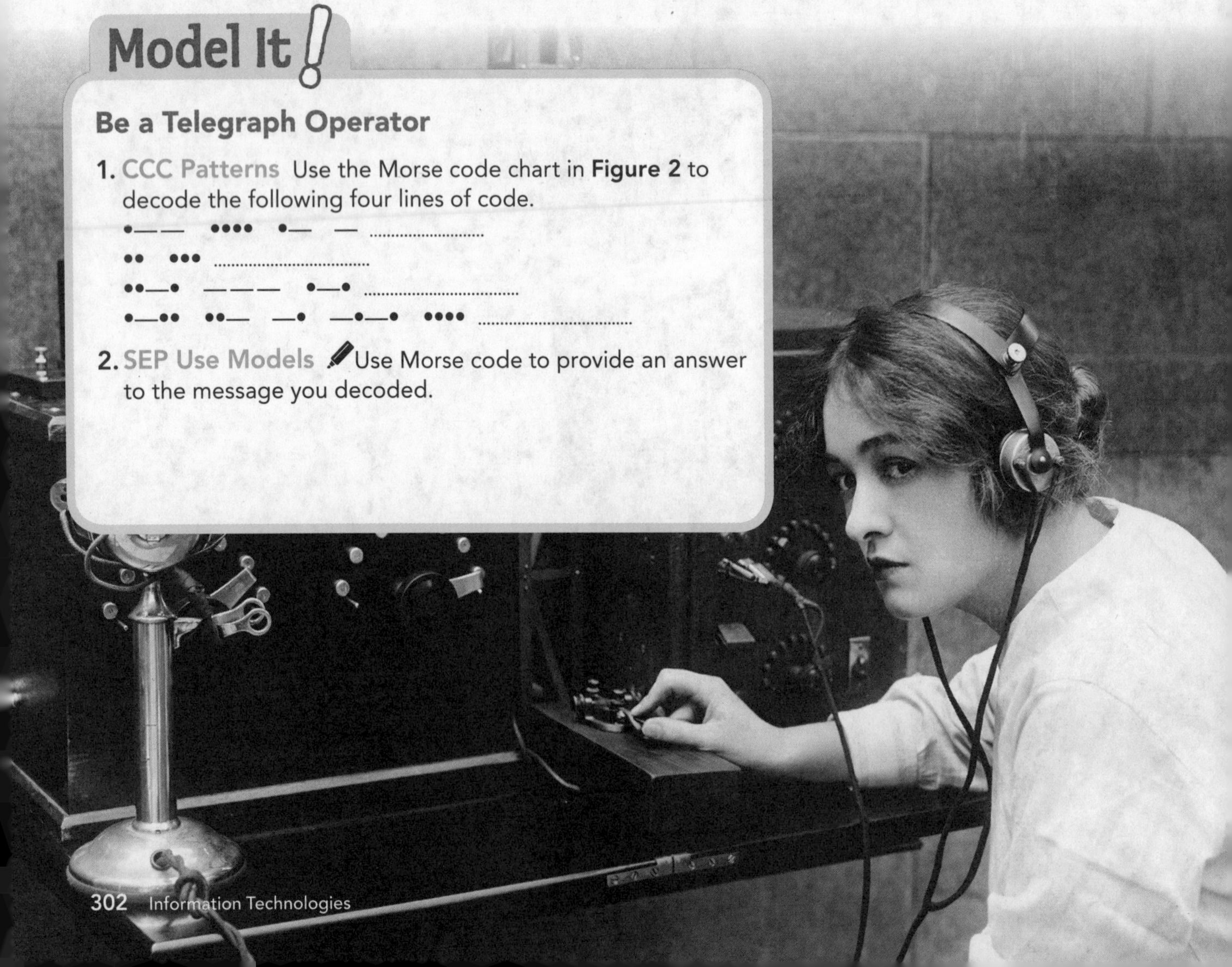

Electronic Signals	Electromagnetic Signals

Electromagnetic Signals

Electromagnetic Signals Information sent as patterns of electromagnetic waves such as visible light, infrared waves, microwaves, and radio waves are **electromagnetic signals**. Modern information technologies use a combination of electronic and electromagnetic signals. In 1895, the first radio station transmitted radio wave signals between two points without using an electrical circuit. This launched wireless forms of communication that allowed messages to be transmitted across the globe. Wireless technologies, such as the ones shown in **Figure 3**, now dominate the telecommunications industry. Electromagnetic signals travel at the speed of light, which is much faster than the speed at which current flows through a circuit.

Different types of electromagnetic signals are used for different purposes. Modern mobile phones communicate using microwaves, which are in the ultra-high frequency (UHF) band of the electromagnetic spectrum. Submarines communicate underwater with extremely low frequency (ELF) waves. Optical fibers use visible and infrared light to transmit large amounts of information.

READING CHECK **Determine Central Ideas** What is an electronic signal?

....

....

From Wired to Wireless

Figure 3 The transition from wired to wireless telecommunications has allowed people to communicate and share information with each other with greater convenience, speed, and quality.

Compare and Contrast Complete the table to compare and contrast electronic and electromagnetic signals.

Types of Signals

Figure 4 Analog signals are continuous, whereas digital signals are discrete.

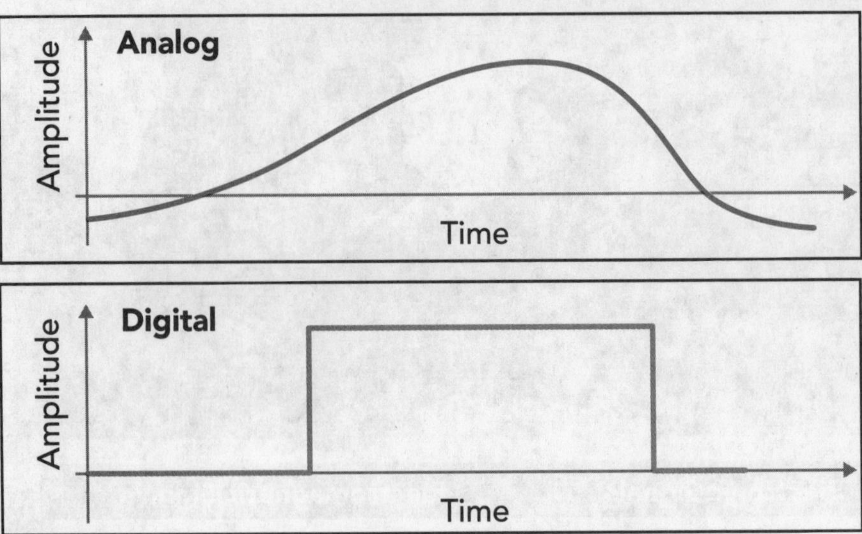

VIDEO

Compare analog sound recording devices to newer digital technologies.

Literacy Connection

Summarize Texts
Underline the sentences that summarize the differences between analog and digital signals.

Analog and Digital Signals

Electronic and electromagnetic signals can carry information from one place to another in two different ways: as analog signals or as digital signals. Both analog and digital signals have strengths and weaknesses, but the power and flexibility of digital signals have made them the foundation of modern information technologies.

Analog Signals An **analog signal** allows for a continuous record of some kind of action (**Figure 4**). For example, when seismic waves from an earthquake cause the ground to move, a seismograph records that continuous motion as an analog signal. The advantage of analog signals is that they provide the highest resolution of an action by recording it continuously. But analog signals can be difficult to record. The signals processed by a seismograph must be recorded with ink on paper as a seismogram. Other examples of analog signals are the recordings of music on vinyl records. You can slow down a record and still hear continuous music. However, vinyl records scratch and warp very easily. Analog media also take up a lot of space, compared to digital media.

Digital Signals A **digital signal** allows for a record of numerical values of an action at a set of continuous time intervals (**Figure 4**). This results in a series of numbers. For example, a digital seismometer can record ground motion by recording the numerical value of the ground height at each second. This produces a list of numbers that shows the ground motion, second by second. The disadvantage of digital signals is that you do not have a record of any signals that occurred in between each sampling. One advantage is that once you have recorded the signal as a set of numbers, you can store it on a computer or other digital device. Digital recordings can also be edited easily by just changing the numbers.

Sampling Rate The quality of digital media depends on the length of the recording intervals. The term *sampling rate* refers to how often a signal is recorded or converted to digital code. More data are captured and recorded the more times the event is sampled (**Figure 5**). For example, a digital music file with a high sampling rate may sound richer and more detailed than a file with a lower sampling rate. The downside of a higher sampling rate is that the file size is larger.

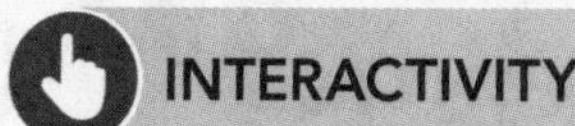

Compare analog and digital signals, and learn about signal noise.

Scientists and music producers have conducted tests with people to find a sampling rate that will produce digital music files that sound realistic without having more data than humans can perceive. If the sampling rate is too high and the files are too large, then the files will waste space on music players, mobile phones, computers, or storage services.

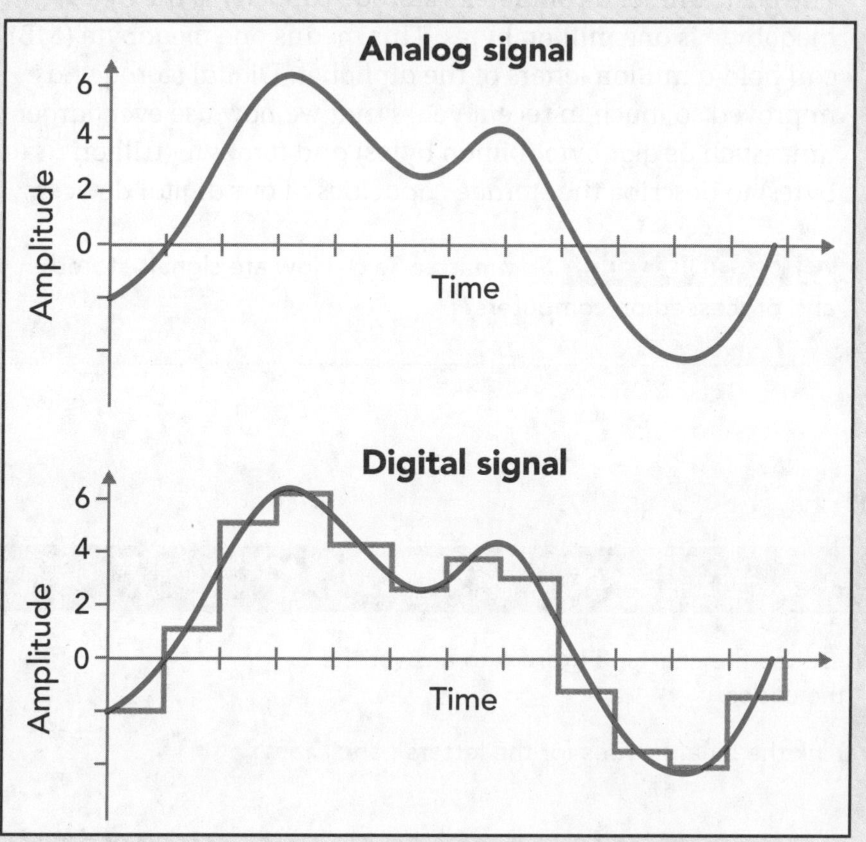

Analog-to-Digital Processing

Figure 5 When an analog signal is converted to a digital signal, what was continuous must be broken into discrete pieces. The higher the sampling rate, the closer the digital signal will come to the analog signal.

SEP Develop Models Draw two digital versions of the original analog signal in the blank graphs: one based on sampling the analog signal 24 times, and the other based on sampling 32 times.

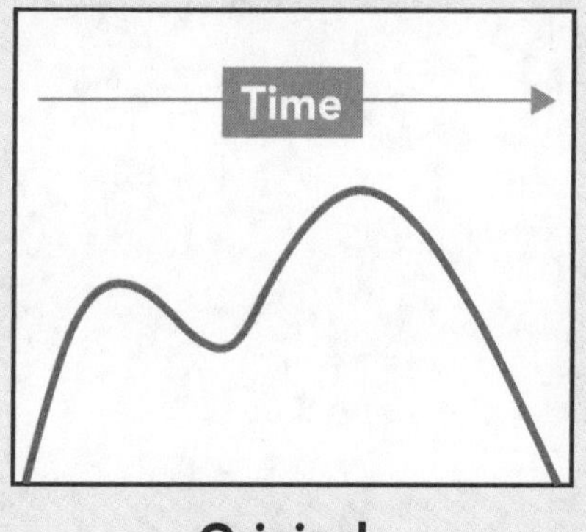

Original

Time

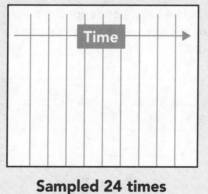

Sampled 24 times

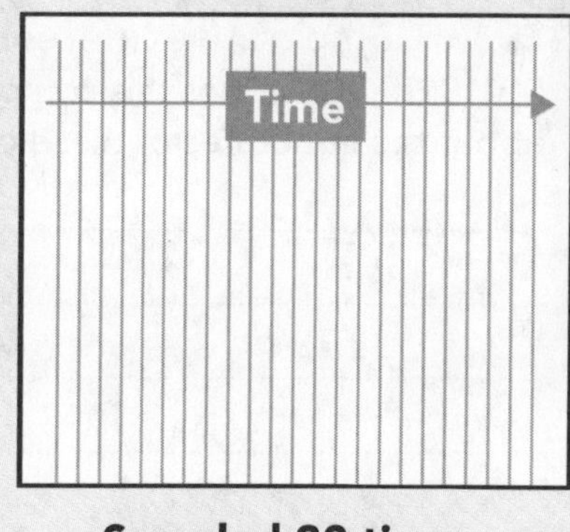

Sampled 32 times

Investigate Explore how analog signals can be converted to digital information.

Binary Signals Recall that Morse code has just two signals—dots and dashes—that are used in different combinations to communicate letters. Computers use a similar system called binary, which consists of ones and zeros. The information that we store on computers is encoded with binary, whether it's a song, a text document, or a movie.

Each number in binary code is a bit of information. Bits are arranged into groups of eight, called bytes. The code for each letter of the alphabet has its own unique byte, as shown in **Figure 6**. The code for a word consists of bytes strung together. For example, as the author wrote this page, a computer program translated the keyboard strokes for the letters in the word *"code"* into bytes.

01100011011011110110010001100101

The basic unit of a computer's storage capacity is the byte. A megabyte is one million bytes. This means one megabyte (MB) can hold a million letters of the alphabet. Digital storage has improved so much in recent years that we now use even larger units such as gigabyte (billion bytes) and terabyte (trillion bytes) to describe the storage capacities of our digital devices.

Binary Code

Figure 6 The binary codes, or bytes, for the first five letters of the alphabet are shown here. Notice that there are different codes for lowercase and uppercase letters.

a = 01100001 A = 01000001
b =01100010 B = 01000010
c = 01100011 C = 01000011
d = 01100100 D = 01000100
e = 01100101 E = 01000101

SEP Interpret Data What would the code be for the word *Dad*?

READING CHECK **Summarize Text** How are signals stored and processed on computers?

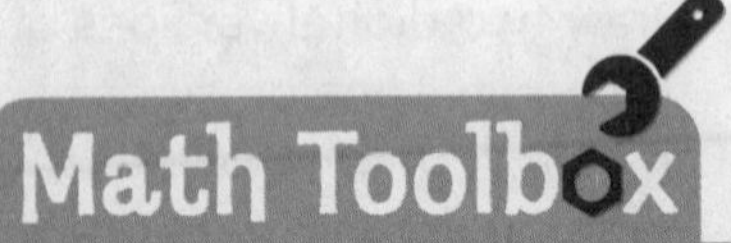

Math Toolbox

Cryptography

Cryptography is the study of codes. Use the chart in **Figure 6** to answer the following questions and "break" the codes.

1. **CCC Patterns** What do you think the binary codes for the letters *f* and *F* are?

2. **Draw Comparative Inferences** The binary code for the number *6* is 00110110. How does this compare to the code for *f*? What can you infer about the structures of these codes?

Transmitting Signals

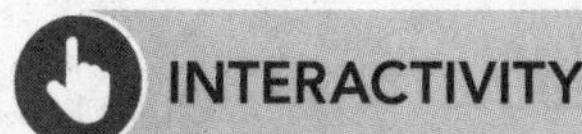

INTERACTIVITY

Analyze a model of how phone calls are made with mobile devices.

Modern forms of communication involve the **transmission** of electronic or electromagnetic signals. Many transmissions are now in digital formats. In some cases, the transmission consists of an entire file, such as a digital song file saved to your phone. In other cases, the transmission is more like a broadcast, such as a live stream.

Academic Vocabulary

In your science notebook, record other uses of the term *transmission* in science. In those other contexts, what's being transmitted?

Sound Information Analog telephones transmit signals by first converting sound waves to electronic wave pulses. Those travel along wires to another phone, which converts the wave pulses back to sound waves. Modern mobile phones convert sound waves to digital data in the form of binary code. The data are transmitted as microwaves, which are converted back to sound waves by another mobile phone. If someone records and sends a voice message from one mobile phone to another, or to a computer, the process is basically the same. Sound waves are the initial signal and the ultimate product.

Digital Audio

Figure 7 To transmit a sound signal from one place to another, the signal must be processed and converted into different forms.

SEP Develop Models Complete the diagram by identifying the type of signals that are being transmitted.

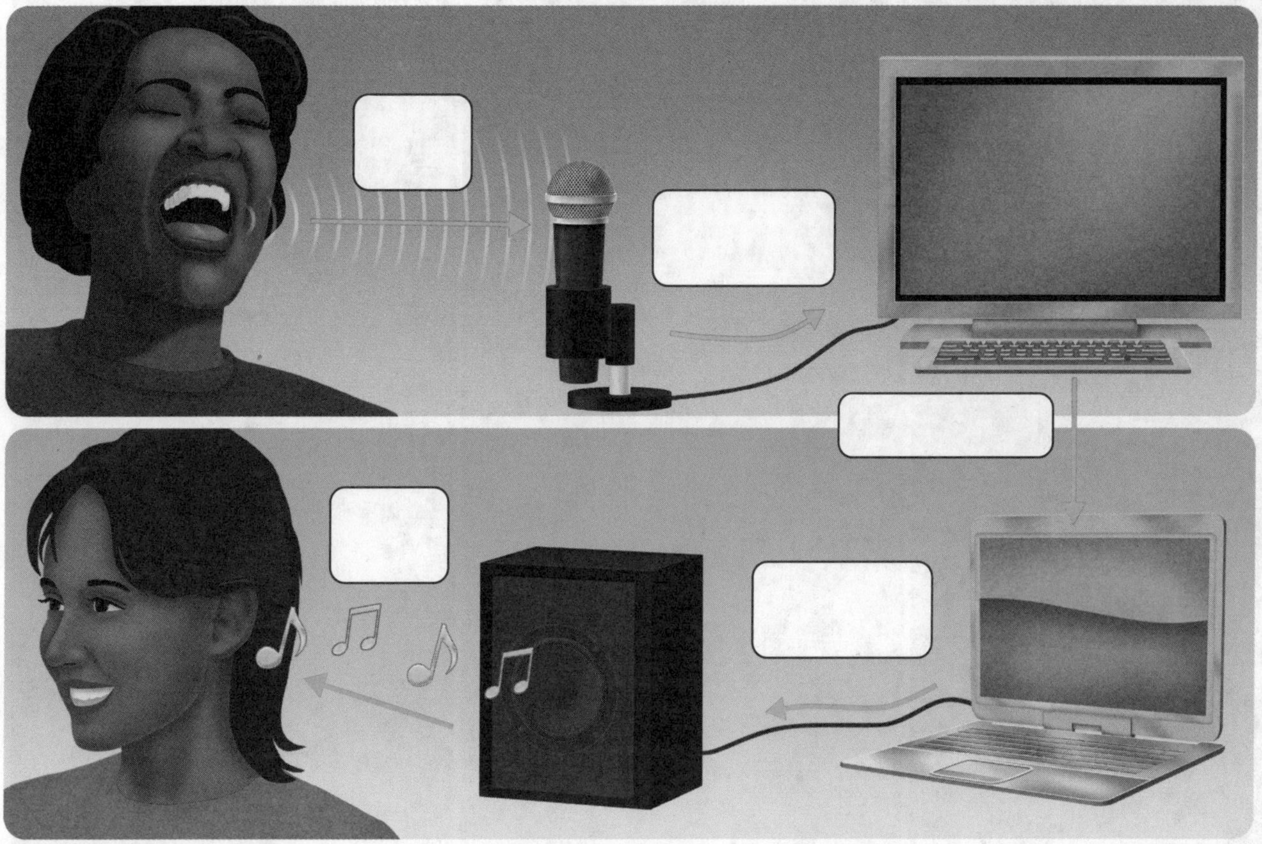

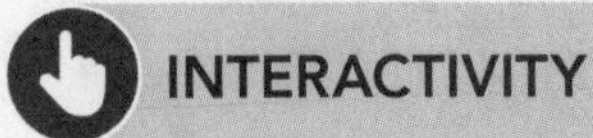

INTERACTIVITY

Model how the number of pixels affects the resolution of digital images.

Visual Information Photographs, printed documents, and other visuals can be digitized and transmitted as well. A digital visual consists of **pixels**, or small uniform shapes that are combined to make a larger image (**Figure 8**). The information that determines a pixel's color and brightness is coded in bytes. The more pixels that are used, the more bytes the digital image file will require. For example, a digital image that is meant to take up a few centimeters on a mobile phone screen may be far less than a megabyte, whereas an image that is meant to be shown on a high-resolution display or printed as a poster can be 50 megabytes and more. Just as audio engineers and music producers try to balance file size with detail that will be audible to human ears, visual artists and engineers must strike a balance too. They don't want their images to appear too "pixilated," but they don't want to waste device storage with too much detail either.

READING CHECK **Summarize Text** How are pixels used to capture and convey visual information with digital technology?

....

....

....

Pixels and File Size

Figure 8 The three images of the flower are copies of the same file. The leftmost image has a low resolution and small file size. The middle image has higher resolution and a larger file size. The rightmost image has the highest resolution and largest file size.

LESSON 2 Check

MS-PS4-3

1. **Identify** Sound waves move from a guitar to a microphone. The microphone converts the sound waves to electronic wave pulses that are transmitted through a wire to a computer. The computer converts the wave pulses to a series of 1's and 0's. The 1's and 0's are packaged as a file and posted online for sale to the guitarist's fans. In this process, when were the signals digital?

2. **SEP Use Mathematics** If one letter of the alphabet is one byte, and the average word consists of five letters, how many words could be encoded in binary and stored on a 1-GB memory card?

3. **Make Comparative Inferences** How is the sampling rate used in recording digital music similar to the number of pixels in a digital image?

4. **CCC Patterns** Compare and contrast Morse code and binary code.

Quest CHECK-IN

In this lesson, you learned about different types of signals and how they are used to record and transmit information.

Evaluate Why is it important to know the different types of signals that can be used to record information?

INTERACTIVITY

Analog and Digital Recordings

Go online to investigate and identify advantages and disadvantages of digital music.

Case Study

MS-PS4-3

Super **Ultra High** Definition!

If your family has purchased a new television recently, you know there are many digital options. In fact, many consumers and digital media providers have sometimes struggled to keep up with the technological changes.

Video resolution is one of the most important factors in digital TV technology. Resolution refers to the number of pixels on the TV screen. The diagram shows the different resolutions currently in use. The numbers shown for each resolution refer to the dimensions of the screen image in pixels. For example, standard-definition resolution (SD) has a 640 × 480 pixel dimension. The image is made up of 480 horizontal lines. Each line contains 640 pixels, for a total of 307,200 pixels.

As resolution increases, image quality increases because there are more pixels to form the image. However, as resolution and image quality increase, file size increases too. Each pixel in the image takes up 1 byte of storage. This means that one frame of an SD image takes up 307,200 bytes, or about 0.3 megabytes (MB) of storage. A moving TV image runs at 30 frames per second, so a one-hour program would take up about 32,400 MB in storage. This is where video codecs come in. A codec is software that digitally encodes and compresses the video signal to reduce its file size without affecting image quality very much.

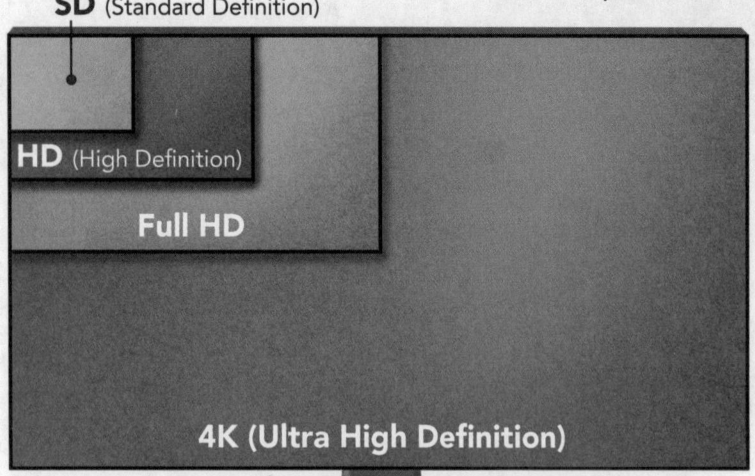

A Streaming Society

Today, many people download or stream TV shows and movies to their televisions and smart devices. Because the higher-quality signals are larger in file size, fast Internet speeds are required to move all the data. Internet speed is generally measured in megabits per second (Mbps). The amount of data that can be transferred at three different speeds is shown here.

Mbps speed	MB transferred per second
1	0.125
50	6.25
100	12.5

Use the text and data to answer the following questions.

1. Use Models A 4K image contains 8,294,400 pixels. What is the corresponding file size?

2. Calculate Suppose you're downloading a movie that is 3.2 GB. Your Internet speed is 50 Mbps. About how long will it take to download the file? Show your work.

3. Patterns Some video engineers are already touting 8K resolution, the next advance in video technology. The image quality of an 8K signal is equal to taking four 4K TVs and arranging them in a 2×2 array. What are the dimensions of an 8K image? Explain.

4. Analyze Properties Television programs used to be transmitted using analog signals. As more people began to buy HD televisions and watch HD programming, TV broadcasters and cable providers switched to digital signals. Why do you think this switch occurred? What advantage does a digital signal have over an analog signal when transmitting HD video?

5. Construct Explanations Most televisions sold now are 4K Ultra HD capable. However, most streaming services and digital TV providers offer little 4K programming. Why do think this is the case?

Communication and Technology

Guiding Questions

- What technologies are used for communication?
- What are the advantages of using digital signals for communications technology?

Connections

Literacy Cite Textual Evidence

Math Analyze Relationships

MS-PS4-3

HANDS-ON LAB

uInvestigate Observe the structure of a vinyl record and predict how it functions.

Vocabulary

information technology
software
noise
bandwidth

Academic Vocabulary

hardware

Connect It!

Circle a symbol on the clay tablet that appears more than once.

Compare and Contrast How is the ancient clay tablet similar to a digital tablet of today? How is it different?

The Information Age

The invention of writing was one of the first examples of information technology. Using a sharpened stick or a finger and some kind of medium such as clay (**Figure 1**) or a stone wall, people were able to record ideas, observations, and other information.

Fast forward to today. Information technology is everywhere, and there many forms and modes of writing. For example, one person typed the text on this page into a computer. The file was then sent via the internet to reviewers and editors. Edited text was then combined with the photograph in a different computer application. Finally, a file was sent to a printer, and a series of pages were put together as a book. What would have taken hours to inscribe in clay or rock can now be recorded and shared much faster, thanks to information technology. Modern **Information technology** consists of computer and telecommunications **hardware** and software that store, transmit, receive, and manipulate information. **Software** refers to programs that encode, decode, and interpret information, including browsers, apps, games, and operating systems. The invention of electronic computers around 1940 helped usher in the information age.

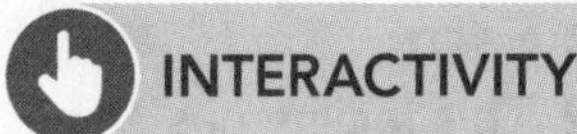

Discuss the encoding and decoding of information with classmates.

Academic Vocabulary

Hardware is an older term. What do you think "hard" refers to in the information technology usage of *hardware*?

....

....

....

Sumerian Tablet

Figure 1 This clay tablet was used to record information 6,500 years ago in Sumer, part of Mesopotamia.

Server Farm

Figure 2 This facility has thousands of computers that store and share the data of millions of people.

SEP Ask Questions Why do think this facility is called a server farm?

INTERACTIVITY

Investigate the development of communications and information transmission technologies.

Literacy Connection

Cite Textual Evidence Underline text that supports the idea that we are in a period of exponential data growth.

Information Technologies Every day, hundreds of millions of e-mails, and billions of text messages are sent. Files are also exchanged online through "clouds" that are accessible from thousands of networks. Every year, trillions of gigabytes of information are produced on Earth, ranging from high-definition movies to printable text documents to brief messages about what to buy at the supermarket.

The software and hardware that power modern information technology (IT) depend on each other. IT hardware is the modern version of clay or stone. It serves as the physical medium where information is stored and altered. Processor chips, batteries, disks, wiring, and other components compose the physical place where software operates. In some cases, the hardware you depend on is "local," such as the processor, display, built-in memory, and other components of your mobile device or computer. Other hardware that you probably use is housed elsewhere, such as the cell phone tower that may be in or near your town, and the "farms" of servers that major telecommunications and computer companies use to store some of your information (**Figure 2**). By accessing data held on a server that is somewhere else, you can watch, listen to, read, or otherwise experience media without actually storing the data locally. We are now in a period of exponential growth of digital information production.

READING CHECK **Summarize Text** What are some examples of hardware used in information technology?

Communications Systems

Learn about the career of a network administrator.

Before the industrial and information ages, long-distance communication methods included smoke signals and handwritten messages carried by pigeons. Today, we depend on three types of transmissions: electronic signals carried by wires, electromagnetic transmissions through the atmosphere, and electromagnetic transmissions through fiber-optic cables.

Digital Data Explosion

With ever-growing numbers of people accessing the Internet, greater and greater amounts of information and data are being produced. The graph shows data production and expected projections for the future.

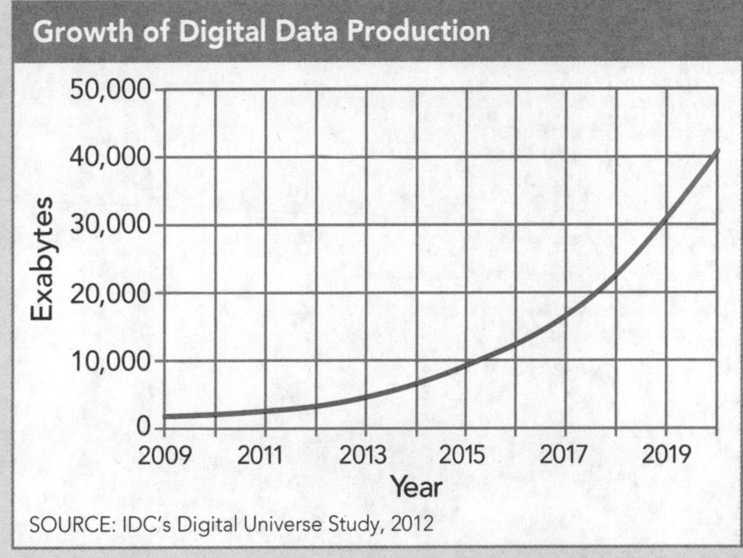

SOURCE: IDC's Digital Universe Study, 2012

1. **Analyze Relationships** Compare the rate of growth from 2011 to 2013 with the rate of growth from 2015 to 2017.

2. **Claim** If the trend continues, how much data do you think will be produced in 2030?

3. **Evidence** How does the data support your claim?

4. **Reasoning** What do you think accounts for the exponential growth of data in recent years?

Roger That!

Figure 3 Communications technologies all have one thing in common—they must move vast amounts of data in our digital world.

SEP Designing Solutions For each type of communications technology, identify a benefit and a drawback of using analog signals and digital signals.

Making a telephone call used to involve a large device mounted on a wall or in a booth, which was wired to a switchboard operator in another location, who would connect your call to a specific person by connecting two circuits. There was no "voicemail" system to record a message. The signal could be poor, making it difficult to hear each other. Nowadays, many people carry phones in their pockets that can connect to other people around the world.

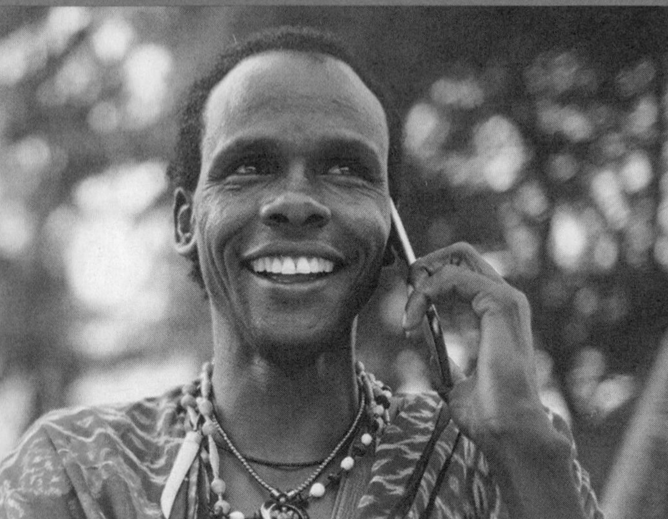

Benefit ....

....

Drawback ....

....

For many years, radio and television broadcasts were transmitted using radio waves. Analog televisions and radios depended on tall towers to broadcast signals over the air. In recent years, television has switched over to digital signal transmissions. Televisions can now handle high definition media.

Benefit ....

....

Drawback ....

....

Telecommunications satellites that orbit Earth can relay signals that cannot be transmitted by wires or towers. Some satellites are used to broadcast television stations and other media, and others are used by government agencies and the military.

Benefit ....

....

Drawback ....

....

Fiber optic technology is based on glass or plastic cables that transmit light at speeds around 200,000 kilometers per second. Fiber-optic cables can carry about a thousand times more information per second than standard copper cable.

Benefit ....

....

Drawback ....

....

The Internet is a complex set of interconnected networks that transmits information, largely through the World Wide Web. The Internet is usually accessed through an application called a browser, which allows people to navigate through the millions of pages. Internet connection used to require a cable plugged into a computer, but now many connections are achieved over wireless "WiFi" networks, or even mobile cellular networks.

Benefit ....

....

Drawback ....

....

Investigate Observe the structure of a vinyl record and predict how it functions.

Advantages of Digital Signals

Although they are not continuous signals, digital signals are more reliable and efficient overall than analog signals, for several reasons.

Compatibility with Computers Computers process digital signals, and computers are everywhere—on laps and desktops, tucked in pockets, in car dashboards, and even on refrigerator doors. It's easier for computers and digital devices to do what we want them to do without having to convert analog signals first. Using digital signals is more efficient.

Noise When an analog signal is transmitted, it can incorporate **noise**—random signals from the environment. This noise can then stay with the signal and alter the output. Static is an example of noise. Because digital signals consist of 0's and 1's, it is more difficult for noise to alter the signal, because binary code is essentially a choice between on and off. Unless noise causes a one to become a zero or vice versa, noise shouldn't affect how the digital signal is received or read.

Model It!

Noise? No Problem!

The first graph shows an analog signal accompanied by noise during transmission. The second graph shows a digital signal also accompanied by noise during transmission.

SEP Develop Models Complete the models by drawing the received analog and digital signals to show how noise affects each one.

Original signal with noise

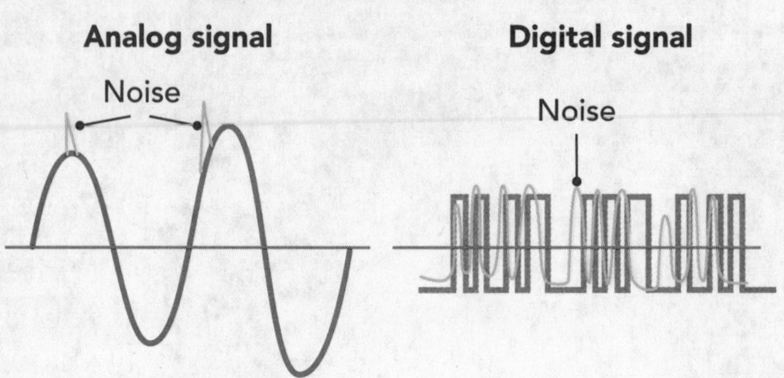

Received signal

Distortion caused by noise

Restored digital signal

Security Although digital signals are encrypted—hidden by binary coding—both analog and digital signals are vulnerable to security breaches. It's relatively easy for someone to tap into an analog phone line and listen to or record the conversation, because the signal is not encrypted. It's more difficult to access digital phone signals or communications, but hacking—stealing of digital information by breaking the codes—is on the rise. Tech experts are continually working to improve digital security.

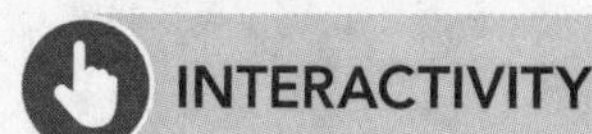

Research the advantages and disadvantages of analog and digital signals.

Bandwidth As illustrated in **Figure 4**, the amount of information that can be transmitted and measured in bits per second is called **bandwidth**. Digital signals carry less information than comparable analog signals, so digital information technology solutions typically have greater bandwidth than analog solutions. For example, a cable that provides a home with television and Internet service can provide those services faster, and allow more data to be downloaded and uploaded, if it carries digital signals. Compression can help with bandwidth as well. For example, if a 1-gigabyte file can be compressed to a smaller file size for transmission and then uncompressed by a computer, the file should download faster.

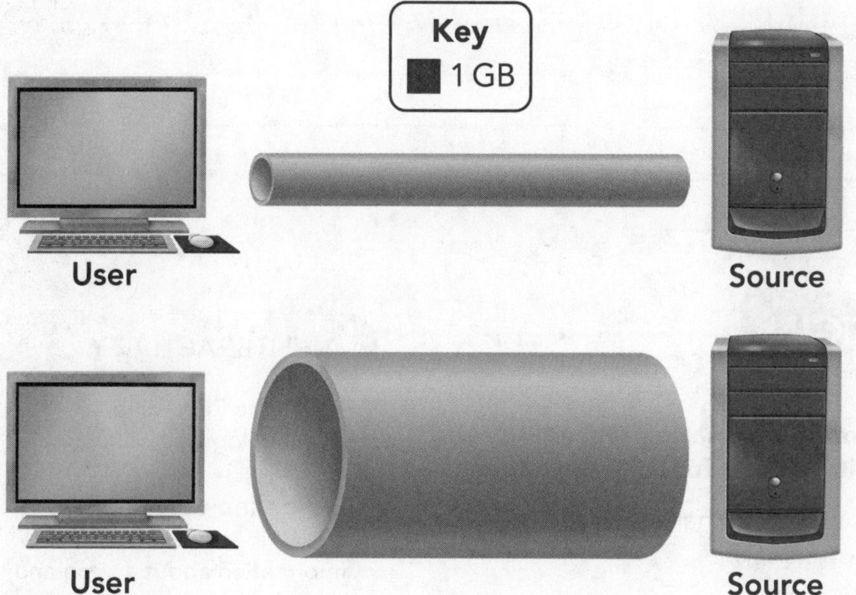

Bandwidth

Figure 4 Narrow bandwidth means slower data transmission, which likely means slower download times.

SEP Develop Models Using the information in the key, model the transmission of 5 GB of data from each source to each user. Your model should demonstrate why narrower bandwidth results in slower download times.

READING CHECK **Cite Textual Evidence** Why are there so many different types of communications technology?

....

....

LESSON 3 Check

MS-PS4-3

1. **Identify** List five different technologies or types of hardware that are used today in communications.

2. **CCC Cause and Effect** Describe how increasing bandwidth and improving compression software can result in a higher quality of hardware and media of higher resolution.

3. **Summarize** What role does software play in information technology?

4. **SEP Construct Explanations** Explain why digital signals are somewhat harder to hack or spy on than analog signals.

Quest CHECK-IN

In this lesson, you learned about information technology and the advantages of using digital signals for communication.

CCC Structure and Function How do hardware and infrastructure affect how we use signals?

INTERACTIVITY

Evaluate Recording Technologies

Go online to research scientific and technical information about analog and digital recording technologies. Then, present your findings in a poster.

MS-PS4-3

Beam Me Up!

It may be hard to believe, but using your phone to make a video call to a friend or family member on the other side of the planet was the stuff of science fiction until about a decade ago. Although the idea for video calls can be traced back to the late 1800s, it required a great deal of scientific advancement and technological progress to become a reality.

In the 1930s, following the development of television, German scientists developed a closed-circuit TV system that allowed people to talk to each other in different cities. Despite plans to expand, the system was shut down in 1940 following the outbreak of World War II.

At the 1964 World's Fair in New York, an American telecommunications company unveiled a picture phone to the world. The system used a regular telephone line with a separate video screen. Since it was very expensive, it did not catch on with the public.

In the 1980s and 1990s, technological advancements, spurred on by the growing popularity of personal computers, led to the development of videoconferencing technology. As electronic devices shrank, it was only a matter of time before the technology made it to the palms of our hands.

MY DISCOVERY

Type "video telephony" into an online search engine to learn more about the history of this technology.

TOPIC 7 Review and Assess

1 Electric Circuits

MS-PS4-3

1. Which of the following is *not* a basic part of an electric circuit?
   A. conducting wires
   B. a transformer
   C. a source of electrical energy
   D. a device that runs on electrical energy

2. In a typical battery,
   A. the negative end has more electrical potential energy than the positive end.
   B. the negative end has the same amount of electrical potential energy as the positive end.
   C. the positive end has more electrical potential energy than the negative end.
   D. voltage determines which end of the battery has more electrical potential energy.

3. The measure of how hard it is for current to flow through an object is called ....

4. **SEP Develop Models** Draw a diagram of a circuit that consists of two lights. The circuit must allow for one light to remain lit if the other light bulb goes out.

2 Signals

MS-PS4-3

5. Digital signals rely on a coding system known as
   A. megabytes.
   B. transmission.
   C. wave pulse.
   D. binary.

6. Which of the following comparisons between analog and digital signals is correct?
   A. Analog signals are electronic signals, while digital signals are electromagnetic signals.
   B. Analog signals are continuous signals, while digital signals are discrete signals.
   C. Analog signals can be stored on computers, while digital signals cannot.
   D. Analog signals store information as numbers, while digital signals do not.

7. **Evaluate Claims** A friend says that digital signals are more exact representations than analog signals. Do you agree? Explain.

8. **SEP Communicate Information** Using a real-world example, identify one advantage of a digital signal over an analog signal.

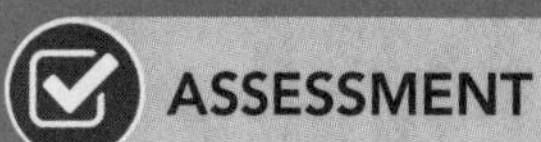

Evaluate your understanding by taking a Topic Test.

3 Communication and Technology

MS-PS4-3

9. Which of the following is *not* an advantage of sending an email over sending a letter through the postal service?
  A. The email is encrypted, making it harder for someone to intercept and read.
  B. The email is easier to store and retrieve, making it less likely to get lost.
  C. The email is more likely to get destroyed.
  D. The email will arrive much faster than the mailed letter.

10. Which of the following statements about signal noise is true?
  A. It affects analog and digital signals in similar ways.
  B. It affects digital signals more than analog signals.
  C. It affects analog signals more than digital signals.
  D. It has little effect on either analog or digital signals.

11. The amount of information that can be transmitted as digital signals over some amount of time is known as
  A. bandwidth. **B.** hardware.
  C. resolution. **D.** noise.

12. Information technology consists of .... and ....that store, manipulate, and transmit information.

13. **CCC Analyze Systems** Why is fiber optic technology an improvement over standard copper cable?

....

....

....

14. **Connect to Nature of Science** Choose an example of a digital technology and describe how it has helped to advance science and scientific investigations.

....

....

....

....

....

....

....

....

15. **SEP Construct Explanations** Explain why digital signals are a more reliable way to conduct a telephone conversation.

....

....

....

....

....

....

....

....

....

TOPIC 7 Review and Assess

MS-PS4-3

Evidence-Based Assessment

A friend of yours lives in a nearby town. The town needs to purchase new two-way radios for its emergency first responders. Town board members are considering replacing the two-way analog radios with digital radios.

However, the digital radios are more expensive. Board members want to know whether the increased costs will bring any benefits before they will vote to approve the measure. Many residents are opposed to spending additional money on new technology.

You and your friend research the issue and find the graph shown here, which compares the range and quality of analog radio signals with digital radio signals.

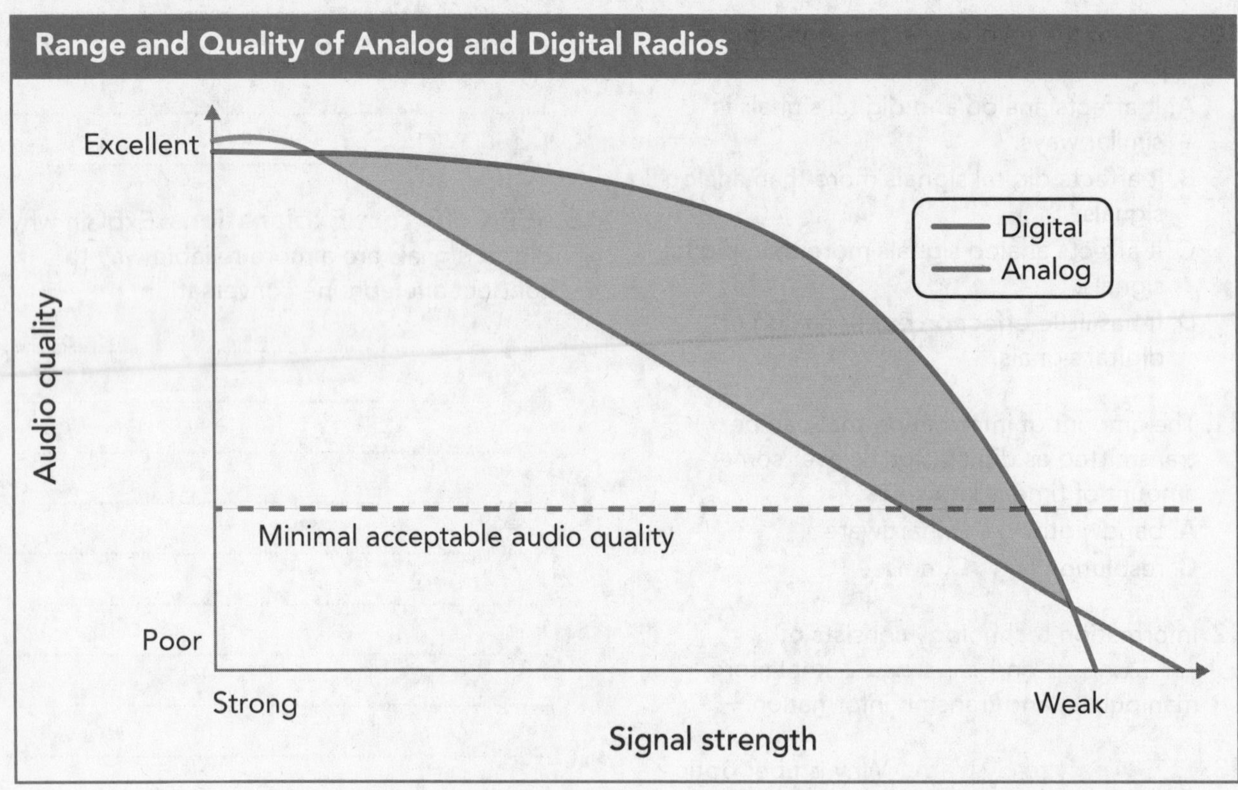

1. **SEP Interpret Data** What does the shaded part of the graph represent?
   A. area in which the audio quality of both radios is not affected by signal strength
   B. area of the digital radio's improved performance over the analog radio
   C. area in which there is no difference in quality between the analog and digital radios
   D. area of the analog radio's improved performance over the digital radio

2. **CCC Patterns** Which of the following statements about the data in the graph are correct? Select all that apply.
   - ☐ The audio quality of the analog radio is slightly better with a very strong signal.
   - ☐ The digital radio has improved audio quality with the very weakest signals.
   - ☐ Both the analog and digital radio have almost the same quality with moderate signal strengths.
   - ☐ The audio quality of the analog radios drops more sharply as signal strength weakens.

3. **Use Graphs** How are signal strength and audio quality related for both analog and digital signals?

4. **SEP Cite Evidence** Use evidence from the graph to explain why the digital radio signals are more reliable than the analog radio signals.

5. **SEP Engage in Argument** What can your friend tell the town board members and residents to persuade them to purchase the digital radios?

Quest FINDINGS

Complete the Quest!

Phenomenon **Determine the best way to present your claim in a multimedia presentation.**

Connect to Society Are there situations in which recording with an analog signal would be more reliable than a digital signal? Explain.

INTERACTIVITY

Reflect on Your Recording Method

uDemonstrate Lab

MS-PS4-3

Over and Out

How can you demonstrate that **digital** signals are a more efficient way to send **information**?

Background

The Center for Information Technology Education will soon open its doors to the public. The center houses a library for students and researchers, as well as a large multimedia theater and exhibit areas. The center has devoted space for hands-on exhibits where visitors can explore communication technology and its history. The center wants you to develop an interactive exhibit that compares and contrasts analog and digital signals. The exhibit's models will allow visitors to send a coded signal designed for each transmission method.

In this investigation, you will design models that help visitors recognize that digital signals are a more reliable way than analog signals to transmit data and information.

(per group)

- spring coil
- small light bulb and socket
- battery (9-volt or type C)
- electrical wire, 10 strips
- electrical switch

Safety

Be sure to follow all safety guidelines provided by your teacher. The Safety Appendix of your textbook provides more details about the safety icons.

In just over 125 years, telephone technology has evolved from large boxes with a lot of wires to small, wireless powerhouses.

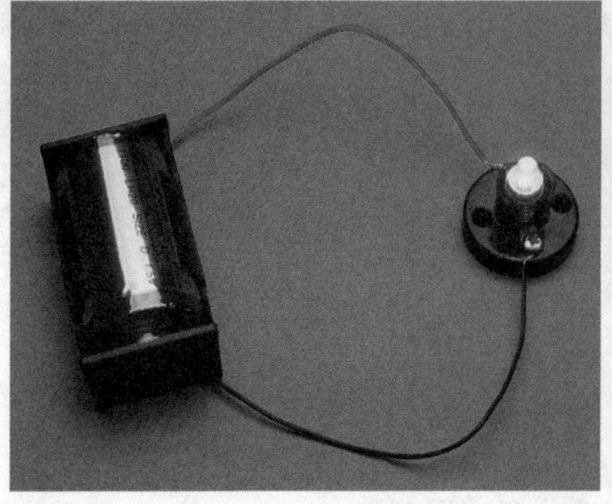

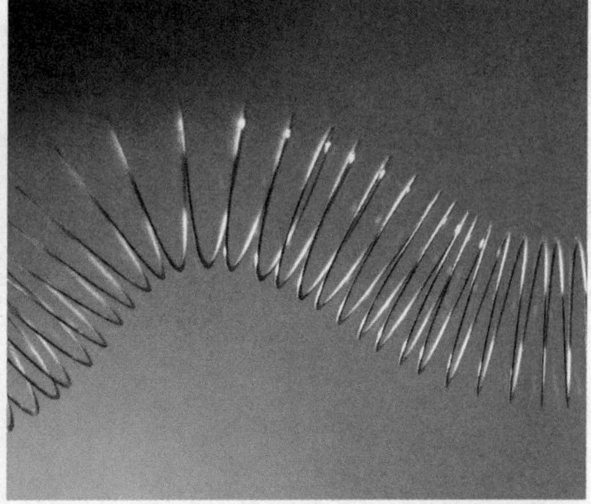

Design Your Exhibit Model

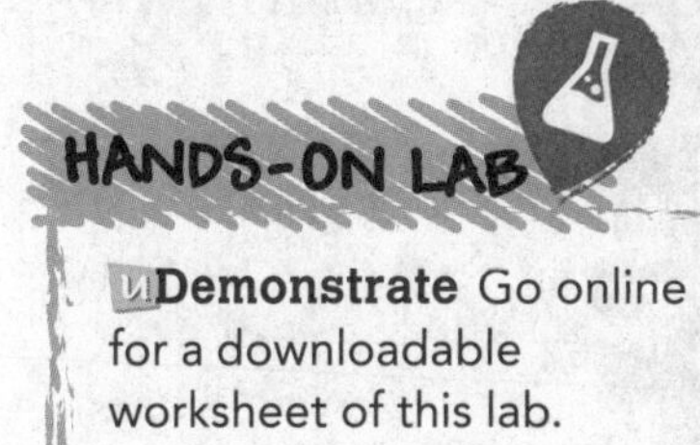

Demonstrate Go online for a downloadable worksheet of this lab.

- [ ] 1. Plan the models you will use in the exhibit. Think about how you can use the available materials to represent two different communication systems: one that models how analog signals send information using continuous wave pulses and one that models how digital signals send information using discrete wave pulses. Consider the following questions as you plan and design your model:
   - Is the spring coil or an electric circuit a better choice to represent the continuous nature of analog signals?
   - Which of these materials is more appropriate to model the discrete nature of digital signals?
- [ ] 2. Develop a code that can be used for the analog system and another one that can be used for the digital system. The data you will transmit is a word made up of four letters: E, T, A, and S. You will need to create a code for each letter. Think about the following questions as you develop the codes:
   - How can you use continuous wave pulses of different amplitudes to represent each letter for the analog system?
   - How can you use discrete wave pulses to represent each letter for the digital system?
- [ ] 3. Sketch your models in the space provided and label the materials you will use. Include descriptions of how the models will operate. Then, complete the table with the codes you developed.
- [ ] 4. After getting your teacher's approval, carry out your investigation. One team member is the transmitter and the other member is the receiver. The transmitter should choose a word, refer to the code, and then transmit the word using the analog system. Repeat the process using a different word for the digital system. You may want to consider using commands to indicate the start and end of transmissions, such as "start transmission" and "end transmission." Run the trial again using the same procedure for each system.

Model Sketches

Data Table and Observations

Letter	Analog Code	Digital Code
E		
T		
A		
S		

Analyze and Interpret Data

1. **SEP Use Models** Describe the results of your investigation and your observations about using each system to transmit information. Which system did you find easier to use? Which system was more accurate? Explain.

2. **Explain Phenomena** Think about the issue of signal noise. How could you incorporate this concept into your models? What effect do you think signal noise would have on the analog system? What effect might it have on the digital system?

3. **SEP Communicate Information** How do your models for the exhibit demonstrate that digital signals are a more reliable way to encode and transmit information than analog signals? Explain.

4. **Identify Limitations** What are some of the challenges you faced as you designed your models and codes? What are some of the drawbacks or limitations of your models?

TOPIC

8

Atoms and the Periodic Table

NGSS PERFORMANCE EXPECTATION

MS-PS1-1 Develop models to describe the atomic composition of simple molecules and extended structures.

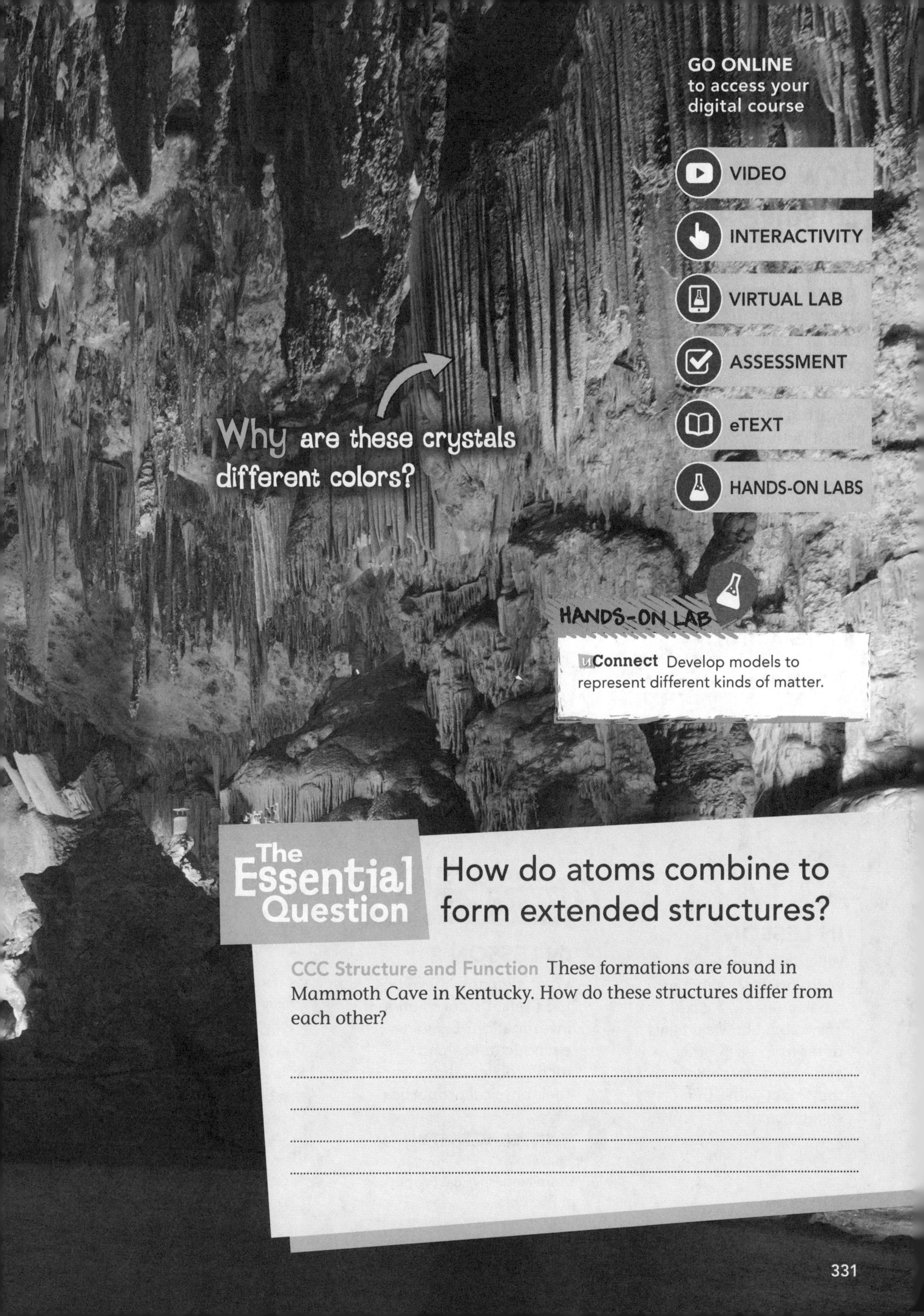

GO ONLINE
to access your
digital course

- VIDEO
- INTERACTIVITY
- VIRTUAL LAB
- ASSESSMENT
- eTEXT
- HANDS-ON LABS

Why are these crystals different colors?

HANDS-ON LAB

uConnect Develop models to represent different kinds of matter.

The Essential Question

How do atoms combine to form extended structures?

CCC Structure and Function These formations are found in Mammoth Cave in Kentucky. How do these structures differ from each other?

....

....

....

....

Quest KICKOFF

How can you use chemistry to solve a culinary mystery?

Phenomenon The baking competition is in an uproar. A confident contestant's cake comes out of the oven in a disastrous state. She cries foul, claiming that her cake has been sabotaged by one of the other contestants. Could it be that one of the other bakers substituted one white powdery ingredient for another, resulting in the spoiled cake? In this problem-based Quest activity, you will be the chemist who determines what substance is in the spoiled cake and which contestant put it there. You will explore and identify the chemical properties of the substances in question. By applying what you learn, you will develop a report about the substance that ruined the cake and which contestant must be guilty.

INTERACTIVITY

Dessert Disaster

MS-PS1-1 Develop models to describe the atomic composition of simple molecules and extended structures.

After watching the Quest Kickoff video, answer the questions. Then turn and share with a partner.

1 **How can chemistry help solve a crime?**

....

....

....

2 **What culinary chemical reactions have you seen that didn't go well or that resulted in a culinary "disaster"?**

....

....

....

IN LESSON 1

Why does it matter which white powdery substance a baker uses in a cake? Think about how elements differ from each other and how differently they react with other substances.

Quest CHECK-IN

IN LESSON 2

What elements make up the five substances under investigation? Examine each substance and record observations of their physical properties.

INTERACTIVITY

Examining Physical Properties of Powders

Quest CHECK-IN

IN LESSON 3

What are the chemical properties of the five substance under investigation? Examine, observe, and record results in a table.

INTERACTIVITY

The Iodine Test for Starch

Chemical reactions are critical to the outcome of all baked products. The ingredients used—and the exact amounts used—contribute to the taste, texture, and appearance of the final product. The wrong ingredient, or the wrong amount, can result in a culinary disaster.

Quest CHECK-IN

IN LESSON 4

How does each of the five substances react with vinegar? How does each respond to heat? Record observations and explain the results of each test.

INTERACTIVITY

The Vinegar Test

Quest CHECK-IN

IN LESSON 5

STEM What is the mystery substance? Draw conclusions from the tests and solve the mystery of the dessert disaster.

HANDS-ON LAB

Solving the Mystery

Quest FINDINGS

Complete the Quest!

Present the findings of your investigation and explain how you arrived at your conclusion.

INTERACTIVITY

Reflect on Your Investigation

uConnect Lab

MS-PS1-1

Modeling Matter

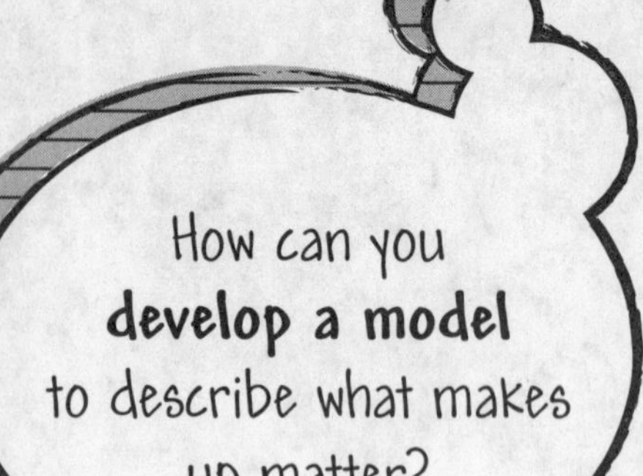

How can you
develop a model
to describe what makes
up matter?

Background

Phenomenon While writing on the board in class one day, the chalk in your hand breaks into tiny pieces. Looking closely, you notice even smaller particles of chalk dust in your hand. Your teacher explains that even smaller particles that you can't see, called atoms, make up the dust particles, as well as all kinds of matter. Your teacher challenges you to develop a model of different kinds of atoms and use them to represent different compounds, including chalk.

Materials

(per group)

- sticky notes in 6 different colors
- colored pencils in 6 different colors

Safety

Be sure to follow all safety procedures provided by your teacher. The Safety Appendix of your textbook provides more details about the safety icons.

Design a Procedure

☐ 1. **SEP Develop a Model** In your models, you will need to represent each of the following elements: hydrogen, oxygen, sodium, chlorine, carbon, and calcium. Write a procedure for how you will use the different colored sticky notes to develop models of different molecules. Include a key to describe which color sticky note represents each element.

☐ 2. Use the following information to develop a model for each molecule using your sticky notes. Write the correct element symbol on each sticky note as you make your model.

Water = 2 hydrogen + 1 oxygen
Salt = 1 sodium + 1 chlorine
Methane = 1 carbon + 4 hydrogen
Chalk = 1 calcium + 1 carbon + 3 oxygen

☐ 3. Draw your models in the Observations section. Be sure to label each model.

Organizing the Elements

Do you organize things according to their properties? Are all of your books together in your locker? Are your clothes organized according to whether they are winter clothes or summer clothes? **Figure 1** shows how sorting recyclable materials puts them into groups that are all recycled the same way.

Organizing things usually makes them easier to use because you can better know their properties, or characteristics. Items grouped together are likely to have some properties that are similar.

Scientists also had a need to organize elements. By 1869, a total of 63 elements had been discovered. A few were gases. Two were liquids. Most were solid metals. Some reacted explosively as they formed compounds. Others reacted slowly. Scientists wondered whether the properties of elements followed a pattern. One of these scientists, Dmitri Mendeleev (men duh LAY ef), discovered a set of patterns that applies to all the elements.

Begin investigating the organization of the periodic table.

Literacy Connection

Determine Central Ideas
In the text, underline a reason that you might organize your DVDs into comedies, dramas, and action movies.

Organizing with a Purpose

Figure 1 Recyclable items must be sorted into groups based on the properties of their materials.

Similar Properties

Figure 2 At room temperature, chlorine is a gas, bromine is a liquid, and iodine is a solid. However, all three elements share some physical properties. They also have very similar chemical properties. They are grouped in the same column on the periodic table. What common property do you observe?

....

....

VIDEO

Watch a video to observe patterns in daily life as they relate to the periodic table.

Mendeleev's Work Mendeleev knew that some elements had similar chemical and physical properties. For example, silver and copper are both shiny metals. Mendeleev thought these similarities were important clues to a hidden pattern. To find that pattern, Mendeleev noted each element's melting point, density, and color. He also included the element's atomic mass.

As you read in the previous lesson, scientists use atomic mass units (amu) to determine the mass of an element. An element's **atomic mass** is the average mass of all the isotopes of that element. Mendeleev noticed that a pattern of properties appeared when he arranged the elements in order of increasing atomic mass. He found that the pattern of the properties repeated regularly.

The Periodic Table The **periodic table** is a chart showing all of the elements arranged according to the repeating pattern of their properties. (The word *periodic* means "in a regular, repeated pattern.") Mendeleev created the first periodic table in 1869. He arranged his table according to each element's atomic mass. **Figure 2** shows three elements that have similar properties and were, therefore, grouped together.

In his periodic table, Mendeleev also left blank spaces. He predicted that the blank spaces would be filled by elements that had not yet been discovered. He even correctly predicted the properties of some of those new elements.

Mendeleev's table has indeed changed over time, as scientists discovered new elements and learned more about atomic structure. We now know that the number of protons in an atom's nucleus, indicated by the atomic number, is related to the chemical properties of an element. Therefore, modern periodic tables are arranged in order of increasing atomic number instead of by increasing atomic mass.

READING CHECK **Explain** How is the modern periodic table different from Mendeleev's periodic table?

....

....

....

....

Using the Periodic Table

The periodic table contains information about each of the known elements. It includes the name of each element, its atomic number, and its atomic mass. It also includes its **chemical symbol**. This symbol is a one- or two-letter abbreviation for the element. **Figure 3** shows the **representation** of the element phosphorus on the periodic table.

Look at the periodic table in **Figure 4** on the next two pages. Notice that the atomic numbers increase from left to right. Also notice that each color-coded region corresponds to a different class of elements—metals, nonmetals, and metalloids.

Academic Vocabulary

How are a symbol and a model both examples of a representation?

....

....

....

....

Information in Each Cell

Figure 3 The periodic table contains one cell for each of the known elements. Each cell provides certain information about the element represented. Study the information shown for the element phosphorus. Then, using **Figure 4**, fill in the information for the element zinc on the cell shown, and label each piece of information.

15

P

30.974

Phosphorus

Atomic Number One piece of information is the atomic number of the element, shown at the top of each cell. For phosphorus, that number is 15. Every phosphorus atom has 15 protons in its nucleus.

Chemical Symbol In the center of each cell is the chemical symbol for the element. A permanent chemical symbol contains either one or two letters. For phosphorus, that letter is "P." Chemical symbols with three letters are temporary and are used until permanent names are assigned to the elements.

Atomic Mass At the bottom of each cell is the average atomic mass of the element. For phosphorus, this value is 30.974 amu (atomic mass units). The atomic mass is an average because most elements consist of a mixture of isotopes.

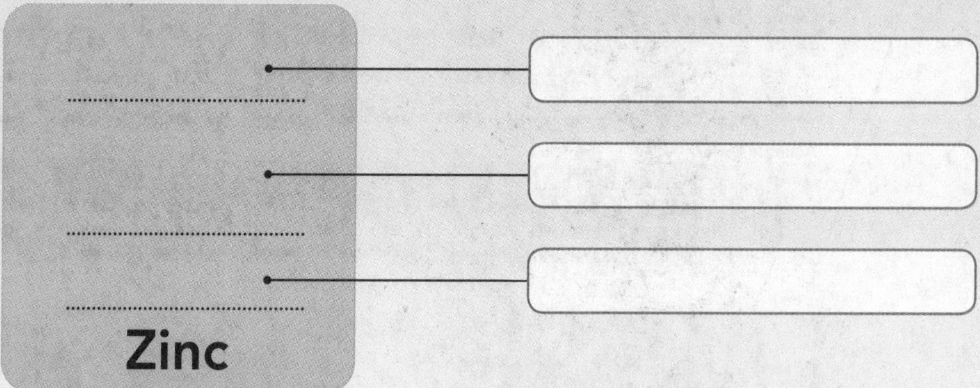

The Periodic Table

Figure 4 The periodic table is one of a chemist's most valuable tools. Find the element identified by the atomic number 51 on the periodic table. Use the information to fill in the blanks below.

Name of element ....

Chemical symbol ....

Atomic mass ....

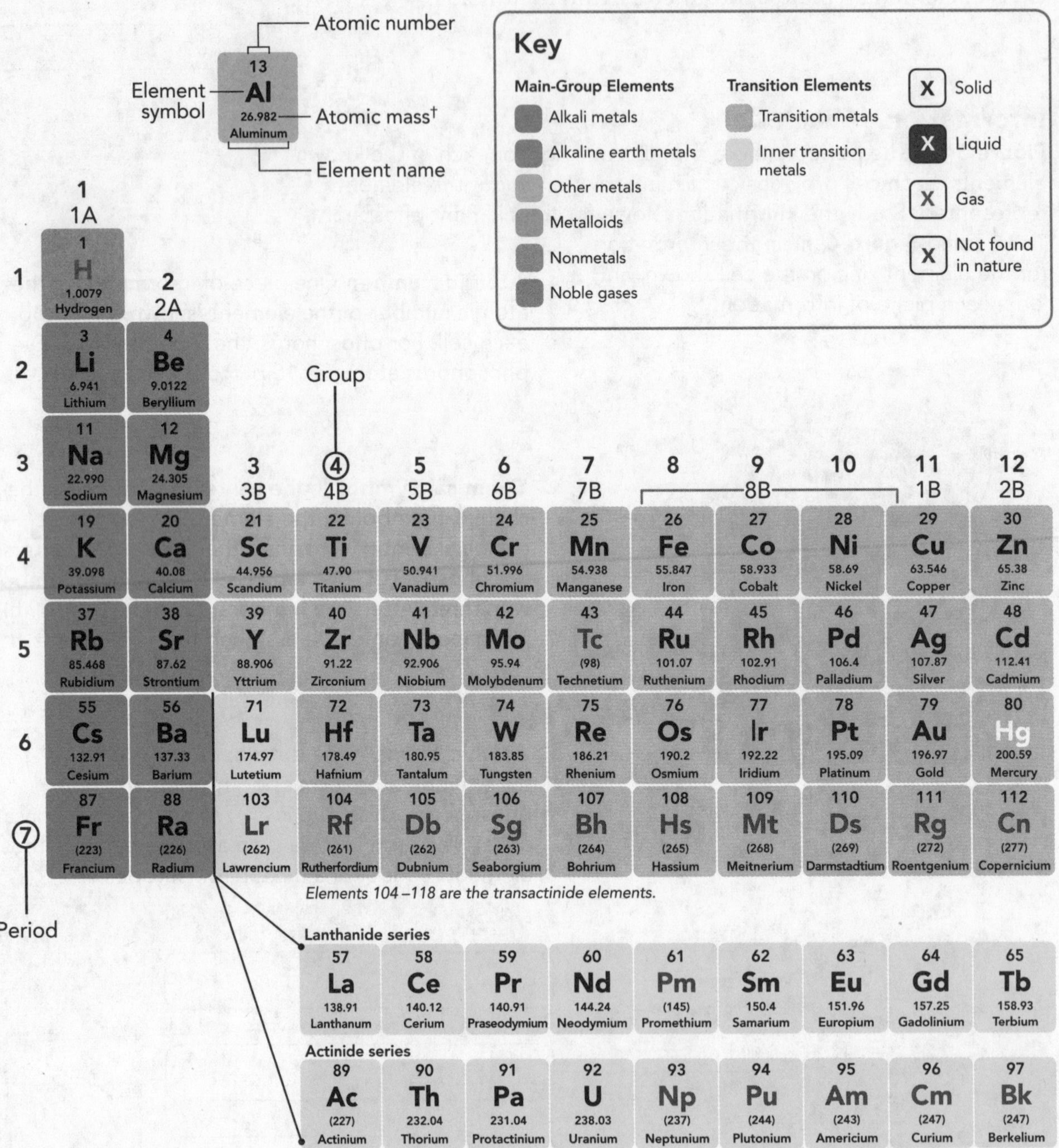

Math Toolbox

Applying the Periodic Table

The order of elements on the periodic table enables scientists to predict properties about the elements. Answer these questions about the periodic table?

1. **SEP Analyze Data** What is the difference of the atomic masses of the heaviest and lightest elements in the table?

   ....

2. **Sequence** Examine the periodic table. Which four pairs of elements would be reversed in order if the elements were listed by increasing atomic mass instead of increasing atomic number?

   ....

   ....

   ....

3. **Predict** When Mendeleev developed the periodic table, the element gallium had not yet been discovered. Without looking at the periodic table on this page, examine the elements surrounding gallium in the diagram below, and predict the atomic number and atomic mass for this element. How does your prediction match the actual atomic number and atomic mass for gallium on the periodic table?

   ....

   ....

   ....

†The atomic masses in parentheses are the mass numbers of the longest-lived isotope of elements for which a standard atomic mass cannot be defined.

13 3A	14 4A	15 5A	16 6A	17 7A	18 8A
					2 He 4.0026 Helium
5 B 10.81 Boron	6 C 12.011 Carbon	7 N 14.007 Nitrogen	8 O 15.999 Oxygen	9 F 18.998 Fluorine	10 Ne 20.179 Neon
13 Al 26.982 Aluminum	14 Si 28.086 Silicon	15 P 30.974 Phosphorus	16 S 32.06 Sulfur	17 Cl 35.453 Chlorine	18 Ar 39.948 Argon
31 Ga 69.72 Gallium	32 Ge 72.59 Germanium	33 As 74.922 Arsenic	34 Se 78.96 Selenium	35 Br 79.904 Bromine	36 Kr 83.80 Krypton
49 In 114.82 Indium	50 Sn 118.69 Tin	51 Sb 121.75 Antimony	52 Te 127.60 Tellurium	53 I 126.90 Iodine	54 Xe 131.30 Xenon
81 Tl 204.37 Thallium	82 Pb 207.2 Lead	83 Bi 208.98 Bismuth	84 Po (209) Polonium	85 At (210) Astatine	86 Rn (222) Radon
113 Nh (284) Nihonium	114 Fl (289) Flerovium	115 Mc (288) Moscovium	116 Lv (292) Livermorium	117 Ts (294) Tennessine	118 Og (294) Oganesson

66 Dy 162.50 Dysprosium	67 Ho 164.93 Holmium	68 Er 167.26 Erbium	69 Tm 168.93 Thulium	70 Yb 173.04 Ytterbium
98 Cf (251) Californium	99 Es (252) Einsteinium	100 Fm (257) Fermium	101 Md (258) Mendelevium	102 No (259) Nobelium

	13 Al 26.982 Aluminum	14 Si 28.086 Silicon
30 Zn 65.38 Zinc	Ga Gallium	32 Ge 72.59 Germanium
48 Cd 112.41 Cadmium	49 In 114.82 Indium	50 Sn 118.69 Tin

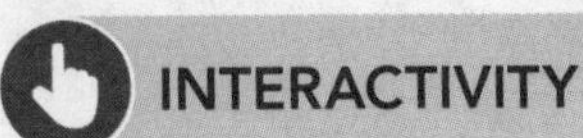

INTERACTIVITY

Explore how atomic mass and other properties of elements determine the organization of the periodic table.

Periods in the Periodic Table

The rows in the periodic table are known as periods. Each **period** contains a series of different elements. Look at the period numbers on the left side of the periodic table in **Figure 4**. As you look from left to right across a period, you will notice that the properties of the elements change in a pattern. Metals are shown on the left of the table, and nonmetals are located on the right. Metalloids are found between the metals and nonmetals. This pattern is repeated in each period. An element's properties can be predicted by its location in the periodic table. This predictability is one reason that the periodic table is so useful to chemists.

Lanthanides and Actinides Under the bottom row of the main part of the periodic table, you can see two additional rows standing alone. These rows are placed off the table to save space and to make the rest of the table easier to read. Follow the line on **Figure 4** to see how these rows fit in the table.

The elements in the top row are the lanthanides. These elements are all found in nature and are sometimes called the "rare earth metals." The most commonly known element in this series is lanthanum (La), for which the series is named. Some uses for lanthanum are shown in **Figure 5**.

Under the lanthanides are the actinides. Uranium and thorium are the only two actinides that are found in significant quantities in nature. Most other actinides are not found in nature, but are made artificially in laboratories. One characteristic that all actinides have in common is that they are radioactive.

....

La

....

Lanthanum

Uses of Lanthanum

Figure 5 Lanthanum (La), like other lanthanides, is a soft, shiny metal. This lanthanide is a major component in batteries for hybrid cars and in permanent magnets. Label the lanthanum cell with the atomic number and atomic mass.

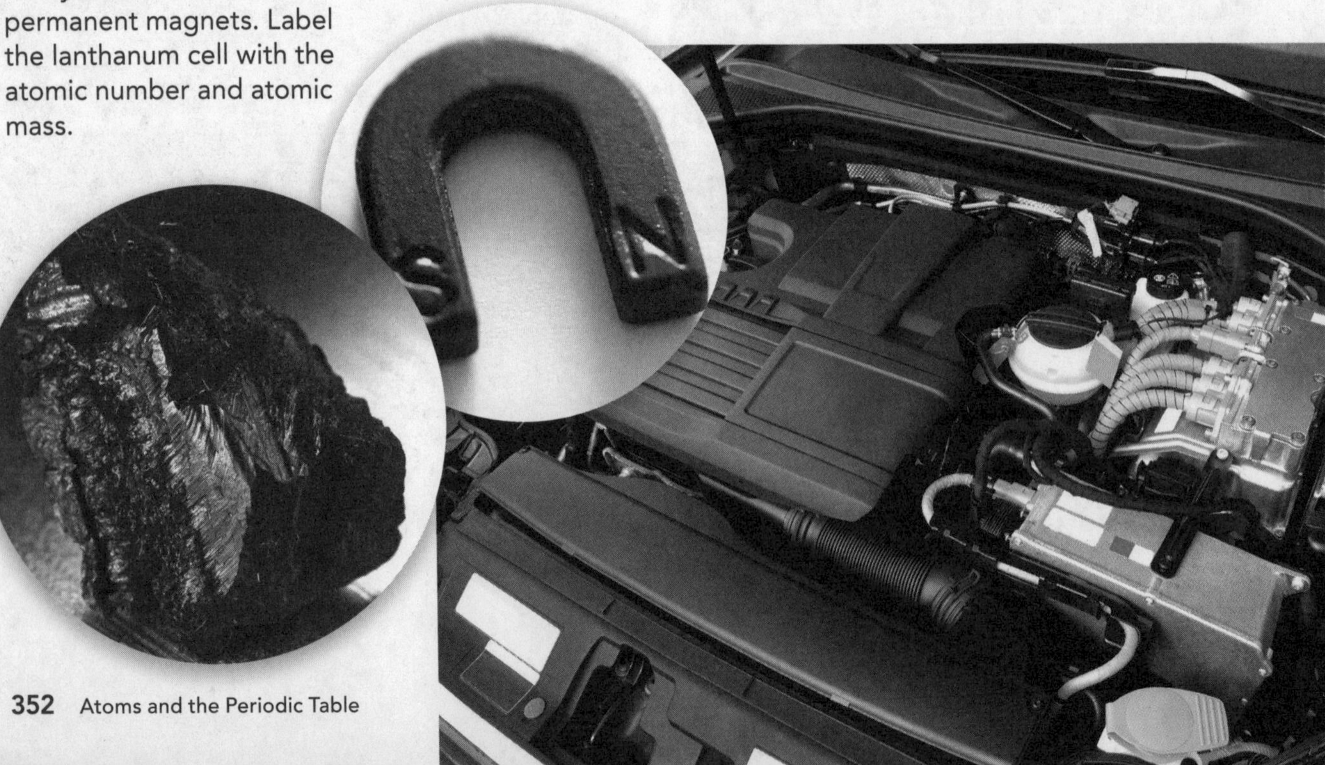

Transuranium Elements The elements that come after uranium (U) in the periodic table are known as transuranium elements. None of these elements is stable, and each of them decays radioactively into other elements. With the exception of small traces of neptunium and plutonium, these elements are not found in nature. They are made in a laboratory when nuclear particles are forced to crash into one another.

Scientists use particle accelerators to make atomic nuclei move at extremely high speeds. If these nuclei crash into the nuclei of other elements with enough energy, the particles can combine into a single nucleus.

In general, the higher the atomic number, the more difficult it is to synthesize new elements. So, this process has taken place only as more powerful particle accelerators have been built. Some of these newly discovered elements do not yet have permanent names or symbols. In the future, scientists around the world will agree on permanent names and symbols for these elements.

See how art and science can come together in the work of an artist.

Question It!

Temporary Element Names

Until scientists assign permanent names to newly discovered elements, the elements are assigned temporary names based on their atomic number. Each digit in the atomic number is assigned the root name for that digit. Then the suffix *-ium* is added to the end of the name. For example, before element 116 got its permanent name, it was called ununhexium from the roots for the digits 1, 1, and 6, followed by the suffix *-ium*.

digit	root	symbol
0	nil	n
1	un	u
2	bi	b
3	tri	t
4	quad	q
5	pent	p
6	hex	h
7	sept	s
8	oct	o
9	en	e

SEP Interpret Data Imagine that three new elements are discovered, and they need temporary names. Use the information in the table to name the yet-undiscovered elements with these atomic numbers. Then, write the three-letter chemical symbol for the element.

Element 119 ....

Element 120 ....

Element 121 ....

HANDS-ON LAB

Investigate Practice arranging and classifying elements in the periodic table.

Groups in the Periodic Table

The modern periodic table has seven periods, each of which follows a pattern. Because the pattern of properties repeats in each period, these patterns can be used to classify elements that have similar characteristics into a specific **group**, or family. There are 18 columns in the table, and so there are 18 groups.

Groups Containing Metals If you examine the periodic table, you can see that metals make up most of the elements. At least one metal is found in every group except Group 18. See **Figure 6** to examine some of the groups that contain metals.

The Metal Groups

Figure 6 The groups shaded on the periodic table below contain the alkali metals, the alkaline earth metals, and the transition metals. Next to each element's name and image, fill in its chemical symbol.

Lithium ....

Alkali Metals
The metals of Group 1, from lithium (Li) to francium (Fr), are called the alkali metals. Alkali metals are so reactive that they are never found as free elements in nature. They are found only in compounds. Some of the alkali metals are shiny and so soft you can cut them with a plastic knife.

Alkaline Earth Metals
The metals of Group 2 are called the alkaline earth metals. These metals are harder and denser, and they melt at higher temperatures than the alkali metals. Alkaline earth metals are very reactive, though not as reactive as the alkali metals. These metals are also never found uncombined in nature.

Magnesium ....

Gold ....

Transition Metals
The elements in Groups 3 through 12 are called the transition metals. They include iron, copper, nickel, gold, and silver. Most of these metals are hard and shiny solids with high melting points. Most are good conductors of heat and electric current. Some transition metals (like gold) can be found in their elemental forms in nature.

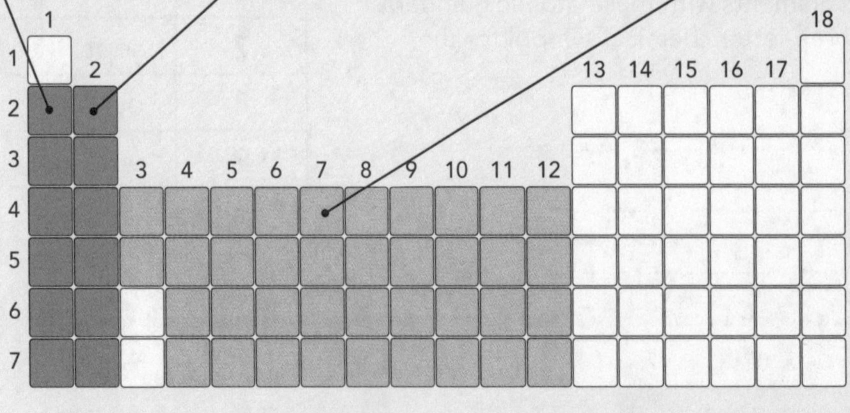

Groups Containing Metalloids and Nonmetals Look back at the periodic table. There are nonmetals in Group 1 and in Groups 14 through 18. Examine **Figure 7**, which shows some groups that contain nonmetals (groups 13 through 16). These groups also contain metalloids, which have some properties of metals and some properties of nonmetals.

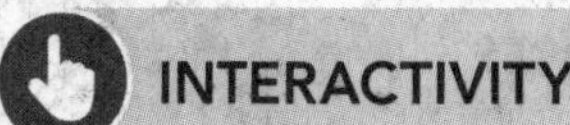

Analyze, identify, and classify elements based on their properties.

Groups with Metalloids and Nonmetals

Figure 7 The groups shaded on the periodic table below contain metals, metalloids, and nonmetals. Write the chemical symbols of the representative elements next to each photo.

The Boron Family Group 13 contains the metalloid boron, followed by post-transition metals. Boron is used in materials of high strength and light weight, such as fiberglass.

Boron ....

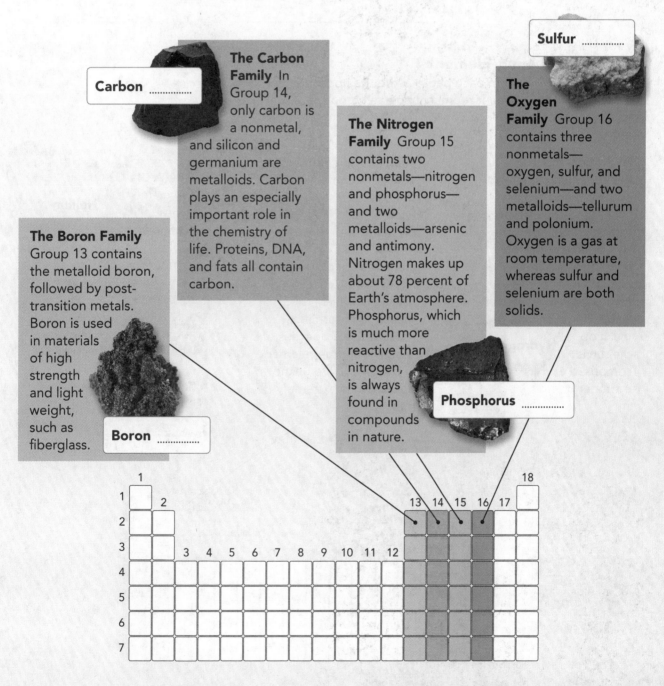

The Carbon Family In Group 14, only carbon is a nonmetal, and silicon and germanium are metalloids. Carbon plays an especially important role in the chemistry of life. Proteins, DNA, and fats all contain carbon.

Carbon ....

The Nitrogen Family Group 15 contains two nonmetals—nitrogen and phosphorus—and two metalloids—arsenic and antimony. Nitrogen makes up about 78 percent of Earth's atmosphere. Phosphorus, which is much more reactive than nitrogen, is always found in compounds in nature.

Phosphorus ....

The Oxygen Family Group 16 contains three nonmetals—oxygen, sulfur, and selenium—and two metalloids—tellurum and polonium. Oxygen is a gas at room temperature, whereas sulfur and selenium are both solids.

Sulfur ....

Reflect How is the periodic table helpful to you? In your science notebook, describe one or two ways the periodic table might help you, and explain how.

Halogens, Noble Gases, and Hydrogen The shaded areas in **Figure 8** contain the halogens, the noble gases, and hydrogen. Halogens are the most reactive nonmetals, while noble gases are the least reactive nonmetals. Hydrogen is a nonmetal that does not fall into a family because its chemical properties are very different from other elements. It is the simplest element, containing only one proton and one electron.

READING CHECK **Determine Central Ideas** What do alkali metals and alkaline earth metals have in common? How are they different?

....

....

....

The Remaining Elements

Figure 8 Next to each photo, write the appropriate symbol of the element representing each group.

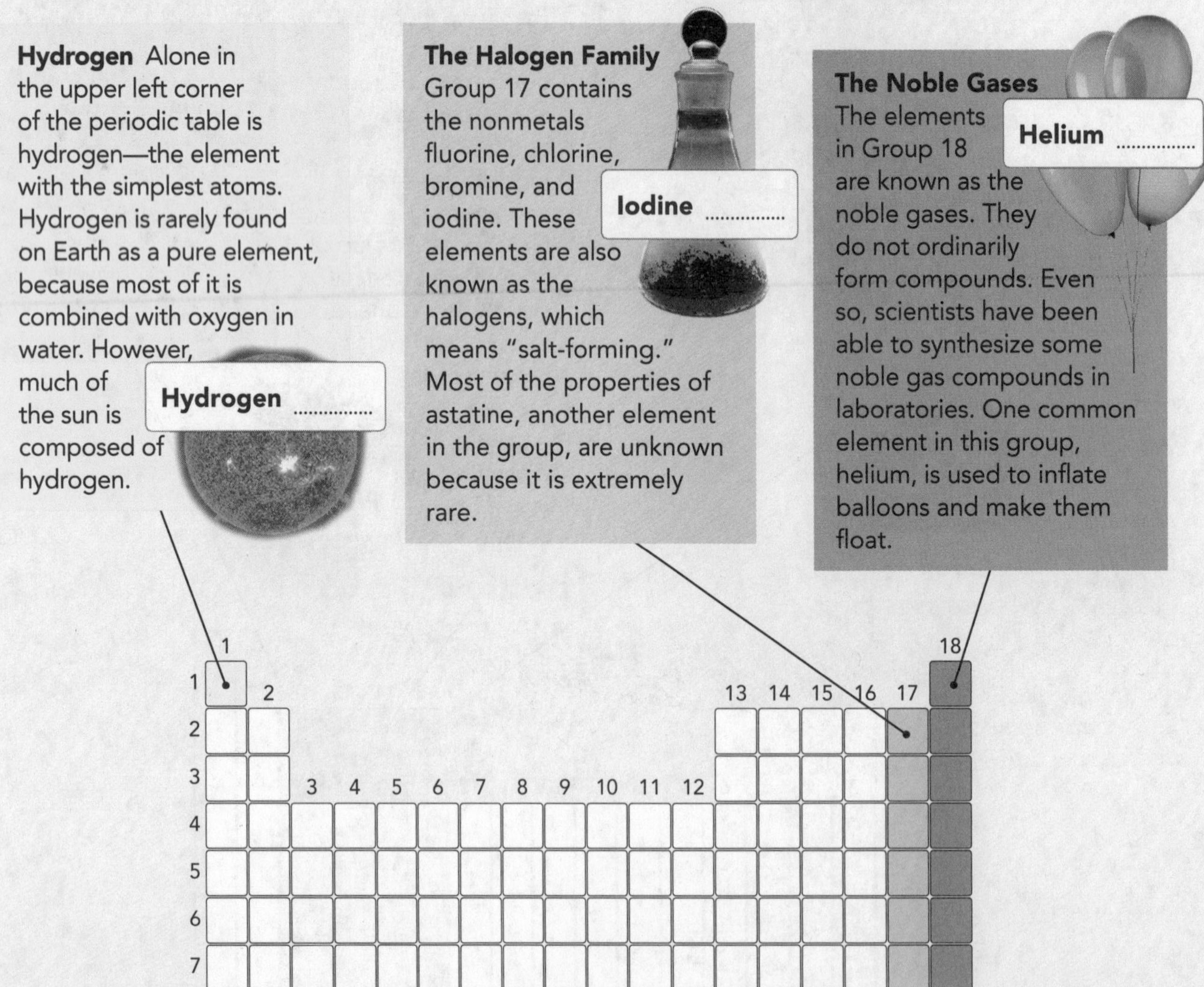

Hydrogen Alone in the upper left corner of the periodic table is hydrogen—the element with the simplest atoms. Hydrogen is rarely found on Earth as a pure element, because most of it is combined with oxygen in water. However, much of the sun is composed of hydrogen.
Hydrogen ....
The Halogen Family Group 17 contains the nonmetals fluorine, chlorine, bromine, and iodine. These elements are also known as the halogens, which means "salt-forming." Most of the properties of astatine, another element in the group, are unknown because it is extremely rare.
Iodine ....
The Noble Gases The elements in Group 18 are known as the noble gases. They do not ordinarily form compounds. Even so, scientists have been able to synthesize some noble gas compounds in laboratories. One common element in this group, helium, is used to inflate balloons and make them float.
Helium ....
1
2
3
4
5
6
7
8
9
10
11
12
13
14
15
16
17
18

LESSON 2 Check

MS-PS1-1

1. **SEP Communicate Information** In addition to properties of elements, list at least two other things or events that are periodic.

2. **Explain Phenomena** Assume that one particular atom of rhodium (Rh) has a mass of 102. Why does this number not exactly match the atomic mass of 102.91 listed on the periodic table for this element?

Use Figure 4 to answer question 3.

3. **CCC Patterns** What element is found in Group 6 and Period 4? Based on its location, is this element more similar to tungsten or to iron? Explain.

4. **SEP Engage in Argument** The noble gases in Group 18 were some of the last natural elements to be discovered. Why do you think this is so?

Quest CHECK-IN

In this lesson, you learned how scientists use the periodic table as a tool to organize elements according to their physical and chemical properties.

Describe If you were given five unknown substances and were asked to describe them by their physical properties, what would you look for? What should you **not** do while observing their physical properties?

INTERACTIVITY

Examining Physical Properties of Powders

Go online to learn more about the physical properties of some common elements and substances.

Bonding and the Periodic Table

Guiding Questions

- What causes atoms to bond together?
- How do valence electrons and bonding affect the properties of elements?

Connection

Literacy Support Claims

MS-PS1-1

HANDS-ON LAB

uInvestigate Explore how to use combustion levels to classify compounds.

Vocabulary

compound
valence electron
reactivity
malleable
ductile
luster
semiconductor

Academic Vocabulary

interpretation
transfer

Connect It!

Circle the part of the image that shows the reactivity of hydrogen.

SEP Analyzing and Interpreting Data Use the periodic table to predict why krypton, another noble gas, is not used in airships.

....

....

Infer How would the results of the spark have been different if the Hindenburg had been filled with helium?

....

....

GO ONLINE
to access your digital course

VIDEO

INTERACTIVITY

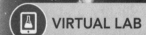

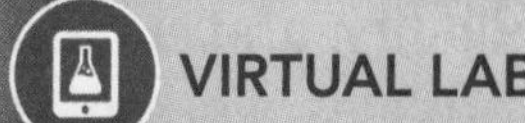
VIRTUAL LAB

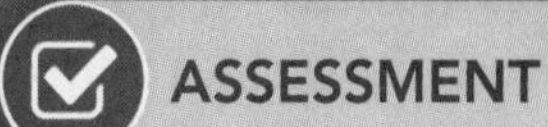
ASSESSMENT

eTEXT

HANDS-ON LABS

What allows these fireflies to glow?

The Essential Question

How can you determine when a chemical reaction has occurred?

CCC Energy and Matter This digitally enhanced image shows fireflies meandering through a forest. The fireflies spend their summers lighting up at night to attract mates. How do you think a firefly is able to make its abdomen glow like this?

Quest KICKOFF

How can you design and build hot packs and cold packs?

Phenomenon Every day, people test the strength, flexibility, and endurance of their bodies. They may be athletes, workers, or simply active kids and adults. When minor injuries occur, applying heat or cold can ease pain, reduce swelling, and help damaged muscle or tissue begin to heal. Chemists and product engineers have designed easy-to-use packs that get hot or cold because of chemical reactions that can activate when users are ready to use the packs. In this problem-based Quest activity, you will design and build a hot or cold pack for the treatment of minor injuries. You will determine which chemicals and materials best meet the criteria and constraints. After exploration, design, and testing, you will reflect on your product and its effectiveness.

INTERACTIVITY

Hot and Cool Chemistry

MS-PS1-6 Undertake a design project to construct, test, and modify a device that either releases or absorbs thermal energy by chemical processes.

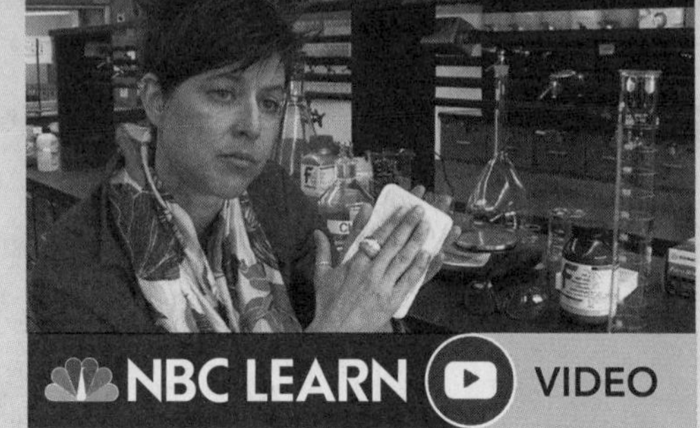

NBC LEARN VIDEO

After watching the Quest Kickoff video, in which a chemist describes chemical processes that release or absorb heat, think of other uses for a product that heats up or cools down. Record three ideas.

1 ....

....

....

2 ....

....

....

3 ....

....

Quest CHECK-IN

IN LESSON 1

How do salts react with water? Explore whether various chemical interactions bring about a release or absorption of energy.

HANDS-ON LAB

Energy Salts

Quest CHECK-IN

IN LESSON 2

STEM Which chemical reaction will achieve the desired results in a hot or cold pack? Devise a plan for your chosen chemical reaction, including a design plan for the pack itself.

INTERACTIVITY

Design Your Pack

Quest CHECK-IN

IN LESSON 3

STEM How can you construct your hot or cold pack? Choose materials, build a prototype using ordinary salt or sugar, and test your product.

HANDS-ON LAB

Pack Building

Instant cold packs don't need to be kept in a freezer or cooler, so they are easier to transport than ice. They can be activated the moment an injury occurs.

Quest CHECK-IN

IN LESSON 4

STEM How can you construct a better prototype? Build an improved prototype using chemical salts and demonstrate the use of the product.

HANDS-ON LAB

Heat It Up or Ice It Down

Quest FINDINGS

Complete the Quest!

Based on results and feedback from your demonstration, evaluate the effectiveness of your hot or cold pack. Reflect on your work.

INTERACTIVITY

Reflect on Your Pack

uConnect Lab

MS-PS1-2

What Happens When Chemicals React?

How can you **observe** some of the changes that happen when two chemicals react?

Background

Phenomenon In this activity, you will observe some of the changes that take place when two substances are combined and chemically react.

Materials

(per group)

- baking soda
- white vinegar
- clear plastic cup
- spoon
- graduated cylinder
- large bowl or sink

Safety

Be sure to follow all safety procedures provided by your teacher. The Safety Appendix of your textbook provides more details about the safety icons.

Design a Procedure

☐ 1. Write a plan to make observations about the characteristics of baking soda and vinegar before they are mixed and after they are mixed. Think about the different characteristics you will observe (i.e., smell, color, etc...). **Do not taste any materials.** Record your plan.

....

....

....

....

....

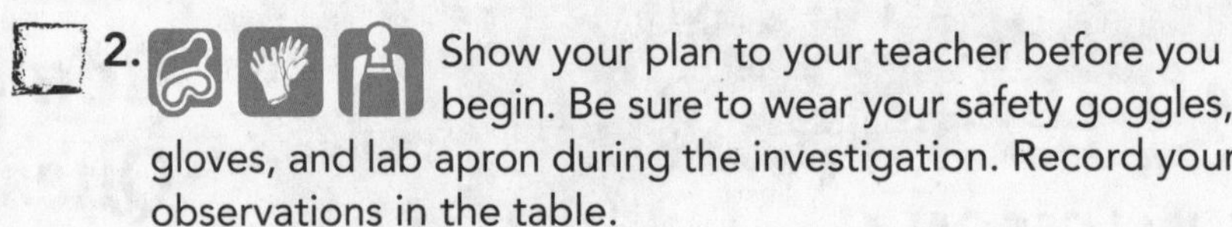

☐ 2. Show your plan to your teacher before you begin. Be sure to wear your safety goggles, gloves, and lab apron during the investigation. Record your observations in the table.

☐ 3. Pour the contents of the cup into the drain, and run some water to wash it down. Wash your hands with soap when you are finished with this activity.

Synthetic Materials

Engage in a class discussion about synthetic materials in your everyday life.

Chemical reactions are constantly happening all around us in nature. Many of the products of naturally occurring reactions have properties that are useful to humans. For instance, plants perform photosynthesis, a chemical reaction that releases oxygen, which we need to survive.

However, not all of the chemicals and materials that humans use come directly from naturally occurring reactions. Instead, they are products of chemical reactions we induce. Such reactions start with substances found in nature, but they result in new materials being formed. For example, glass is made from sand and other minerals that are melted together.

Chemicals and resources made by humans are called **synthetic** materials. Synthetic materials, such as the tartrazine in **Figure 1**, have a wide variety of uses and have enabled great advances in engineering and technology. Chemists are always trying out new chemical reactions to produce new materials for our ever-changing needs.

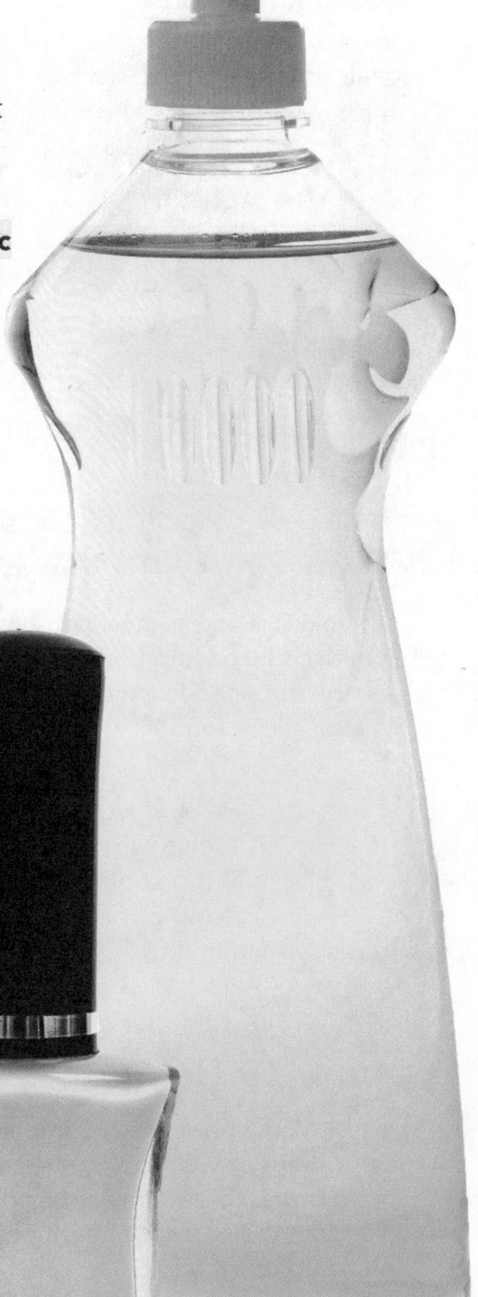

Making Colors in the Lab

Figure 1 Tartrazine is a synthetic coloring agent. It is used in products ranging from foods to medicines and cosmetics.

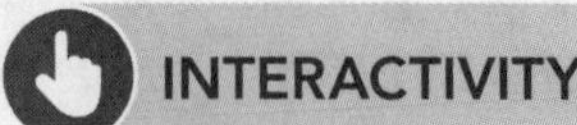

INTERACTIVITY

Explore the relationship between natural resources and synthetics in medicine.

Academic Vocabulary

Replicate means to copy or repeat. Use the word replicate in a sentence.

....

....

Natural Resources as Building Blocks All the useful materials we benefit from are synthesized from natural resources. A **natural resource** is anything naturally occurring in the environment that humans use. These resources may be pure elements, simple molecules, or complex molecules.

Chemists assemble synthetic materials in an ordered set of steps, using chemical reactions to create the desired material. The process can be **replicated** at a later time or by another lab to produce the same results. Just the way you would build a house one brick at a time, a chemist synthesizes a material by adding molecular "blocks" one step at a time. You build the house by moving the bricks into place by hand. The chemist relies upon chemical reactions to move molecules into place.

Math Toolbox

Nutrient Concentration

Vitamin C is an essential nutrient for a healthy, functioning body. This vitamin can be obtained from food sources or in a synthetic form in a tablet.

A tablet with a mass of 500 mg contains about 450 mg of synthetic vitamin C.

A 180-g (180,000-mg) orange contains about 106 mg of vitamin C.

1. Use Ratio Reasoning Compare the concentrations of vitamin C in the tablet and in the orange. To determine the concentration, calculate the percent of each object that is made up of vitamin C.

....

....

....

....

2. SEP Interpret Data About how many oranges would you need to eat to get the same amount of vitamin C in one tablet?

....

3. Analyze Quantitative Relationships A carton of navel oranges has a mass of 18.2 kilograms. How much vitamin C do the oranges contain?

....

Properties of Pure Substances

Properties of Pure Substances Every pure substance has characteristic physical and chemical properties that you use to identify it. Substances react in characteristic, predictable ways, forming new materials with physical and chemical properties different from the original substances. For example, sodium is a soft metal with a low melting point, and chlorine is a toxic gas. When sodium burns in chlorine gas, the product formed by the reaction is sodium chloride (NaCl). As you may recall, sodium chloride is table salt. The reaction of two substances produces a new material with completely different properties, and we can eat it!

With the knowledge of the physical and chemical properties of substances and how they chemically react with each other, chemists can combine substances to produce materials that have specific structures and that serve particular functions. This isn't to say that all synthetic materials are created on purpose, as shown in **Figure 2**.

VIDEO

Watch a video to clear up misconceptions about synthetics.

Accidental Synthetics

Figure 2 Many synthetic materials were created accidentally in the lab. Use what you know about each of these products to write their properties.

SEP Evaluate Information Use library or Internet resources to check your answers and find out more about each synthetic product. Make sure to evaluate the credibility of the sources you use.

Synthetic and How It Was Discovered	Useful Properties
Superglue In the 1940s, a chemist working on plastic gun sights synthesized a material called cyanoacrylate that frustratingly stuck to everything it touched. A few years later, the chemist came up with an important purpose for the sticky material. 	
 **Non-stick Coating** In the 1930s, a chemist working on a new refrigerant came back to his lab to find small white flakes in a container instead of a gas he had been experimenting with. The chemist had unintentionally synthesized a new non-stick substance.	
Artificial Sweetener In the late 1800s, a chemist was working on an experimental compound. Forgetting to wash his hands before eating, he noticed that everything he ate tasted very sweet. 	

Investigate Discover how to make plastic from starch.

Polymers Many natural and artificial materials are made of **polymers**. Polymers are long chains of molecules that are made up of repeating units called monomers. Polymers occur naturally and have been used by people for centuries. They include wool, silk, rubber, and cellulose. Polymers have many different and important properties, such as strength, flexibility, and elasticity, all due to the structure of long molecule chains. Polymers that don't occur naturally are synthesized in large quantities to provide clothes, building materials, and most of our material goods. Plastic water bottles and toothbrushes (**Figure 3**) are made of polymers.

The most common synthetic polymers are plastics. Plastics are moldable substances that are strong but flexible. These synthetic materials are usually made from petroleum, a natural resource. While plastics have revolutionized our lives, they also are generally resistant to breaking down and biodegrading. They contribute to pollution when they are not recycled.

READING CHECK **Summarize** Why do chemists synthesize polymers in the lab?

....

....

....

Model It!

The Structure of Polymers

Figure 3 The composition of a polymer such as plastic may be very simple, but the number of molecules may be huge, containing millions of atoms!

SEP Develop Models Use the model of the monomer to create a model of a polymer.

Monomer

Polymer

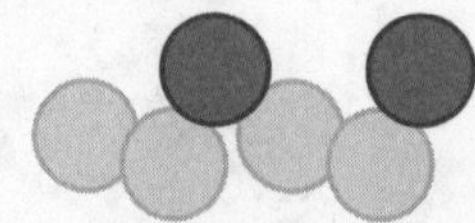

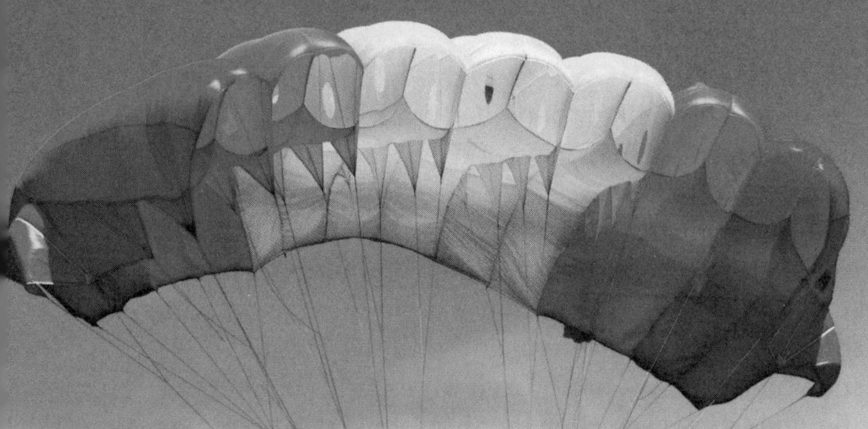

Impact of Synthetic Materials

Synthetic materials allow very large numbers of people to be clothed, housed, and fed. Many of the medical, technological, and societal advances that have occurred during the last 200 years are due in large part to synthetic materials.

Synthetic Fibers Naturally occurring fibers such as cotton, wool, and silk have been used for thousands of years, but they can be expensive. In part, that is because each can be grown or raised only in certain parts of the world. Synthetic fibers, such as acrylic, nylon, polyester, spandex, and rayon, replicate or improve the characteristics of natural fibers. In addition, they generally are much less expensive to produce. Synthetic fibers last longer, dry more quickly, and clean more easily than natural fibers, although they often burn more easily.

Synthetic Foods Synthetic food products include flavorings, colorings, and preservatives. Many foods we eat would rot or decay quickly without synthetic preservatives. And yet, some preservatives have been found to cause health problems. Vanillin is a synthetic flavor designed as a substitute for the natural flavor of the vanilla bean. But the vanilla bean grows only on a few particular orchids in places such as Mexico and Madagascar. It would be too costly and time-consuming to meet the world demand for natural vanilla flavoring.

Producing and Using Synthetic Food Products	
Benefits	**Drawbacks**

INTERACTIVITY

Describe the impact of synthetics on society.

Nylon

Figure 4 The polymer nylon is used to make parachutes because of its strength and resistance to tearing.

Literacy Connection

Evaluate Information
Suppose you were asked to research information about a potentially dangerous synthetic food product. How would you evaluate the credibility of the sources you found?

....

....

....

....

Preserving Food

Figure 5 Potassium sorbate is a synthetic food preservative often used in cheese, yogurts, and other dairy products to prevent mold growth. In the table shown, identify some benefits and drawbacks of producing and using synthetic food products.

Write About It How do you think the ability of chemists to synthesize compounds has affected the field of medicine? Write your thoughts in your science notebook.

Synthetic Medicines If you have ever taken medicine for an illness, you have likely benefited from chemical synthesis in the form of pharmaceuticals. Many synthetic chemicals are used to cure or reduce the effects of diseases and illnesses. Many medical compounds have been discovered in plants. Chemists can determine the chemical formula of these natural compounds and then produce them in large amounts and in safer forms through chemical synthesis. *Digitalis lanata,* shown in **Figure 6**, produces a compound that benefits cardiac patients. However, the plant is highly toxic to humans and animals. Chemists have isolated and synthesized the compound, called digoxin, that provides the benefits without the toxic side effects.

Synthetic Fuels One day, the world will run out of petroleum. Cars and trains can run on electricity, but how will we power planes and boats? Synthetic fuels of many kinds are made through chemical reactions. Chemists have been exploring how to synthesize resources such as plants, animal oils, coal, algae, or other materials into fuels.

READING CHECK **Evaluate Information** A website publishes an article arguing that synthetic materials do not benefit society because they are created in a lab. Do you think the website is a reliable source? Explain.

....

....

....

....

Safer Synthetics

Figure 6 This plant is *Digitalis lanata,* also known as Grecian foxglove. Eating even a small portion of the plant itself can be fatal. However, a compound from this plant is used to help patients with heart conditions. Chemists synthesize the compound into digoxin tablets that are safe to consume.

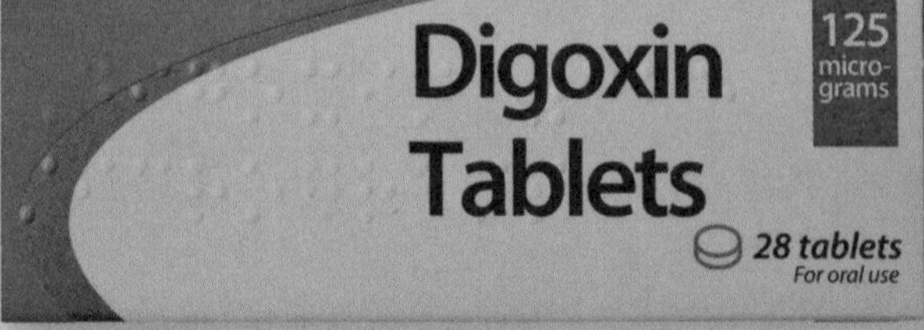

Digoxin
Tablets
125
micro-
grams
28 tablets
For oral use

LESSON 4 Check

MS-PS1-3

1. **Identify** What is a synthetic material?

2. **Write Informative Texts** What type of change must occur for pure substances to combine into new materials? Name a few kinds of synthetic materials that can be produced by this type of change.

3. **CCC Patterns** What is the difference between the structures of monomers and polymers?

4. **SEP Structure and Function** Describe how the structure of polymers helps to make them useful materials.

5. **SEP Engage in Argument** How would you respond to a friend's claim that chemists don't know what to expect when synthesizing new materials?

Quest CHECK-IN

In this lesson, you learned how chemists produce synthetic materials. You also investigated how synthetic materials have impacted society.

SEP Communicate Information What are some of the benefits and drawbacks of using synthetic materials, such as plastic bags, in your pack design?

HANDS-ON LAB

Heat It Up or Ice It Down

Go online to download the lab worksheet. Retest and refine your pack to make sure it meets the criteria of the challenge. Then demonstrate your final version.

Case Study

MS-PS1-3

Is Plastic Really So Fantastic?

Chemists use crude oil to make plastics in a lab.

Look around your classroom or community, and you will likely see many things made from plastic.

Most plastic is synthesized from petroleum, or crude oil. This natural resource is a mixture of thousands of different compounds. To make plastic from it, these compounds have to be processed.

Oil is a mixture of carbon and hydrogen atoms, which differ in size and structure. These atoms form simple monomers. Through several chemical reactions, the monomers form large chains of polymers, and you end up with plastic.

The Benefits of Plastic

Plastic has had a profound impact on society. It is very durable and fairly inexpensive to produce. Plastic is much lighter than metal, and it can be molded into just about any shape. These properties work to our advantage in a wide variety of applications. Many auto parts are plastic because they increase fuel efficiency by decreasing the mass of the car.

The Drawbacks of Plastic

While plastic is a world-changing synthetic material, it has its share of problems. Plastic materials do not biodegrade readily. Landfills are overflowing with plastic items that will be around for many hundreds of years. Plastic refuse also has ended up in the oceans, impacting the survival of fish and other aquatic organisms.

One way to deal with the negative impacts of plastics is to recycle as much of it as possible. The table shows how the recycling of different types of plastic bottles has changed from 2013 to 2014.

	Postconsumer Plastics Recycled in U.S., 2013–2014		
	Plastic Bottle Type	**Plastic Recycled (millions of pounds)**	**Recycling Rate**
2013	PET	1798	31.2%
2013	HDPE Natural	440.4	28.0%
2013	HDPE Pigmented	605.0	34.9%
2013	Total Bottles	1045.4	31.6%
2014	PET	1812	31.0%
2014	HDPE Natural	464.4	29.9%
2014	HDPE Pigmented	643.0	36.8%
2014	Total Bottles	1107.4	33.6%

Use the table to answer the following questions.

1. CCC Patterns What patterns do you observe among the data in the table?

2. SEP Use Mathematics What do you think the recycling data will look like in 2020? Explain. Do a calculation that predicts what the percentage will be.

3. SEP Plan an Investigation Describe an experiment that could be conducted to investigate how long it takes different plastics to break down.

4. CCC Cause and Effect What are some ways you can think of to get people to recycle more plastic instead of allowing it to end up in a landfill or the ocean?

☑ TOPIC 9 Review and Assess

1 Mixtures and Solutions

MS-PS1-2

1. In a heterogeneous mixture, the substances
   A. can be physically separated.
   B. are chemically combined.
   C. can only be separated through chemical processes.
   D. break down into new substances.

2. Which of the following statements is true?
   A. A solution is a pure substance.
   B. A solution is a mixture.
   C. The solvent is dissolved in the solute.
   D. A solution has the same properties as a colloid.

3. Milk and sugar water are both (mixtures / pure substances). However, milk is a (colloid / solution) and sugar water is a (colloid / solution).

4. **SEP Analyze Data** Examine the data table. Why is ethylene glycol used in de-icing fluid for airplanes and other vehicles?

Ethylene Glycol in Water (%)	Freezing Point (°C)
0	0
10	–2
20	–8
30	–16
40	–25

....

....

5. **CCC Structure and Function** What factors affect the properties of a solution?

....

....

....

....

2 Chemical Change

MS-PS1-2

6. Which of the following is an example of a chemical change?
   A. breaking a rock into smaller pieces
   B. burning a candle
   C. stirring butter and sugar together
   D. adding food coloring to water

7. In general, what happens to the rate of reaction when you decrease the temperature of a chemical reaction?
   A. it decreases
   B. it increases
   C. it is unaffected
   D. it increases, and then decreases

8. Burning a log is an example of
   A. an endothermic reaction.
   B. a solution.
   C. a catalyst.
   D. an exothermic reaction.

9. All chemical changes result in

....

10. **SEP Communicate Information** Milk contains bacteria that carry out chemical reactions to live and reproduce. Why is milk kept in the refrigerator?

....

....

....

....

....

....

....

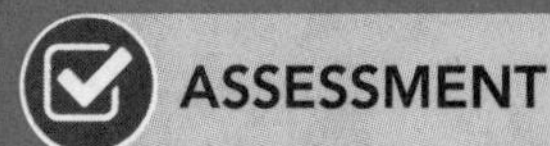

ASSESSMENT

Evaluate your understanding by taking a Topic Test.

3 Modeling Chemical Reactions

MS-PS1-5

11. In the chemical equation shown, what are the reactants?

$$4\ Al + 3\ O_2 \longrightarrow 2\ Al_2O_3$$

A. Al_2O_3
B. Al_2O_3 and Al
C. Al and O_2
D. $Al_2O_3$and O_2

12. You run an experiment in which two substances chemically react in a closed system. You run the same experiment in an open system. How would the masses of the products in each experiment compare? Explain.

....

....

....

....

13. SEP Use Models A model of a reaction is shown below. In the reaction, 1 nitrogen molecule (N_2) and 3 hydrogen molecules (H_2) react to form 2 ammonia molecules (NH_3). Complete the model of the reaction. Then, explain how the model demonstrates the conservation of mass.

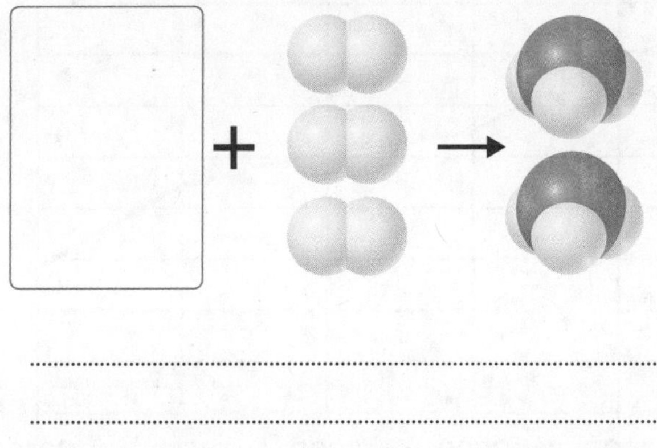

....

....

....

....

4 Producing Useful Materials

MS-PS1-3

14. Which of the following statements about synthetic materials is true?
A. Synthetic materials are never harmful to the environment.
B. Synthetic materials are pure substances found in nature.
C. Synthetic materials have properties that are different from those of the natural materials used to produce them.
D. Synthetic materials are not different from natural materials.

15. Which of the following is a valid explanation for why people produce synthetic materials?
A. Synthetic materials always biodegrade easily.
B. Synthetic materials do not require any natural resources to produce.
C. Synthetic materials are less artificial than natural resources.
D. Synthetic materials help meet societal demand for materials that are in short supply in nature.

16. Chemists can synthesize new materials using chemical reactions because pure substances form new materials that have (the same/ different) physical and chemical properties.

17. CCC Structure and Function Explain why the structure of a polymer such as plastic makes it such a useful material for society.

....

....

....

....

....

....

TOPIC 9 Review and Assess

MS-PS1-2, MS-PS1-5

Evidence-Based Assessment

Human industries and agriculture produce carbon dioxide (CO_2) gas that enters the atmosphere. About a quarter of the CO_2 is absorbed by Earth's ocean. Once the CO_2 dissolves in the seawater, it can react with water (H_2O) to produce carbonic acid (H_2CO_3). The equation shown below represents this reaction. The data table lists some of the properties of CO_2, H_2O, and H_2CO_3.

$$CO_2 + H_2O \rightarrow H_2CO_3$$

Properties of Compounds

	Carbon Dioxide (CO_2)	Water (H_2O)	Carbonic Acid (H_2CO_3)
Density*	0.00198g/cm^3	1.000g/cm^3	2.54g/cm^3
Melting Point	−56.6°C	0°C	856°C
Boiling Point	−78.5°C (sublimes)	100°C	Not applicable
Solubility	Soluble in water	Not applicable	Soluble in water

* Densities taken at standard temperature and pressure.

In water, carbonic acid produces hydrogen ions. The higher the concentration of these ions, the lower the pH of the seawater. The pH scale can be used to measure the acidity of a substance. If a substance has a lower pH, it is more acidic. This graph shows ocean pH levels near Hawaii.

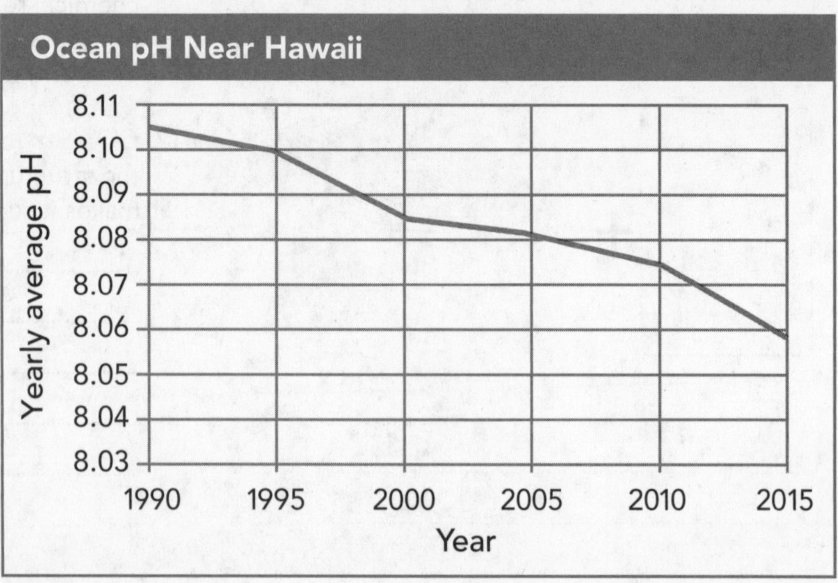

1. **SEP Analyze Data** How did the pH of the ocean change from year 1990 to year 2015?
   A. It increased by about 0.05
   B. It decreased by about 0.05
   C. It increased by about 0.5
   D. It decreased by about 0.5

2. **Quantify Change** In which five-year period did ocean pH decline at the fastest rate?
   A. 1990–1995
   B. 2000–2005
   C. 2005–2010
   D. 2010–2015

3. **SEP Use Models** Is mass conserved in the chemical equation shown? How can you tell?

4. **SEP Evidence** Based on the chemical equation and data table, provide two pieces of evidence that suggest a chemical change is occurring between dissolved CO_2 and H_2O in the oceans.

5. **SEP Construct Explanations** Since preindustrial times, the pH of the Earth's ocean has decreased significantly. Explain one reason why Earth's ocean is becoming more acidic and why you think this might be a problem.

Quest FINDINGS

Complete the Quest!

Phenomenon **Determine the best way to present your design to the class and demonstrate the effectiveness of your pack.**

Apply Concepts In this Quest, you dissolved salts in water to cause your pack to heat up or cool down. How might using different substances in the pack increase its effectiveness?

INTERACTIVITY

Reflect on Your Pack

MS-PS1-2

Evidence of Chemical Change

How can you **determine** when a **chemical reaction** has occurred?

Background

Phenomenon Quiet on the set! You have been asked to create a video for a science channel to show and explain the differences between physical and chemical changes. In this investigation, you will observe how different substances interact. You will use this information to develop a script for the video that explains how to determine when a chemical change has occurred.

(per group)

- 3 100-mL beakers
- baking soda (1 teaspoon)
- vinegar (10 mL)
- potato (2-cm cube)
- hydrogen peroxide (25 mL)
- sugar (1 teaspoon)
- iodine (10 mL)
- 3 plastic spoons
- graduated cylinder

Be sure to follow all safety guidelines provided by your teacher. The Safety Appendix of your textbook provides more details about the safety icons.

Design an Experiment

Demonstrate Go online for a downloadable worksheet of this lab.

1. Design a procedure using the listed materials that lets you observe interactions of the pairs of substances listed in the table. Here are some questions that might help you to write your procedures:
    - At what points in each experiment might you need to make observations?
    - What evidence will you specifically look for?
    - When is the best time to make your prediction?
    - How will you determine whether the interaction has resulted in a physical or chemical change?
    - How might you determine when a reaction is complete?

Interactions		
Interaction 1	**Interaction 2**	**Interaction 3**
baking soda and vinegar	sugar and iodine	potato and hydrogen peroxide

2. Record your predictions and observations in the data table.

3. Get your teacher's approval of your procedure. Then run your experiments.

uDemonstrate Lab

Procedure

Data Table

Interaction	Prediction	Observations
1		
2		
3		

Analyze and Interpret Data

1. **CCC Patterns** What similarities and differences did you observe among the three interactions?

2. **Make Observations** In each case, how did the properties of the substances before the interaction compare to the properties of the substances after the interaction?

   Interaction 1:

   Interaction 2:

   Interaction 3:

3. **Apply Scientific Reasoning** Which of the three interactions result in chemical changes? Were your predictions correct? Explain how observing the properties of substances before and after the interactions helped you to determine whether a chemical change occurred.

4. **SEP Construct Explanations** With your group, use the data and your observations from your experiment to develop a video script. Write it in your notebook. Your script should identify the substances in each interaction, demonstrate the interaction, and then explain how to determine whether a chemical reaction has occurred.

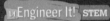

TOPIC 10

Forces and Motion

NGSS PERFORMANCE EXPECTATIONS

MS-PS2-1 Apply Newton's Third Law to design a solution to a problem involving the motion of two colliding objects.

MS-PS2-2 Plan an investigation to provide evidence that the change in an object's motion depends on the sum of the forces on the object and the mass of the object.

MS-PS2-4 Construct and present arguments using evidence to support the claim that gravitational interactions are attractive and depend on the masses of interacting objects.

MS-PS3-1 Construct and interpret graphical displays of data to describe the relationships of kinetic energy to the mass of an object and to the speed of an object.

MS-PS3-2 Develop a model to describe that when the arrangement of objects interacting at a distance changes, different amounts of potential energy are stored in the system.

What forces act on these skydivers?

HANDS-ON LAB

uConnect Determine a reference point for two different observers.

The Essential Question

How is the motion of an object affected by forces that act on it?

SEP Construct Explanations Just for thrills, skydivers leap from a helicopter and fall to the ground. They fall faster and faster until they reach a top speed of 195 km/h (122 mi/h)! Think about the forces that act on the skydivers. Why do they reach a top speed instead of continuing to accelerate?

Quest KICKOFF

How can you take the crash out of a collision?

Phenomenon When engineers design amusement park rides, they have to consider all of the forces that will be acting on riders and make sure the rides are safe. Engineers test their designs with dummies to ensure that riders will not fall out of their seats and collisions will not be harmful to them. In this problem-based Quest activity, you will apply your knowledge of Newton's laws of motion to design a bumper car ride that is safe—for both the rider and the bumper car. You will explore forces and Newton's third law of motion as you design, build, test, and refine a model bumper car.

INTERACTIVITY

Build a Better Bumper Car

MS-PS2-1 Apply Newton's Third Law to design a solution to a problem involving the motion of two colliding objects.

NBC LEARN VIDEO

After watching the Quest Kickoff video, which examines forces and the laws of motion, think about amusement park rides. Complete the 3-2-1 activity.

3 things riders want to experience

....

....

....

2 ways that rides keep riders safe

....

....

1 way in which riders sometimes get injured

....

....

Quest CHECK-IN

IN LESSON 1

STEM What criteria and constraints must engineers consider when designing a safe ride? Think about the goals of the project and how you will ensure a positive outcome.

INTERACTIVITY

Define Criteria and Constraints

Quest CHECK-IN

IN LESSON 2

How do mass and speed affect collisions? Observe and collect data on how mass and speed affect collisions.

HANDS-ON LAB

Mass, Speed, and Colliding Cars

Quest CHECK-IN

IN LESSON 3

STEM How do varying masses and rates of speed affect bumper cars and their riders? Develop and evaluate a design for a safe and fun bumper car.

INTERACTIVITY

Apply Newton's Laws of Motion

Every time a bumper car moves forward and hits another car, there is an equal push in the opposite direction. That is part of what makes riding bumper cars fun.

Quest CHECK-IN

IN LESSON 4

STEM How do the action-reaction forces affect bumper cars and their riders? Build, test, evaluate, and improve your bumper car model.

HANDS-ON LAB

Bumping Cars, Bumper Solutions

Quest FINDINGS

Complete the Quest!

Present your final design and explain how you applied Newton's third law of motion as you developed your design.

INTERACTIVITY

Reflect on Your Bumper Car Solution

uConnect Lab

Identifying Motion

How can you **model** how the change in an object's motion depends on its position relative to a reference point?

Background

Phenomenon Your class visited an aviation event, where pilots exhibited aeronautical feats by participating in an aerobatic competition. Pilots performed rolls, verticals, loops, and figure eights. Judges scored the figures to identify the most skilled pilot. When your class returned to school and compared observations, it was apparent that descriptions of the figures performed were reported differently by different students. To help explain why an observer's reference point can affect how the observer perceives the motion of an object, your group will design and carry out a model to demonstrate this phenomenon.

Materials

(per group)

- tennis ball

Safety

Be sure to follow all safety procedures provided by your teacher. The Safety Appendix of your textbook provides more details about the safety icons.

Design a Procedure

☐ 1. **SEP Plan an Investigation** Write a procedure to show that the perceived motion of a tennis ball depends on its position relative to the reference point of the observer. Your procedure must include four trials, with each student having a different reference point relative to the motion of the ball for each trial. A different student will be responsible for moving the ball during each trial.

....

....

....

....

....

....

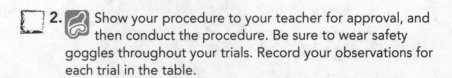

☐ 2. Show your procedure to your teacher for approval, and then conduct the procedure. Be sure to wear safety goggles throughout your trials. Record your observations for each trial in the table.

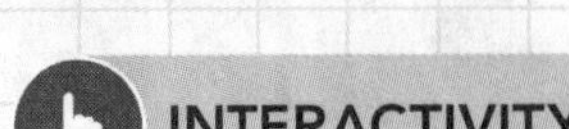

MS-PS2-1

GENERATING ENERGY from Potholes

INTERACTIVITY

Explore how Newton's laws can be used to design more fuel-efficient vehicles.

Traveling in a car over uneven road surfaces and potholes can make for a bouncy ride. How can you capture the energy generated by that bouncing motion? You engineer it!

The Challenge: To convert the motion of a car into electrical energy.

With electromechanical shock absorbers, the energy generated by bumps and potholes can be transformed into electrical energy.

Phenomenon When a car travels down the road, the car exerts an action force on the road, and the road exerts a reaction force on the wheels of the car. A bumpy road occasionally exerts a stronger force than a smooth road, which means an uncomfortable ride for passengers. That's where shock absorbers come in. Shock absorbers are part of a car's suspension system, and they cause the body of the car to react slowly to bumps. This decreases the force exerted on a car by the road.

With traditional shock absorbers, the energy that is absorbed is then released as heat. Auto engineers have now found a way to use their understanding of the Law of Conservation of Energy to harness this energy. They have developed electromechanical shock absorbers that use a lever arm to capture the up-and-down motion of the wheels. A device called an alternator transforms this kinetic energy into electricity. The engineers hope that this electrical energy can be used to increase the fuel efficiency of cars.

Can you build a shock absorber? Go to the Engineering Design Notebook to find out!

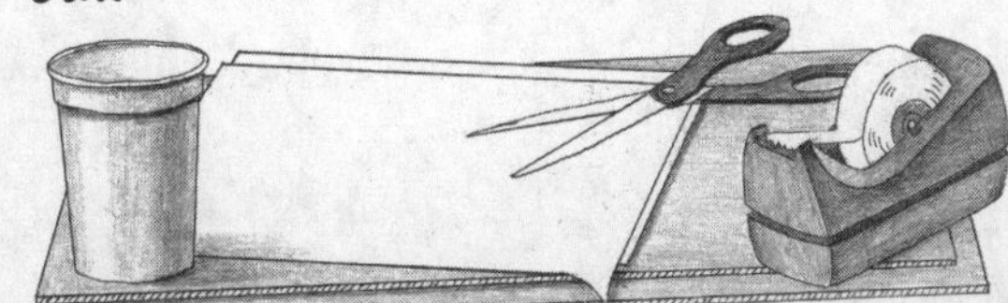

LESSON

Friction and Gravitational Interactions

Guiding Questions

- What factors affect the different types of friction?
- What factors affect gravity?
- How are gravity and friction related to motion and energy?

Connections

Literacy Write Arguments

Math Analyze Relationships

MS-PS2-4, MS-PS3-1, MS-PS3-2

HANDS-ON LAB

uInvestigate Explore how friction is affected by different surfaces, and investigate how the force of friction affects the motion of objects.

Vocabulary

weight

Academic Vocabulary

associate

Connect It!

Circle two areas that show what causes the bike to slow down.

Identify What force is responsible for stopping the bike?

....

SEP Engage in Argument Is this force a contact or noncontact force? Explain.

....

....

Factors That Affect Friction

Describe your experiences riding a bicycle on different surfaces.

Recall that the force two surfaces exert on each other when they rub against each other is the contact force called friction. For example, if you slide a book across a table, the surface of the book rubs against the surface of the table. The resulting force is friction. This force acts in a direction opposite to the motion of the book and eventually stops the book.

Two Factors Both the types of surfaces involved and how hard the surfaces are pushed together affect the friction between two surfaces. The bicyclist in **Figure 1** is using friction to slow his bicycle. One place where friction occurs on the bicycle is between the tires and the ground. Have you ever examined the surface of a tire? The tread on the tire results in more friction between the tire and the ground. A tire on a mountain bike has more tread on it than a regular bike tire, so a lot of friction is produced between a mountain bike tire and the ground. In general, smoother surfaces produce less friction than rougher surfaces.

In this instance, friction also occurs between the brake pads and the wheels. This friction prevents the tire from turning. The harder the bicyclist applies the brakes, the more quickly the bike will come to a stop. Friction increases as surfaces push harder against each other.

Friction acts in a direction opposite to the direction of the object's motion. Without friction or some other force acting in the opposite direction, a moving object will not stop until it strikes another object.

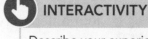

Skidding to a Stop

Figure 1 This mountain biker applies his brakes and skids to slow down.

Types of Friction

Use **Figure 2** to find out more about four different types of friction.

READING CHECK **Write Arguments** How can you be sure that the skater leaping through the air is moving faster than the one speeding along the ground?

....

....

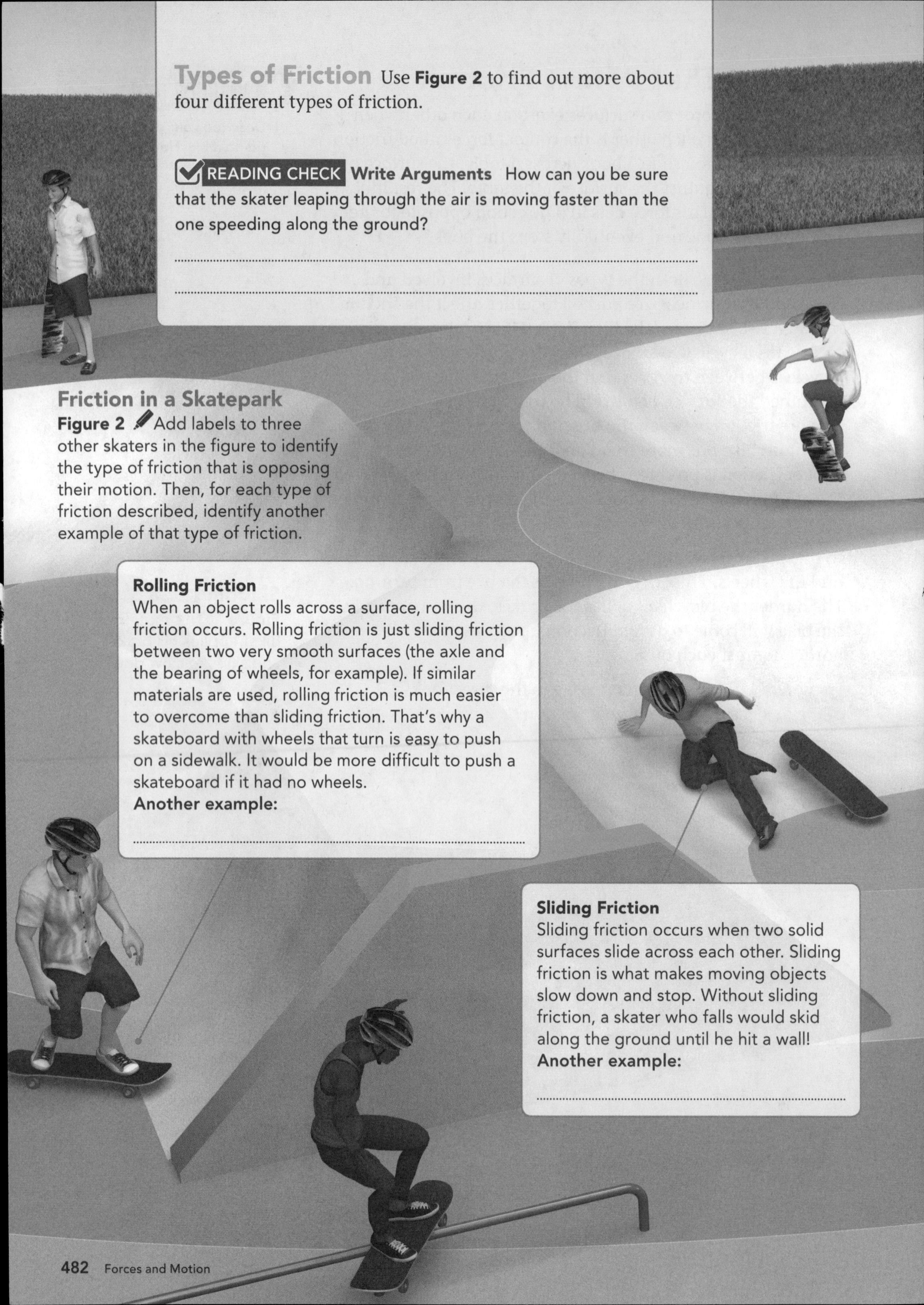

Friction in a Skatepark

Figure 2 ✎ Add labels to three other skaters in the figure to identify the type of friction that is opposing their motion. Then, for each type of friction described, identify another example of that type of friction.

Rolling Friction
When an object rolls across a surface, rolling friction occurs. Rolling friction is just sliding friction between two very smooth surfaces (the axle and the bearing of wheels, for example). If similar materials are used, rolling friction is much easier to overcome than sliding friction. That's why a skateboard with wheels that turn is easy to push on a sidewalk. It would be more difficult to push a skateboard if it had no wheels.
Another example:

....

Sliding Friction
Sliding friction occurs when two solid surfaces slide across each other. Sliding friction is what makes moving objects slow down and stop. Without sliding friction, a skater who falls would skid along the ground until he hit a wall!
Another example:

....

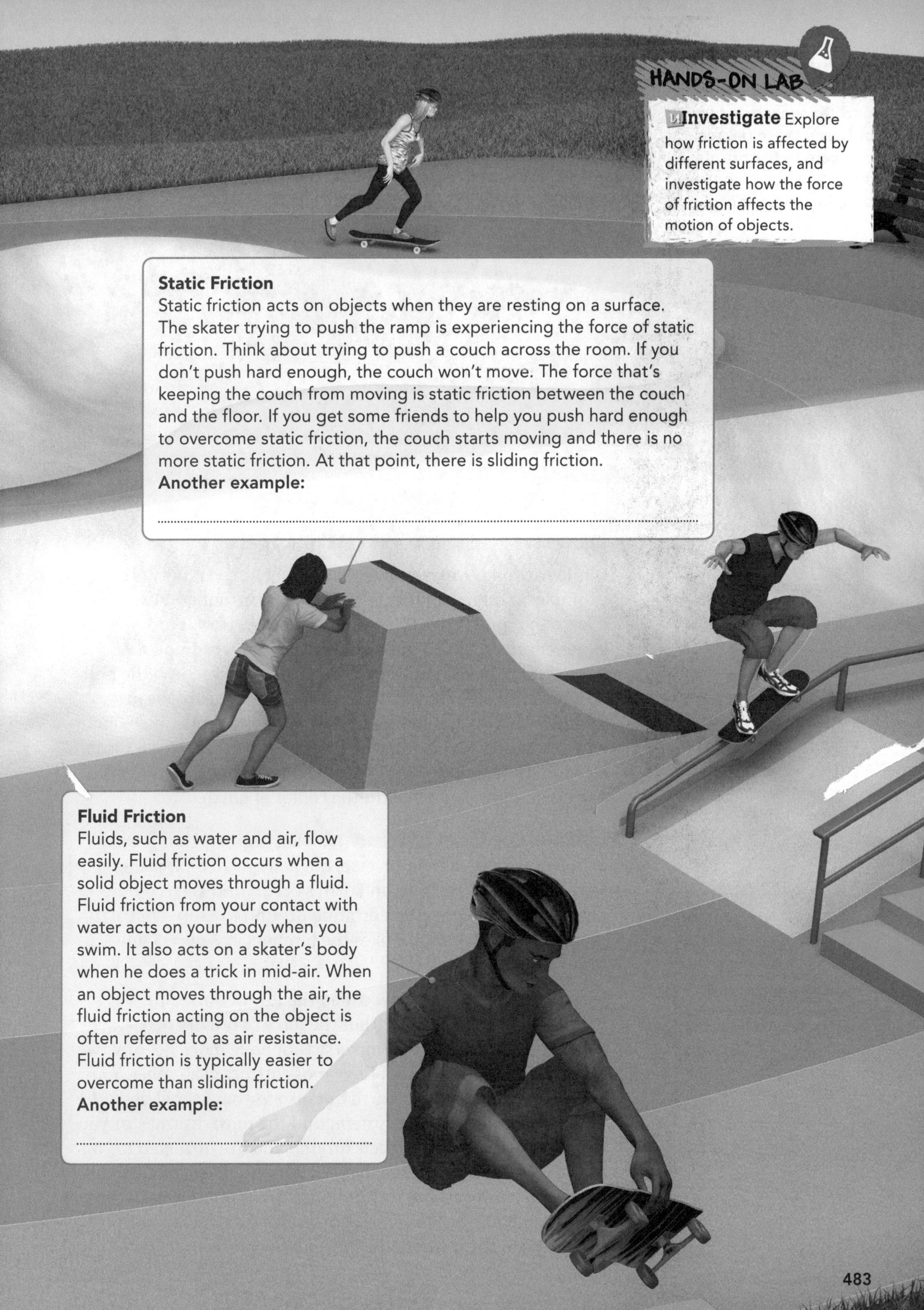

HANDS-ON LAB

Investigate Explore how friction is affected by different surfaces, and investigate how the force of friction affects the motion of objects.

Static Friction
Static friction acts on objects when they are resting on a surface. The skater trying to push the ramp is experiencing the force of static friction. Think about trying to push a couch across the room. If you don't push hard enough, the couch won't move. The force that's keeping the couch from moving is static friction between the couch and the floor. If you get some friends to help you push hard enough to overcome static friction, the couch starts moving and there is no more static friction. At that point, there is sliding friction.
Another example:

....

Fluid Friction
Fluids, such as water and air, flow easily. Fluid friction occurs when a solid object moves through a fluid. Fluid friction from your contact with water acts on your body when you swim. It also acts on a skater's body when he does a trick in mid-air. When an object moves through the air, the fluid friction acting on the object is often referred to as air resistance. Fluid friction is typically easier to overcome than sliding friction.
Another example:

....

Universal Gravitation

Figure 3 How does the gravitational attraction between these people compare to the gravitational attraction between the people and Earth?

VIDEO

Explore why the moon is able to circle Earth without falling toward it.

Factors That Affect Gravity

While friction is an example of a contact force, gravity is an example on a non-contact force. Remember that gravity is a force that pulls objects toward each other. How is gravity experienced on Earth? You could name many examples. A basketball player shoots a ball toward the basket, and the ball falls toward Earth. Rain falls from the sky to Earth. We are so familiar with objects falling that we may not think much about why they fall. One person who thought about this was Sir Isaac Newton. He concluded that a force called gravity acts to pull objects straight down toward the center of Earth.

Universal Gravitation Newton realized that gravity acts everywhere in the universe, not just on Earth. It is the force that causes the tides in Earth's ocean and keeps all the planets in our solar system orbiting around the sun. On Earth, gravity is the force that makes the jumpers in **Figure 3** fall toward the water.

READING CHECK **Summarize** What is the law of universal gravitation?

Newton's realization is now called the law of universal gravitation. This law states that the force of gravity acts between all objects in the universe that have mass. So, any two objects in the universe that have mass attract each other. You are attracted not only to Earth but also to your school desk, the other planets in the solar system, and the most distant star you can see. Earth and the objects around you are attracted to you as well. You can clearly see the gravitational effect of Earth on an object. However, you do not notice the attraction between objects on Earth because these forces are extremely small compared to the attraction between the objects and Earth itself.

Factors Affecting Gravity

What factors control the strength of the gravitational force between two objects? These factors are the mass of each object and the distance between them.

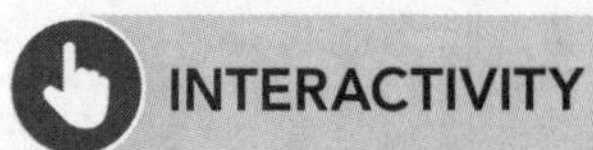

Investigate how gravity affects falling objects.

The more mass an object has, the greater the gravitational force between it and other objects. Earth's gravitational force on nearby objects is strong because the mass of Earth is so large. Gravitational force also depends on the distance between the objects' centers. As distance increases, gravitational force decreases. What happens when you drop your cell phone? You see your cell phone fall to Earth because Earth and your cell phone are close together. If your cell phone were on the moon, Earth would not exert a visible gravitational attraction to it because Earth and the phone would be so far apart. The phone would be visibly attracted to the moon instead.

Literacy Connection

Write Arguments Write an argument supported by evidence that explains why the pencil and notebook resting on your desk are not being pulled together by the force of gravity between them.

....

....

....

....

....

....

Weight and Mass

Mass is sometimes confused with weight. Mass is a measure of the amount of matter in an object. **Weight** is a measure of the force of gravity on an object. Since weight is a measure of force, the SI unit of weight is a newton (N). If you know the mass of an object in kilograms, you can calculate its weight on Earth using Newton's second law. The acceleration due to gravity at Earth's surface is 9.8 m/s². The force is the weight of the object.

Net force = Mass × Acceleration

When you stand on a bathroom scale, it displays your weight—the gravitational force that Earth is exerting on you. On Earth, 1 pound equals 4.45 newtons. If you could stand on the surface of Jupiter, which has a mass around 300 times the mass of Earth, your mass would remain the same, but your weight would increase. This is because the gravitational force exerted on you is greater on Jupiter than on Earth.

Describing g-Forces

Figure 4 A lowercase g is used as the symbol for acceleration due to gravity at Earth's surface (9.8 m/s²). This symbol is used in the field of space engineering, where acceleration is often measured in "g"s. Engineers must design space shuttles considering the acceleration and forces that the crew and the shuttle itself would experience during flight.

The Relationship Between Weight and Mass

Weight varies with the strength of the gravitational force. This baby elephant weighs 480 pounds on Earth, and its mass is 218 kilograms. On the moon, he would weigh about one-sixth of what he does on Earth. On Mars, he would weigh just over one-third of what he does on Earth. On Jupiter, he would weigh approximately 2.5 times as much as he does on Earth.

Analyze Relationships Complete the table using the information about the baby elephant.

Location	Earth	Moon	Mars	Jupiter
Mass (kg)				
Weight (lbs)				

Energy, Forces, and Motion

By now, you can see how forces such as gravity and friction relate to motion. Recall that forces and motion are also related to energy.

Gravitational Potential Energy As you know, the potential energy of an object is the energy stored in the object. There are several different types of potential energy, based on different types of forces. The type of potential energy that we **associate** with gravity is called gravitational potential energy. On Earth, gravitational potential energy (GPE) is based on an object's position. In general, the higher up an object is, the greater its GPE. For example, as a diver climbs the ladder to a diving board, her GPE increases. The GPE of a skydiver increases as he rides the helicopter to his jumping point. You can calculate the GPE of an object on Earth based on the mass of the object, the acceleration due to gravity (9.8 m/s^2), and the height of the object above Earth's surface.

$$\text{Gravitational potential energy (GPE)} = \text{Mass} \times \text{Acceleration due to gravity} \times \text{Height}$$

Academic Vocabulary

Used as a verb, *associate* means to connect something to something else in one's mind. Write a sentence using *associate* as a noun.

....

....

....

....

Forces and Motion When a skydiver jumps from a helicopter, a net force acts on his body as he falls. This net force is a combination of gravity and friction. Gravity pulls him down toward the ground, and fluid friction acts on him in the opposite direction as he falls through the air. However, these forces are unbalanced—the force of gravity is stronger than the air resistance, so he accelerates downward. Net force works on him as he falls, so his GPE transforms to kinetic energy, the energy of motion. As a result, his speed increases throughout his fall. As the skydiver accelerates, the force of air resistance increases until it is equal to the force of gravity. At this point, the forces on the skydiver are balanced and he falls at a constant speed the rest of the way down. This top speed is called terminal velocity. It only takes about 15 seconds for skydivers to reach 99% of their terminal velocity of 195 km/h (122 mi/h)! When skydivers open a parachute, air resistance increases. This causes the forces acting on the skydiver to balance at a much slower terminal velocity.

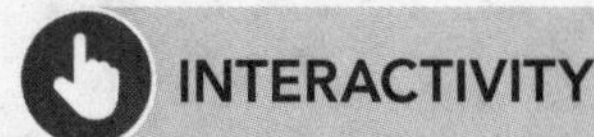

Explore the relationships among friction, gravity, tides, and Earth's rotation.

Model It!

SEP Develop Models Use what you know about energy, forces, and motion to develop a model of a falling object. Add labels to your sketch to show locations of maximum and minimum gravitational potential energy, kinetic energy, and speed. Label areas of acceleration. Draw arrows to represent the forces acting on the object. Write a caption to explain what your model shows.

LESSON 4 Check

MS-PS2-4, MS-PS3-2

1. **Synthesize Information** What is the difference between weight and mass?

2. **CCC Stability and Change** Snow has been lying on a mountainside. Suddenly, it starts to move down the mountain. Which types of friction are observed in this avalanche? Where does each type occur?

3. **Apply Scientific Reasoning** Give a real-life example of fluid friction.

4. **Explain Phenomena** A 4-kg ball is 2 cm away from one 1-kg ball and 6 cm away from another 1-kg ball. Use the relationships among the balls to describe two factors that affect gravity. Also explain why the balls do not move toward each other unless acted upon by another force.

5. **SEP Construct Explanations** Rather than push a heavy box from one room to another, a worker chooses to place the box on a wheeled cart. In terms of friction, explain why moving the box on the wheeled cart is easier than pushing.

Quest CHECK-IN

In this lesson, you learned how different types of friction affect the movement of objects. You also learned about universal gravitation and how this scientific law applies to objects on Earth and elsewhere in the universe.

Evaluate How might friction affect the movement of bumper cars? What role does gravity play in how bumper cars move? How might you use these concepts to make bumper cars safer?

HANDS-ON LAB

Bumper Cars, Bumper Solutions

Go online to download the worksheet for this lab. Learn how friction and gravity affect vehicles on different surfaces. Then brainstorm how these factors influence the speed and direction of bumper cars.

Graphing Kinetic Energy

When a moving object collides with an obstacle, it may cause a certain amount of damage. It will cause even more damage if it is moving faster or if it has more mass. The kinetic energy of an object (the energy due to the object's motion) depends on both the mass and the speed of the object, but not necessarily in the same way. How, exactly, do the mass and speed of an object affect kinetic energy? You can use graphs to see this relationship.

In the following scenario, Michael and Manuel are studying kinetic energy by observing sleds slide down a snowy hill. First they push one sled at different speeds down the hill and record the kinetic energy and speed. Then they push sleds of different masses down the hill and record the kinetic energy and masses. They put together two tables of data as shown using generic units.

Kinetic Energy and Speed					
KE	1	4	9	16	25
Speed	1	2	3	4	5

Kinetic Energy and Mass					
KE	1	2	3	4	5
Mass	1	2	3	4	5

Analyze Data

1. **Construct Graphs** On a piece of graph paper, construct a graph of kinetic energy versus speed from the first data table.
2. **SEP Interpret Graphs** Interpret the shape of the graph.
3. **CCC Scale, Proportion, and Quantity** Explain what the graph shows about the relationship between kinetic energy and speed.
4. **Construct Graphs** On a piece of graph paper, construct a graph of kinetic energy versus mass from the second data table.
5. **SEP Interpret Graphs** Interpret the shape of the graph.
6. **CCC Scale, Proportion, and Quantity** Explain what the graph shows about the relationship between kinetic energy and mass.

Conclusion How do Michael and Manuel's data show the relationship between kinetic energy, mass, and speed? Given the graphs, what do you think would cause more damage in a collision: a faster object or a heavier object?

TOPIC 10 Review and Assess

1 Describing Motion and Force

MS-PS2-2

1. A girl pushes on the classroom door to open it. Which two terms accurately describe the net force acting on the door?
   A. contact and balanced
   B. contact and unbalanced
   C. noncontact and balanced
   D. noncontact and unbalanced

2. A dog is pulling on a leash while walking down the sidewalk. What frame of reference would indicate that the dog is not moving?
   A. A nearby building
   B. A tree
   C. The leash
   D. The sidewalk

3. Two dogs pull on a rope. One dog pulls with a force of 5 N to the left, and the other dog pulls with a force of 3 N to the right. What is the result?
   A. The rope remains in place.
   B. The rope moves to the left.
   C. The rope moves to the right.
   D. The rope has a balanced force applied to it.

4. **SEP Develop Models** Using pictures, labels, and arrows, model a box that has two forces acting on it, 12 N to the right and 4 N to the left. Also show the net force on the box.

2 Speed, Velocity, and Acceleration

MS-PS2-2

5. A bus driver drove from Philadelphia to Washington D.C. He drove the first 100 km in 2 hours, the next 55 km in 1 hour, and the final 75 km in 2 hours. What is the average speed of the bus throughout the trip?
   A. 46 km/h
   B. 50 km/h
   C. 77 km/h
   D. 81 km/h

6. Which statement about acceleration is always true?
   A. The unit m/s is the SI unit of acceleration.
   B. For objects to accelerate, they must speed up.
   C. Either a change in speed or a change in direction causes acceleration.
   D. Both speed and direction must change for acceleration to occur.

7. A cross-country runner runs 4 km in 15 minutes. What can you calculate using this information?
   A. acceleration
   B. force
   C. speed
   D. velocity

8. You can find the speed on a distance-versus-time graph by finding the .... of the line.

9. **SEP Ask Questions** A woman is taking a walk, moving at a rate of 80 m/min. What additional information would you need to determine her velocity?

....

....

....

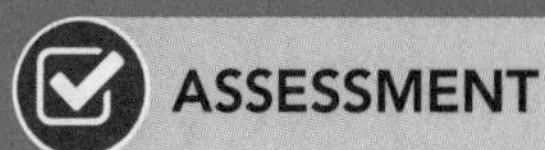

Evaluate your understanding by taking a Topic Test.

3 Newton's Laws of Motion

MS-PS2-2

10. A soccer player kicks a ball. Which of the following describes the reaction force to this kick?
A. friction between the ball and the foot
B. friction between the ball and the ground
C. force applied to the ground by the foot
D. force applied to the foot by the ball

11. Which term describes resistance to change in motion?
A. Acceleration
B. Inertia
C. Net force
D. Velocity

12. The acceleration of a baseball after it is hit by a bat depends on the mass of the ball and the net force on the ball. This example best illustrates what law?
A. Newton's first law of motion
B. Newton's second law of motion
C. Newton's third law of motion
D. Newton's law of universal gravitation

13. Integrate Information Describe how each of Newton's laws may be observable during a car trip.

....

....

....

....

....

....

....

....

....

4 Friction and Gravitational Interactions

MS-PS2-4, MS-PS3-1, MS-PS3-2

14. When is there static friction between your desk chair and the floor?
A. when the chair sits still
B. when the chair falls to the floor
C. when you lift the chair
D. when you slide your chair under your desk

15. What is the relationship between the kinetic energy of an object and the mass of an object? Assume the speed is constant.
A. Kinetic energy gets bigger at the same rate as the mass of an object.
B. Kinetic energy gets bigger at a faster rate than the increase of a mass of an object.
C. Kinetic energy decreases as the mass of an object increases.
D. Kinetic energy decreases at a faster rate than the increase of a mass of an object.

16. After an initial push, a sled begins to move downhill at 1 m/s. A few seconds later its kinetic energy has increased. The sled now has 64 times more kinetic energy than it did right after the push. How fast it it going?
A. 64 times faster
B. 8 times faster
C. 4,096 times faster
D. 32 times faster

17. SEP Construct Explanations Using examples, explain how each of the four types of friction are present during lunch time in the school cafeteria.

....

....

....

....

....

....

MS-PS2-1, MS-PS2-2, MS-PS2-4

Evidence-Based Assessment

In 2005, NASA sent a robotic spacecraft called DART to a satellite that was orbiting Earth. DART was supposed to demonstrate that it could move around the satellite and communicate with it, without a human on board. The spacecraft was supposed to come close to the satellite without actually touching it.

Here is how the DART system works: The spacecraft's navigation system estimates its position and speed. Then, commands are sent to the thrusters to keep the spacecraft along its intended path. Force from the thrusters causes a change in motion. If the GPS system communicates incorrect navigation data to the spacecraft, then it will travel incorrectly and use up its fuel.

DART made it into space, but then its navigation system failed, providing incorrect data on its position and speed. This failure caused DART to bump into the satellite. The force of the collision changed the motion of the satellite. Luckily it remained in orbit around Earth, but the mission was deemed a failure. Though NASA has had many successes, the science and engineering work involved with space exploration is extremely complex, and sometimes even the best-planned projects fail.

The diagram below shows the relative positions of DART, and the satellite before the collision.

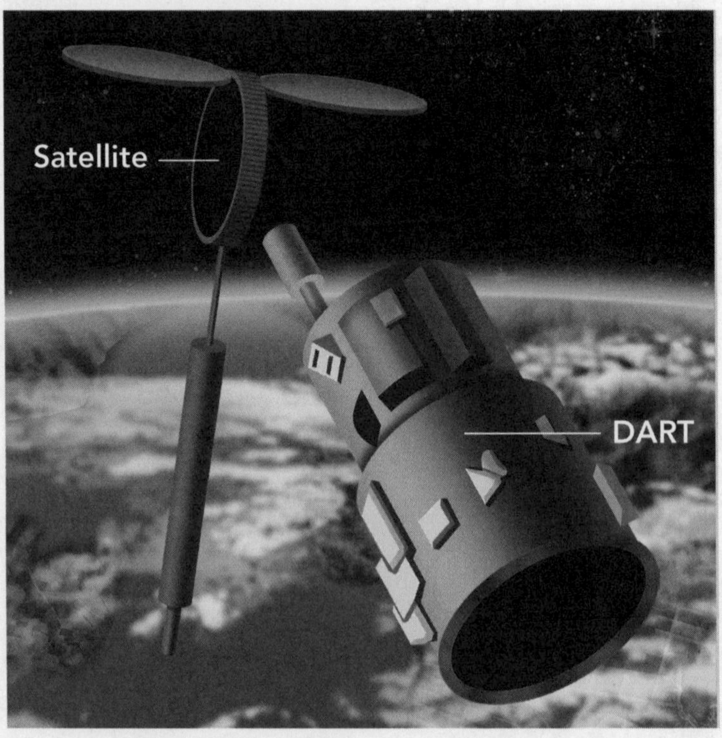

1. **Apply Scientific Reasoning** If the satellite had less mass, but the force of the collision was the same, then the collision would have
   A. caused the satellite to accelerate more quickly.
   B. caused the satellite to accelerate more slowly.
   C. caused the satellite to accelerate at the same rate.
   D. had no effect on the satellite's original motion.

2. **Cite Evidence** Did DART apply a balanced or unbalanced force to the satellite during the collision? What evidence supports your answer?

3. **Draw Comparative Inferences** Describe the action-reaction forces during the collision between DART and the satellite.

4. **CCC Scale, Proportion, and Quantity** Which do you think is stronger—the gravitational attraction between DART and Earth, or the gravitational attraction between DART and the satellite? Explain your answer.

5. **SEP Develop Models** What labels and symbols could you add to an image to represent the forces acting on DART and the satellite during the collision? Describe what you would draw and write.

Quest FINDINGS

Complete the Quest!

Phenomenon Design a way to present your new bumper car design and the results of your testing to your class. Be sure to include how you applied Newton's third law of motion to your design.

Synthesize Information Bumper cars have safety features to protect both the riders and the cars themselves. These features are built around how forces and the laws of motion affect the movement of the cars. What is another example of how forces and laws of motion impact your safety in your daily life?

INTERACTIVITY

Reflect on Your Bumper Car Solution

MS-PS2-1, MS-PS2-2, MS-PS2-4, MS-PS3-2

Stopping on a Dime

How can you **design** a **basketball court** so that players don't run into band members and other spectators near the court lines?

(per group)

- tape measure
- 2 stopwatches or watches with second hands

Background

Phenomenon Imagine your school is hosting a championship basketball game, and the school band will be playing at the game. The band director wants the band to set up its instruments very close to the out-of-bounds line of the basketball court, so that the band will be front and center during the game. Some people at the school, however, have raised concerns about this plan. They feel that having band members so close to the court is unsafe because the members might be hit by players running off the court.

You and some of your fellow science students have been asked to design and conduct an experiment to determine whether or not the band director's plan is safe for both the band members and the players. In this experiment, you will investigate how time, distance, and average speed relate to changes in motion, and you will apply these concepts to the players on the basketball court.

Design Your Investigation

To model the basketball players running off the court, you will determine the speed of someone running a distance of 10 meters. You will also determine how far it takes the runner to come to a complete stop after hitting the 10-meter mark. Discuss with your group how you will design and conduct the investigation. As you plan, consider the following questions with your group:

Demonstrate Go online for a downloadable worksheet of this lab.

- [ ] 1. What three properties of the players in motion do you need to consider?
- [ ] 2. What do you need to know to calculate the speed of a runner?
- [ ] 3. What tests will you perform?
- [ ] 4. How many trials of each test will you perform?
- [ ] 5. What type of data will you be collecting? How will you collect, record, and organize your data?
- [ ] 6. What evidence will you need to present after your investigation?
- [ ] 7. How will you present your evidence to communicate your results effectively?

Write your plan in the space provided on the next page. After getting your teacher's approval, conduct your investigation. Record the data you collect in your group data table.

Procedure

Data Table

Speed (m/s)

Stopping Distance (m)

Analyze and Interpret Data

1. **SEP Carry Out Investigations** Why was it important to carry out the steps of your procedure multiple times with each participant?

2. **CCC Stability and Change** How are unbalanced forces at work when a runner attempts to stop quickly after reaching the 10-m mark?

3. **SEP Interpret Data** Do your data seem reasonable for representing speeds and distances traveled by basketball players on a court? Explain why or why not.

4. **Provide Critique** Compare your procedure with the procedure of another group. What did that group do differently? What would you suggest to improve that group's procedure?

5. **SEP Construct Arguments** Write a proposal to the school that explains the importance of making sure the basketball court has enough space around it. In your proposal, suggest a strategy for making the court safer. Cite data from your investigation as evidence to support your points.

SEP.1, SEP.8

The Meaning of Science

Science Skills

Reflect Think about a time you misplaced something and could not find it. Write a sentence defining the problem. What science skills could you use to solve the problem? Explain how you would use at least three of the skills in the table.

Science is a way of learning about the natural world. It involves asking questions, making predictions, and collecting information to see if the answer is right or wrong.

The table lists some of the skills that scientists use. You use some of these skills every day. For example, you may observe and evaluate your lunch options before choosing what to eat.

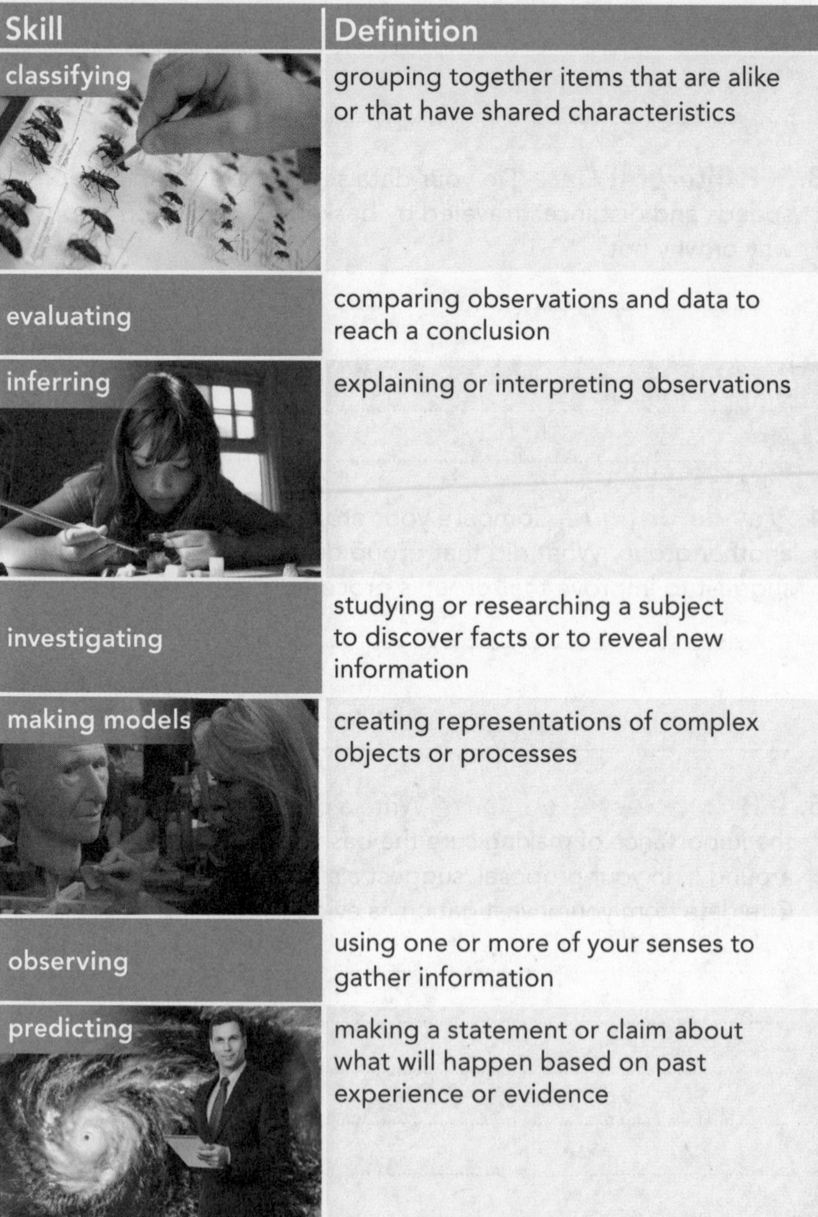

Skill	Definition
classifying	grouping together items that are alike or that have shared characteristics
evaluating	comparing observations and data to reach a conclusion
inferring	explaining or interpreting observations
investigating	studying or researching a subject to discover facts or to reveal new information
making models	creating representations of complex objects or processes
observing	using one or more of your senses to gather information
predicting	making a statement or claim about what will happen based on past experience or evidence

Scientific Attitudes

Curiosity often drives scientists to learn about the world around them. Creativity is useful for coming up with inventive ways to solve problems. Such qualities and attitudes, and the ability to keep an open mind, are essential for scientists.

When sharing results or findings, honesty and ethics are also essential. Ethics refers to rules for knowing right from wrong.

Being skeptical is also important. This means having doubts about things based on past experiences and evidence. Skepticism helps to prevent accepting data and results that may not be true.

Scientists must also avoid bias—likes or dislikes of people, ideas, or things. They must avoid experimental bias, which is a mistake that may make an experiment's preferred outcome more likely.

Make Meaning

Think about a bias the marine biologist in the photo could show that results in paying more or less attention to one kind of organism over others. Make a prediction about how that bias could affect the biologist's survey of the coral reef.

Scientific Reasoning

Scientific reasoning depends on being logical and objective. When you are objective, you use evidence and apply logic to draw conclusions. Being subjective means basing conclusions on personal feelings, biases, or opinions. Subjective reasoning can interfere with science and skew results. Objective reasoning helps scientists use observations to reach conclusions about the natural world.

Scientists use two types of objective reasoning: deductive and inductive. Deductive reasoning involves starting with a general idea or theory and applying it to a situation. For example, the theory of plate tectonics indicates that earthquakes happen mostly where tectonic plates meet. You could then draw the conclusion, or deduce, that California has many earthquakes because tectonic plates meet there.

In inductive reasoning, you make a generalization from a specific observation. When scientists collect data in an experiment and draw a conclusion based on that data, they use inductive reasoning. For example, if fertilizer causes one set of plants to grow faster than another, you might infer that the fertilizer promotes plant growth.

Write About It

Suppose it is raining when you go to sleep one night. When you wake up the next morning, you observe frozen puddles on the ground and icicles on tree branches. Use scientific reasoning to draw a conclusion about the air temperature outside. Support your conclusion using deductive or inductive reasoning.

SEP.1, SEP.2, SEP.3, SEP.4, CCC.4

Science Processes

Scientific Inquiry

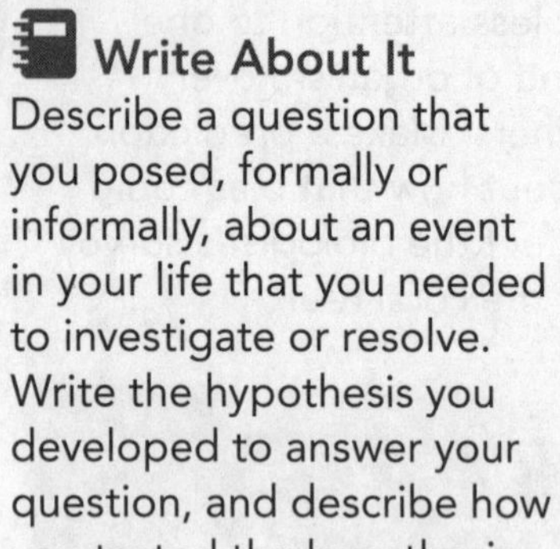

Write About It Describe a question that you posed, formally or informally, about an event in your life that you needed to investigate or resolve. Write the hypothesis you developed to answer your question, and describe how you tested the hypothesis.

Scientists contribute to scientific knowledge by conducting investigations and drawing conclusions. The process often begins with an observation that leads to a question, which is then followed by the development of a hypothesis. This is known as scientific inquiry.

One of the first steps in scientific inquiry is asking questions. However, it's important to make a question specific with a narrow focus so the investigation will not be too broad. A biologist may want to know all there is to know about wolves, for example. But a good, focused question for a specific inquiry might be "How many offspring does the average female wolf produce in her lifetime?"

A hypothesis is a possible answer to a scientific question. A hypothesis must be testable. For something to be testable, researchers must be able to carry out an investigation and gather evidence that will either support or disprove the hypothesis.

Scientific Models

Models are tools that scientists use to study phenomena indirectly. A model is any representation of an object or process. Illustrations, dioramas, globes, diagrams, computer programs, and mathematical equations are all examples of scientific models. For example, a diagram of Earth's crust and mantle can help you to picture layers deep below the surface and understand events such as volcanic eruptions.

Models also allow scientists to represent objects that are either very large, such as our solar system, or very small, such as a molecule of DNA. Models can also represent processes that occur over a long period of time, such as the changes that have occurred throughout Earth's history.

Models are helpful, but they have limitations. Physical models are not made of the same materials as the objects they represent. Most models of complex objects or processes show only major parts, stages, or relationships. Many details are left out. Therefore, you may not be able to learn as much from models as you would through direct observation.

Reflect Identify the benefits and limitations of using a plastic model of DNA, as shown here.

Science Experiments

An experiment or investigation must be well planned to produce valid results. In planning an experiment, you must identify the independent and dependent variables. You must also do as much as possible to remove the effects of other variables. A controlled experiment is one in which you test only one variable at a time.

For example, suppose you plan a controlled experiment to learn how the type of material affects the speed at which sound waves travel through it. The only variable that should change is the type of material. This way, if the speed of sound changes, you know that it is a result of a change in the material, not another variable such as the thickness of the material or the type of sound used.

You should also remove bias from any investigation. You may inadvertently introduce bias by selecting subjects you like and avoiding those you don't like. Scientists often conduct investigations by taking random samples to avoid ending up with biased results.

Once you plan your investigation and begin to collect data, it's important to record and organize the data. You may wish to use a graph to display and help you to interpret the data.

Write About It
List four ways you could communicate the results of a scientific study about the health of sea turtles in the Pacific Ocean.

Communicating is the sharing of ideas and results with others through writing and speaking. Communicating data and conclusions is a central part of science.

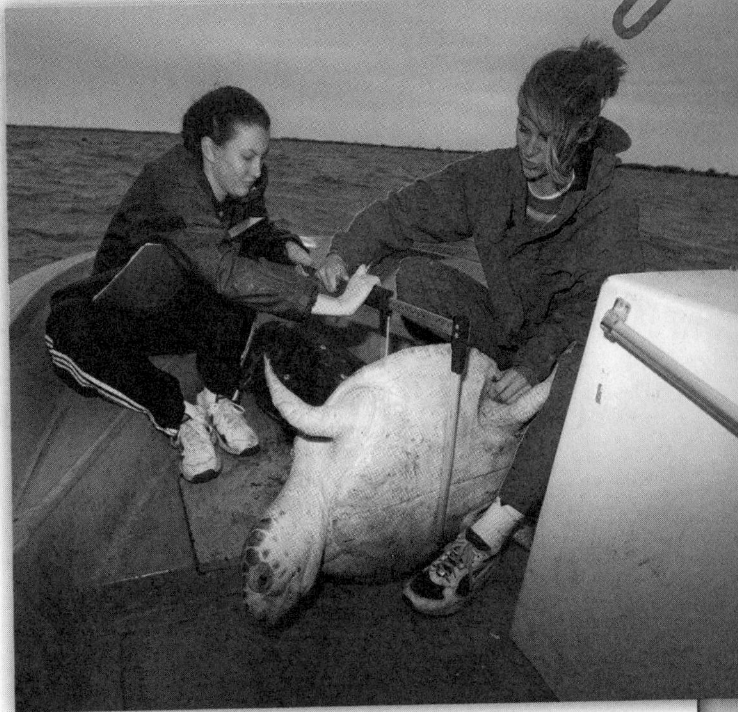

Scientists share knowledge, including new findings, theories, and techniques for collecting data. Conferences, journals, and websites help scientists to communicate with each other. Popular media, including newspapers, magazines, and social media sites, help scientists to share their knowledge with nonscientists. However, before the results of investigations are shared and published, other scientists should review the experiment for possible sources of error, such as bias and unsupported conclusions.

SEP.1, SEP.6, SEP.7, SEP.8

Scientific Knowledge

Scientific Explanations

Suppose you learn that adult flamingos are pink because of the food they eat. This statement is a scientific explanation—it describes how something in nature works or explains why it happens. Scientists from different fields use methods such as researching information, designing experiments, and making models to form scientific explanations. Scientific explanations often result from many years of work and multiple investigations conducted by many scientists.

Scientific Theories and Laws

A scientific law is a statement that describes what you can expect to occur every time under a particular set of conditions. A scientific law describes an observed pattern in nature, but it does not attempt to explain it. For example, the law of superposition describes what you can expect to find in terms of the ages of layers of rock. Geologists use this observed pattern to determine the relative ages of sedimentary rock layers. But the law does not explain why the pattern occurs.

By contrast, a scientific theory is a well-tested explanation for a wide range of observations or experimental results. It provides details and describes causes of observed patterns. Something is elevated to a theory only when there is a large body of evidence that supports it. However, a scientific theory can be changed or overturned when new evidence is found.

Write About It
Choose two fields of science that interest you. Describe a method used to develop scientific explanations in each field.

SEP Construct Explanations Complete the table to compare and contrast a scientific theory and a scientific law.

	Scientific Theory	Scientific Law
Definition		
Does it attempt to explain a pattern observed in nature?		

Analyzing Scientific Explanations

To analyze scientific explanations that you hear on the news or read in a book such as this one, you need scientific literacy. Scientific literacy means understanding scientific terms and principles well enough to ask questions, evaluate information, and make decisions. Scientific reasoning gives you a process to apply. This includes looking for bias and errors in the research, evaluating data, and identifying faulty reasoning. For example, by evaluating how a survey was conducted, you may find a serious flaw in the researchers' methods.

Write About It
Suppose the conservation committee of a town wants to gauge residents' opinions about a proposal to stock the local ponds with fish every spring. The committee pays for a survey to appear on a web site that is popular with people who like to fish. The results of the survey show 78 people in favor of the proposal and two against it. Do you think the survey's results are valid? Explain.

Evidence and Opinions

The basis for scientific explanations is empirical evidence. Empirical evidence includes the data and observations that have been collected through scientific processes. Satellite images, photos, and maps of mountains and volcanoes are all examples of empirical evidence that support a scientific explanation about Earth's tectonic plates. Scientists look for patterns when they analyze this evidence. For example, they might see a pattern that mountains and volcanoes often occur near tectonic plate boundaries.

To evaluate scientific information, you must first distinguish between evidence and opinion. In science, evidence includes objective observations and conclusions that have been repeated. Evidence may or may not support a scientific claim. An opinion is a subjective idea that is formed from evidence, but it cannot be confirmed by evidence.

Make Meaning
Explain what empirical evidence the photograph reveals.

SEP.3, SEP.4

Tools of Science

Measurement

Making measurements using standard units is important in all fields of science. This allows scientists to repeat and reproduce other experiments, as well as to understand the precise meaning of the results of others. Scientists use a measurement system called the International System of Units, or SI.

For each type of measurement, there is a series of units that are greater or less than each other. The unit a scientist uses depends on what is being measured. For example, a geophysicist tracking the movements of tectonic plates may use centimeters, as plates tend to move small amounts each year. Meanwhile, a marine biologist might measure the movement of migrating bluefin tuna on the scale of kilometers.

Units for length, mass, volume, and density are based on powers of ten—a meter is equal to 100 centimeters or 1000 millimeters. Units of time do not follow that pattern. There are 60 seconds in a minute, 60 minutes in an hour, and 24 hours in a day. These units are based on patterns that humans perceived in nature. Units of temperature are based on scales that are set according to observations of nature. For example, 0°C is the temperature at which pure water freezes, and 100°C is the temperature at which it boils.

Measurement	Metric units
Length or distance	meter (m), kilometer (km), centimeter (cm), millimeter (mm) 1 km = 1,000 m 1 cm = 10 mm 1 m = 100 cm
Mass	kilogram (kg), gram (g), milligram (mg) 1 kg = 1,000 g 1 g = 1,000 mg
Volume	cubic meter (m^3), cubic centimeter (cm^3) 1 m^3 = 1,000,000 cm^3
Density	kilogram per cubic meter (kg/m^3), gram per cubic centimeter (g/cm^3) 1,000 kg/m^3 = 1 g/cm^3
Temperature	degrees Celsius (°C), kelvin (K) 1°C = 273 K
Time	hour (h), minute (m), second (s)

Write About It
Suppose you are planning an investigation in which you must measure the dimensions of several small mineral samples that fit in your hand. Which metric unit or units will you most likely use? Explain your answer.

Math Skills

Using numbers to collect and interpret data involves math skills that are essential in science. For example, you use math skills when you estimate the number of birds in an entire forest after counting the actual number of birds in ten trees.

Scientists evaluate measurements and estimates for their precision and accuracy. In science, an accurate measurement is very close to the actual value. Precise measurements are very close, or nearly equal, to each other. Reliable measurements are both accurate and precise. An imprecise value may be a sign of an error in data collection. This kind of anomalous data may be excluded to avoid skewing the data and harming the investigation.

Other math skills include performing specific calculations, such as finding the mean, or average, value in a data set. The mean can be calculated by adding up all of the values in the data set and then dividing that sum by the number of values.

Hour	Number of Ducks Observed at a Pond
1	12
2	10
3	2
4	14
5	13
6	10
7	11

SEP Use Mathematics The data table shows how many ducks were seen at a pond every hour over the course of seven hours. Is there a data point that seems anomalous? If so, cross out that data point. Then, calculate the mean number of ducks on the pond. Round the mean to the nearest whole number.

....

Graphs

Graphs help scientists to interpret data by helping them to find trends or patterns in the data. A line graph displays data that show how one variable (the dependent or outcome variable) changes in response to another (the independent or test variable). The slope and shape of a graph line can reveal patterns and help scientists to make predictions. For example, line graphs can help you to spot patterns of change over time.

Scientists use bar graphs to compare data across categories or subjects that may not affect each other. The heights of the bars make it easy to compare those quantities. A circle graph, also known as a pie chart, shows the proportions of different parts of a whole.

Write About It
You and a friend record the distance you travel every 15 minutes on a one-hour bike trip. Your friend wants to display the data as a circle graph. Explain whether or not this is the best type of graph to display your data. If not, suggest another graph to use.

SEP.1, SEP.2, SEP.3, SEP.6

The Engineering Design Process

Engineers are builders and problem solvers. Chemical engineers experiment with new fuels made from algae. Civil engineers design roadways and bridges. Bioengineers develop medical devices and prosthetics. The common trait among engineers is an ability to identify problems and design solutions to solve them. Engineers use a creative process that relies on scientific methods to help guide them from a concept or idea all the way to the final product.

Define the Problem

To identify or define a problem, different questions need to be asked: *What are the effects of the problem? What are the likely causes? What other factors could be involved?* Sometimes the obvious, immediate cause of a problem may be the result of another problem that may not be immediately apparent. For example, climate change results in different weather patterns, which in turn can affect organisms that live in certain habitats. So engineers must be aware of all the possible effects of potential solutions. Engineers must also take into account how well different solutions deal with the different causes of the problem.

Reflect Write about a problem that you encountered in your life that had both immediate, obvious causes as well as less-obvious and less-immediate ones.

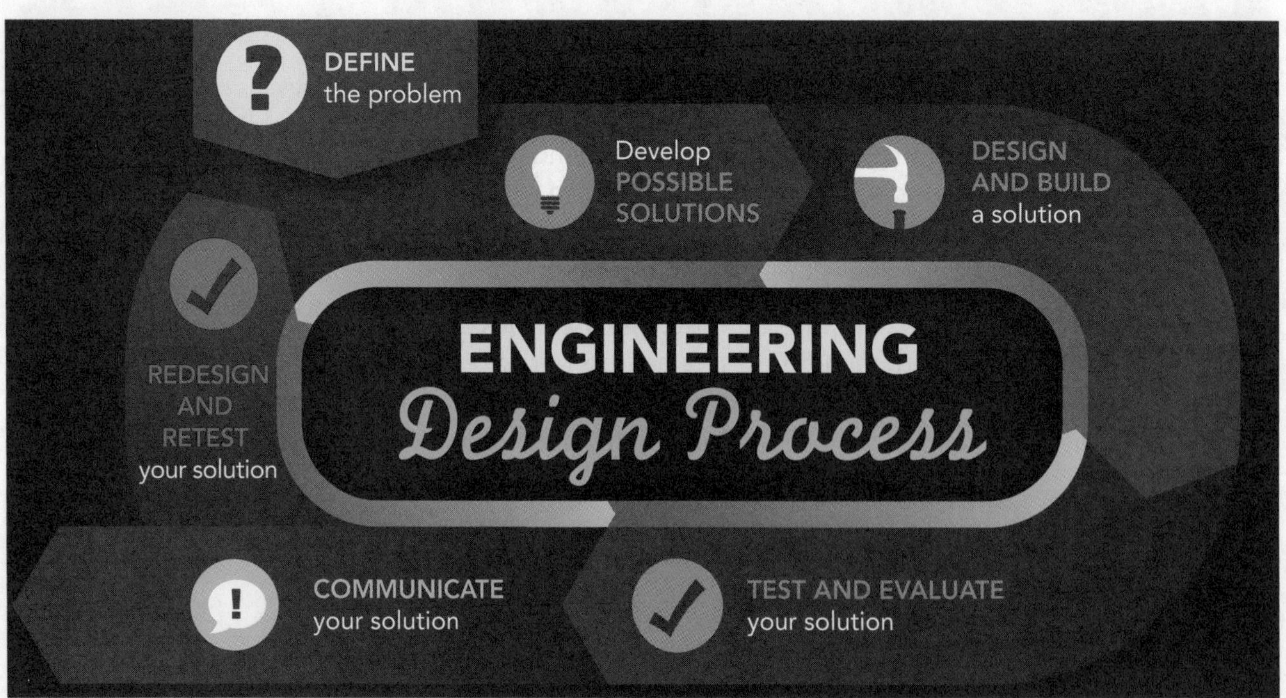

As engineers consider problems and design solutions, they must identify and categorize the criteria and constraints of the project.

Criteria are the factors that must be met or accomplished by the solution. For example, a gardener who wants to protect outdoor plants from deer and rabbits may say that the criteria for the solution are "plants are no longer eaten" and "plant growth is not inhibited in any way." The gardener then knows the plants cannot simply be sealed off from the environment, because the plants will not receive sunlight and water.

The same gardener will likely have constraints on his solution, such as budget for materials and time that is available for working on the project. By setting constraints, a solution can be designed that will be successful without introducing a new set of problems. No one wants to spend $500 on materials to protect $100 worth of tomatoes and cucumbers.

Develop Possible Solutions

After the problem has been identified, and the criteria and constraints identified, an engineer will consider possible solutions. This often involves working in teams with other engineers and designers to brainstorm ideas and research materials that can be used in the design.

It's important for engineers to think creatively and explore all potential solutions. If you wanted to design a bicycle that was safer and easier to ride than a traditional bicycle, then you would want more than just one or two solutions. Having multiple ideas to choose from increases the likelihood that you will develop a solution that meets the criteria and constraints. In addition, different ideas that result from brainstorming can often lead to new and better solutions to an existing problem.

Make Meaning

Using the example of a garden that is vulnerable to wild animals such as deer, make a list of likely constraints on an engineering solution to the problem you identified before. Determine if there are common traits among the constraints, and identify categories for them.

Design a Solution

Engineers then develop the idea that they feel best solves the problem. Once a solution has been chosen, engineers and designers get to work building a model or prototype of the solution. A model may involve sketching on paper or using computer software to construct a model of the solution. A prototype is a working model of the solution.

Building a model or prototype helps an engineer determine whether a solution meets the criteria and stays within the constraints. During this stage of the process, engineers must often deal with new problems and make any necessary adjustments to the model or prototype.

Test and Evaluate a Solution

Make Meaning Think about an aluminum beverage can. What would happen if the price or availability of aluminum changed so much that cans needed to be made of a new material? What would the criteria and constraints be on the development of a new can?

Whether testing a model or a prototype, engineers use scientific processes to evaluate their solutions. Multiple experiments, tests, or trials are conducted, data are evaluated, and results and analyses are communicated. New criteria or constraints may emerge as a result of testing. In most cases, a solution will require some refinement or revision, even if it has been through successful testing. Refining a solution is necessary if there are new constraints, such as less money or available materials. Additional testing may be done to ensure that a solution satisfies local, state, or federal laws or standards.

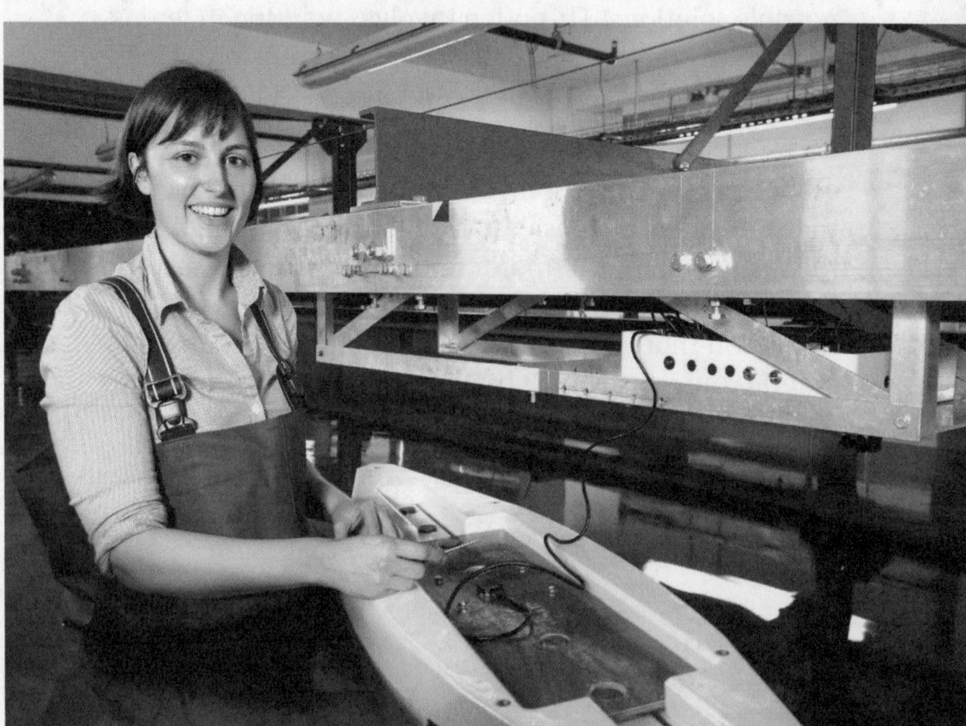

A naval architect sets up a model to test how the the hull's design responds to waves.

Communicate the Solution

Engineers need to communicate the final design to the people who will manufacture the product. This may include sketches, detailed drawings, computer simulations, and written text. Engineers often provide evidence that was collected during the testing stage. This evidence may include graphs and data tables that support the decisions made for the final design.

If there is feedback about the solution, then the engineers and designers must further refine the solution. This might involve making minor adjustments to the design, or it might mean bigger modifications to the design based on new criteria or constraints. Any changes in the design will require additional testing to make sure that the changes work as intended.

Redesign and Retest the Solution

At different steps in the engineering and design process, a solution usually must be revised and retested. Many designs fail to work perfectly, even after models and prototypes are built, tested, and evaluated. Engineers must be ready to analyze new results and deal with any new problems that arise. Troubleshooting, or fixing design problems, allows engineers to adjust the design to improve on how well the solution meets the need.

Communicate Suppose you are an engineer at an aerospace company. Your team is designing a rover to be used on a future NASA space mission. A family member doesn't understand why so much of your team's time is taken up with testing and retesting the rover design. What are three things you would tell your relative to explain why testing and retesting are so important to the engineering and design process?

Safety Symbols

These symbols warn of possible dangers in the laboratory and remind you to work carefully.

Safety Goggles Wear safety goggles to protect your eyes in any activity involving chemicals, flames or heating, or glassware.

Lab Apron Wear a laboratory apron to protect your skin and clothing from damage.

Breakage Handle breakable materials, such as glassware, with care. Do not touch broken glassware.

Heat-Resistant Gloves Use an oven mitt or other hand protection when handling hot materials, such as hot plates or hot glassware.

Plastic Gloves Wear disposable plastic gloves when working with harmful chemicals and organisms. Keep your hands away from your face, and dispose of the gloves according to your teacher's instructions.

Heating Use a clamp or tongs to pick up hot glassware. Do not touch hot objects with your bare hands.

Flames Before you work with flames, tie back loose hair and clothing. Follow your teacher's instructions about lighting and extinguishing flames.

No Flames When using flammable materials, make sure there are no flames, sparks, or other exposed heat sources present.

Corrosive Chemical Avoid getting acid or other corrosive chemicals on your skin or clothing or in your eyes. Do not inhale the vapors. Wash your hands after the activity.

Poison Do not let any poisonous chemical come into contact with your skin, and do not inhale its vapors. Wash your hands when you are finished with the activity.

Fumes Work in a well-ventilated area when harmful vapors may be involved. Avoid inhaling vapors directly. Test an odor only when directed to do so by your teacher, and use a wafting motion to direct the vapor toward your nose.

Sharp Object Scissors, scalpels, knives, needles, pins, and tacks can cut your skin. Always direct a sharp edge or point away from yourself and others.

Animal Safety Treat live or preserved animals or animal parts with care to avoid harming the animals or yourself. Wash your hands when you are finished with the activity.

Plant Safety Handle plants only as directed by your teacher. If you are allergic to certain plants, tell your teacher; do not do an activity involving those plants. Avoid touching harmful plants such as poison ivy. Wash your hands when you are finished with the activity.

Electric Shock To avoid electric shock, never use electrical equipment around water, when the equipment is wet, or when your hands are wet. Be sure cords are untangled and cannot trip anyone. Unplug equipment not in use.

Physical Safety When an experiment involves physical activity, avoid injuring yourself or others. Alert your teacher if there is any reason you should not participate.

Disposal Dispose of chemicals and other laboratory materials safely. Follow the instructions from your teacher.

Hand Washing Wash your hands thoroughly when finished with an activity. Use soap and warm water. Rinse well.

General Safety Awareness When this symbol appears, follow the instructions provided. When you are asked to develop your own procedure in a lab, have your teacher approve your plan.

APPENDIX B

Using a Laboratory Balance

The laboratory balance is an important tool in scientific investigations. Different kinds of balances are used in the laboratory to determine the masses and weights of objects. You can use a triple-beam balance to determine the masses of materials that you study or experiment with in the laboratory. An electronic balance, unlike a triple-beam balance, is used to measure the weights of materials.

The triple-beam balance that you may use in your science class is probably similar to the balance depicted in this Appendix. To use the balance properly, you should learn the name, location, and function of each part of the balance.

Triple-Beam Balance

The triple-beam balance is a single-pan balance with three beams calibrated in grams. The back, or 100-gram, beam is divided into ten units of 10 grams each. The middle, or 500-gram, beam is divided into five units of 100 grams each. The front, or 10-gram, beam is divided into ten units of 1 gram each. Each gram on the front beam is further divided into units of 0.1 gram.

Apply Concepts What is the greatest mass you could find with the triple-beam balance in the picture?

....

Calculate What is the mass of the apple in the picture?

....

The following procedure can be used to find the mass of an object with a triple-beam balance:

1. Place the object on the pan.
2. Move the rider on the middle beam notch by notch until the horizontal pointer on the right drops below zero. Move the rider back one notch.
3. Move the rider on the back beam notch by notch until the pointer again drops below zero. Move the rider back one notch.
4. Slowly slide the rider along the front beam until the pointer stops at the zero point.
5. The mass of the object is equal to the sum of the readings on the three beams.

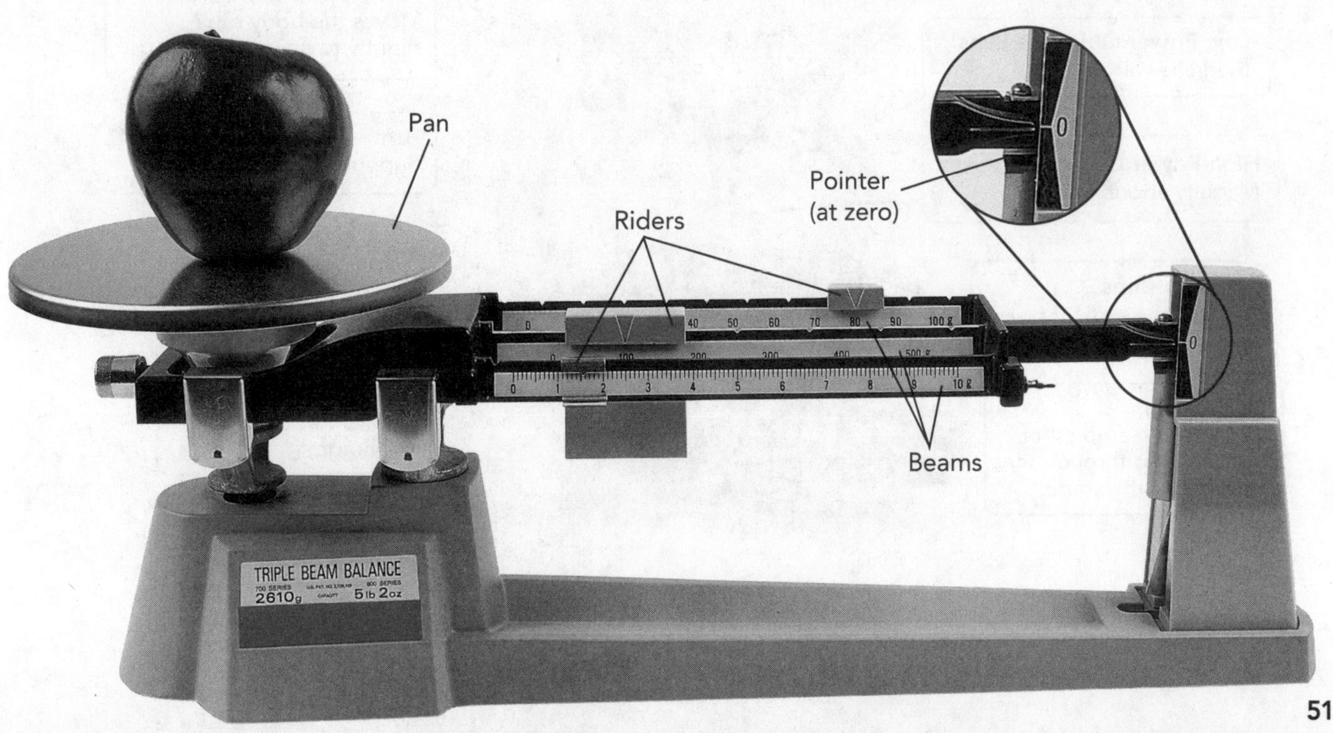

APPENDIX C

Using a Microscope

The microscope is an essential tool in the study of life science. It allows you to see things that are too small to be seen with the unaided eye.

You will probably use a compound microscope like the one you see here. The compound microscope has more than one lens that magnifies the object you view.

Typically, a compound microscope has one lens in the eyepiece (the part you look through). The eyepiece lens usually magnifies 10×. Any object you view through this lens will appear 10 times larger than it is.

A compound microscope may contain two or three other lenses called objective lenses. They are called the low-power and high-power objective lenses. The low-power objective lens usually magnifies 10×. The high-power objective lenses usually magnify 40× and 100×.

To calculate the total magnification with which you are viewing an object, multiply the magnification of the eyepiece lens by the magnification of the objective lens you are using. For example, the eyepiece's magnification of 10× multiplied by the low-power objective's magnification of 10× equals a total magnification of 100×.

Use the photo of the compound microscope to become familiar with the parts of the microscope and their functions.

The Parts of a Microscope

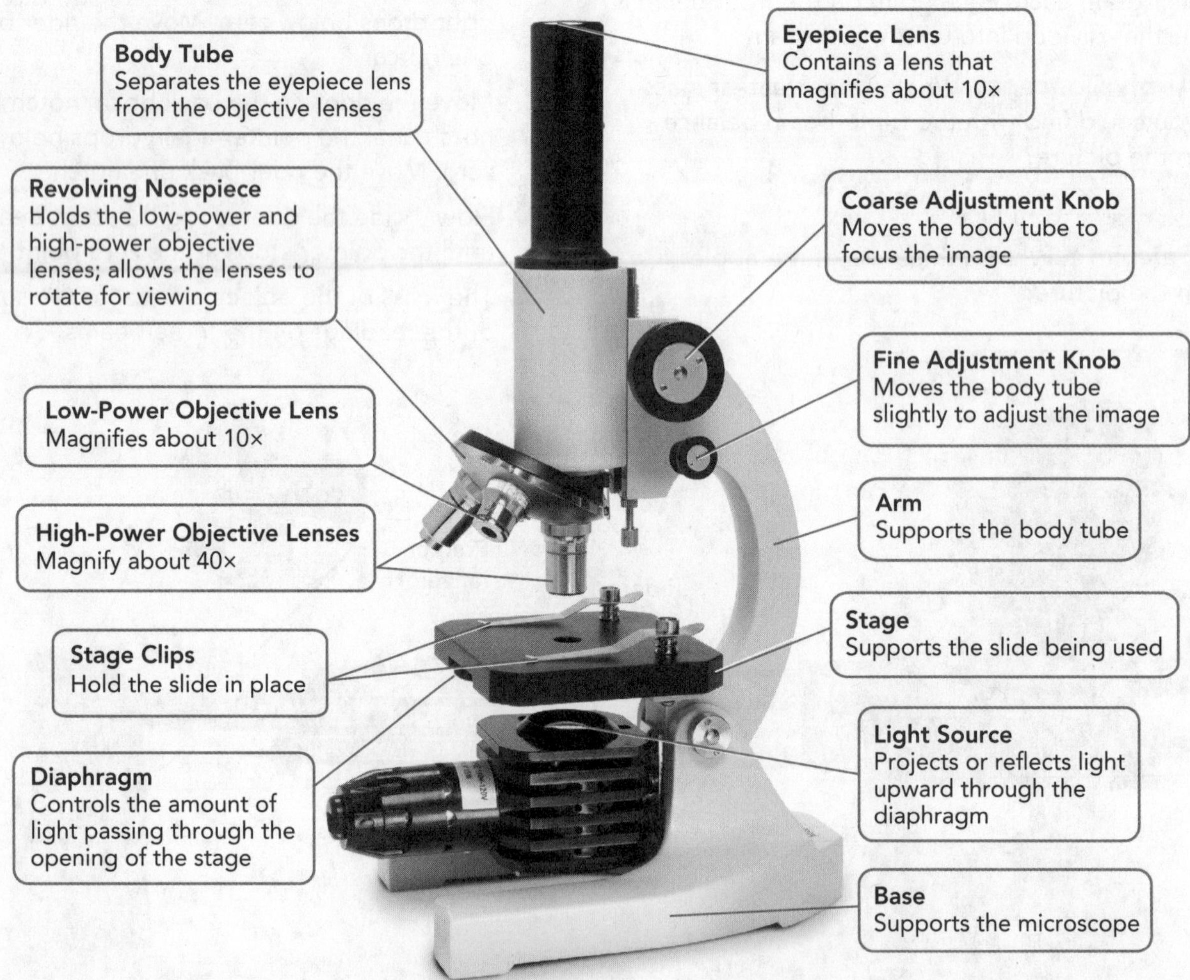
Body Tube
Separates the eyepiece lens from the objective lenses
Revolving Nosepiece
Holds the low-power and high-power objective lenses; allows the lenses to rotate for viewing
Low-Power Objective Lens
Magnifies about 10×
High-Power Objective Lenses
Magnify about 40×
Stage Clips
Hold the slide in place
Diaphragm
Controls the amount of light passing through the opening of the stage
Eyepiece Lens
Contains a lens that magnifies about 10×
Coarse Adjustment Knob
Moves the body tube to focus the image
Fine Adjustment Knob
Moves the body tube slightly to adjust the image
Arm
Supports the body tube
Stage
Supports the slide being used
Light Source
Projects or reflects light upward through the diaphragm
Base
Supports the microscope

Using the Microscope

Use the following procedures when you are working with a microscope.

1. To carry the microscope, grasp the microscope's arm with one hand. Place your other hand under the base.
2. Place the microscope on a table with the arm toward you.
3. Turn the coarse adjustment knob to raise the body tube.
4. Revolve the nosepiece until the low-power objective lens clicks into place.
5. Adjust the diaphragm. While looking through the eyepiece, adjust the mirror until you see a bright white circle of light. **CAUTION:** Never use direct sunlight as a light source.
6. Place a slide on the stage. Center the specimen over the opening on the stage. Use the stage clips to hold the slide in place. **CAUTION:** Glass slides are fragile.
7. Look at the stage from the side. Carefully turn the coarse adjustment knob to lower the body tube until the low-power objective almost touches the slide.
8. Looking through the eyepiece, very slowly turn the coarse adjustment knob until the specimen comes into focus.
9. To switch to the high-power objective lens, look at the microscope from the side. Carefully revolve the nosepiece until the high-power objective lens clicks into place. Make sure the lens does not hit the slide.
10. Looking through the eyepiece, turn the fine adjustment knob until the specimen comes into focus.

Making a Wet-Mount Slide

Use the following procedures to make a wet-mount slide of a specimen.

1. Obtain a clean microscope slide and a coverslip. **CAUTION:** Glass slides and coverslips are fragile.
2. Place the specimen on the center of the slide. The specimen must be thin enough for light to pass through it.
3. Using a plastic dropper, place a drop of water on the specimen.
4. Gently place one edge of the coverslip against the slide so that it touches the edge of the water drop at a 45° angle. Slowly lower the coverslip over the specimen. If you see air bubbles trapped beneath the coverslip, tap the coverslip gently with the eraser end of a pencil.
5. Remove any excess water at the edge of the coverslip with a paper towel.

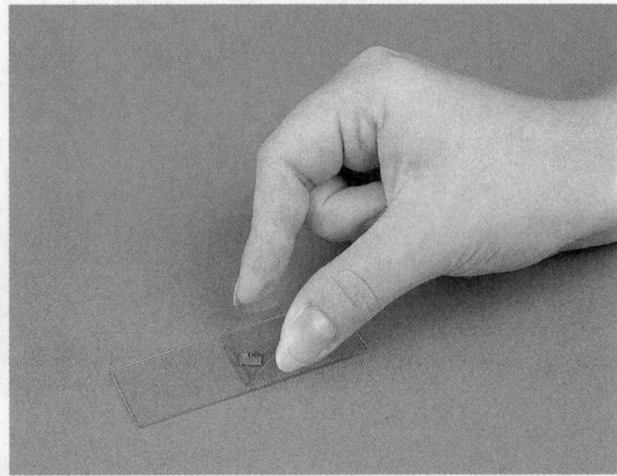

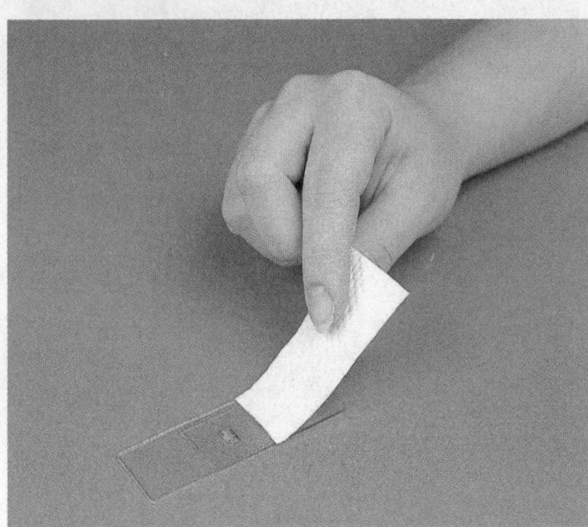

APPENDIX D

Periodic Table of Elements

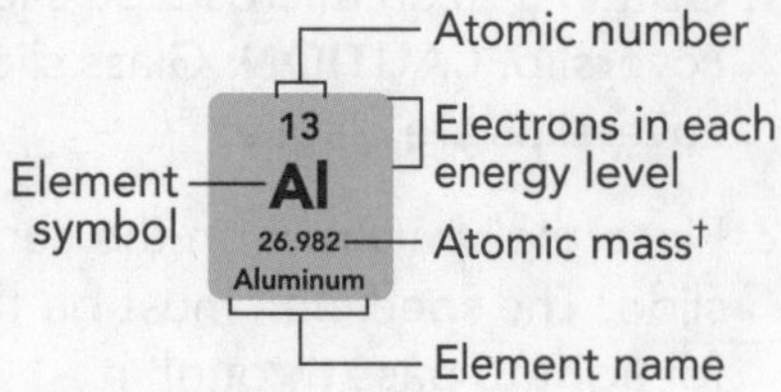

Key

Main-Group Elements
- Alkali metals
- Alkaline earth metals
- Other metals
- Metalloids
- Nonmetals
- Noble gases

Transition Elements
- Transition metals
- Inner transition metals

- X Solid
- X Liquid
- X Gas
- X Not found in nature

Period	1 1A	2 2A	3 3B	4 4B	5 5B	6 6B	7 7B	8	9 8B	10	11 1B	12 2B
1	1 H 1.0079 Hydrogen											
2	3 Li 6.941 Lithium	4 Be 9.0122 Beryllium										
3	11 Na 22.990 Sodium	12 Mg 24.305 Magnesium										
4	19 K 39.098 Potassium	20 Ca 40.08 Calcium	21 Sc 44.956 Scandium	22 Ti 47.90 Titanium	23 V 50.941 Vanadium	24 Cr 51.996 Chromium	25 Mn 54.938 Manganese	26 Fe 55.847 Iron	27 Co 58.933 Cobalt	28 Ni 58.69 Nickel	29 Cu 63.546 Copper	30 Zn 65.38 Zinc
5	37 Rb 85.468 Rubidium	38 Sr 87.62 Strontium	39 Y 88.906 Yttrium	40 Zr 91.22 Zirconium	41 Nb 92.906 Niobium	42 Mo 95.94 Molybdenum	43 Tc (98) Technetium	44 Ru 101.07 Ruthenium	45 Rh 102.91 Rhodium	46 Pd 106.4 Palladium	47 Ag 107.87 Silver	48 Cd 112.41 Cadmium
6	55 Cs 132.91 Cesium	56 Ba 137.33 Barium	71 Lu 174.97 Lutetium	72 Hf 178.49 Hafnium	73 Ta 180.95 Tantalum	74 W 183.85 Tungsten	75 Re 186.21 Rhenium	76 Os 190.2 Osmium	77 Ir 192.22 Iridium	78 Pt 195.09 Platinum	79 Au 196.97 Gold	80 Hg 200.59 Mercury
7	87 Fr (223) Francium	88 Ra (226) Radium	103 Lr (262) Lawrencium	104 Rf (261) Rutherfordium	105 Db (262) Dubnium	106 Sg (263) Seaborgium	107 Bh (264) Bohrium	108 Hs (265) Hassium	109 Mt (268) Meitnerium	110 Ds (269) Darmstadtium	111 Rg (272) Roentgenium	112 Cn (277) Copernicium

Elements 104–118 are the transactinide elements.

Lanthanide series

57	58	59	60	61	62	63	64	65
La 138.91 Lanthanum	Ce 140.12 Cerium	Pr 140.91 Praseodymium	Nd 144.24 Neodymium	Pm (145) Promethium	Sm 150.4 Samarium	Eu 151.96 Europium	Gd 157.25 Gadolinium	Tb 158.93 Terbium

Actinide series

89	90	91	92	93	94	95	96	97
Ac (227) Actinium	Th 232.04 Thorium	Pa 231.04 Protactinium	U 238.03 Uranium	Np (237) Neptunium	Pu (244) Plutonium	Am (243) Americium	Cm (247) Curium	Bk (247) Berkelium

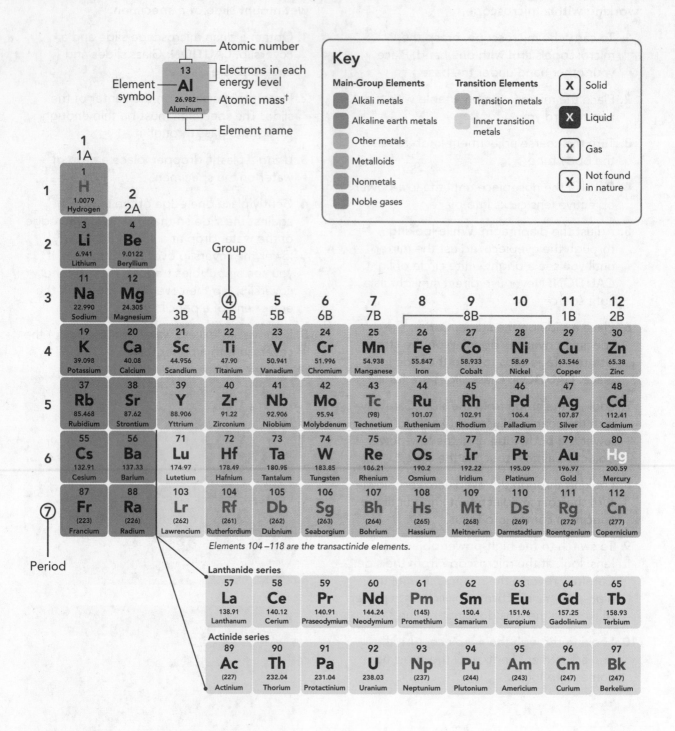

†*The atomic masses in parentheses are the mass numbers of the longest-lived isotope of elements for which a standard atomic mass cannot be defined.*

13 3A	14 4A	15 5A	16 6A	17 7A	18 8A
					2 He 4.0026 Helium
5 B 10.81 Boron	6 C 12.011 Carbon	7 N 14.007 Nitrogen	8 O 15.999 Oxygen	9 F 18.998 Fluorine	10 Ne 20.179 Neon
13 Al 26.982 Aluminum	14 Si 28.086 Silicon	15 P 30.974 Phosphorus	16 S 32.06 Sulfur	17 Cl 35.453 Chlorine	18 Ar 39.948 Argon
31 Ga 69.72 Gallium	32 Ge 72.59 Germanium	33 As 74.922 Arsenic	34 Se 78.96 Selenium	35 Br 79.904 Bromine	36 Kr 83.80 Krypton
49 In 114.82 Indium	50 Sn 118.69 Tin	51 Sb 121.75 Antimony	52 Te 127.60 Tellurium	53 I 126.90 Iodine	54 Xe 131.30 Xenon
81 Tl 204.37 Thallium	82 Pb 207.2 Lead	83 Bi 208.98 Bismuth	84 Po (209) Polonium	85 At (210) Astatine	86 Rn (222) Radon
113 Nh (284) Nihonium	114 Fl (289) Flerovium	115 Mc (288) Moscovium	116 Lv (292) Livermorium	117 Ts (294) Tennessine	118 Og (294) Oganesson

66 Dy 162.50 Dysprosium	67 Ho 164.93 Holmium	68 Er 167.26 Erbium	69 Tm 168.93 Thulium	70 Yb 173.04 Ytterbium
98 Cf (251) Californium	99 Es (252) Einsteinium	100 Fm (257) Fermium	101 Md (258) Mendelevium	102 No (259) Nobelium

GLOSSARY

A

absorption The transfer of energy from a wave to a material that it encounters. (191)
acceleration The rate at which velocity changes. (463)
acid A substance that tastes sour, reacts with metals and carbonates, and turns blue litmus paper red. (379)
amplitude The maximum distance the particles of a medium move away from their rest positions as a longitudinal wave passes through the medium. (180)
analog signal A signal that allows for a continuous record of some kind of action. (304)
atom The basic particle from which all elements are made; the smallest particle of an element that has the properties of that element. (8, 336)
atomic mass The average mass of all the isotopes of an element. (348)
atomic number The number of protons in the nucleus of an atom. (341)

B

bandwidth The amount of information that can be transmitted in bits per second. (319)
base A substance that tastes bitter, feels slippery, and turns red litmus paper blue. (382)
boiling point The temperature at which a liquid boils. (60)
Boyle's Law A principle that describes the relationship between the pressure and volume of a gas at constant temperature. (71)

C

Charles's Law A principle that describes the relationship between the temperature and volume of a gas at constant pressure. (69)
chemical change A change in which one or more substances combine or break apart to form new substances. (27, 410)
chemical energy A form of potential energy that is stored in chemical bonds between atoms. (112)
chemical property A characteristic of a substance that describes its ability to change into different substances. (7)
chemical symbol A one- or two-letter abbreviation for an element (349)
closed system A system in which no matter is allowed to enter or leave. (425)
colloid A mixture containing small, undissolved particles that do not settle out. (401)
compound A substance made of two or more elements chemically combined in a specific ratio, or proportion. (10, 360)

concave A mirror with a surface that curves inward or a lens that is thinner at the center than at the edges. (224)
condensation The change in state from a gas to a liquid. (62)
conduction The transfer of thermal energy from one particle of matter to another. (149)
conductor A material that conducts heat well. (159); A material that allows electric charges to flow. (245)
convection The transfer of thermal energy by the movement of a fluid. (149)
convection current The movement of a fluid, caused by differences in temperature, that transfers heat from one part of the fluid to another. (149)
convex A mirror that curves outward or lens that is thicker in the center than at the edges. (223)
corrosive The way in which acids react with some metals so as to wear away the metal. (380)
covalent bond A chemical bond formed when two atoms share electrons. (372)

D

decibel (dB) A unit used to compare the loudness of different sounds. (204)
density The measurement of how much mass of a substance is contained in a given volume. (18)
diffraction The bending or spreading of waves as they move around a barrier or pass through an opening. (191)
diffuse reflection Reflection that occurs when parallel light rays hit an uneven surface and all reflect at different angles. (222)
digital signal A signal that allows for a record of numerical values of an action at a set of continuous time intervals. (304)
Doppler effect The change in frequency of a wave as its source moves in relation to an observer. (206)
ductile A term used to describe a material that can be pulled out into a long wire. (363)

E

elastic potential energy The energy of stretched or compressed objects. (105)

electric current The continuous flow of electrical charges through a material. (244)

electric field The region around a charged object where the object's electric force is exerted on other charged objects. (242)

electric force The force between charged objects. (242)

electric motor A device that transforms electrical energy to mechanical energy. (269)

electrical circuit A complete, unbroken path through which electric charges can flow. (291)

electrical energy The energy of electric charges. (113)

electromagnet A magnet created by wrapping a coil of wire with a current running through it around a core of material that is easily magnetized. (263)

electromagnetic induction The process of genrating an electric current from the motion of a conductor through a magnetic field. (270)

electromagnetic radiation The energy transferred through space by electromagnetic waves. (113, 179)

electromagnetic signal Information that is sent as a pattern of electromagnetic waves, such as visible light, microwaves, and radio waves. (303)

electromagnetic spectrum The complete range of electromagnetic waves placed in order of increasing frequency. (213)

electromagnetic wave A wave made up of a combination of a changing electric field and a changing magnetic field. (209)

electromagnetism The relationship between electricity and magnetism. (259)

electron A tiny particle that moves around the outside of the nucleus of an atom. (241, 337)

electronic signal Information that is sent as a pattern in a controlled flow of current through a circuit. (302)

element A pure substance that cannot be broken down into other substances by chemical or physical means. (8)

endothermic reaction A reaction that absorbs energy. (414)

energy The ability to do work or cause change. (91)

evaporation The process by which molecules at the surface of a liquid absorb enough energy to change to a gas. (60)

exothermic reaction A reaction that releases energy, usually in the form of heat. (414)

F

focal point The point at which light rays parallel to the optical axis meet, after being reflected (or refracted) by a mirror (or lens). (223)

force A push or pull exerted on an object. (92, 453)

freezing point The temperature at which a liquid freezes. (59)

frequency The number of complete waves that pass a given point in a certain amount of time. (182)

friction The force that two surfaces exert on each other when they rub against each other. (454)

G

galvanometer A device that uses an electromagnet to detect small amounts of current. (268)

gamma rays Electromagnetic waves with the shortest wavelengths and highest frequencies. (215)

gas A state of matter with no definite shape or volume. (53)

generator A device that transforms mechanical energy into electrical energy. (273)

gravitational potential energy Potential energy that depends on the height of an object. (104)

gravity The attractive force between objects; the force that moves objects downhill. (454)

group Elements in the same vertical column of the periodic table; also called family. (354)

H

heat The transfer of thermal energy from a warmer object to a cooler object. (141)

GLOSSARY

I

indicator A compound that changes color in the presence of an acid or a base. (381)
inertia The tendency of an object to resist a change in motion. (472)
information technology Computer and telecommunication hardware and software that store, transmit, receive, and manipulate information. (313)
infrared rays Electromagnetic waves with shorter wavelengths and higher frequencies than microwaves. (214)
insulator A material that does not conduct heat well. (159)
intensity The amount of energy per second carried through a unit area by a wave. (203)
interference The interaction between waves that meet. (192)
ion An atom or group of atoms that has become electrically charged. (370)
ionic bond The attraction between ions with opposite charges. (371)
isotope An atom with the same number of protons and a different number of neutrons from other atoms of the same element. (342)

K

kinetic energy Energy that an object has due to its motion. (101)

L

law of conservation of energy The rule that energy cannot be created or destroyed. (122)
law of conservation of mass The principle that the total amount of matter is neither created nor destroyed during any chemical or physical change. (424)
liquid A state of matter that has no definite shape but has a definite volume. (51)
longitudinal wave A wave that moves the medium in a direction parallel to the direction in which the wave travels. (181)
loudness The perception of the energy of a sound. (203)
luster The way a mineral reflects light from its surface. (363)

M

magnet Any material that attracts iron and materials that contain iron. (251)
magnetic field The region around a magnet where the magnetic force is exerted. (253)
magnetic force A force produced when magnetic poles interact. (252)
magnetic pole The ends of a magnetic object, where the magnetic force is strongest. (252)
magnetism The force of attraction or repulsion of magnetic materials. (251)
malleable A term used to describe material that can be hammered or rolled into flat sheets. (363)
mass A measure of how much matter is in an object. (15)
mass number The sum of protons and neutrons in the nucleus of an atom. (342)
matter Anything that has mass and takes up space. (5)
mechanical energy Kinetic or potential energy associated with the motion or position of an object. (109)
mechanical wave A wave that requires a medium through which to travel. (179)
medium The material through which a wave travels. (113, 179)
melting point The temperature at which a substance changes from a solid to a liquid; the same as the freezing point, or temperature at which a liquid changes to a solid. (58)
microwaves Electromagnetic waves that have shorter wavelengths and higher frequencies than radio waves. (214)
mixture Two or more substances that are together in the same place but their atoms are not chemically bonded. (11, 399)
molecule A neutral group of two or more atoms held together by covalent bonds. (9, 372)
motion The state in which one object's distance from another is changing. (91, 451)

N

natural resource Anything naturally occuring in the environment that humans use. (430)

net force The overall force on an object when all the individual forces acting on it are added together. (455)

neutralization A reaction of an acid with a base, yielding a solution that is not as acidic or basic as the starting solutions were. (383)

neutron A small particle in the nucleus of the atom, with no electrical charge. (340)

newton A unit of measure that equals the force required to accelerate 1 kilogram of mass at 1 meter per second per second. (453)

noise Random signals from the environment that can alter the output of a signal. (318)

nonpolar bond A covalent bond in which electrons are shared equally. (373)

nuclear energy The potential energy stored in the nucleus of an atom. (110)

nucleus 1. The central core of an atom which contains protons and neutrons. (338)

O

Ohm's law The law that staes that resistance in a circuit is equal to voltage divided by current. (294)

opaque A type of material that reflects or absorbs all of the light that strikes it. (219)

open system A system in which matter can enter from or escape to the surroundings. (425)

P

parallel circuit An electric circuit in which different parts of the circuit are on separate branches. (296)

period A horizontal row of elements in the periodic table. (352)

periodic table An arrangement of the elements showing the repeating pattern of their properties. (348)

physical change A change that alters the form or appearance of a material but does not make the material into another substance. (25, 409)

physical property A characteristic of a pure substance that can be observed without changing it into another substance. (6)

pitch A description of how a sound is perceived as high or low. (205)

pixel A small, uniform shape that is combined with other pixels to make a larger image. (308)

polar bond A covalent bond in which electrons are shared unequally. (373)

polyatomic ion An ion that is made of more than one atom. (370)

polymer A long chain of molecules made up of repeating units. (432)

potential energy The energy an object has because of its position; also the internal stored energy of an object, such as energy stored in chemical bonds. (103)

power The rate at which one form of energy is transformed into another. (96)

pressure The force pushing on a surface divided by the area of that surface. (67)

product A substance formed as a result of a chemical reaction. (410)

proton A small, positively charged particle that is found in the nucleus of an atom. (338)

R

radiation The transfer of energy by electromagnetic waves. (149)

radio waves Electromagnetic waves with the longest wavelengths and lowest frequencies. (213)

reactant A substance that enters into a chemical reaction. (410)

reactivity The ease and speed with which an element combines, or reacts, with other elements and compounds. (362)

reference point A place or object used for comparison to determine whether an object is in motion. (451)

reflection The bouncing back of an object or a wave when it hits a surface through which it cannot pass. (189)

refraction The bending of waves as they enter a new medium at an angle, caused by a change in speed. (190)

resistance The measurement of how difficult it is for charges to flow through an object. (293)

resonance The increase in the amplitude of a vibration that occurs when external vibrations match an object's natural frequency. (195)

S

salt An ionic compound made from the neutralization of an acid with a base. (383)

semiconductor A substance that can conduct electric current under some conditions. (365)

series circuit An electic circuit in which all parts are connected one after another along one path. (295)

slope The steepness of a graph line; the ratio of the vertical change (the rise) to the horizontal change (the run). (461)

software Programs that encode, decode, and interpret information. (313)

solenoid A coil of wire with a current. (262)

solid A state of matter that has a definite shape and a definite volume. (48)

solubility A measure of how much solute can dissolve in a given solvent at a given temperature. (404)

solute The part of a solution that is dissolved by a solvent. (402)

solution A mixture containing a solvent and at least one solute that has the same properties throughout; a mixture in which one substance is dissolved in another. (402)

solvent The part of a solution that is usually present in the largest amount and dissolves a solute. (402)

specific heat The amount of heat required to raise the temperature of 1 kilogram of a material by 1 kelvin, which is equivalent to 1°C. (160)

speed The distance an object travels per unit of time. (459)

standing wave A wave that appears to stand in one place, even though it is two waves interfering as they pass through each other. (194)

static electricity A buildup of charges on an object. (246)

sublimation The change in state from a solid directly to a gas without passing through the liquid state. (63)

substance A single kind of matter that is pure and has a specific set of properties. (5)

surface tension The result of an inward pull among the molecules of a liquid that brings the molecules on the surface closer together; causes the surface to act as if it has a thin skin. (52)

suspension A mixture in which particles can be seen and easily separated by settling or filtration. (401)

synthetic Created or manufactured by humans; not found occuring in nature (429)

T

temperature How hot or cold something is; a measure of the average energy of motion of the particles of a substance; the measure of the average kinetic energy of the particles of a substance. (57, 142)

thermal energy The total kinetic and potential energy of all the particles of an object. (57, 111, 141)

thermal expansion The expansion of matter when it is heated. (161)

transformer A device that increases or decreases voltage, which often consists of two separate coils of insulated wires wrapped around an iron core. (274)

transluscent A type of material that scatters light as it passes through. (219)

transparent A type of material that transmits light without scattering it. (219)

transverse wave A wave that moves the medium at right angles to the direction in which the wave travels. (180)

U

ultraviolet rays Electromagnetic waves with wavelengths shorter than visible light but longer than X-rays. (215)

V

valence electron The electrons that are in the highest energy level of an atom and that are involved in chemical bonding. (360)

vaporization The change of state from a liquid to a gas. (60)

velocity Speed in a given direction. (462)

viscosity A liquid's resistance to flowing. (52)

visible light Electromagnetic radiation that can be seen with the unaided eye. (214)

voltage The difference in electrical potential energy per charge between two places in a circuit. (292)

volume The amount of space that matter occupies. (15)

wave A disturbance that transfers energy from place to place. (179)

wave pulse A pulse of energy that travels through an electric circuit when it is closed. (302)

wavelength The distance between two corresponding parts of a wave, such as the distance between two crests. (182)

weight A measure of the force of gravity acting on an object. (15, 485)

work Force exerted on an object that causes it to move. (93)

X-rays Electromagnetic waves with wavelengths shorter than ultraviolet rays but longer than gamma rays. (215)

INDEX

Page numbers for key terms are printed in boldface type.

A

B

C

D

INDEX

Page numbers for key terms are printed in boldface type.

E

F

G

H

I

K

L

INDEX

Page numbers for key terms are printed in boldface type.

N

O

P

INDEX

Page numbers for key terms are printed in boldface type.

S

INDEX

Page numbers for key terms are printed in boldface type.

T

U

ACKNOWLEDGEMENTS

Photographs

Photo locators denoted as follows: Top (T), Center (C), Bottom (B), Left (L), Right (R), Background (Bkgd)

Front Cover: Miguel Sotomayor/Moment/Getty Images

Back Cover: Marinello/DigitalVision Vectors/Getty Images

Front Matter

vi: sokkajar/Fotolia; vii: Makieni/Fotolia; viii: David Jones/PA Images/Alamy Stock Photo; ix: fabriziobalconi/Fotolia; x: Paul Melling/Alamy Stock Photo; xi: Perry van Munster/Alamy Stock Photo; xii: Raimundas/Shutterstock; xiii: Alexander Cher/Shutterstock; xiv: HTU/Shutterstock; xv: Matteo Arteni/Shutterstock

Topic 1

xviii: sokkajar/Fotolia; 002: stock_colors/E+/Getty Images; 004: Sami Sarkis RM CC/Alamy Stock Photo; 006 Bkgrd: lazyllama/Shutterstock; 006 BL: subinpumsom/Fotolia; 007 BL: borroko72/Fotolia; 007 BR: Arpad NagyBagoly/Fotolia; 008 BR: anyka/123RF; 008 C: James Steidl/Shutterstock; 010 TC: smereka/Shutterstock; 010 TR: GIPhotoStock/Science Source; 011 TCR: Bert Folsom/123RF; 011 TR: lepas2004/iStock/Getty Images; 013 BC: SuperStock; 013 Bkgrd: Massimo Pizzotti/AGE Fotostock/SuperStock; 013 TR: David L. Ryan/The Boston Globe/Getty Images; 014: Michelle McMahon/Moment/Getty Images; 016 T: Martin Shields/Alamy Stock Photo; 016 TR: Martin Shields/Alamy Stock Photo; 017 BR: leungchopan/Fotolia; 017 CR: GIPhotoStock/Science Source; 017 L: hitandrun IKON Images/Newscom; 018: SchulteProductions/E+/Getty Images; 020 CR: RF Company/Alamy Stock Photo; 020 L: Denis Radovanovic/Shutterstock; 020 R: Siim Sepp/Alamy Stock Photo; 020 T: victor21041958/Fotolia; 022: U.S. Coast Guard Photo; 025: Fuse/Corbis/Getty Images; 026: Sergey Dobrydnev/Shutterstock; 027 BCL: Vinicef/Alamy Stock Photo; 027 BCR: Vinicef/Alamy Stock Photo; 027 BL: Stephanie Frey/Fotolia; 027 BR: kzen/Shutterstock; 028 CL: Fuse/Corbis/Getty Images; 028 CR: Charles D. Winters/Science Source; 028 TL: studio on line/Shutterstock; 028 TR: 123RF; 030 Bkgrd: Peter Barritt/Alamy Stock Photo; 030 BL: Paul Souders/Alamy Stock Photo; 031: byrdyak/123RF; 033: Kiyoshi Takahase Segundo/Alamy Stock Photo; 035: Shaiith/iStock/Getty Images; 038: Torontonian/Alamy Stock Photo; 039: USantos/Fotolia

Topic 2

042: Makieni/Fotolia; 044: Studio 8/Pearson Education Ltd.; 046: Kendall Rittenour/Shutterstock; 048: Dmytro Skorobogatov/Alamy Stock Photo; 049 BL: Marco Cavina/Shutterstock; 049 BR: CrackerClips Stock Media/Shutterstock; 049 T: Erika8213/Fotolia; 050 BCL: Robyn Mackenzie/Shutterstock; 050 BL: Fototrips/Fotolia; 051 BL: Kropic/Fotolia; 051 BR: Rony Zmiri/Fotolia; 052 BL: Wiklander/Shutterstock; 052 BR: Oriori/Fotolia; 053 T: Sutichak/Fotolia; 053 TL: Hudiemm/Getty Images; 055 BCR: Özgür Güvenç/Fotolia; 055 CR: Xiaoliangge/Fotolia; 056: WavebreakMediaMicro/Fotolia; 060 TC: PhotoAlto/Odilon Dimier/Getty Images; 060 TL: Petr Malyshev/Fotolia; 060 TR: Uygaar/Getty Images; 062 B: Michael Hare/Shutterstock; 062 CR: Cultura Creative (RF)/Alamy Stock Photo; 063: Charles D. Winters/Science Source; 066: Ronstik/Fotolia; 068 T: Saap585/Shutterstock; 068 TC: Eric Audras/PhotoAlto/AGE Fotostock; 068 TL: Gudellaphoto/Fotolia; 068 TR: Peterspiro/iStock/Getty Images; 071: Cebas/Shutterstock; 073 B: Faded Beauty/Fotolia; 073 CL: Alexmit/iStock/Getty Images; 076 Bkgrd: Physicx/Shutterstock; 076 BL: Mara Zemgaliete/Fotolia; 076 TL: Denisfilm/Fotolia; 078 BC: Pakhnyushcha/Shutterstock; 078 C: Reika/Shutterstock; 078 CR: Richard Megna/Fundamental Photographs, NYC; 082: Pakhnyushcha/Shutterstock; 083: Bestphotostudio/Fotolia

Topic 3

086: David Jones/PA Images/Alamy Stock Photo; 088: Jeffrey Coolidge/Getty Images; 090: Derek Watt/Alamy Stock Photo; 094: Hero Images/Getty Images; 095 BC: Steven May/Alamy Stock Photo; 095 BL: WavebreakMediaMicro/Fotolia; 095 BR: Monkey Business/Fotolia; 096 BL: Ben Schonewille/Shutterstock; 096 BR: Andrey Popov/Shutterstock; 097: Egmont Strigl/imageBROKER/Alamy Stock Photo; 098 TCL: Ariel Skelley/Blend Images/Getty Images; 098 TL: B Christopher/Alamy Stock Photo; 100: AFP/Getty Images; 103: Feng Yu/Fotolia; 104: Anatoliy Gleb/Fotolia; 107: Sportpoint/Fotolia; 108: fhm/Moment/Getty Images; 109: Steve Byland/Shutterstock; 111: Paul Vinten/Fotolia; 112: Toa55/Shutterstock; 117 B: John Lund/Marc Romanelli/Blend Images/Getty Images; 117 TR: Hero Images Inc./Alamy Stock Photo; 118: Holger Thalmann/Cultura RM/Alamy Stock Photo; 120 BL: Richard Megna/Fundamental Photographs; 120 BR: Kim Karpeles/Alamy Stock Photo; 122: Parker Photography/Alamy Stock Photo; 124: Ian McDonnell/iStock/Getty Images; 126: Blackpixel/Shutterstock; 132: Stockbyte/Getty Images

Topic 4

136: fabriziobalconi/Fotolia; 138: Ragnar Th Sigurdsson/Arctic Images/Alamy Stock Photo; 140: Andrew Cline/Alamy Stock Photo; 143: Yanika Panfilova/123RF; 147 B: Jim West/Alamy Stock Photo; 147 TR: Evgeny Itsikson/Shutterstock; 149: EduardSV/Fotolia; 153: Alextype/Fotolia; 158: Zavgsg/Fotolia; 161 BR: Tom Uhlman/Alamy Stock Photo; 161 T: Coffeemill/Shutterstock; 162: Juice Images/Getty Images; 163: NASA; 167 BL: Panther Media GmbH/Alamy Stock Photo; 167 CL: Jason Bazzano/Alamy Stock Photo; 167 TL: Halfpoint/Fotolia; 170: Hugo Felix/Shutterstock

Topic 5

174: Paul Melling/Alamy Stock Photo; 176: Losevsky Pavel/Shutterstock; 178: Mark Leary/Getty Images; 179: NOAA; 180: Wavebreak Media Ltd./123RF; 186: imageBROKER/Jim West/Newscom; 188: Brian Maudsley/Shutterstock; 191 BCL: Science Source; 191 BCR: Kenny10/Shutterstock; 191 BL: Roberto Lo Savio/Shutterstock; 191 BR: Nublee bin Shamsu Bahar/Shutterstock; 193: Denis Gladkiy/Fotolia; 195: Sergey Nivens/Fotolia; 197 CR: Graham Oliver/123RF; 197 TR: Lionel Le Jeune/Fotolia; 199: LightField Studios/Shutterstock; 200: Lipsett Photography Group/Shutterstock; 202 B: Andrey Kuzmin/Shutterstock; 202 C: Mike Flippo/Shutterstock; 202 T: pukach/Shutterstock; 203: Goran Djukanovic/Shutterstock; 204: mr_sailor/iStock/Getty Images; 205: vvoennyy/123RF; 208: U.S. Navy; 213: gaspr13/Getty Images; 214 B: Arno Vlooswijk/TService/Science Source; 214 TL: Chuck Franklin/Alamy Stock Photo; 215: Anton Petrus/Fotolia; 217 B: Andrey Armyagov/123RF; 217 TR: Blend Images/Alamy Stock Photo; 219: Sirtravelalot/Shutterstock; 220: Yellow Cat/Shutterstock; 221 B: Falk/Shutterstock; 221 C: Havoc/Shutterstock; 222 B:

Anne08/Shutterstock; 222 T: Tusharkoley/Shutterstock; 223 B: Yuelan/123RF; 223 T: TLF Design/Alamy Stock Photo; 224 B: Mediaphotos/iStock/Getty Images; 224 T: Photo Researchers; 232: Amirul Syaidi/Fotolia; 233: EpicStockMedia/Shutterstock

Topic 6

236: Perry van Munster/Alamy Stock Photo; 238: Tingimage/Alamy Stock Photo; 240: Ali Kabas/Alamy Stock Photo; 245 BCR: Boonchuay1970/Shutterstock; 245 BR: All Canada Photos/Alamy Stock Photo; 245 TCR: Bokeh Blur Background/Shutterstock; 245 TR: Rassul Azadi/Shutterstock; 247: Andy Crawford/Dorling Kindersley/Science Source; 249: Radius Images/Alamy Stock Photo; 251: Siiixth/Shutterstock; 253: Claire Cordier/Dorling Kindersley/Science Source; 255: Bart Sadowski/Shutterstock; 256: Steve Bloom Images/Alamy Stock Photo; 258: KarlFriedrich Hohl/Getty Images; 263 BR: Valentinrussanov/Getty Images; 263 CR: China Images/Alamy Stock Photo; 263 TR: Simon Turner/Alamy Stock Photo; 265 B: Dave Higginson/Getty Images; 265 TR: Hero Images Inc./Alamy Stock Photo; 267: Tom Wang/Shutterstock; 272: Martin Shields/Alamy Stock Photo; 276: NASA Graphic/NASA Langley/Advanced Concepts Lab, AMA, Inc.

Topic 7

286: Raimundas/Shutterstock; 288: Smolaw/Shutterstock; 290: Room27/Shutterstock; 294: F.G.I CO., LTD./Alamy Stock Photo; 300: imageBROKER/Alamy Stock Photo; 302: Everett Collection/Shutterstock; 303 CR: Sirtravelalot/Shuttertock; 303 TL: Monkey Business Images/Shuttertock; 303 TR: Pressmaster/Shutterstock; 308: Marcio Jose Bastos Silva/Shutterstock; 313: CSP_Elly_l/AGE Fotostock; 314: Dotshock/Shutterstock; 316 BL: Tempura/Getty Images; 316 CR: Ruslan Ivantsov/Shutterstock; 316 TCR: Gallofoto/Shutterstock; 317 CR: Asharkyu/Shutterstock; 317 R: David Ducros/Science Photo Library/Getty Images; 321 B: Bettmann/Getty Images; 321 T: Jacob Lund/Shutterstock; 327 TL: Doug Martin/Science Source; 327 TR: Richard Megna/Fundamental Photographs

Topic 8

330: Alexander Cher/Shutterstock; 332: Peter Dazeley/Iconica/Getty Images; 334: vodolaz/Fotolia; 337: Bon Appetit/Alamy Stock Photo; 341: David Tipling/DigitalVision/Getty Images; 344: John S. Zeedick/Hulton Archive/Getty Images; 346: Billy Hustace/Photographer's Choice/Getty Images; 348: Chip Clark/Fundamental Photographs; 352 BC: photoeverywhere/Fotolia; 352 BL: SPL/Science Source; 352 BR: Asturcon/Shutterstock; 354 BC: SPL/Science Source; 354 CL: SPL/Science Source; 354 CR: Burmakin Andrey/123RF; 355 BL: SPL/Science Source; 355 BR: SPL/Science Source; 355 CL: SeDmi/Shutterstock; 355 CR: Tom Grundy/Shutterstock; 356 C: Charles D. Winters/Science Source; 356 CL: NASA/SDO (AIA). Courtesy of NASA/SDO and the AIA, EVE, and HMI science teams.; 356 CR: blackpixel/Shutterstock; 358: GL Archive/Alamy Stock Photo; 363 Bkgrd: sakda2527/Fotolia; 363 BL: dgool/123RF; 363 BR: Matthew Howard/123RF; 363 CR: Eddie Phantana/Shutterstock; 365: dpa picture alliance archive/Alamy Stock Photo; 367 CR: generalfmv/iStock/Getty Images; 367 TR: Newscom; 368: Lightspringd/Shutterstock; 371 Bkgrd: Radu/Fotolia; 371 C: Andrew Lambert Photography/Science Source; 371 CL: SPL/Science Source; 372: Charles D. Winters/Science Source; 373 BL: Ryan McVay/Photodisc/Getty Images; 373 BR: michaelstephanfotografie/Shutterstock; 374: sciencephotos/Alamy Stock Photo; 375: Sciencephotos/Alamy Stock Photo; 378: Martyn Williams/Alamy Stock Photo; 379: Robert Harding/Alamy Stock Photo; 380: Alessia Pierdomenico/Bloomberg/Getty Images; 381 BL: 256261/Shutterstock; 381 TR: Gilbert S. Grant/Science Source; 382 BCL: Focal Point/Shutterstock; 382 BR: Nikola Bilic/Shutterstock; 382 TC: Lana Langlois/Shutterstock; 382 TR: Petr Malyshev/Fotolia; 383: Oleksandr Lysenko/Alamy Stock Photo; 390: Alexey Protasov/Fotolia; 391: Andrew Lambert Photography/Science Source

Topic 9

394: HTU/Shutterstock; 395: Anita Patterson Peppers/Shutterstock; 396: Steve Hix/Getty Images; 398: djgis/Shutterstock; 399: Alexander Bark/Shutterstock; 401 BC: Gareth Boden/Pearson Education Ltd.; 401 BL: Jim West/The Image Works; 401 T: DarKinG/Shutterstock; 404: Alexey Lysenko/Shutterstock; 405: imageBROKER/Alamy Stock Photo; 407: Jake Lyell/Alamy Stock Photo; 408: Lew Robertson/Photographer's Choice/Getty Images; 411: Richard Megna/Fundamental Photographs; 414 TC: Charles D. Winters/Science Source; 414 TR: serezniy/123RF; 417: MGPicturesProd/Shutterstock; 419 BL: John Lund/The Image Bank/Getty Images; 419 BR: akgimages/Interfoto/Hermann Historica; 420: Anastasios71/Shutterstock; 423: Chepko Danil Vitalevich/Shutterstock; 425 BC: Patrick Moynihan/pyronious/Getty Images; 425 BR: vlorzor/Fotolia; 426: 123RF; 428: Vidady/Fotolia; 429 BCR: gamjai/Fotolia; 429 CL: thewet/Fotolia; 429 R: Feng Yu/Alamy Stock Photo; 431 BC: Thomas J. Peterson/Alamy Stock Photo; 431 CL: Shyripa Alexandr/Shutterstock; 431 TL: naretev/Fotolia; 432 BL: Mau Horng/Shutterstock; 432 L: monticello/Shutterstock; 433 BR: Nils Z/Shutterstock; 433 TL: Borodin Denis/Shutterstock; 434 BL: Oscar Dominguez/Alamy Stock Photo; 434 BR: Nigel Wilkins/Alamy Stock Photo; 436 Bkgrd: Alain Machet/Alamy Stock Photo; 436 CR: Roman. SPhotographer/Shutterstock; 436 TR: loonger/E+/Getty Images; 442: jordeangjelovik/Shutterstock; 443: Charles D. Winters/Science Source

Topic 10

446: Matteo Arteni/Shutterstock; 448: Heiner Heine/imageBROKER/Alamy Stock Photo; 450: Seth K. Hughes/Image Source/Alamy Stock Photo; 452: Marcio Jose Bastos Silva/Shutterstock; 453 CR: WilleeCole Photography/Shutterstock; 453 TCR: Sonya Etchison/Fotolia; 453 TR: dmussman/iStock/Getty Images; 454 BL: gbh007/Getty Images; 454 BR: Monkey Business Images/Shutterstock; 458: Ian Lishman/Juice Images/Getty Images; 460: Scott A. Miller/ZUMA Press/Newscom; 461: Jim Zuckerman/Alamy Stock Photo; 462: Emma Yacomen/Alamy Stock Photo; 464 TC: WING/UPPA/Photoshot/Newscom; 464 TL: John Ewing/Portland Press Herald/Getty Images; 464 TR: Jim Cummins/The Image Bank/Getty Images; 468 Bkgrd: hkeita/Shutterstock; 468 CL: BLACKDAY/Shutterstock; 470: Isantilli/123RF; 472 CL: Janet Horton/Alamy Stock Photo; 472 TL: Hero Images Inc/Alamy Stock Photo; 473: Sorin Papuc/Alamy Stock Photo; 474: omgimages/123RF; 475 BL: Janet Horton/Alamy Stock Photo; 475 C: Jiang Dao Hua/Shutterstock; 476: imageBROKER/Alamy Stock Photo; 477 B: D. Trozzo/Alamy Stock Photo; 477 TR: full image/Fotolia; 479 CR: ScofieldZa/Shutterstock; 479 TCR: Barry Blackburn/Shutterstock; 480: kuznetsov_konsta/

Fotolia; 484: Robert Daly/OJO Images/Getty Images; 489 B: Andrey Volodin/Alamy Stock Photo; 489 CR: koya979/Fotolia; 494: Jason O. Watson (Sports)/Alamy Stock Photo; 495: Gary Hamilton/Icon SMI/Icon Sport Media/Getty Images

End Matter
336: WaterFrame/Alamy Stock Photo; 498 BCL: Philippe Plailly & Elisabeth Daynes/Science Source; 498 BL: EHStockphoto/Shutterstock; 498 TCL: Cyndi Monaghan/Getty Images; 498 TL: Javier Larrea/AGE Fotostock; 499: WaterFrame/Alamy Stock Photo; 500: Africa Studio/Shutterstock; 501: Jeff Rotman/Alamy Stock Photo; 502: Grant Faint/Getty Images; 503: Ross Armstrong/Alamy Stock Photo; 504: geoz/Alamy Stock Photo; 507: Martin Shields/Alamy Stock Photo; 508: Nicola Tree/Getty Images; 509: Regan Geeseman/NASA; 511: Pearson Education Ltd.; 512: Pearson Education Ltd.; 513 BR: Pearson Education Ltd.; 513 CR: Pearson Education Ltd.

Program graphics:
ArtMari/Shutterstock; BeatWalk/Shutterstock; Irmun/Shutterstock; LHF Graphics/Shutterstock; Multigon/Shutterstock; Nikolaeva/Shutterstock; silm/Shutterstock; Undrey/Shutterstock

Take Notes

Use this space for recording notes and sketching out ideas.

Take Notes

Use this space for recording notes and sketching out ideas.

Take Notes

Use this space for recording notes and sketching out ideas.

Take Notes

Use this space for recording notes and sketching out ideas.